THE CHURCH OF THE ANCIENT COUNCILS

ARCHBISHOP PETER L'HUILLIER

THE CHURCH OF THE ANCIENT COUNCILS

The Disciplinary Work of the First Four
Ecumenical Councils

ST VLADIMIR'S SEMINARY PRESS
575 SCARSDALE ROAD
CRESTWOOD, NEW YORK 10707
1996

Library of Congress Cataloging-in-Publication Data

L'Huillier, Peter, 1926-
    The church of the ancient councils : the disciplinary work of the first four
ecumenical councils / Peter L'Huillier.
        p.   cm.
Based on the author's thesis (doctoral) — Theological Academy of Moscow.
Includes bibliographical references and index.
ISBN 0-88141-007-1
    1. Canon law—Sources.   2. Canon law—History.
3. Church discipline—History—Early church, ca. 30-600.
4. Councils and synods, Ecumenical.   5. Council of Nicea (1st: 325).
6. Council of Constantinople (1st: 381).   7. Council of Ephesus (431).
8. Council of Chalcedon (451).   I. Title.
LAW
262.9.22—dc20   95-50117
                                                                      CIP

THE CHURCH OF THE ANCIENT COUNCILS

ST VLADIMIR'S SEMINARY PRESS

ISBN 0-88141-007-I

All Rights Reserved

PRINTED IN THE UNITED STATES OF AMERICA

Table of Contents

PRINCIAL ABBREVIATIONS

ACO .... *Acta Conciliorum Oecumenicorum*, ed. E. Schwartz, Strasbourg, 1914- .

Acta Selecta .... *Patriarchatus Constantinopolitani Acta Selecta*, ed. (= Pontificia Commissione per la Redazione del Codice di Diritto Canonico Orientale, *Fonti*, Sr. II, fasc. 4, pt. 2).

BTr .... *Bogoslovskie Trudy*, Moscow.

BZ .... *Byzantinische Zeitschrift*, Leipzig, 1892ff., Munich, 1950.

CCL .... *Corpus Christianorum, Series Latina*, Turnhout.

CJ .... *Codex Justinianus* (= *CJC* vol. 2).

CJC .... *Corpus Juris Civilis*, 3 vols., Berlin, 1954-59.

COeD .... *Conciliorum Oecumenicorum Decreta*, Freiburg-in-Br., 1962.

CT .... *Codex Theodosianus*, Berlin.

CSEL .... *Corpus Scriptorum Ecclesiasticorum Latinorum*.

DDC .... *Dictionnaire de Droit Canonique*, Paris, 1935-1965.

DGA .... *Discipline générale antique*, ed. P.P. Joannou (= Pontificia Commissione per la Redazione del Codice di Diritto Canonico Orientale, *Fonti*, fasc. IX), 2 vols. Grottaferrata, 1962-64.

DOP .... *Dumbarton Oaks Papers*, Cambridge, Mass., then Washington, D.C.

DTC .... *Dictionnaire de Theologie Catholique*, Paris.

EQ .... *Echos d'Orient*, Paris.

GCS .... *Die griechischen Christlichen Schriftsteller der ersten drei Jahrhunderte*.

Hefele-Leclercq ...... C.J. Hefele and J.M. Leclercq, *Histoire des conciles*.

HTR .... *Harvard Theological Review*, Cambridge, Mass.

JTS .... *Journal of Theological Studies*, London.

Lexicon .... *A Patristic Greek Lexicon*, ed. G.W.H. Lampe, Oxford.

Lexilogion .... E. Roussos, *Lexilogion ekklesiastikou dikaiou (byzantinon dikaion)*, Athens.

MGH .... *Monumenta Germaniae Historica*.

Mansi .... J.D. Mansi, *Sacrorum conciliorum nova et amplissima collectio*, Florence and Venice, 1759 ff.

Messager .... *Messager de l'Exarchat du Patriarche russe en Europe occidentale*, Paris.

Monumenta .... *Ecclesiae occidentalis monumenta antiquissima*, ed. C.H. Turner, Oxford, 1899-1930.

OCA .... *Orientalia Christiana Analecta*, Rome, 1935 ff.

OCP .... *Orientalia Christiana Periodica*, Rome, 1935 ff.

Oxford Dictionary ... *Oxford Dictionary of the Christian Church.*
PBE .... *Pravoslavnaia Bogoslovskaia Entsiklopedia,* Petrograd, 1900-1910.
PG .... *Patrologia series graeca,* ed. J.P. Migne, Paris, 1857-66.
PL .... *Patrologia series latina,* ed. J.P. Migne, Paris, 1844-55.
Pravila .... Nikodim Milash, *Pravila Pravoslavnoi Tserkvi s Tolkovaniami,* St. Petersburg.
Pauly-Wissowa ...... Pauly, Wissowa, Kroll, *Realencyclopaedie der Classischen Altertumswissenchaft,* Stuttgart, 1894-1980.
RDC .... *Revue de Droit Canonique,* Strasbourg, 1951ff.
REB .... *Revue des Etudes Byzantines.*
Regestes .... *Les Regestes des actes du Patriarcat de Constantinople,* vol. I: Les actes des patriarches, fasc. 1-7, 1932ff. 2 ed., rev. 1972- .
Rhalles-Potles .... Γ.Α. Ράλλη-Μ. Πότλῆ, *Σύνταγμα τῶν Θείων καὶ ἱερῶν κανόνων,* I-VI, Athens, 1852-9.
RHE .... *Revue d'Histoire Ecclesiastique,* Louvain, 1900ff.
RSPT .... *Revue des Sciences Philosophiques et Theologiques,* Paris.
SC .... *Sources chretiennes.*
Beveridge .... Beveridge, *Synodikon, sive Pandectae,* Oxford, 1672.
Strewe .... A. Strewe, *Die Canonessammlung des Dionysius Exiguus in der ersten Redaktion,* Berlin, 1931.
Synagoga .... *Joannis Scholastici Synagoga L. Titulorum,* ed. V. Beneševič, Munich.
Syntagma .... *Syntagma XIV Titulorum sine scholiis secundum versionem Palaeo-Slovenicam,* ed. V. Beneševič, St. Petersburg, 1906.
T.S.C.B. .... *Textus selecti ex operibus commentatorum byzantinorum,* ed. (= Pontificia Commissione per la Redazione del Codice di Diritto Canonico Orientale, *Fonti,* ser. 1 v. fasc. 9), Grottaferrata.
Th.ith.E. .... Θρησκευτικὴ καὶ Ἠθικὴ Ἐγκυκλοπαιδεία, Athens.
TU .... *Texte und Untersuchungen.*
VV .... *Vizantiiskii Vremennik,* St. Petersburg, then Moscow, 1894-1927.
Zepos .... J. and P. Zepos, *Jus Graecoromanum,* Athens, 1931.
ZK .... *Zeitschrift für Kirchengeschichte,* Stuttgart, 1876ff.
ZhMP .... *Zhurnal Moskovskoi Patriarkhii,* Moscow, 1931ff.

FOREWORD

"Just as the four books of the holy gospel, so also I confess to receive and venerate four councils." With these words Pope St. Gregory the Great of Rome (*Ep.* I.24) expressed his respect for the authority of the four most ancient ecumenical councils: Nicea (325 AD), Constantinople (381), Ephesus (431) and Chalcedon (451). These councils not only defined trinitarian and christological dogma in terms which ever since have been regarded as normative by the major Christian confessions of East and West. They also laid down canons and disciplinary decrees which constitute a milestone in the history of church order, signaling as they do a shift from the multifarious customary law of earlier centuries to a written law universally applicable throughout the Church. But these ancient canons have more than merely historical interest. Their continuing influence can still be felt in the modern codifications of the Roman Catholic Church and elsewhere among Western Christians. For the Orthodox East, their importance is even greater. Constituting the core of the *corpus canonum* common to all the Orthodox Churches, these canons remain the primary point of reference for their institutional life.

Given the great importance of these canons of the ancient ecumenical councils, what precisely do they say and mean? What was the intention of their authors, the fathers of those councils? With the present work, His Eminence Archbishop Peter (L'Huillier) has given the English-speaking world authoritative answers to such questions. After providing an historical overview of each of the four councils, he meticulously examines their canons one by one. He translates them into clear and readable English on the basis of the best modern critical editions; he explains the sometimes ambiguous terminology of the original texts; he explores the historical circumstances which gave rise to these canons in the first place; and he also indicates some of the ways in which they have been reinterpreted (and sometimes misinterpreted) in later centuries.

It would be difficult to overestimate the magnitude of this undertaking. As the voluminous notes suggest, it required the critical evaluation of a vast body of scholarly literature in many different languages. In his own Foreword, His Eminence indicates that he has not undertaken a systematic updating of the work since it was originally written nearly two decades ago. Yet while a certain number of relevant books and articles have been published in the interval, the most important of these have in fact been taken into consideration. In any case, little has appeared—or is likely to appear in the foreseeable future—that would require significant modification of the author's presentation. This is above all because of the very judicious approach which the author adopts. Always attentive to the text itself, to variant readings and ambiguities in vocabulary or syntax, he indicates when more than one interpretation of a given text is possible, and he offers his own judgment as to which interpretation is more plausible only after reviewing and evaluating the circumstantial evidence on all sides. In a word, His Eminence assiduously avoids ungrounded speculation. Unlike some who invoke the Holy Canons, he does not pile hypothesis on hypothesis in order to advance a personal theory or agenda. Neither does he claim to give answers to all the questions which we today might wish that the ancient canons addressed. Rather, as a scholar, he seeks to engage others in the challenges which honest scholarship poses, to lead them into the world of the ancient councils in order to discover the *mens legislatoris.* And at the same time, as a bishop, he seeks to discern the continuing significance of the ancient canons for the life of the Church today. His critical study of *The Church of the Ancient Councils,* subtitled *The Disciplinary Work of the First Four Ecumenical Councils* will long remain an essential reference work for historians and churchmen alike.

John H. Erickson
St. Vladimir's Orthodox Theological Seminary
The Feast of the Nativity of the Theotokos
September 8, 1995

PREFACE

The present work was originally elaborated and written in France during the seventies as a doctoral thesis in Canon Law for the Theological Academy of Moscow. Therefore, this work was composed in French and subsequently translated into Russian. As a consequence of my episcopal transfer to America in 1979, the defense of this thesis was delayed and eventually took place in June 1985. Meanwhile, the late Frs. A. Schmemann and J. Meyendorff suggested the publication of this work in English. It was decided that the title would be *The Church of the Ancient Councils*; the subtitle remaining the original one, viz. *The Disciplinary Work of the First Four Ecumenical Councils*. The English rendition was not an easy task, especially because it implied a good knowledge of French and English as well as an acquaintance with technical terminology in both languages and required several verifications. Furthermore, as above-mentioned, I had prepared this study almost two decades earlier and the following problem arose: Was an updating necessary? Fortunately, in the area of Eastern Canon Law of the epoch under investigation, nothing significant has been published about primary sources since *Concilia Africae* (1947), the critical edition by C. Munier, which I had been able to use while still living in Paris. About secondary works addressing some specific issues, the situation was somewhat different. I had to rewrite partly my commentary on canon 3 of Nicea because serious studies published after the redaction of this part of my thesis provided a fresh view on the origins of permanent continence of the clergy in the West. On other points of less importance I did not deem it indispensable to modify the text already printed. Suffice it to mention that, having read the article of T.D. Barnes, "The Date of the Council of Gangra" (J.T.S., N.S. 40, 1989), I agree with his conclusion which places chronologically this synod ca. 355. Further, I give more credence to the opinion that in the mind of the authors of canons 9 and 17 of Chalcedon appeals in the East can be addressed in any case to the See of Constantinople.

Finally, I would like to express my deep thanks to those who encouraged me to undertake this study, especially the ever-memorable Metropolitans Nikodim Rotov and Nikodimos Galiatsatos. I should also extend my thanks to the late Fr. Darrouzes who drew my attention to works uneasily accessible in the West and communicated to me unpublished notes written by the late Fr. V. Laurent. I have not forgotten the help I received from R.-G. Coquin for the Syriac rendition of the canons of Nicea according to the edition of F. Schulthess (Göttingen 1908).

I wish also to give special thanks to Fr. Steven Bigham for doing the initial work on the translation and to Dr. William Churchill for his editorial assistance. Furthermore, I thank my colleague and friend Professor John Erickson of St. Vladimir's Seminary for reading the text and making editorial suggestions, and Mr. Ted Bazil, Managing Director of the Seminary's Press, as well as Amy Odum for her index. Finally, I have a thought of acknowledgement for the late Fr. Alexander Schmemann who first suggested the publication of this work by St. Vladimir's Seminary Press.

INTRODUCTION

In the area of church discipline, the work of the first four ecumenical councils has an obvious interest for the knowledge of the law and institutions of early Christianity. During this period, 325 to 451, which corresponds to the flowering of the great patristic literature, we can follow—through the canonical legislation of the Councils of Nicea, Constantinople, Ephesus, and Chalcedon as well as other decisions made by these assemblies on specific questions—the evolution of the structures of the Church, of her discipline, and of her relations with the surrounding society. If we compare this and the ante-Nicene period, we see that all sorts of new problems come up while others fade in importance. The canons issued by these councils constitute the core of Church Law in the Christian East, even today. They also formed an important part of the Western Church's law during the first millennium and influenced, in no small way, the western medieval synthesis.

In considering the canonical legislation elaborated and approved by the first four ecumenical councils, it appears quite clear that this was a period of particularly fruitful creativity in the field of the Eastern Church's written law. Although it was not the intention of the Fathers gathered at Nicea to substitute a written, universal law for the already existing customary law with its local variants, many factors since then have turned the scales in favor of written law. In the first place, the unequaled prestige of this "great and holy council" conferred an unquestioned authority on its legislation. Thus around 330, Eusebius of Caesarea, having been asked to become bishop of Antioch, refused the offer by invoking the regulation established by the Fathers of Nicea.[1] St. Basil, writing to a priest to order him to stop living with a woman, expressly made reference to the canon of Nicea relevant to this case.[2] In the West, the regulations of the great council were held in equally high esteem. Pope Julius spoke of "divine inspiration" in referring to canon 5.[3] As for Pope Leo, he declared the legislation of Nicea to be inviolable.[4]

1

Another factor favored the predominance of written law. During the first centuries of Christianity, the consciousness of a permanent disciplinary tradition was very strong in each local Church. In the fourth century, many new dioceses were created due to missionary expansion on the one hand and to the reinforcement of one or another theological trend during the Arian crisis on the other. For the same reasons, episcopal transfers, completely exceptional in earlier times, became more numerous; this phenomenon contributed to the breakdown of the links between the bishop and his church. Structures of common and coordinated action were set up, and the working of these new organs had to be made clear. Under these conditions, it was no longer possible to appeal solely to ancient customs; it was necessary to issue regulations intended to apply to the whole Church. Finally the tendency which was sketched out after the reign of Constantine and which took final form under Theodosius I—namely, giving the force of state law to the decisions of the church hierarchy—implied the existence of a body of canonical law.[5] This evolution was later fully established by the legislation of the Emperor Justinian which confirmed the juridical validity of the canons issued by the Councils of Nicea, Constantinople, Ephesus, and Chalcedon as well as of those local councils accepted by these ecumenical assemblies.[6]

In many cases, the canons merely endorsed customs which were seen to be legitimate. To the extent that written law (canons and imperial laws) gained ground, custom was more or less limited to the domain of precedents. We could, it is true, quote the statement of Metropolitan Zachary of Chalcedon at the time of the Council of St. Sophia (879-880): "custom has a tendency to outweigh canons,"[7] but we must not overestimate the significance of a statement formulated during a discussion or take it as a fundamental principle of Byzantine church law. Appealing to custom remains limited, as we can clearly see in reading the *Nomocanon in XIV Titles* and the commentaries of Balsamon on this work.[8]

In the Byzantine East, there was no break in continuity between Late Antiquity and the Middle Ages on the political and socio-cultural level, as there was in the West, but there was constant evolution. The Church had to make concrete adaptations of the old canonical regulations to meet new situations. Canonical creativity was certainly not extinguished after the end of the ninth century, but it was limited to certain areas, principally to marriage and monastic law. No council issued regulations changing church structures already established by the end of the ancient period. Since the canons of Late Antiquity and the early Middle Ages had hardly touched the question of patriarchal privileges,[9] it is, therefore, not surprising to find that many Byzantine interpretations of the canons on this question appear to us to be arbitrary and erroneous.[10] Many other canons created problems in regard to their meaning and applicability. Given their respect for tradition and their uncontestable legal formalism, the Byzantines avoided as much as possible an appeal to the idea of laws being "out of date."

After the eleventh century, Byzantium more and more felt the need to have authorized commentaries on the canons. Probably the renaissance of legal studies stimulated an interest in the serious exegesis of canonical texts.[11] But we have to wait until the twelfth century to see the first systematic work on this subject. Between 1118 and 1143, Alexis Aristenos, deacon and nomophylax of the Great Church, at the request of the Emperor John II Comnenus, wrote some concise annotations on the *Synopsis* which was compiled in the sixth or seventh century by Stephen of Ephesus and completed during the second half of the tenth century by Simeon "magistros and logothete."[12] Not very long after 1159, no doubt, John Zonaras wrote his commentary (Ἐξήγησις) on the canons, a work which has always been well-received and rightly so. Zonaras classified the canonical documents of the *Syntagma in XIV Titles* according to an order of the weightiness of the sources. He placed the Canons of the Holy Apostles first; then came those of the ecumenical councils and the general councils of 861 and 879-880. Zonaras put the canons of the local councils and of the Holy Fathers last.[13] Although this classification had already been used previously, he made it, henceforth, the accepted order. Zonaras was above all concerned to set out the exact meaning of the texts, also giving necessary clarifications. When required, he compared canons on the same subject and proposed a reasoned reconciliation.[14]

While he was still deacon and nomophylax in Constantinople, Theodore Balsamon, at the request of the Emperor Manuel Comnenus (1143-1180) and the Ecumenical Patriarch Michael III (1169-1176), elaborated his commentaries on the *Nomocanon in XIV Titles*. In his interpretation of the canons he showed little originality; he often followed Zonaras to the letter but differed from him in consciously referring to the case law of his time. At the same time, Balsamon was concerned with relating the canons and the civil laws, in conformity with the main goal of his work.[15]

In Byzantium, the interpretations of these three canonists had a quasi-official position[16] and have continued in subsequent periods to be given great weight. Consequently they have influenced the canonical praxis of the whole Orthodox Church. For the historian of institutions, these commentaries are especially interesting in that they show how their authors understood the ancient canons and also how they applied them. Furthermore, references in Balsamon's commentaries to decisions of the patriarchal synod in Constantinople are very valuable for the study of jurisprudence in Byzantium. These works, however, have only a limited use in trying to determine the real thinking of the Fathers who issued these ancient canons.

We must not neglect the anonymous scholia (explanatory notes) found in the manuscripts. We can say the same thing for these notes that was said for the interpretations of the great Byzantine commentators. Nevertheless, it is fitting to underline the fact that these notes are strictly the private opinions of their authors.[17]

The "Syntagma arranged in alphabetical order according to subject" (Σύνταγμα κατὰ στοιχεῖον) by hieromonk Matthew Blastares occupies a singular place. This work, written in Thessalonica around 1335, is a collection of canons, civil laws, synodical decrees and commentaries.[18] Because of its convenient ordering and the richness of its content, this work was a great success not only among the Greeks but also among the southern Slavs and later among the Russians and Romanians.

The era of Ottoman domination is far from being devoid of interest for the historian of canon law. Nonetheless, even more than in the Middle Ages, the actions of the hierarchy on this subject were taken in the field of case law.[19] We have to wait till the turn of the eighteenth century to see the appearance of a new commentary on the corpus of received canons in the Greek Orthodox Church. In 1800, the first edition of the *Pedalion* was published.[20] The text of each canon is followed by a paraphrase in modern Greek along with a commentary often based on Byzantine canonists. Moreover, we find disgressions on different canonical or liturgical points among these numerous and often wordy notes. According to the title of the work, the editors were hieromonk Agapios and the monk Nicodemus (St. Nicodemus the Hagiorite). In reality the essential parts of the work are the work of the latter.[21] After some delays, the book received the official approval of the Patriarchate of Constantinople. The reservations set out in the letter of Patriarch Neophyte VII, August, 1902, concerned only changes introduced by hieromonk Theodoret without the knowledge of the authors.[22]

The *Pedalion* has always enjoyed a great reputation in Greek-speaking Churches; this is obvious from its many reprintings, without, of course, the far-fetched additions of Theodoret. We can explain this success in different ways: the translation of the canons was done in paraphrases; the commentaries and the notes make for relatively easy reading, even for churchmen and monks having little education. The liturgical and pastoral directives, as well as other additional material, are of obvious practical interest for the clergy. This recension of the canons is on the whole correct, as we can see by comparing the present text with critical editions which we now have. St. Nicodemus the Hagiorite was no stranger to the concerns of textual criticism; this is obvious from his notes, which give the most characteristic variants of the recension of John the Scholastic. Having said this, we must not, however, overestimate the value of the *Pedalion*. It constitutes, first and foremost, a valuable witness for the understanding of the milieu in which it was formed.[23] As for treating the *Pedalion* as the perfect and therefore untouchable expression of Orthodox canon law, such an attitude is a manifest exaggeration which we often meet in a strict, integrist environment. St. Nicodemus' position on the invalidity of Roman Catholic baptism is particularly appreciated in that milieu.[24]

For a long time, the Orthodox Slavs were content to reproduce translations of the works of Byzantine commentators on the canons. But in the nineteenth century, Slavic canonists took over the first place. Chronologically speaking, it is proper to mention first the work of Archimandrite John Sokolov, published in St. Petersburg in 1851.[25] Nicodemus Milash rightly considered this Russian canonist as the father of Orthodox canonical studies in the modern period.[26] Fr. G. Florovsky underlined the scientific value of this work; he wrote that "for the first time, the ancient and fundamental canons of the Church were presented in Russian more in historical than in doctrinal fashion."[27]

A work consisting of the canons of the Orthodox Church with commentaries was published in 1895-6 by Nicodemus Milash, who later became Bishop of Dalmatia;[28] this work is still of great interest today and shows itself as the fruit of considerable study.[29] The interpretations and explanations found in this work, although they must obviously be revised and completed on the basis of more recent studies, are not at all to be minimized. Moreover, it is still used today as a reference work by Orthodox canonists. As for canonical commentaries in Romanian, we can mention the works of Metropolitan Andrew Saguna, N. Popovici, and C. Dron.[30]

In the West, starting with the seventeenth century, we find some quite worthy works which interpret the ancient canons. We can mention the names of Christian Wolf[31] and John Cabassut;[32] William Beveridge particularly stands out because of the value of his study of the canons. When he was vicar of Ealing, later Bishop of St. Asaph (1704), this erudite Anglican clergyman published his Συνοδικόν.[33] It was successful not only in the West but also in the Orthodox East. Patriarch Dositheos of Jerusalem (1669-1707) sent a copy of Beveridge's *Synodikon* to Patriarch Adrian of Moscow (1690-1700) so that the latter could correct the text of the *Kormchaya Kniga*.[34] Zeger-Bernard Van Espen (1646-1728), the most famous canonist of the old University of Louvain, found himself entangled in the controversies of his time between the advocates and opponents of the absolute authority of the Roman pontiff; he resolutely took the side of the opponents.[35] Van Espen's commentary on the canons is found among the posthumous works of this great scholar; in this work, his point was to make known the authentic church discipline which was eclipsed in the medieval West by canons based on the False Decretals.[36] It is not at all surprising, then, that from that time on the works of this Belgian canonist were put on the Index by the Roman curia.

We should also note the work of William Bright, professor at Oxford from 1868-1901.[37] His commentaries on the canons of the first four ecumenical councils are still of scholarly interest.[38] Henri Leclercq was often inspired by this work. Karl-Joseph Hefele (1809-1898), professor at Tübingen and later bishop of Rottenburg, was the author of a great scholarly work on *The History of the Councils*, published in seven volumes from 1855 to 1874.[39] Even though it has been surpassed on many points by subsequent scientific studies, this work remains a classic reference work. In 1907 the Benedictine monk, Henri Leclercq d'Ornancourt undertook a French translation of the *Conciliengeschichte* of Hefele,[40] which was really to be a complete reworking and enlargement of the German scholar's work.[41]

Finally, we can mention the book of Henry R. Percival, which constitutes volume 14 in *The Nicene and Post-Nicene Fathers,* second series.[42] It is true that this volume is not an original work, properly speaking, since the comments are completely drawn from the works of ancient and modern canonists. However, we believe it is necessary to note this book because the *excursus* often represent the personal synthesis of the author. Moreover, the volume is readily available.

The disciplinary legislation issued by the first four Ecumenical Councils undoubtedly constitutes the historical core of Orthodox canon law. This appears to be even more obvious if one takes into account the canonical legislation of the local synods contained in the collection used and therefore approved by the Fathers of Chalcedon.[43] Subsequent legislation universally accepted in the Orthodox Church did not introduce basic alterations.[44] Such alterations would not have been accepted in the East because of a widespread feeling that not only the Church kerygma but also the fundamental norms of Church order were part and parcel of Holy Tradition. The Fathers of the Seventh Ecumenical Council, with some exaggeration, applied the words of Deuteronomy in the Torah to canonical rules: "To them nothing is to be added, and from them nothing is to be taken away."[45] Thus, changes are always presented as duly justified adjustments of particular details.[46] Nowadays, in the light of historical data, we share a far more nuanced view of the real evolution of ecclesiastical institutions. Be that as it may, in Byzantine times and even later on no doubts affecting the validity of the old legislation were expressed.

The understanding of the ancient canons does not interest just the historians of institutions but also all Orthodox practitioners of canon law, since the canons' stipulations constitute the core of all legitimate law still in force.[47]

The point of all interpretations is obviously to determine the exact meaning of each canon. We must, therefore, investigate the intention of the legislator, *mens legislatoris*. This is not always an easy task, not just because of the time that separates us from them. Research must be concerned as much with the historical context as with the canonical text itself; we must carefully investigate what the lawgiver wanted to correct, suppress, add, or simply recall to mind. We also properly take into account that the technical terms in canon law had not yet been rigidly fixed.[48] Moreover, we must not forget either that the Holy Fathers, the authors of the canons, were not necessarily specialists in legal terminology. Consequently we cannot automatically apply to canon law principles of interpretation established by specialists in civil law. For example, we would really be misled if we strictly applied the rule which says that the lawmaker always "expresses what he wants to say and refrains from saying what he does not want to say."[49] In some cases, uncertainties flow from the wording, which can be understood in several ways due to editorial ambiguities in grammatical construc-

tion or punctuation.[50] The exact meaning of terms must be determined by taking factors of time and place into account. To neglect
these data and arbitrarily put elements together necessarily leads to
serious misinterpretations.[51] Research into the *mens legislatoris* inter-
ests the historian and the canonists, but the canonist has another
preoccupation. It is frequently the case that a canon is presented as an
act involving a local and limited situation; can we, then, consider it as
a law in the proper sense, which has general application? Certainly,
there are some cases where the purely limited nature of the canon
evidently stands out.[52] Sometimes only a knowledge of the historical
context permits us to affirm that despite its formulation, a canon has
an application strictly limited to a moment in church history.[53]   One
of the essential, and at the same time most delicate, problems in interpreting the canons is the use of analogy. There is no doubt at all that
this method is perfectly legitimate in itself since, taken in their individual cases, the canons are only concrete expressions on a given subject
of the Church's general order. The ancient legal adage is applicable to
canon law: *Non ex regula ius sumatur sed ex iure quod est, regula
fiat*.[54] It is even possible that this definition has influenced the usage
which eventually restricted the term to disciplinary rulings of church
authorities.[55] The application of analogy to the canons is nonetheless
delicate; it supposes that the canon in question is perfectly clear.[56]
Moreover, the similarity of each case must be solidly grounded. We
must correctly avoid any subjectivism which in a particular case
argues on the basis of superficial resemblances.[57] Therefore, an analogical interpretation, also called "extensive," is not arbitrary as long as it
conforms to the general intention of the legislator, even if that interpretation materially goes beyond his thought.[58]

In what measure can we categorically affirm that an ancient canon
ought no longer to be applied? In principle, such is the case when a
disciplinary measure has been abrogated or modified by a canon
adopted in some later time; this is in line with the adage *lex posterior
derogat priori*, which assumes that the conciliar authority issuing the
abrogation or modification possess the necessary authority.[59] It is still
necessary to take into account the reasons underlying the more recent
canon. Thus, canon 8 of the Synod in Trullo begins by recalling the
norm which requires semiannual synods in each province. However,
in the face of a practical impossibility (ἀδυνάτως), such as barbarian
invasions, the Fathers of the Synod in Trullo decided in favor of a single
annual session.[60] It is clear that the meeting of semiannual synods is still

preferred and must be held unless there are major obstacles.[61]

An ancient canon can partially or fully lose its legal force; partially when it is only capable of being applied analogically[62] or else when an ecclesiological principle is decreed on the occasion of a strictly limited decision.[63]

Let us also note although "economy" excludes by nature an automatic application of analogy, a canon concerning an individual case can serve as an indication to help resolve comparable cases.[64] It would appear logical to allow without restriction the principle that abrogates a canon when its *ratio legis* disappears; that is, the reason which prompted its adoption in the first place. But a long tradition expressing a consensus in the Church can block the application of this principle. Thus the first place of the See of Constantinople is not really in question even though this city has long since ceased to be "honored by the presence of the emperor and the senate."[65] In reality, the primacy of honor of the Archbishop of Constantinople is most probably founded on the extension to his see of the axiom applied by the Fathers of Nicea to the privileges of Rome, Alexandria and Antioch: "Let the ancient customs be maintained."[66] Total nullity is certain when a canon shows itself to apply only to a specific case and not capable of being extended by an analogical interpretation.[67] Nullity can result automatically from the disappearance of an institution: thus canon 15 of Chalcedon which fixes the minimum age of forty for deaconesses lost its force after the Church ceased to ordain deaconesses.[68]

Investigation into the meaning and extent of a canon requires, as we have said above, research into the social and historical background as well as an analysis of the texts themselves. It is very evident that these exegetical studies suppose previous enquiries into the value of the texts which we have received through time. In this case, when dealing with the canonical stipulations of the first four ecumenical councils the investigator does not run up against insurmountable obstacles. These texts have on the whole been rather faithfully transmitted in the Greek manuscript tradition. This is true first of all due to the nature of the subject. As P.P. Joannou pertinently noted:

> The letter of a legal text is of prime importance; it is quite normal, therefore, in the innumerable manuscripts of these canonical collections to find a very careful transcription which has been done by a copyist familiar with the material or else reviewed and corrected by a jurist. From one manuscript to another, we can expect to find very few variants that

deeply alter the sense of the text.[69]

Let us add that the ancient canons and especially those of the ecumenical councils were considered to have been issued under divine inspiration, which explains the great care taken to preserve the exactness of the texts.[70]

From the beginning of this century on, a remarkable job has been carried out in establishing a critical edition of ancient canonical collections. It is, of course, these works that we have primarily used in our research. We must first mention the excellent editions of the *Synagoge* and of the *Syntagma in XIV Titles* done by V.N. Beneševič.[71] For the disciplinary ruling issued by the Councils of Ephesus and Chalcedon, we also have the monumental work of Edward Schwartz.[72] With certain exceptions, the Greek text of the canons of the first four ecumenical councils found in *Fonti* is that of the *Synagoge*, sometimes with some interesting variants; it is nonetheless difficult to appreciate their importance because of deficiencies in the way the critical apparatus is set out.[73] The old Latin versions of the canons, above all those of Nicea I, are worthy of careful consideration. Certain ones in fact show signs of being based on a Greek text earlier than those which have come down to us. At least in the one case, the old Latin text allows us to reconstruct with near certainty the original form of the canon and to understand the *mens legislatoris*.[74] We can also add that the old Latin versions have an interest all their own. The variety of Latin translations of Greek terms found in these versions calls for theological reflection.[75] Moreover, certain interpretive translations, indeed additions, constitute precious testimony to the history of Church institutions in the West.[76] The research of Strewe[77] and, above all, the work of Turner,[78] as complete as it is serious, give the scholar access to correctly edited Latin texts. The Syriac translation of the canons done at Hierapolis of Euphratesia (500-501) is far from being as interesting as the old Latin versions. It is in fact very close to the oldest Greek editions we have. At the most, when a variant is found simultaneously in this Syriac version and in the Latin translations of Dionysius Exiguus, we can infer that it must reflect the text of the Antiochian *Graeca auctoritas*. The critical edition of the manuscript containing the Syriac translation mentioned above has been published by F. Schulthess.[79]

We have already drawn attention to the work of Stephen of Ephesus, the *Synopsis*, edited by Aristenos and completed by Symeon the Logothete. No critical edition of this *Epitome canonum* exists; we have, therefore, used the work of Rhalles and Potles. We have done the same for the commentaries of Aristenos, Zonaras, and Balsamon.[80] For the anonymous scholia, we have used the publication of V.N. Beneševič.[81]

ENDNOTES

[1]*...τὸν κανόνα τῆς ἐκκλησιαστικῆς ἐπιστήμης, De vita Const.* III, 61, PG 2020, col. 1133B; ... τὸν θεσμόν *Ἐκκλησίας, ibid.* 62, col. 1137A. Although the reference to canon 15 of Nicea I is not explicit, allusion to it is certain.

[2]Letter to the priest Gregory—can. 88, *Synt.* pp. 515-6.

[3]Literally "not without the will of God" (*οὐκ ἄνευ Θεοῦ βουλήσεως*) ap. Athanasius, *Contra Arianos* 22, PG 25, col. 284C.

[4]He wrote to Archbishop Anatolius of Constantinople that these rules must remain in force *usque in finem mundi ACO* II, IV, p. 61.

[5]See E. Schwartz, *Die Kanonessamlungen der alten Reichskirche, Gessammelte Schriften* IV (Berlin, 1960), pp. 155-275.

[6]Nov. CXXXI, *praef., CJC* III, pp. 654-55.

[7]Mansi, 12A-18A, col. 457D.

[8]See *Rhalles-Potles* I, pp. 38-42: *Nomocanon in XIV Titles* I, 3; J. Gaudemet rightly underlines patristic proofs showing that Christian antiquity was reserved in its references to custom: *La Formation du droit séculier et du droit de l'Eglise au IVᵉ et Vᵉ siècles*, 2nd edition (Paris, 1979), pp. 187-188.

[9]On the interpretation of canon 6 of Nicea and canon 28 of Chalcedon see our commentaries below. We also mention canon 15 of the "First-Second" Council, *C.S.P.* pp. 473-475, as well as canon 1 of the Council of St. Sophia, *ibid.* pp. 482-4. This last ruling concerned, *ad litteram,* the unique relations between the Sees of Rome and Constantinople, but Balsamon correctly thought that an analogical application should be made concerning the relations between the patriarchs, *Rhalles-Potles* II, pp. 706-7.

[10]For example, see the documents 2, 3, 4, 5, published by J. Darrouzès, *Documents inédits d'ecclésiologie byzantine* (Paris, 1966), pp. 116-237.

[11]See W. Wolska-Conus, *L'Ecole de Droit et l'enseignement du Droit à Byzance au XIᵉ siècle: Xiphilin et Psellos,* in *Travaux et Memoires* 7 (Paris, 1979).

[12]*Textus selecti,* pp. 21-38.

[13]The idea of establishing a hierarchy among the canonical sources is found already at the beginning of the fifth century in St. Augustine, *De bapt. contra Donat.* II, 3, 4, *CSEL* 51, p. 178.

[14]*Textus selecti,* pp. 23-4.

[15]*Ibid.* pp. 24-6. Also see G.P. Stevens, *De Theodoro Balsamone, Analysis operum ac mentis iuridicae* (Rome, 1969).

[16]See M. Krasnozhen, *Tolkovateli kanonicheskogo kodeksa vostochnoi Tserkvi, Aristin, Zonara i Valsamon* (Moscow, 1892), p. 198.

[17]*TSCB.* p. 9. On the influence of these scholia in the works of Aristenos, Zonaras and Balsamon, see M. Krasnozhen, *op. cit.* p. 56.

[18]*Rhalles-Potles* VI, pp. 1-518. On Matthew Blastares, see pp. 31-32. It should be noted that the correct form of his name is *Βλαστάρης* and not *Βλάσταρις.*

[19]On the canonical works of this period found in the East under the Ottoman yoke, see A.P. Christophilopoulos, Ἑλληνικόν ἐκκλησιαστικὸν Δίκαιον, 2nd ed. (Athens, 1965), pp. 63-66. For the documents of the Patriarch of Constantinople's chancery, we have the precious work of M. Gedeon, *Κανονικαὶ διατάξεις* II (Constantinople, 1888-89).

[20]The choice of the term *Πηδάλιον* was probably suggested by the title of the Slavic canonical collection "Kormchaya Kniga." Such was the opinion of E. Golubinsky, *Istoriia Russkoï Tserkvi,* 2nd ed. (Moscow, 1901), p. 660. Nicodemus Milash also thought the same thing: *Pravoslavno tskverno Pravo,* 3rd ed. (Belgrade, 1926), p. 202.

[21]On the personality and work of Agapios, see the article of L. Petit, "Le canoniste Agapios Leonardos," *EO* 2 (1898-1899), pp. 204-6. On St. Nicodemus the Hagiorite, see the work of the monk Theoclitos Dionysiatis, Ἅγιος Νικόδημος ὁ Ἁγιορίτης (Athens, 1959).

[22]See the letter of Neophyte VII, 6th ed., *Pedalion* (Athens, 1957), pp. IV-X.

[23]See M.-J. Le Guillou, "Aux sources du mouvement spirituel de l'Eglise Orthodoxe de Grèce: La renaissance spirituelle du XVIIIe siè*cle," Istina* (1960), pp. 95-128, especially p. 125.

[24]In particular consult the above-mentioned edition of the *Pedalion*, pp. 58-9 and 164-65. An English edition of the *Pedalion, The Rudder*, has been published by D. Cummings (Chicago, 1957). This translation has popularized the ideas of St. Nicodemus on this point in certain parts of the English-speaking Orthodox world.

[25]*Opyt kursa Tserkovnogo zakonovedeniia*, vol. 2 (St. Petersburg, 1851). On this canonist who died in 1869 as bishop of Smolensk, see the article of J. Pokrovsky, *PBE* vol. 7, col. 141-56. Also see G. Florovsky, *Ways of Russion Theology* I (Belmont, MA, 1979), pp. 260-2.

[26]*Pravila* I, p. 5.

[27]*Op. cit.* p. 261.

[28]See the article of the hierodeacon Kalinić, "Episkop Dalmatinski-Istriiskii Dr. Nikodim Milash", *ZhMP*, 1975, 12, pp. 63-64.

[29]*Pravila pravoslavne tskrve s tumachenima* vol. 2 (Novi-Sad, 1895-1896). Our references to this article are taken from the Russian translation published in St. Petersburg, 1911-1912, *Pravila pravoslavnoi Tserkvi s tolkovaniiami*.

[30]Andrei Saguna (1805-1873), *Enchiridion* (Sibiu, 1871). This work contains an interpretation of the canons (Tîlcuirea canoanelor). N. Popovici (1836-1938), *Canoanele Bicericii Ortodoxe însotide de comentarii*, 4 vols. (Arad, 1930, 1931, 1934, 1936). C. Dron, *Traducere a canoanelor însotita de comentarii*. On these authors and their works, see Liviu Stan, "Contributions des theologiens roumains aux problèmes de droit canon et leur position dans ce domaine." This article is found in the collection entitled: *De la théologie orthodoxe roumaine des origines à nos jours* (Bucharest, 1974), pp. 382-421.

[31]Christianus Lupus, *Synodorum generalium ac provincialium decreta et canones* (Louvain, 1665). See the article "Wolf" by J. Mercier, *DTC* XV, 2, col. 3583.

[32]J. Cabassutius, *Notitia ecclesiastica historiarum conciliorum et canonum* (Lyon, 1680). See the article "Cabassut" by A. Ingold, *DTC* II, 2 col. 1297.

[33]Beverigius, Συνοδικὸν sive Pandectae, 2 vols. (Oxford, 1672). In this second volume, we find his own annotations on the canons. On this point, see H.R. Percival, *The Seven Ecumenical Councils of the Undivided Church* (Grand Rapids, Michigan, reprinted in 1977), pp. XVII-XIX. Also see the article "Beveridge" in the *Oxford Dictionary of the Christian Church* 2nd ed. (Oxford, 1974), p. 166.

[34]J. Žužek, *Kormčaja Kniga, Studies of the Chief Code of the Russian Canon Law, OCA* 168 (1964), p. 56.

[35]See the masterful study of Michael Nuttinck, *La vie et l'oeuvre de Zeger-Bernard Van Espen: Un canoniste janséniste, gallican et régalien à l'Université de Louvain* (1646-1728) (Louvain, 1969).

[36]*Commentarius in canones et decreta juris veteris ac novi* (Louvain, 1753). In volume III, we find his commentaries on the canons "juris veteris."

[37]*Oxford Dictionary*, p. 201.

[38]William Bright, *The Canons of the First Four General Councils of Nicaea, Constantinople, Ephesus, and Chalcedon, with notes,* 2nd ed. (Oxford, 1892).

[39]See the article "Héfele" by E. Mangenot, *DTC* IV, 2, col. 2111-2113.

[40]*Histoire des conciles, d'après les documents originaux* (Paris, 1907).

[41]"...a completely recast French edition of K.J. Héfele's Conciliengeschichte," *Oxford Dictionary*, article "Leclercq," p. 808.

[42]*The Seven Ecumenical Councils of the Undivided Church, Their Canons and Dogmatic Decrees together with the Canons of all the local synods which have received ecumenical acceptance* (reprinted Grand Rapids, Michigan, 1977).

[43]It is true that the brief title of canon 1 of Chalcedon would not permit us, by itself, to establish the official nature of this reception, but we properly take into account the non-contested use—at least by the Easterners—of this *"codex canonum"* during several council sessions. This is also what stands out in the Novella XXXI of Justinian, previously mentioned. For canon 1 of Chalcedon, see our analysis of this text below.

[44]Let us be very precise as to how we understand "canonical legislation universally accepted." We mean what is contained in the last redaction of the *Syntagma in XIV Titles*, dated 882-3.

[45]Deut. 13: 1 (LXX, 13: 32). Nicea II, canon 1, *Synt.* p. 205. On the underlying theory, see R. Sohm, *Kirchenrecht* II (Munich-Leipzig, 1923), *passim*, especially pp. 95-98. Also see N. Afanasiev, "The Canons of the Church: Changeable or Unchangeable," *St. Vladimir's Seminary Quarterly* II (1967), pp. 54-68.

[46]See for example the wording of canon 12 of the Synod in Trullo concerning the forbidding of bishops to live with their wives, *Synt.*, pp. 151-52. We note this sentence: "We say that not to abolish or reverse the apostolic legislative rulings (τῶν ἀποστολικῶν προνενομοθετημένων), but to obtain the people's salvation and their advancement in goodness," *loc. cit.*, p. 152.

[47]We insist on the word "legitimate" because the expression "law now in force" is often used to designate the presently existing statutes and regulations of autocephalous and autonomous Churches. The *jus novum* is far from always conforming to the authentic canonical tradition of the Church such as we find it in the *jus vetus*, which has never been abolished yet to which modern church laws often refer in a purely formal manner.

[48]Thus the verbs χειροτονεῖν and χειροθετεῖν, contrary to the usage which prevailed subsequently, are completely synonymous. The idea of "deposition" is frequently referred to by paraphrases.

[49]On this formula, see Charles Lefebvre, *Histoire du Droit et des Institutions de l'Eglise en Occident* vol. 7 (Paris, 1965), p. 449. A typical example of how this exegetical norm does not apply is given in canon 3 of the first ecumenical council.

[50]On this matter, we can refer to canon 6 of Nicea, and canons 9 and 17 of Chalcedon.

[51]This is what happened in medieval Byzantium with the terms ἔξαρχος in canons 9 and 17 of Chalcedon. Certain authors linked this term with that used in the Greek recension of canon 6 of Sardica.

[52]Thus, for example, canon 11 of Nicea, canon 5 of Constantinople, canons 1-6 of Ephesus, and canon 30 of Chalcedon. In addition, we properly note that, excepting the previously mentioned canon of Nicea, no other canons that we refer to were initially presented with this qualification.

[53]This is the case for canon 12 of Nicea.

[54]*Dig.* L, 17, 1, *Paulus, Libro sexto decimo ad Plautium, CJC* I, p. 920.

[55]On this meaning of the word κανών-*regula* see L. Wenger, *Canon in den römischen Rechtsquellen und in den Papyri* (Vienna-Leipzig, 1942) and by the same author, *Die Quellen des römischen Rechts* (Vienna, 1953). See also *C.S.P.* pp. 299-502 and A.P. Christophilopoulos, Ἑλληνικόν ἐκκλησιαστικόν δίκαιον 2nd ed. (Athens, 1965), p. 39.

[56]At the time of Nicea II, canon 8 of Nicea I, dealing with the reception of Novatianist clergy, served as a reference for Patriarch Tarasius to permit the reception of repentant iconoclast bishops by a rite of reconciliation and not by reordination. But the premise of analogical reasoning was doubtful, for Patriarch Tarasius maintained that the imposition of hands refered to by canon 8 was not an ordination rite. On this see our analysis of Nicea I.

[57]The advocates of rebaptizing Latins cite the ancient canonical texts which mention that heretics baptizing with only one immersion. But this type of argument does not take into account what the heretics referred to, the Eunomians wanted to emphasize by only one immersion: their distance from the trinitarian baptism of the Church.

[58]See P. Andrieu-Guitrancourt, *Introduction a l'étude du droit en général et du droit canonique contemporain* (Paris, 1963), p. 965.

[59]The canons issued or approved by the general councils cannot be abrogated or modified except by another general council. See for example canons 6 and 12 of the Synod in Trullo.

[60]The prescription of the synod in Trullo is recalled by canon 6 of Nicea II, which gives fatigue which the bishops are exposed to and their inability to move around as reasons for having a single annual synod.

[61]The author of the *Epitome* (ἐπει μή δυνατόν...) points out very clearly in the wording of canon 6 of the seventh ecumenical council that holding a single annual synod is a concession. *Rhalles-Potles II*, p. 579.

[62]For example, we can deduce from canon 19 of Nicea that according to the doctrine of the Church, the use of a properly worded formula in the administration of baptism by a heretical group is without sacramental effect if it is not accompanied by a basic, trinitarian orthodox belief. As for the Paulianist sect directly refered to in the canon of Nicea, it has not existed for fifteen centuries.

[63]Canon 8 of Nicea, setting out the ways of receiving into the Church clergy coming from the Novatianist group, establishes the fundamental principle according to which there must be only one bishop in each city. Canons 7 of Nicea and 12 of Chalcedon firmly maintain that in particular situations there must be one primatial jurisdiction in a prescribed territory.

[64]See for example the letter of the Council of Ephesus to the synod of Pamphylia about Eustathius.

[65]Chalcedon, canon 28; cf. Constantinople, canon 3; synod in Trullo, canon 36.

[66]Nicea, canon 6. It is curious to observe that in our time, in order to justify the primacy of Constantinople, most Orthodox canonists refer to the canons mentioned in the preceding note and do so from a clear perspective of legal positivism. Note the very appropriate comment of Fr. J. Meyendorff: "...since Byzantium does not exist anymore, it is simply meaningless to attempt a definition of the rights of the Ecumenical Patriarchate in Byzantine terms," in "The Ecumenical Patriarch, seen in the light of Orthodox Ecclesiology and History," *The Greek Orthodox Theological Review* 24 (1979), pp. 222-244, *loc. cit.* p. 243.

[67]Cf. note 52 above.

[68]If in the future a female diaconate were re-established, this canon would apply in principle, unless a general council issued different norms.

[69]*DGA* p. 5.

[70]On the inspiration of the prescriptions of the ancient canons, see Y. Congar, *La Tradition et les traditions, Essai historique* (Paris, 1960), pp. 157-58. The special authority of the first four ecumenical councils was a familiar idea to western canonists of the Early Middle Ages. See Ch. Lefebvre, *op. cit.* pp. 324-5.

[71]*Johannis Scholastici Synagoga L. titulorum caeteraque eiusdem opera iuridica* (Munich, 1937). *Syntagma XIV titulorum sine scholiis secundum versionem palaeoslavicam adiecto texto greco e vetustissimis codicibus manuscriptis* (St Petersburg, 1906). On the work of this great scholar, who was born in 1874 and died in 1943, see Ivan Seredny, *Trudy russkikh kanonistov V.N. Beneshevicha, I.S. Berdnikova, A.S. Pavlova i S.V. Troitskogo* (Leningrad, 1969, typed thesis presented to the Church Academy of that city), pp. 155-94 and pp. 262-76. See also T. Granstrem, "Vladimir Nikolaevich Beneševič (k 100-letiiu so dnia roždeniia)," *Vr.* 35 (1973), pp. 235-243. Although Beneševič did not edit the *Recensio Trullana,* we can get a pretty clear idea of the primitive redaction (*Recensio Trullana*) contained in the Codices Patmiaci 172-73, by means of the footnotes indicating the variant readings of the two manuscripts.

[72]*ACO* I, 5 vol. II, 6 vol. (Berlin, 1927-38).

[73]*Fonti,* fasc. IX, *Discipline générale antique* I, 1: *Les canons des conciles oecumeniques* (Rome, 1962).

[74]Reference to canon 6, Nicea. On this subject see our analysis of this text.

[75]We are thinking in particular of the different ways the Greek participle ἀκυρωθέντων has been translated into Latin in canon 4 of Constantinople; on the subject of the consecrations of Maximus the Cynic and ordinations performed by him, see our analysis of this canon.

[76]On this, the best example is still that of canon 6 of Nicea.

[77]A. Strewe, *Die Canonessamlung des Dionysius Exiguus in der ersten Redaktions* (Berlin, 1931).

[78]C.H. Turner, *Monumenta Juris Ecclesiae occidentalis antiquissima* 2 vol. (Oxford, 1899-1939).

[79]F. Schulthess, *Die syrischen Kanones der Synoden von Nicaea bis Chalcedon* (Berlin, 1908). The reference here is to a codex in the British Museum, Add. 14528. Thanks to the kind help and competence in Syriac of Mr. R-G Coquin, we were able to consult the work of F. Schulthess. We wish to thank him very heartily.

[80]In the *Syntagma* of Athens (*Rhalles-Potles* II and III), the text of the canons, based on a manuscript from Trebizond dated 1311, is followed by the commentaries of Zonaras and Balsamon. Then comes the text of the *Epitome* with the commentary of Aristenos. To avoid confusion, note that the name of Aristenos is placed before that of the *Epitome*.

[81]*Kanonicheskii Sbornik xiv Titulov, Prilozheniia* (St Petersburg, 1904), pp. 3-80.

CHAPTER I

THE COUNCIL OF NICEA

SECTION 1: THE BACKGROUND AND PROCEEDINGS

Orthodox Christianity has always considered itself to be the legitimate extension and the complete fulfillment of the religion of the Old Testament. According to the words of St. Paul, the Christian people are "the Israel of God."[1] Consequently, Christianity has claimed from the beginning to be strictly monotheistic, but the New Testament categorically affirms the divinity of Jesus Christ. The problem which, of necessity, had to be faced by theological thinking was the following: From within inherited Jewish monotheism, as set out in the Bible and obstinately defended against the pagans, how is it possible to proclaim the oneness of God while at the same time insisting on the divine nature of a being distinct from God the Father?[2] If the trinitarian faith of the Church was well established, the theological interpretation of this faith during the period before the Council of Nicea was nonetheless full of trial and error. In the third century, a cleavage appeared between popular belief and reflective theology.[3] It would be erroneous to oppose these two trends completely and to see in the second a source of all the Church's problems. Popular belief was not at all free from serious deformations; then again, reflective theology could not be reduced to any one single current. It is an established historical fact that the Arian heresy had the thinking of the school of Antioch as its breeding ground, more specifically the ideas of Lucian, martyred in 312. Moreover, Arius and his adversaries were in agreement on the source of the Arian orientation.[4] The Collucianists, as the disciples of Lucian liked to call themselves, claimed to base their doctrinal affirmations on a scriptural exegesis they designated as rational, that is, methodical and literal.[5] Probably around 318, Arius, who was a priest of the church of Baucalis, came into open conflict with his bishop, Alexander of Alexandria.[6] Arius denied the eternity and the real divine nature of the Word.[7] He was condemned by a council of one hundred bishops from Egypt and Libya under the presidency of Alexander, but Arius refused to submit to the decision and looked for support primarily among his former fellow disciples in the school of Antioch. He also found support among certain Origenists who along with their Alexandrian master emphasized the instrumental role of the Word in the creation of the world.[8] Thus the dispute quickly spread all over the Greek East. The emperor Constantine at first thought that the controversy was of little importance and that it would be resolved through conciliation. Seeing that this was not at all possible and after consulting his ecclesiastical advisors, he decided to call a general council. It seems that at first Ancyra in Galatia, where a council had already been held, was to be the site of the future assembly,[9] but Nicea appeared to be preferable. It was the second city of Bithynia, and the emperor had a palace there. It was relatively easy to get to for the bishops coming from the other side of the straits and besides, it was close to Nicomedia, where Constantine most often held his court, and this was a great advantage for him.[10]

How many bishops took part in the council? More than 250 according to Eusebius, 270 according the Eustathius of Antioch, more than 300 according to Constantine. St. Athanasius spoke of about 300 in one of his writings; in another place, he said 318, a figure stated for the first time by Hilary of Poitiers around 359/60.[11] This number, which recalls the number of Abraham's servants, was adopted and passed on to posterity.[12] Even though the emperor gave the bishops and their entourages the privileges of the *evectio,* that is, they could use the *cursus publicus,* difficult traveling conditions explain the great disproportion in the geographical distribution of the churches represented. The great majority of the fathers came from Asia, Pontus and Syro-Phoenicia. The representation from the Latin West was numerically weak.[13] We must note that Arianism had not yet penetrated those regions; nonetheless, western influence was not negligible due to the personality of Ossius of Cordova, Constantine's chief ecclesiastical advisor.[14] Pope Sylvester declined to come because of his great age, but he sent two legates, the priests Vito and Vincent.[15] Basing himself on the approximate number of existing bishops at the time, V.V. Bolotov estimated that a sixth of the world-wide episcopate took part in the council.[16]

The fathers of Nicea did not call their assembly "ecumenical"; rather, they often used the expression "great and holy council."[17] They had, however, the unquestionable awareness of representing the moral consciousness of the whole Church; this was clearly shown by the ending of the symbol of faith they worked out.[18] Eusebius of Caesarea was the first to call the Council of Nicea "ecumenical."[19] It is proper to note that not until later did the term "ecumenical council" receive specific acceptance by being exclusively applied to a very definite type of church assembly.[20] The opening of the council took place on May 20, 325, and the meetings were held in the imperial palace, which was the only place large enough to accommodate the bishops and their attendants. It is, in fact, probable that the cathedral had been destroyed in the recent persecution and had not yet been fully reconstructed. We do not know how long the council sat: no doubt at least three months if we admit that the creed was edited on June 19 and that the closing took place on August 25.[21]

Who presided at the meetings of the council? The lack of clarity, indeed the silence, of the most ancient sources does not allow us to answer that question with any precision. It seems quite possible that Constantine himself assumed the presidency for most of the sessions,[22] but who among the bishops had the honorary first position? We can even ask if any one of the fathers held that position in a permanent way. Eusebius stated that the emperor, after having given his speech, gave the floor τοῖς τῆς συνόδου προέδροις.[23] The plural form here does not permit us, however, to affirm categorically that several bishops had the first position because the term πρόεδρος at that time was often a synonym for ἐπίσκοπος.[24] In the lists of signatures, the first name is that of Ossius of Cordova, Constantine's official ecclesiastical counselor. Later on, it was to be claimed, without proof, that he was a representative of the Roman see along with the two priestly legates.[25] Eustathius of Antioch, as much from the weight of his personality as from the importance of his see, was destined to play a very important role in the council; the same could be said for Alexander of Alexandria.[26]

The primary task of the fathers was to make the trinitarian doctrine of the Church very precise in the face of the Arian heresy. This they did by issuing a symbol of faith based on baptismal creeds of the Syro-Palestinian region, adequately completed of course. The key word of the Nicene symbol is the adjective "consubstantial," ὁμοούσιος, used to indicate the relation between the Father and the Son.[27] It was around this term that theological debate polarized in the fifty years following the council.

According to its agenda, the council was also supposed to resolve the thorny problem about the date of Pascha.[28] The first controversy about Pascha shook the Church in the second century: the Asiatic communities celebrated the great feast on the fourteenth of Nisan whatever the day of the week it might fall on.[29] Other churches which followed the Asiatic practice finally adopted the general usage. From then on there was only a minority who refused to conform. These Quartodecimans, Τεσσαρεσκαιδεκατῖται, as they were called, constituted tiny dissident groups whose followers at least later were received into the catholic Church by unction with chrism after renouncing their former position.[30] During the debates raised by the particular customs of the Asiatics, no one accused them of being Judaizers because no one questioned the method of calculating the Jewish Passover; it was by this method that everyone calculated the annual date of the great Christian feast. However, using the Jewish method of calculation soon raised its own questions. After the crushing defeat of the revolt of Simon Bar Kochba in 135, Judaism, in fact, lost its contact with Palestine. Now if the Bible clearly indicates when to celebrate Passover, it makes no explicit reference to the equinox, but, looking forward to the expected offering of the first fruits of the harvest, a celebration before this time would have been impossible.[31] Such a criterion, though, lost its exactness with the disappearance of a geographical center, and a variety of calculations began to be used, producing contrasting results.

At the end of the second century or the beginning of the third Jewish authorities established a new system for fixing the date of Passover. This new system did not take the vernal equinox into account, so that once every three years Passover came before it.[32] Many Christians were troubled by this: why, they asked, should they celebrate the memorial of the passion and resurrection on the basis of a calendar calculation that was not in use in the time of Jesus? Then again, in the new Jewish system, following a calculation based only on the equinox, there could be a double anomaly: Passover could be celebrated twice in one twelve month period, that is, from one vernal equinox to the next, or it could not be celebrated at all from one to the other. On the whole, Christians gave great weight to the relation between Pascha and the vernal equinox because the time of the passion itself was linked to the six days of creation.[33]

Moreover, as the distance between the synagogue and the Church grew, it seemed abnormal to the majority of Christians to depend on the Jews for the determination of the date of Pascha. This feeling provoked many authors to write works during the third century,

West as well as East.[34] Thus an Alexandrian scientist, Anatolius, who became bishop of Laodicea in Syria, used a cycle of nineteen years, discovered by the Athenian astronomer Meto in 432 BC, to determine the date of Pascha.[35] This cycle was to be imposed on the whole Christian world later on, but according to this system, Pascha was always celebrated after the vernal equinox.

At the beginning of the fourth century, the Jews modified their method of calculating Passover so that all the possible dates of the feast would fall in the single month of March; this change gave greater weight to the calculation which favored having Passover before the equinox.[36] However, while the majority of churches had long since stopped following the Jewish method of dating Passover, a relatively strong minority around Antioch continued to follow it. The followers of this practice attributed the following saying to the apostles: "As for you, do not make calculations. But when your brothers of the circumcision celebrate their Passover, celebrate yours also...and even if they are wrong in their calculation, do not worry about it."[37]

Alongside this important difference, there existed, sometimes, slight variations in the date of Pascha betweeen Rome and Alexandria.[38] In 314, the Council of Arles suggested that the bishop of Rome indicate the annual date of the feast to all the churches.[39] The emperor Constantine was not only preoccupied by the disagreement over the divine nature of the Logos but also by the different dates of Pascha. According to the historian Sozomen, he may have sent Bishop Ossius of Cordova to Alexandria to examine these two problems.[40]

The whole affair was thus submitted to the fathers gathered in Nicea. No authentic acts of the council exist. If there were any minutes of the meetings taken, they have not survived. The only documents unquestionably coming from the council are the symbol of faith, the twenty canons, the certainly incomplete list of members, and a synodal letter addressed to the Church of Alexandria.[41] The document about Pascha which John the Scholastic made into an appendix to the *Synagoge* and which some authorities identify with the decree that the fathers of the Council of Antioch referred to is not, properly speaking, a falsification; it is a redactional arrangement, of unknown origin, compiled from authentic documents which themselves have come down to us.[42] As such, this document does not tell us much more than the originals themselves. Here is the content of the text:

From the holy council of Nicea concerning the holy Pascha: Thus we have put into effect the opinion of everyone gathered together at the holy council in the time of the pious and great emperor Constantine who not only convoked the undersigned bishops to give peace to our nation but also attended the meetings himself; he examined with them what was good for the catholic Church. Therefore, after having examined the question of the duty of the whole Church under heaven to celebrate Pascha on the same date, we found that the three parts of the universe were agreed with the Romans and the Alexandrians; only one eastern region disagreed. It was judged good and proper, all questions and contradictions being left aside, that the eastern brothers follow the example of the Romans and Alexandrians and all the others so that everyone should let their prayers rise to heaven on one single day of holy Pascha. And all the easterners who had a different practice signed the document.[43]

Was there a written document, a decree, whose text may have been lost? It is difficult to give a categorical answer. If there was a real decree, it is hard to understand how such an important document could have gotten lost while the twenty conciliar canons were preserved. It is true that the Council of Antioch mentioned τόν ὅρον τῆς Ἁγίας καί Μεγάλης Συνόδου τῆς ἐν Νικαίᾳ συγκροτηθείσης. . .περὶ τῆς ἁγίας ἑορτῆς τοῦ σωτηριώδους Πάσχα.[44] In addition, St. Athanasius in his De synodis made reference to a text, unknown elsewhere, which began with the words: Ἔδοξε τὰ ὑποτεταγμένα.[45] These witnesses are to be taken seriously because of their origin and their antiquity. The Council of Antioch which issued the canon about Pascha must not be confused with the synodus in encaeniis which took place in that city in 341. It was held ten years earlier, putting it very close to Nicea in time.[46] But the term ὅρος could have had the meaning of "decision," "adopted measure," and did not necessarily imply a written decree. As for the reference found in the De synodis written in 359, it is much too vague for us to deduce that it referred to the supposed decree. A passage from the Panarion of St. Epiphanius established a distinction among the decisions made by the fathers of Nicea:

At the time of the council, they issued some ecclesiastical rulings; but at the same time concerning Pascha, they prescribed (ὥρισαν) unity and agreement on the holy and very virtuous Day of God.[47]

It seems clear that, as with the Meletian schism, there was not a decree, as such, about one uniform date for Pascha. Nonetheless, it is possible on the basis of certain testimony to know what was decided on this question. The synodal letter to the Church of Alexandria stated the following:

All our eastern brothers who up till now have not been in agreement with the Romans or you or with all those who from the beginning have done as you do, will henceforth celebrate Pascha at the same time as you.[48]

The circular letter of the emperor Constantine to the churches about the Council of Nicea, of course, touched on the paschal question and indicated the solution arrived at:[49]

Christian Pascha must be celebrated on the same day by everyone; and for the calculation of the date, no reference should be made to the Jews. Such would be humiliating and moreover it is possible for them to have two Passovers in one single year. [We have seen what this assertion signified.] Consequently, the churches must conform to the practice followed by Rome, Africa, Italy, Egypt, Spain, Gaul, Britain, Libya, Greece, Asia, Pontus, and Cilicia.

St. Athanasius himself cited Cilicia as one of the regions where the date of Pascha was calculated according to the Jewish method.[50] In fact, different practices existed there, as in other places, as we learn from Socrates.[51] Canon 1 of the Council of Antioch mentioned the ruling of Nicea without making the wording precise; this council threatened grave sanctions—excommunication for laymen, deposition for clergy—against anyone who henceforth contravened this ruling by celebrating Pascha "with the Jews." The *Apostolic Constitutions*, compiled in the second half of the fourth century, shows us to what extent the text of the earlier *Didascalia* was reworked on the question of Pascha so it would harmonize with Nicea. We read:

You, brothers, celebrate Pascha with minute care according to the equinox so as not to commemorate the Passion two times in one year. In one year, you will remember only one time him who suffered only once and you will no longer seek to celebrate with the Jews.[52]

The Canons of the Holy Apostles found at the end of the *Apostolic Constitutions* came out of the same north Syrian milieu. Canon 7 declares: "If a bishop, a priest, or a deacon celebrates the holy day of Pascha before the vernal equinox, with the Jews, let him be deposed."[53] St. Epiphanius, refuting the position on Pascha taken by the Audian sect, reminds us of the three principles which must guide the orthodox in determining the date of Pascha: (1) the full moon, (2) equinox, and (3) Sunday.[54]

We can, therefore, reconstruct the elements of the decision of the first ecumenical council on Pascha in the following way: (1) This feast must be celebrated on the same Sunday by all the churches. (2) It must take into account the full moon that follows the vernal equinox. (3) Consequently, the eastern churches who followed the Jews in calculating the date must abandon this usage. However, the council did not enter into details of the method of calculation and, therefore, did not impose the use of the nineteen-year cycle. As Professor D.M. Ogitsky correctly notes,

> a detailed and exhaustive ordering of all the technical aspects
> of the computation of Pascha (including the problems raised
> by the inexactness of the Julian calendar) was not in the
> competence of the council.[55]

However, little by little the idea was introduced that the Alexandrian cycle of nineteen years had been sanctioned by the fathers of Nicea. It seems that this was already the opinion of St. Ambrose.[56] This belief was definitively implanted by the beginning of the sixth century. Dionysius Exiguus affirmed in no uncertain terms that the cycle in question had been established by the fathers of Nicea *non tam peritia saeculari quam Sancti Spiritus illustratione.*[57] In the seventh century, the author of the *Chronicon Paschale* maintained that this cycle, which he called "admirable and worthy of eternal memory," had been adopted by the first ecumenical council under divine inspiration (Θεοπνεύστως).[58] Dionysius' influence in the West was such that the cycle of nineteen years spread everywhere; by the reign of Charlemagne, it had been imposed on the whole of Latin Christianity. From then on, there was complete agreement about the date of Pascha between the Latin West and the Byzantine East. This situation was maintained until 1582 when the Roman Catholic Church introduced the Gregorian calendar.

The refusal to celebrate Pascha "with the Jews" (μετὰ τῶν Ἰουδαίων) meant that, in the ancient canonical texts, we were not to celebrate this feast by basing its date on the method of calculation of the Jews. But, contrary to what was believed later, this refusal in no way was aimed at avoiding an accidental celebrating of Pascha and Passover together. This is clearly shown by the fact that during the fourth century after Nicea, Christian and Jewish Paschas coincided several times.[59] St. Athanasius, speaking of those who followed the Jewish method of calculating the date of Pascha and who were later called the Protopaschites, did not say that they celebrated this feast on the same day as the Jews but only during the same period.[60] In the Middle Ages, when it became impossible to celebrate the Jewish and Christian Paschas together because of the loss of time in the Julian calendar, the idea that a concelebration of the feasts had been forbidden by church law was generally accepted; this idea, however, was based on a literal but erroneous understanding of the expression μετὰ τῶν 'Ιουδαίων. Thus Zonaras in commenting on canon 7 of the Holy Apostles stated concerning the Jews that their non-festal Pascha (ἀνέ-ορτον ἑορτὴν) must come first and then our Pascha should follow.[61] Matthew Blastares, who summed up the knowledge and opinions of his time on the Pascha question, indicated that one of the norms to follow in determining the date of Pascha is the non-coincidence of Pascha and Passover.[62]

The decisions of the Council of Nicea to bring the Protopaschites into line with the general practice ran up against serious resistance. Canon 1 of Antioch gives us the most ancient evidence on this matter. Theodoret of Cyrus wrote the following about an anchorite named Abraham:

His simplicity of mind at first led him to celebrate Pascha ahead of time, being apparently ignorant of what the fathers of Nicea had stipulated; he wanted to follow the ancient usage. Moreover, many others in that time were in the same state of ignorance.[63]

In certain cases, it was a conscious refusal to abide by Nicea; such was the case of the Audians. They went so far as to accuse the official Church of having changed the method of calculating the date of Pascha to please the emperor Constantine, which was completely wrong.[64] The Jewish calculation had an unquestioned attraction for the Christian communities of the civil Diocese of the East, especially when the Alexandrian calculation led to a late Pascha, that is, a month after the equinox. That created a real problem. Such was the case in 387 when the Christian Pascha fell on April 25 while the Jewish feast had already been celebrated on March 20. St. John Chrysostom, then a priest in Antioch, gave a speech entitled Εἰς τοὺς τὰ πρῶτα νηστεύον-τας. He made reference to the decisions of Nicea; and, taking a purely disciplinary point of view, he said that "even if the Church made a

mistake, exactness in the observance of times would not be as important as the offense caused by this division and this schism."[65] The late
date of Pascha that year also furnished us with a very interesting homily.[66] The author, an unknown easterner, went to great effort to establish the correctness of the equinoxal principal. Here is how he
summed up the rules which must be observed:

> In effect, the whole thing is to make sure that the fourteenth of
> the month does not precede the vernal equinox, that the Sun-
> day of the resurrection be freed from dependence on the four-
> teenth. It is this that gives problems to those who calculate
> improperly. It is necessary, in effect, that the fourteenth fall in
> the week which precedes the day fixed for the resurrection. If it
> falls in the middle of the week, the solution is easily found; if
> on the contrary, it falls on Sunday, there must be a meticulous
> application because those who do not make a careful inquiry
> sometimes commit the error of believing that it is the fifteenth
> and not the fourteenth. This is precisely what has happened in
> the present case.[67]

This text shows us how in the East the orthodox understood and
applied the Nicene ordinance. With time the Protopaschite practice
disappeared. Moreover, civil legislation contributed to its fading away;
a law of March 21, 413, punished with exile anyone who celebrated
Pascha on a date other than the one of the catholic Church. This
stipulation was taken up again in another law of June 8, 423.[68]

The fathers of Nicea also took measures to end the trouble over
Meletius and his followers, who already for twenty years had been
seriously disturbing the life of the Church in Egypt.[69] In 305 Meletius,
bishop of Lycopolis in the Thebaid, taking as his pretext the persecution then battering the Church and depriving communities of their
pastors, arrogated to himself the right to ordain bishops and priests
for that region.[70] Four imprisoned bishops, Phileas, Hesychius, Pacho-
mius, and Theodore, wrote a letter to him in which they demanded
that he stop his irregular actions, which ran roughshod over the rights
of the bishop of Alexandria.[71] Meletius did not pay any attention to
these appeals. He came to Alexandria and got scandalously mixed up
in the administration of the church which Bishop Peter, constrained to
hide because of the persecution, was not able to assume directly. Meletius set aside the priests that Peter had designated and put in his own
men. Peter ordered the faithful of Alexandria to hold back from
communion with the usurper.[77] When the persecution abated a bit,

Bishop Peter took back the effective direction of his church and proceded to regulate the question of the lapsed Christians. At Pascha 306, he wrote an encyclical letter on this subject. He fixed the penances which the lapsed had to carry out if they wanted to be readmitted to communion.[73] If the defections were soundly condemned, the sanctions set out were inspired by a spirit of mercy. Then Meletius made himself the champion of rigorism and thus attracted to himself and his faction all the advocates of severity. From all this, the conflict gained new life and the conflict hardened into schism. Meanwhile, the persecution also regained vigor in Egypt at the instigation of the emperor Maximinus Daia. Meletius was deposed by a synod presided over by Peter of Alexandria for this transgressions of church laws.[74] He was later arrested and sent to the mines of Phaino in Palestine like many other Christians. His deposition took place in 306 and the deportation in 308. In the spring of 311, following the edict of Galerius, Meletius was liberated and returned to Egypt bathed in the glory of a confessor. He pursued his schismatic activity, opposing his group, called the church of the martyrs, to the catholic Church. In this respect, the Meletian attitude was not without similarity to the Donatists of North Africa at the same time. However, Maximinus renewed the persecution, and Peter of Alexandria died a martyr on November 25, 311. At the time of the Council of Nicea, the Meletians had thirty-five bishops.[75]

Ought we to see in this affair a conflict between the centralizing tendency, which sought to give the bishop of Alexandria control over all episcopal consecrations, and the party of those who wanted to establish the provincial system? Certainly Meletius' overstepping the boundaries of his own jurisdiction was a challenge to the authority of the see of Alexandria, but nothing allows us to affirm that Meletius represented a decentralizing tendency. He did not limit his actions to the Thebaid, which would have been his metropolitan district, but he tried to present himself as the head of the hierarchy for the whole of Egypt.[76] Even if his rigorist attitude regarding the reconciliation of the lapsed resulted from his own inner conviction and was not simply a pretext to oppose Peter of Alexandria and his legitimate successors, it remains certain that the personal ambition of the bishop of Lycopolis played an essential role in his schismatic scheming.[77] Achillas, who succeeded Peter, was bishop for only a few months. Alexander followed him on the primatial see of Alexandria, which he occupied until his death on April 17, 328.

The Council of Nicea tried to put an end to the Meletian schism

first of all by solemnly confirming the customary right by which the
see of Alexandria had the primacy over episcopal consecrations in
Egypt, Libya, and the Pentapolis.[78] The council equally decided the
status of Meletius and the bishops he had ordained. These measures,
no less than in the case of Pascha, were not embodied in a specific
decree, but they were mentioned in the synodal letter to the churches
of Egypt, Libya and the Pentapolis.[79] Here is the extract from that
letter on this matter:

> It has therefore been decided that Meletius—though the council
> has been moved to clemency since according to the norm ($\kappa\alpha\tau\grave{\alpha}$
> $\tau\grave{o}\nu \, \dot{\alpha}\kappa\rho\iota\beta\tilde{\eta} \, \lambda\acute{o}\gamma o\nu$) he deserved no pardon—should remain in his
> city and that he should have no power to make promotions or
> ordinations. He shall not appear in the country or in another city
> claiming such ordinations or promotions as his pretext to be
> there. Only the dignity of the name of bishop shall be given to
> him. In addition those who were established by him, after hav-
> ing been confirmed by a holier imposition of hands ($\mu\upsilon\sigma\tau\iota\kappa\omega$-
> $\tau\acute{e}\rho\alpha \, \chi\epsilon\iota\rho o\tau o\nu\acute{\iota}\alpha \, \beta\epsilon\beta\alpha\iota\omega\theta\acute{e}\nu\tau\alpha\varsigma$), will be admitted to commun-
> ion, which means that afterwards they will conserve their rank
> and their function, but they will obviously be second behind
> those who were approved and ordained by our very honorable
> concelebrant Alexander in each district and church. They will
> have no power to promote those whom they will or to pro-
> pose their names nor to do any thing without the consent of
> the bishops of the catholic and apostolic church under Alex-
> ander. Those who by the grace of God and your prayers have
> not been found in schism but have been without blemish in
> the catholic and apostolic church have the right to promote
> and propose the names of those worthy of being clerics and to
> do everything that is permitted by the law and church ordi-
> nance. If it happens that someone of those in the church dies,
> then those who were recently received have the right to suc-
> ceed to the dignity of the deceased only on condition that they
> seem worthy of such a dignity and that the people choose
> them and the bishop of the catholic church of Alexandria
> gives his consent and confirmation. This ruling has been made
> for all except Meletius because of his manifest lack of disci-
> pline from the very beginning and also because of his rash and
> fiery character, so that no power of promotion be given to a
> man apt to commit again the same acts of lawlessness.[80]

The fathers of Nicea clearly disassociated the personal case of Meletius from the bishops he had ordained. The clemency of the council in his case consisted only in considering him as an honorary bishop when in the light of his deposition he should have had the status of a layman according to strict law. But nothing more was allowed to him at that time or for the future. As for the bishops installed by him, after receiving an imposition of hands, they were allowed to exercise their episcopal ministry as auxiliaries of the local bishops with the inherent limitations of that position. This provided for only one ruling bishop in each church; canon 8 of Nicea expressly makes reference to this case in regulating the integration of the Novatianist clergy into the Church. In the case of a vacancy in a see, this auxiliary would be the normal successor to the ruling bishop. However, the promotion was not automatic; the people had to elect the new bishop, and the bishop of Alexandria had to install him.

In order to be admitted to the exercise of their functions in the Church, the Meletian bishops had to be confirmed by an imposition of hands designated as μυστικωτέρα χειροτονία. This comparative grammatical form shows that the imposition of hands in question was an ordination and not a penitential action. It was an affirmation which said that the previous ordination conferred in an irregular manner was deficient. It was obviously so since it was done without the indispensable approval of the legitimate primate, the bishop of Alexandria. It is proper here to connect this action with what the fathers of Nicea stipulated in canon 6, having exactly the situation of Egypt in mind: "If anyone became a bishop without the consent of the metropolitan, the great council decrees that such a person is not even a bishop."

Two more remarks about the expression μυστικωτέρα χειροτονία: First, it would not be at all inexact to translate this expression as "by a more sacramental ordination."[81] Secondly, the comparative form allows us to suppose that the fathers of Nicea did not want to affirm categorically the absolute nullity of the ordinations conferred by Meletius without at the same time recognizing them due to the intrinsically ecclesial character of the idea of ministry. The conditions of integration made for the Meletian bishops differed from those for Novatianist bishops in that for the second group, they were only guaranteed a priestly status while the first group was assured of having the status of bishops. We also note that the Novatianist clergy were required to make a written statement of acceptance of the doctrine and practice of the catholic Church on remarriage and the reconciliation of the lapsed

Christians. Nothing of the sort was demanded of the Meletians, which seems to prove that the origin of the schism was not doctrinal. Meletius had committed a double offense by having intruded into the affairs of the church and by not having taken into account the traditional perogatives of the see of Alexandria.

Immediately after Nicea, the schism seemed to be healing, Meletius himself gave to Alexander the list of his clergy and remained at Lycopolis as he had been ordered until his death two or three years later; he at least died before Alexander, who died on April 17, 328. The Meletians were solidly planted in Egypt, and the restriction of the rights of their bishops as decreed by the Council of Nicea was not well received by them; and so there was a resurgence of the schism after the election of St. Athanasius to the see of Alexandria. The Meletians made a tactical alliance with the Arians and were the tenacious adversaries of Athanasius. Their communities existed at least until the eighth century.[82]

The fathers of Nicea took advantage of their meeting to discuss a number of points concerning church discipline. Their intention was not at all to introduce a new law but to recall rules sometimes neglected, indeed contested, to resolve problems rising out of concrete situations. They also confirmed rather than created a form of coordination in the organization of the Church by sanctioning the metropolitan system.

The authentic canons of Nicea are twenty in number. If, in several ancient Latin collections, we find a different number, it is the result of different ways of dividing the texts or from omissions.[83] Then again at Rome, the canons of Sardica were joined to those of Nicea and were very soon confused with them.[84] In the non-Greek East, some Syriac and Arabic canons were erroneously attributed to the fathers of Nicea.[85]

The twenty canons can be classified according to subject in the following way: Canons 1, 2, 9 and 10 deal with the conditions of ordination. Canons 4, 5, 6 and 7 deal with hierarchical structures. Canons 3, 15, 16 and 17 have to do with the life and status of clerics. Canons 11, 12, 13 and 14 concern the penance and the reconciliation of lapsed Christians. Canons 8 and 19 set out the ways to admit dissidents. Canons 18 and 20 settle two points of liturgical discipline.

SECTION 2: THE CANONS OF THE COUNCIL

The Canons of the 318 fathers gathered at Nicea under the consulate of the illustrious Paulinus and Julian in the year 536 of the Alexandrian era, the 19th of the month of Desius, the 13th day of the Kalends of July.[86]

1

If anyone has been maimed by doctors at the time of an illness or has been castrated by barbarians, let him remain a cleric; but if anyone, already being a cleric and in good health, castrates himself, he must be excluded from the clergy and in the future no such person shall be ordained. As it is obvious that what has been said above concerns those who act on their own volition and who have dared to castrate themselves, the ruling permits, therefore, those who have been made eunuchs by barbarians or by their masters to become clerics, if on other grounds they are judged to be worthy.

First of all we need to determine the meaning of certain terms used in this and other canons of Nicea. We have translated the Greek expression ἐν τῷ κλήρῳ ἐξεταζόμενον by "being a cleric." The verb ἐξετάζω in the passive form here means "to be reckoned as, to be registered as"; this meaning was already attested in the classical period.[87] As for the word κλῆρος and its derivative κληρικός as well as their Latin counterparts *clerus* and *clericus,* we encounter them from the third century in the specific meaning of "clergy" and "cleric."[88] Concerning self-mutilation, let us call attention to what Zonaras has to say: "The canon is aimed not only at those who have themselves perpetrated the act but of course at those also who have voluntarily submitted to such an operation."[89] About the expression πεπαῦσθαι προσήκει, we can observe that the verb παύω is one of the terms used in the ancient canonical texts to designate the action of deposing a cleric.[90] The word κανὼν when it is related to a disciplinary ruling, as it is in this case, has the meaning for the fathers of Nicea of a well determined norm regardless of how it got that way. Very soon in church parlance, the term took on a very precise meaning: it designated a legislative action being part of written law. According to what is stipulated in canon 1 of Nicea, the fact of being a eunuch is not considered as an impediment *ex defectu* to becoming a cleric; on the contrary, it constitutes a permanent irregularity *ex delicto* for those who may have intentionally castrated themselves. The theory lying behind the decision adopted at Nicea is clearly set out in the Canons of the Holy Apostles. Canon 22 of this collection states that "anyone who castrates himself, let him not become a cleric because he is a murderer of himself and an enemy of the creation of God." Canon 23 declares that "if a cleric castrates himself, let him be deposed because he is his own murderer."[91]

Did the fathers of Nicea have concrete cases of their own time in view, or did they remember the controversy between Demetrius of Alexandria and the Palestinian bishops about the ordination of Origen?[92] We can only offer hypotheses. Following Beveridge, it is often affirmed that the affair of Leontius was behind the promulgation of this particular canon.[93] This Leontius, born in Phrygia and a cleric in Antioch, lived with a woman *subintroducta*[94] by the name of Eustolia. Refusing to separate from her, he castrated himself, following which his bishop, Eustathius, deposed him. Despite this, the emperor Constantine in 344 promoted him to be bishop of Antioch.[95] But in 325 Leontius was still a person too insignificant to have been himself the only cause of the promulgation of this canon. Without a doubt, there were at that time a certain number of analogous cases among Christians influenced by extreme currents of asceticism. St. Epiphanius mentions the Valesian sect, where castration was systematically practiced.[96]

Was the ruling issued by Nicea scrupulously observed? The above-mentioned case of Leontius, who was raised to the episcopate despite such an impediment, does not prove anything, because he was an Arian, and he obviously rejected the legislation of Nicea. We must call attention on the one hand to the civil laws severely banning castration, but, on the other, to the fact that they were often renewed; this shows that they were not very well applied.[97] The fathers of the "First-Second Council of 861 thought it good to recall the incompatibility of being a cleric and being a eunuch, if it was a question of voluntary castration. Such a reminder lets us suppose that the canons were not always carefully observed on this point.[98]

2

Whether by necessity or by the weight of human frailties, several things have come about contrary to the general order

of the Church. Thus, spiritual washing has been given and, along with this baptism, the episcopate or the priesthood has been given to men who have only been recently received from pagan life to the faith and have not been sufficiently instructed. It seems right and proper that such things not happen anymore. These men, in effect, must remain catechumens for a certain time and after baptism submit to a still longer period of probation. The apostolic statement in this matter is very clear: "Let him not be a neophyte for fear that by pride he fall into judgment and into the trap of the devil."[99] If, during this probation period, he is found to be guilty of some fault affecting his soul and which is attested to by two or three witnesses, let him be excluded from the clergy. If anyone acts contrary to this ordinance, as much as he opposes himself in that to the great council, he is in danger of being excluded from the clergy.

The expression ψυχικόν τι ἁμάρτημα is difficult to understand, and the scholiasts, ancient as well as modern, have only been able to give personal opinions.[100] The Latin versions do not shed much light on the subject: some are literal or nearly so, and others are interpretative translations which simply show the doubt in the translators' minds as to the meaning that the fathers of Nicea wanted to give to this expression.[101] In our opinion, the truest meaning in this case is that which takes the context into account; therefore, it must mean serious sin that a cleric commits in the exercise of his functions by pride or lack of sound judgement. His becoming a priest too quickly did not allow these faults to be seen. Perhaps we must connect this canon with what we read in canon 5 which makes reference to the case of a bishop who excommunicates someone "on the basis of his own lack of courage, his quarrelsome spirit, or by some feeling of dislike." As Hefele properly stated, the threat of deposition is directed as much against the one ordained as against the ordaining bishop.[102]

Canon 80 of the Canons of the Holy Apostles, which in principle condemned the promotion of neophytes to the episcopate, introduced, however, a restriction by the following formula: "unless such a thing happens by divine grace." Effectively, many historical witnesses show us how Christians were sensitive to divine signs in the choice of their bishops and priests. This shows the fundamental belief that the election of sacred ministers comes from God.[103] Whatever may have been the case, one thing is certain: the ruling issued by Nicea was not con-

sidered as an absolutely constraining factor. We know of the case of
Ambrose of Milan. Still more characteristic is the case of Nectarius,
elected bishop of Constantinople by the council of 381. We must not
deduce from these exceptions, however, that church practice did not
take into account the principle set out by the fathers of Nicea. On the
contrary, the Council of Laodicea, in its canon 3, recalled "that those
who have been very recently baptized should not be elevated to be a
cleric."[104]

The Nicene canon does not specify the length of time for the
catechumenate. The time was, moreover, variable according to the
Church, and it was admitted besides that the bishop could shorten or
lengthen the time according to the circumstances and the frame of
mind of the catechumen.[105] As for the lapse of time between the baptism of a person and his becoming cleric, this was not fixed either; it
was only required that it be longer than that of the catechumenate.
Canon 10 of the Council of Sardica stipulates that it is necessary,
before being promoted to the episcopate, to remain a certain time in
each degree of the ministry. The East never felt itself strictly bound by
this obligation even though it was restated by canon 17 of the First-
Second Council.[106]

3

**The great council absolutely forbids any bishop, priest, dea-
con, or any other member of the clergy to have a woman
living with him, unless she is a mother, a sister, an aunt, or
any other woman completely above suspicion.**

The Greek text of this canon admits of several variants; the only
one to have an influence on the meaning involves the omission of the
conjunction ἤ in front of, ἃ μόνα πρόσωπα,[107] which would mean that
the only women who are above suspicion are a mother, sister or aunt.
But this reading is not in agreement with the totality of the ancient
Latin versions or with the reference to this conciliar resolution in the
Corpus Juris Civilis.[108] In addition, we find this addition in the recension of John the Scholastic at the end of the canon: "These women
and those who are closely related to them (παραπλήσια) are above
suspicion."[109]

The key word for determining the meaning of this canon is the term
συνείσακτος. In Antioch from the third century on, a virgin or a
widow living with a man was designated by this term, both having
vowed to live in continence.[110] The term with this meaning soon

spread throughout the whole Greek East along side the synonyms ἐπείσακτος and ἀγαπητή;[111] in the Latin world, however, eventually these women were habitually called *subintroductae*.[112] Such unions were not rare during the first centuries of Christianity. People have supposed that those who lived in this way based themselves on a false interpretation of two passages taken from 1 Corinthians.[113] The church authorities disapproved, on the whole, of these unions, as the correspondence of St. Cyprian shows,[114] as well as the letter of the Council of Antioch in 268 concerned with the doctrine and behavior of Paul of Samosata.[115] Canon 19 of the Council of Ancyra in 314 forbade virgins to live with men ʻas sisters."[116]

Despite the great authority of the Council of Nicea, it was difficult to eradicate this shocking custom. In a letter to a certain priest Gregory, Basil the Great wrote the following:

> We have not been the first nor the only one, my dear Gregory, to decree that women cannot cohabitate with men. Read the canon promulgated by our holy fathers at the Council of Nicea, which forbade most clearly the introduction of women into one's house.[117]

Jerome deplored "the plague of the *agapetae*"[118] (celibate men and women living together); John Chrysostom also reacted energetically against this custom.[119] Civil law expressly reinforced the prohibition of cohabitation as made by the fathers of Nicea; this civil law was adopted in 420.[120] Canon 5 of the synod in Trullo takes up the same interdiction. Inspired by analogous considerations, the fathers of the seventh ecumenical council forbade women to live in a bishop's residence and opposed mixed monasteries.[121]

The Nicene canon does not mention the legitimate wife among the women who may properly live with a cleric; must we deduce that the fathers of the first ecumenical council wanted to impose celibacy or a separation from their wives on the members of the clergy? Such an interpretation is totally excluded. First of all, it seems hardly believable that a decision of such importance would not have been clearly formulated if that had been the intention of the fathers of Nicea. An innovation of that importance is completely inconceivable on the part of the council, whose primary preoccupations, on the canonical level, were to maintain the ancient customs and to eliminate abuses. Moreover, if the council had really introduced such a modification in the discipline in practice, we would find echoes of this decision in the writings of the time. The church authorities of the fourth century who leaned toward permanent celibacy of clerics functioning in holy orders would have been only too happy to make reference to the prestigious authority of the great and holy council. In fact, the question in all probability was not even touched on at Nicea. The anecdote reported by Socrates, taken up again by Sozomen and Gelasius of Cyzicus, about the favorable intervention on behalf of maintaining the ancient marriage discipline for the clergy made by a certain Paphnutius, bishop of the Upper Thebaid, is probably only a legend fabricated in the East at the beginning of the fifth century. It constituted one form of censure in the face of attempts by Rome to impose permanent celibacy on clerics in holy orders.[122] As for canon 33 attributed to the council held in Elvira, today Grenada, around 306-311, which made a law to this effect, it is part of the group of canons added at a later time. Only the first twenty-one canons were issued by the above mentioned council.[123]

Under these conditions, it is certain that the fathers of Nicea had no other intention than to forbid celibate clerics to live with women under suspicious conditions. That must have been evident to the contemporaries of the council, especially because of the use of the term συνείσακτος.

4

It is preferable that a bishop be established by all the bishops of a province; but if this appears difficult because of a pressing necessity or because of the distance to be traveled, at least three bishops should come together; and, having the written consent of the absent bishops, they may then proceed with the consecration. The confirmation of what takes place falls to the metropolitan bishop of each province.

Before analyzing this fundamental ruling concerning the organization of the Church as envisioned by the fathers of Nicea, let us study certain terms. We have translated καθίστασθαι by "be established." This verb has reference to the whole procedure for becoming a bishop: the election, the sacramental consecration and the installation. Καθιστάναι and the noun of the same root κατάστασις were usually employed to designate the official installation in a public charge. Moreover, we find the verb with this meaning in the New Testament.[124] It was used from the beginnings of Christianity to refer to the entry into a church function.[125] Further on in the same canon, we find the expression χειροτονίαν ποιεῖσθαι, which according to the context seems to indicate the performing of an ordination rite. Though the *Kormchaia* in Old Slavonic says *postavliennie tvoriti*, we read *sovershati rukopolozhenie* in the *Kniga Pravil*.[126] If this difference in translation seems justified here, we must say that at the time we are considering, χειροτονεῖν was often a synonym for καθιστάναι, or more precisely it referred to the canonical election, as for example, in canon 19 of the Council of Antioch. In the New Testament, the verb χειροτονεῖν is found twice: Acts 14:23 indicates the naming of presbyters by Paul and Barnabas, and 2 Corinthians 8:19 says that Titus was chosen by the suffrage of the churches. This same meaning is found in the *Didache*.[127] Without losing this meaning, χειροτονεῖν and χειροτονία also acquired, from the third century on, the sense of "to ordain" and "ordination." This meaning is finally the only one which has endured.[128] Etymologically χειροτονεῖν means "to extend the hand." Since this was the normal way of voting in Greek antiquity, the verb naturally took on the meaning of "to elect." As for the second sense, that of conferring a church function, we have seen that we do not encounter it at the very beginning of Christian history. It is by the related expressions ἐπίθεσις τῶν χειρῶν and ἐπιτιθέναι τὰς χεῖρας that the New Testament designates the action of imposing hands for the conveying of a ministry.[129] We are not here dealing with an innovation either, for in Judaism at the time of Christ doctors and judges were installed in their position by an imposition of hands (*semikah*).[130]

In canon 4 of Nicea, we see for the first time the term "metropolitan bishop" μητροπολίτης ἐπίσκοπος, a very rare expression.[131] We more often find the expression "bishop of the metropolitan city," ἐπίσκοπος τῆς μητροπόλεως.[132] Finally, a shorter form became the most widely used: the metropolitan, ὁ μητροπολίτης. We find it already in canon 6 of Nicea, and it was also introduced into later editions of canon 4. The two Latin versions of Dionysius and the one called "Cecilian" are on this point only calques of the original Greek editions and use the expression *metropolitanus episcopus*.[133] Rufinus did the same.[134] Other Latin versions made use of periphrases,[135] while still others used the simple term *metropolitanus*.[136] We note also that in these cases no classification of these diverse forms according to a chronology of the Latin recensions can be made.

Concerning the establishment of bishops, canon 4 of Nicea introduced an important ruling about the composition of the college of bishops who elect the new bishop: they are to be of the civil province where a see is vacant. In addition, the confirmation of the election must be given by the bishop of the capital of the province. This last stipulation is repeated in the second part of canon 6 where we read the following: "It is clearly evident that if anyone has become a bishop without the consent of the metropolitan, the great council decides that such a person is not even a bishop."[137] The requirement of having a majority of bishops consent to the installation of a new colleague is solidly anchored in Holy Tradition.[138] Generally these bishops came from the surrounding area and belonged to the same province; such is the witness of St. Cyprian,[139] but this last point did not yet constitute a binding rule. As for the participation of the whole episcopate of a province, it must have been a rather rare exception during the ante-Nicene period. Canon 1 of the Holy Apostles, probably belonging to the oldest layer of the writings erroneously attributed to the apostles, only requires the participation of three, indeed only two, bishops. Canon 20 of the Council of Arles, 314, requires that the principal consecrator be assisted by seven other bishops or, where impossible, by at least three.[140] This requirement about the majority of bishops being needed for the installation of a new bishop is based on ecclesiological principles: it highlights the collegial character of the episcopate, and it also underlines the necessity of showing the sacramental unity of a local church with the others.

The requirement of canon 4 of Nicea imposing the election of a bishop by all the bishops of the province concerned, his ordination by at least three consecrators and his approval by the metropolitan had as its goal, besides the above-mentioned reasons, avoidance of hasty promotions to the episcopate as well as eventual challenges following from them. Canon 4 of Nicea, therefore, determines the composition of the college of electing bishops: they are those of the civil province where there is a vacant see, and it is the bishop of the capital who is to confirm the election. This decision implied that the civil provinces (ἐπαρχίαι, *provinciae*) constituted the geographical boundaries on which the territorial organization of the Church was henceforth to be modeled.[141]

In what sense was there something new in this ruling? In this instance, we cannot give a clear and direct answer. The provincial capital had often been the first locality to receive the Christian message and to transmit it to other towns and surrounding areas.[142] Thus, even on a strictly religious level, the metropolis could appear as the "mother city." From the anti-Nicene period on, the opinion of the bishops of these capital cities as to the choice of other bishops of the same province must have been frequently taken into account.[143] Besides, the adminstrative reform of the emperor Diocletian (285-305), consisting mainly of multiplying the number of provinces, resulted in making smaller districts and thus facilitated contacts.[144] We cannot say, therefore, that the legislation of Nicea constituted a complete innovation; it rather gave an official stamp of approval to an already functioning procedure, at least in the East. Nicea legitimized the intervention of the metropolitan in the choice of the bishops of his province; it also made obligatory the participation of all the bishops of the province in the election of bishops. This last injunction constituted without a doubt the canon's most innovative feature, and after Diocletian's reform, its implementation, as we have seen, became a practical possibility.

Was the ruling of the fathers of Nicea wholly and universally applied? Let us note first that the principle of territorial accommodation was regarded as a norm, not excluding certain exceptions. Besides those very important ones expressly mentioned in canon 6, other very minor exceptions existed.[145] The first one, like the second, was founded on custom. In the eastern half of the empire, the stipulation of the Council of Nicea sanctioned only one state of affairs; thus, it was rather generally and rapidly applied even though here and there we see some hesitation on the part of some bishops since it was necessary to urge them to apply the rule more fully.[146] In the West, where conditions were a bit different, the metropolitan system took form more slowly. Africa adopted it with one notable exception: leaving aside Proconsular Africa where the bishop of Carthage exercised the prerogatives of a metropolitan, the primatial authority in each province reverted to the bishop with the most seniority.[147] Conceived essentially on the basis of the administrative geography of the Roman Empire, this system of dividing up metropolitan districts was not always transferable elsewhere. However, the prestige of the Council of Nicea was such that it was accepted in principle everywhere, though at the price of adapting it to local conditions. The church in Persia introduced the metropolitan system in 410 when the council of Seleucia accepted the whole of the Nicene legislation.[148]

Certain delicate problems arose sometimes about the practical application of the system; the civil provinces did not constitute unchangeable territorial entities. What was the proper thing to do when civil provinces were divided or united? This was the case in 372 when Cappadocia was divided in two; there were, henceforth, a Cappadocia Prima whose capital was Caesarea and a Cappadocia Secunda whose capital was Tyana. As soon as Anthimus, bishop of this new civil capital, claimed that he was no longer a suffragan bishop of Basil of Caesarea and rallied several bishops to his cause, St. Basil, far from accepting such a claim, forcefully sought to strengthen his position in Cappadocia Secunda. He then created an episcopal see in the market town of Sasima and wanted to install St. Gregory Nazianzus.[149] At the beginning of the following century, Pope Innocent I writing to Bishop Alexander of Antioch affirmed in a rather peremptory way that the Church was not required to duplicate metropolitan districts on the basis of civil provinces when the limits of these provinces are modified.[150] Since this was and is not a dogmatic question, the Church has in practice adopted various positions according to local circumstances. Canons 12 and 17 of Chalcedon are related to two specific aspects of this very problem; we shall speak about it when we analyze these canons.

The means of becoming a bishop set out by the fathers of Nicea do not make any allusion to the participation of other clerics or of laymen. Does this mean that such a participation was implicitly excluded? If such had been the case, canon 4 would have marked a rupture with previous tradition.[151] But this interpretation cannot be maintained first of all because it is shown to be false by the letter of the council to the churches of Egypt, in which the role of the laity is mentioned in this matter.[152] In addition, we have formal testimony about the participation of the clergy and the people in the choice of bishops during the time following the council of Nicea.[152a] In fact, the canon concerns only two points considered henceforth as obligatory: (1) all the bishops of a province must take part in the election of a new bishop when a vacancy in a see occurs, and (2) confirmation of this election falls by right to the metropolitan. As an addendum, the requirement of having at least three consecrators is recalled as the norm. As for the role of other clerics and laymen in the choice of their bishop, the fathers of Nicea do not speak about it because no doubt they did not want to introduce any modifications in the existing practice either by suppressing it or by making specific procedures apply to everyone. In effect, there was no one unique practice established by general custom; sometimes the clergy and faithful would suggest a candidate to the neighboring bishops, sometimes these bishops would take the initiative in choosing, with the clergy and laity giving their assent afterwards, indeed after the consecration; no doubt this could lead to difficulties for the new bishop. Canon 18 of Ancyra envisioned the situation where bishops were not accepted by the communities for which they were named and forbade these bishops to cause trouble by trying to impose themselves elsewhere. Canon 18 of Antioch authorized a bishop whose people refused to receive him to keep the honors of his rank while not interfering with the affairs of the church where he found himself and waiting for a decision of the council of the province. As for canon 36 of the Holy Apostles, it provides sanctions for the clergy who do not try to stop the rebellion of the people against a new bishop who, because of this fact, cannot exercise his functions.[153] Even though the ruling established by the Council of Nicea and completed and made precise by the Council of Antioch did not abolish the participation of the laity in the choice of bishops, it nevertheless underlined the decisive role of the hierarchy. This corresponds to an evolution in the circumstances of the fourth century: (1) the new type of relations between the Church and the state, (2) the great increase in the number of faithful, bringing with it a decline in the spiritual quality of the faithful. These two factors modified the previous conditions. St. Gregory of Nazianzus expressed very well the apprehensions of fervent Christians when he sadly noted that episcopal elections often depended on the influence of rich and powerful people or on the passions of the crowd.[154] Byzantine civil legislation reserved the right of presentation only to the *clericos et primates civitatis*,[155] which shows the increasing reticence of the church authorities about the participation of the laity.[156] However, such participation has never been universally suppressed in Orthodoxy; several autocephalous churches have preserved it or reintroduced it in our time.[157]

5

Concerning those who have been excommunicated, either among the clergy or the laity, let the sentence that was given by the bishops of each province remain in force; let this be in conformity with the regulation which requires that those so excluded by some bishops must not be received by others. But let each case be examined to see if those involved were excluded for a cowardly reason, from a quarrelsome spirit, or from some feeling of dislike on the part of the bishop. Therefore, so that a proper inquiry may take place, it seems good and proper that in each province there be a synod two

times a year so that all the bishops of the province sitting together may examine such questions and thus those who, according to the general opinion, may have disobeyed their bishop will be properly considered as excommunicate by all until such time as all the bishops see fit to render a more merciful sentence. Let the synods be held as follows: one before the fortieth day so that, all cowardly feelings being set aside, a pure offering may be made to God; the second during the fall.

Let us first of all examine the problems posed by the text and the translation of this canon. We have followed the standard text, that is, the one established in the Byzantine tradition from the sixth century on; different readings in later manuscripts are minor. Certain pieces of evidence allow us to affirm that the primitive text was different on several points from the text which finally prevailed: When we read μέχρις ἄν τῷ κοινῷ τῶν ἐπισκόπων δόξη ("until such time as all the bishops see fit"), the original must have said μέχρις ἄν τῷ κοινῷ ἤ τῷ ἐπισκόπῳ δόξη ("the lifting of the excommunication can be decided either by the college of bishops of the province or by the bishop who first took the action"). This reading, attested to by Gelasius, is confirmed by the whole of the Latin versions; it also conforms to the Syriac translation.[158] Let us add that the text so restored is in full conformity with the spirit of the canonical legislation; we can notably relate it to what canon 6 of the Council of Antioch requires:

> Whoever has been excommunicated by his own bishop cannot be received by others before he is readmitted by his own bishop unless, by presenting himself to the assembled synod, he gives his defense and by convincing the synod, he obtains another decision on this matter. . .[159]

We have translated προσκρούειν by "to disobey." Etymologically this verb means "to bump against," from which we get "to quarrel," "to be in disagreement," "to give offense," and "to offend." It is clear that the fathers of Nicea wanted to indicate by this word not just a minor disagreement but rather an act which seriously threatened the bishop's authority.

The expression πρὸ τῆς τεσσαρακοστῆς seems at first glance not to present any difficulties; we are normally inclined to understand it to mean "before Lent." In effect, this interpretation was not slow in prevailing, but it is not at all certain that such was the exact meaning.[160]

The existence of a fasting period in preparation for Pascha forty days long was not at all a general practice in the Church. Consequently, a reference to such an institution without other details would not have been clearly understood in many regions. Besides if we admit that πρὸ τῆς τεσσαρακοστῆς means "before Lent," we cannot fail to observe that this stipulation is not in harmony with what other ancient canonical documents prescribe. We read in canon 20 of Antioch the following:

> As is required by the needs of the Church and for the resolving of contested matters, it seems good and proper that the bishops of the province come together in a synod twice a year: the first time after the third week that follows Pascha so that the synod may take place during the fourth week of Pentecost; the bishop of the capital must announce this to his fellow bishops in the province; the second synod will take place at the *ides* of October, that is the fifteenth of the month of Hyperberetaeus....

Many of the rulings set out by the Council of Antioch were intended to enforce the application of the disciplinary decisions adopted at Nicea;[161] this is notably the case here. The lapse of time between Antioch and Nicea makes it certain that the fathers of Antioch were interpreting correctly the meaning of the canons of Nicea.[162] Moreover, canon 37 of the Holy Apostles equally sets the first of the semiannual synods at the same time, that is, during the fourth week of Pentecost. Seeing that the collection of which this canon is a part took its final form in the second half of the fourth century, it would be very surprising if its editors did not take into consideration the date set out by the fathers of Nicea for the holding of the first semiannual synod. Let us add that there is agreement among Nicea, Antioch and the Holy Apostles concerning the ruling for the second synod.[163] Later on, when it became possible to hold only one annual synod, it was decided that it would take place in any case after Pascha.[164] Besides, it is hardly likely that the fathers of Nicea would have required the first semiannual synod to be held before Lent, in the present understanding of the term; this would have meant a meeting in winter, a season in which traveling was extremely difficult in many regions. If in canon 5 τεσσαρακοστή refers to the fortieth day after Pascha, then Ascension is meant. Such a designation for this feast is corroborated by many ancient witnesses.[165]

In issuing this canon, the fathers of Nicea first of all wanted to recall a fundamental principle of church discipline: a sanction pronounced by one bishop against a cleric or a layman under his authority must be taken as valid for the whole of the episcopate. It is possible that before Nicea, the Council of Elvira had already formulated this injunction,[166] and the ruling was often reiterated subsequently,[167] because even if it was not contested in theory by anyone, certain bishops did not take it into account when they thought that a sentence issued by a fellow bishop was not well founded. Sadly, we know all too well that in this area, even in our own time, infractions of this canon are not at all rare. The fathers of Nicea adopted an important measure to avoid arbitrary actions: unjustified penalties inflicted by a bishop can be set aside, while those judged too severe can be reduced. This canon constitutes the basis in canon law of the appeal legislation which was extended and clarified during the fourth century.[168]

This canon, if we go just by the letter, envisions the meeting of only two semiannual provincial synods to review sentences given out by the bishops. This does not mean at all that the fathers of Nicea wanted to limit the competence of such assemblies to this judicial area. If they issued this ruling, it was because the provincial synods seemed to them to be the normal vehicle for the bishops to manifest their collegiality. The Council of Constantinople in 381, making reference to this canon of Nicea, understood it in the sense of "competence" and enlarged it to take in all churchly questions arising in each province.[169] Canon 20 of Antioch, whose beginning we cited above, continues on with a stipulation recalling that of Nicea: "Thus the priests, deacons, and everyone who claims to have been improperly treated shall appear before these synods and their causes will be re-examined by the synod."[170] This canon correctly sets the judicial activity of the provincial synod within a general context mentioned at the beginning: "As is required by the needs of the Church and for the resolving of contested matters." As for canon 37 of the Holy Apostles, it gives to the semiannual synods the task of examining doctrinal matters and resolving conflicts which may have arisen in the Church.[171]

The fixing of the geographical boundary of a province as the basis for holding periodic synods was in conformity with the ideas of the fathers of Nicea about the organization of the Church. There was nothing innovative in this ruling because, since the second century, bishops in each province were accustomed to meet when it was necessary.[172] As for the composition of the college of bishops who elected a new bishop, we can also say that in this case the principle of territorial accommodation naturally imposed itself due to a number of natural relationships and not because of any *jus scriptum*.[173] As for following the geography of the civil provinces of the Roman Empire, it is not totally deniable.[174] However, this principle did not represent a decisive factor because "conciliarity" belongs to the very nature of the Church, and it was concretely manifested right from the apostolic period.[175] In decreeing that the bishops of each province had to hold semiannual meetings, the fathers of Nicea established one new norm about how often they should meet—unless we admit that canon 37 of the Holy Apostles was written before Nicea. Moreover, let us note that the fixing of a semiannual frequency could hardly have been thinkable for practical reasons even outside the times of persecution before the administrative reform of Diocletian, which increased the number of provinces and, therefore, reduced their geographic dimension.

The ruling of Nicea was not well observed. Canon 19 of Chalcedon deplores the fact that "in the provinces, the councils of bishops required by the canons have not been held."[176] Canon 8 of Trullo, taking into account the problems of its own historical era, allowed that only one meeting of the synod be held each year,[177] and this ordinance was repeated in canon 6 of the seventh ecumenical council.[178]

6

> **Let the ancient customs be maintained in Egypt, in Libya, and in the Pentapolis so that the bishop of Alexandria has authority over all these territories, since for the bishop of Rome there is a similar practice and the same thing concerning Antioch; and in other provinces, let the prerogatives of the churches (of the capitals) be safeguarded.**
>
> **Moreover, let this matter be completely clear: If anyone becomes a bishop without the consent of the metropolitan, the great council decrees that such a person is not even a bishop. In addition, if, after a common vote of all has taken place knowingly and in conformity with the church regulation, two or three, for reasons of personal ill will, refuse the decision, then let everyone go along with the majority vote.**

This canon is no doubt the most famous of the canons issued by Nicea. It has often been invoked, but in so doing a meaning has been attributed to it which does not correspond exactly to the *mens legislatoris*. This fluidity in interpretation appeared very quickly in the East as well as in the West and is easily accounted for: the publication of this canon had been motivated by very particular and transitory circumstances. These were soon forgotten, so that the canon was interpreted independently of its historical context. In addition, the rapid evolution of institutional structures tending to favor the formation of large church districts (exarchates and patriarchates) caused the stipulations of this canon to be understood in relation to the new situation. From Nicea on, people saw this canon as the charter which sanctioned the existence of higher jurisdictions.[179] The text itself was modified in the direction of this interpretation, but then the agreement between the two parts of the canon appears less clear. And so we get the tendency to break up the text.[180] Consequently, in order to recapture its original meaning and scope, we have to submit the data given to us by the documents that have come down through history to careful, critical study. It is equally indispensable that we put this canon back into its historical framework, that is, eliminate the influence of subsequent institutional development on our thinking. The very valuable studies done in our own time in the area of textual criticism of the canons of Nicea as well as the area of the institutions of that era permit us to arrive at positive results even if certain secondary points remain open to debate.[181]

The object of canon 6 is the official recognition by the council of the rights of the bishop of Alexandria over several civil provinces, and thus it runs counter to the general principle set out in the two previous canons, according to which each civil province constitutes a church district *sui iuris*. Rome and Antioch were mentioned only for the sake of comparison; that is why the territories over which these sees exercised jurisdiction were not set out as was the case for Alexandria. What was the nature of this authority (ἐξουσία) recognized as belonging to the bishop of Alexandria on the basis of the "ancient customs" (τὰ ἀρχαῖα ἔθη)? Was it a question of a jurisdiction identical to that of the metropolitans such as is set out by canon 4 but extending to several civil provinces, or was it a jurisdiction above the metropolitans analogous to that which subsequent patriarchs had? According to this latter hypothesis, the second half of the canon meant that the higher authority of the bishop of Alexandria did not abolish the prerogatives of the metropolitans in the election of bishops.[182] Such an interpretation is hardly likely. The existence of a metropolitan organization in the territories mentioned cannot be proved because the witnesses invoked by the advocates of this thesis are related to a later period.[183]

On the contrary, a whole series of concordant points lead us to give an opposing answer concerning the situation at the time of the Council of Nicea. The reform of Diocletian had profoundly changed the political and administrative status of Egypt by attaching it to the diocese of the East and also introducing the provincial system,[184] but the tradition of centralization in the church around Alexandria was too deeply anchored for the division into civil provinces to have had many consequences in this field. All the more, let us not forget that before Nicea, the principle of territorial accommodation was not yet considered as normative. The catholic bishops of Egypt seemed, all during this period, very firmly grouped around one single primate, the bishop of Alexandria. When the Meletian schism broke out. some bishops made a great deal out of the traditional prerogatives of the see of Alexandria concerning episcopal consecrations.[185] This piece of information is fully corroborated by what we can read in a letter written by a dissident bishop who had been reconciled to the catholic Church.[186] In addition, if we search through the works of St. Athanasius, we find nothing that indicates the slightest hint of a division of sees by metropolitan districts. However, the wording of the canon itself gives us a decisive argument: to justify respecting the ancient customs giving to the bishop of Alexandria jurisdiction over several provinces, the fathers of Nicea based themselves first and foremost on the example of Rome. Now we know with sufficient certitude that at that time the bishop of the capital exercised the authority of a metropolitan over all the civil territories dependent on the *vicarius urbis*, that is, over central and southern Italy as well as over Sicily, Sardinia and Corsica.[187] Several ancient Latin translations in paraphrase of this canon highlight quite accurately that we are not dealing with a wider zone over which the see of Rome extended its influence and which later would correspond to the patriarchate of the West. In these translations, it is a matter of *loca suburbicaria*, of the *vicinae provinciae*, and of the *suburbicariae ecclesiae*.[188]

What motivated this conciliar clarification of the authority of the bishop of Alexandria? The reason generally put forward is the danger to the primacy of Alexandria which the Meletian schism posed. Perhaps we hear the echo of such a preoccupation in the second half of the canon, but we properly observe that this split led by Meletius had not at all been provoked by claims of provincial autonomy. His bishops were spread all over Egypt and not just in the Thebaid, where Meletius had his see.[188] Absolutely nothing allows us to suppose that the Meletians had a metropolitan organization.

The fact that the canon expressly mentions Libya and the Pentapolis deserves our attention. This region was located very far geographically from Alexandria and was separated from the city by a great expanse of desert. Moreover, the authority that the bishop of Alexandria exercised there is well attested in the third century, and it was not linked to political factors because at the time the surrounding countryside was administratively attached to Crete.[190] This situation was modified by Diocletian's reform. Thus the province of Libya very soon found itself divided into *Libya Superior*, called the Pentapolis in the canon, and *Libya Inferior*, called simply Libya. The primatial authority of Alexandria no doubt ran counter to certain separatist tendencies, and canon 4 would have easily been able to give them a legitimation from which comes the reference to the "ancient customs" to justify the jurisdictional powers of the bishop of Alexandria over these two provinces.[191]

How should we understand the reference to Antioch? Later on, this reference was to be used as a recognition of the suprametropolitan rights of the bishop of this city over the whole diocese of the East.[192] Such was certainly not in the intention of the fathers of Nicea. If we take for granted that the main object of canon 6 was the question of Alexandria, the phrase ὁμοίως δὲ καὶ κατὰ τὴν Ἀντιόχειαν must be linked to what precedes. When we do this we get a perfectly logical and coherent meaning: the reference to Antioch in this case is made to complete the one referring to Rome.[193] The fact that the territories in question are not clearly set out, as in the reference to Rome, shows clearly that it was not a question of a disputed problem requiring clarification. But unlike the cases of Rome and Alexandria, we do not have information from other sources that tells us what those territories were. In his gloss on this canon, the author of the Latin version called Gallo-Hispana speaks of *totam Coelem* in this regard.[194] However this rather late piece of information is valueless because at the time of the Council of Nicea, Coelosyria still formed a single province.[195] Now if the jurisdiction of the bishop of Antioch did not go beyond the border of one province, it would be nothing more or less than the authority assigned to each metropolitan by canon 4, and the reference here to Antioch would not make any sense. It seems probable, therefore, that the bishops of Antioch, by virtue of ancient customs, confirmed the elections of bishops of a certain number of sees beyond the limits of Coelosyria.

Continuing the reading of the canon, we find ourselves faced with a particularly obscure passage, at leat in the Greek text which has come down to us: ...καὶ ἐν ταῖς ἄλλαις ἐπαρχίαις τὰ πρεσβεῖα σῴζεσθαι ταῖς ἐκκλησίαις. If we link this to what precedes it, we must then translate it thus: "[In the same way as at Antioch] and in the other provinces, let the prerogatives of the churches be safeguarded." By disassociating the reference to Antioch from the one to Rome, a serious blow is laid to the argument based on a double analogy to justify the rights of Alexandria; but by uniting the phrase about Antioch to what precedes and separating it from what follows, we get a perfectly coherent meaning. But then what does this phrase mean: "and in the other provinces, let the prerogatives of the churches be safeguarded"? Is it a question of an order of precedence among the churches?[195] The term τὰ πρεσβεῖα indicated normally the pre-eminence of one episcopal see over others;[196] but this interpretation does violence to the rules of grammar: in Greek, the dative when not preceded by a preposition cannot give such a meaning. If there were not the article ταῖς, we could strictly understand the expression indicating that certain churches not mentioned also normally exercised a primatial authority beyond the boundary of a single province; the presence, solidly attested to in the textual tradition, of the article before ἐπαρχίαις and ἐκκλησίαις makes such an interpretaion hardly likely. This seems to have missed the advocates of this opinion.[176] We must note besides that the Fathers of Nicea seemed little inclined to multiply the exceptions to the norm set out by canon 4. This stands out quite clearly from the fact that they did not even allow an exception for the venerable Church of Jerusalem.

We would have to forget completely about finding a satisfactory meaning to this passage if the most ancient Latin translations of this canon had not furnished us with the solution. There is in effect every reason to think, as E. Schwartz has convincingly shown, that these translations faithfully reflect, in this instance, the wording of the original Greek text.[199] We read the following translation in the *Codex Ingilrami*, which was in use in Italy from the fourth century on, *et in ceteris provincii primatus habeant ecclesiae civitatum ampliorum*. The expression *civitates ampliores* was then an equivalent Latin expression for the Greek word μητροπόλεις. If this testimony were presented by itself, we would not be able to give it much credence, all the more because this version is far from always being faithful to the original. But the same passage is rendered in the following way in the *Interpre-

tatio caeciliani, done independently of the preceding one and in use in
Africa from the fourth century on: *et in aliis provinciis propria iura
serventur metropolitanis ecclesiis*.[200] At the time of the famous controversy about Apiarius, the African bishops requested that the authentic
text of the canons of Nicea be sent to them from the East. Now in the
version based scrupulously on the copy that Atticus of Constantinople
sent to them in 419, the passage is as follows: *et in ceteris provinciis
privilegia propria reserventur metropolitanis aecclesiis*.[201] This translation gives an essentially satisfactory meaning and harmonizes well
with the general orientation of the Nicene legislation; the exceptions to
the norm according to which the capital of each civil province is at the
same time the see of the metropolitan, are strictly limited to the three
cases expressly mentioned. In addition, this reconstitution of the primitive text allows us to see more clearly the link between the two halves
of the canon.

The change in the original text in which the term τῶν μητροπόλεων
was suppressed did not happen by accident; it comes from Antioch
and was part of the systematic effort of the bishops of that city, from
the end of the fourth century on, to control the election of the metropolitans in the whole diocese of the East.[202] The Greek text of canon
6, such as it has come down to us, is taken from the *Synagoge*, composed around 550 by John the Scholastic when he was the apocrisiary
of the patriarch of Antioch, Domnus III, in Constantinople.[203] This
recension of the canons is, therefore, Antiochian. The absence of the
mention of the metropolitan cities in canon 6 was spread throughout
all the translations based on the Antiochian codex or influenced by it.
Consequently, we are not surprised to find this omission in the ancient
Syriac version edited at Hierapolis around 500[204] as well as in several Latin versions,[205] the *Graeca auctoritas* which Dionysius referred
to as being the canonical collection of the Church of Antioch.[206]

The second half of canon 6 reaffirms the principle set out in canon
4: no one can become a bishop without the consent of the metropolitan. But whereas canon 4 only formulated the principle, here it is
specified that whoever would proceed without such consent "would
not even be a bishop."[207] This difference is easily explained by the
similarity in sound and writing of the Greek forms μηδὲ and μὴ δεῖν.
This only slightly affects the meaning of the statement. We note that
according to the canon, as according to others of a similar kind elsewhere, the irregularity is supposed to bring with it nullity, without
being precise as to whether such nullity involves an invalidity or only a

reparable defect.[208]

The canon also envisions the eventuality of disputes raised by some bishops in the electing college based on purely personal motivations. It is stated that in such a case the vote of the majority must prevail. This ruling is repeated in canon 19 of the Council of Antioch. We must not deform the thought of the fathers of Nicea and Antioch by unduly giving an enlarged scope to this stipulation. It is only aimed at an objectively unjustified opposition. If some bishops, even a minority in the synod, present reasons based on the canons against the promotion of a candidate and despite their objection the majority proceeds, the election is nonetheless essentially tainted with irregularity. The second half of canon 6 is not completely independent of the first half, but does it follow that the second half does not directly concern the rights of the bishop of Alexandria? The fact that he is called a metropolitan does not constitute in itself a valid argument for rejecting this interpretation, for the bishop of Alexandria effectively exercized the authority of a metropolitan over several civil provinces. Arsenius, a Meletian bishop reconciled to the catholic Church, call St. Athanasius, "the bishop of the metropolitan city" ($\tau o\tilde{u}$ $\tau\tilde{\eta}\varsigma$ $\mu\eta\tau\rho o\pi\acute{o}$-$\lambda\varepsilon\omega\varsigma$ $\dot{\varepsilon}\pi\iota\sigma\kappa\acute{o}\pi o u$).[209] The context supposes a relation with what is set out in canon 6. It is highly probable that the situation in Egypt was the occasion for this solid clarification concerning the rights of metropolitans, since it implied the nullity of the ordinations done by Meletios.[210] However, we do not see why such a ruling would not have a universal scope, so much more because the first half of the canon, in its original wording, contained an affirmation of the rights of the metropolitans. Moreover, some years after the first ecumenical council, the fathers of Antioch promulgated an ordinance taking up again the rulings of canons 4 and 6 of Nicea.[211]

At the beginning of our commentary on canon 6, we showed how there came to be a fluidity in its understanding. In the East as well as in the West, we see in this canon the legal charter forming the basis for the existence of higher ecclesiastical jurisdictions. It is true that the canon could lend itself to such a reading if we do not take into account the particular circumstances which were at the basis of its promulgation; this is even more possible seeing that the canon does not indicate any reasons about the motivation behind the ruling. We have every reason to think that from the end of the fourth century on, this interpretation was admitted by everyone.[212] At the beginning of the following century, Pope Innocent took this canon as the basis of the efforts of the see of Antioch to assure to itself the control of the whole diocese of the East.[213] In the systematic collection of John the Scholastic, the first half of canon 6 is cited in the section given over to a discussion of the rights of the patriarchs.[214] In the Middle Ages, this interpretation seemed so evident that neither Zonaras nor Balsamon took the trouble to justify it, and from this point of view, they deduced that this canon confers on the bishops of Rome patriarchial jurisdiction over the whole of the West.[215]

At the Council of Chalcedon, at the time of the debates about the prerogatives of the see of Constantinople, the papal legate Paschasinus cited canon 6 in the Latin recension; the first half of the text was identical to what we read in the *Codex Ingilrami* and carried the following preamble: *Ecclesia Romana semper habuit primatus.*[216] It is certain that in the middle of the fifth century, this formula was understood in Rome as a affirmation of the Roman supremacy. The significance of the canon, in this altered form, was profoundly modified; while for the fathers of Nicea, the reference to Rome was concerned with the setting out of a matter of fact and was put in only as an analogy, this editing of the text made it seem that the privileges of Alexandria and Antioch flowed from those of the Roman see. Such was at least the underlying idea.[217] However, the introduction of this preamble, going back no doubt to the second half of the fourth century, certainly dealt with more modest concerns. It has been properly noted that the term *primatus,* especially in the plural, did not at that time have the meaning that it acquired later. It was related to the primatial prerogatives of each metropolitan bishop.[218] Under the pontificate of Liberius and at the beginning of that of Damasus, the Roman Church, torn by conflict, had lost much of its prestige in Italy; in addition, the weighty influence of the see of Milan contributed to a veritable eclipse of papal authority in the north of the peninsula.[219] It is very probable that this is the context in which we must understand the addition made to canon 6 in Rome. This preamble must be related to the titles given to the canon in certain collections, for example, the Isidoriana: *De praecipuis honoribus qui maiores ecclesias gubernantibus episcopis constituti sunt.*[220] This is seen even more in the Prisca collection: *De primatu ecclesiae Romanae vel aliarum civitatum episcopis.*[221] At the beginning of the sixth century, the Dionysian translations supplanted the ancient versions in Rome, and there was a text based on the Antiochian recension, which was accepted a little while later in the patriarchate of Constantinople. As we have said above, it differed from the Nicene original in that the term τῶν μητροπόλεων had disappeared from canon 6.

7

Since custom and ancient tradition have prevailed according to which the bishop of Aelia is honored, let him enjoy the honor that flows from his position, while the dignity proper to the metropolitan city is safeguarded.

After having made the prerogatives of the bishop of Alexandria very clear in canon 6 by comparing them with those exercised by the bishops of Rome and Antioch, the fathers of Nicea dealt with the question of the Church of Aelia. In this case it was a question of clarifying the status of the bishop of that city in the framework of the province of Palestine. In order to understand the nature of the problem, it is necessary to look at the historical data.

In 70 A.D., at the end of violent fighting, Roman troops captured Jerusalem, which had in large part been destroyed. Before the siege, the local Christian community left and regrouped at Pella in Decapolis, east of the central valley of the Jordan beyond the area held by the rebels. This should not be taken to mean that the Jewish Christians were uninterested in the fate of their people, but they were completely opposed to the zealots who had provoked the anti-Roman rebellion. When peace was re-established, a part of the Jewish-Christian community went to live in what was left of the city and the surrounding area. The Jewish religious authorities took an even more hostile attitude than before to the Christians, and they took the initiative to bring about a total rupture in the form of an excommunication.[222]

At the time of his trip throughout the East, 120-131 A.D., the emperor Hadrian decided to create a Roman city on the site of Jerusalem. This was no doubt one of the causes of the new rebellion of the Jews under the direction of Simon BarKochba. This insurrection, which broke out in 132, was not completely crushed until 135. A little while later a whole new city was constructed and carried the name of Colonia Aelia Capitolina in honor of the victorious emperor, Aelius Hadrianus, and everything was done to mark the rupture with the past. The site of the temple was occupied by a pagan sanctuary dedicated to Jupiter Capitolinus. An imperial decree forbade the Jews not only to enter the city but even to come near.[223] Nearly immediately, a group of Christians, obviously Gentiles, established themselves in Aelia;

however, we cannot know exactly when an organized community was set up. Eusebius clearly noted that formerly the bishops of Jerusalem had been of the circumcision (τῶν ἐκ περιτομῆς ἐπισκόπων), but now this was no longer the case. The first bishop of this new line was named Mark.[224] Even if from the point of view of civil law, the city was considered as having an absolutely new foundation, for the Christians there existed a spiritual and canonical continuity, symbolized by the presence in the church of the "chair of James."[225] Moreover, Eusebius ·ometimes calls the city Aelia, sometimes Jerusalem.[226] Although Eusebius himself was the bishop of Caesarea, capital of the province of Palestine, he gives a detailed list of the bishops of the holy city as he does for Rome, Alexandria and Antioch, thereby marking the importance of this see, which he considers to be an "apostolic throne."[227]

It was inevitable that canonical relations between Caesarea and Aelia should be clouded in ambiguity: on the one hand, even before the explicit ratification by the fathers of Nicea, it was generally admitted that the bishops of the civil capitals possessed certain primatial prerogatives in the boundaries of the provinces; on the other hand, the see of Jerusalem-Aelia was the recipient of a prestige which gave to it a moral authority going far beyond the boundaries of Palestine. This ambiguity was clearly shown in the order of precedence at the time of conciliar meetings. At one time, the precedence went to the bishop of Caesarea, at another time it went to the bishop of Aelia. It is not possible apart from the historical data to indicate on which principle this diversity of practice was based.[228] Canon 7 properly speaking did not introduce any new element; it merely ratified the *status quo*. However, it was made expressly clear that the right of the metropolitan city, in this case Caesarea, must remain intact. Thus, concerning the prerogatives exercized by the bishop of the capital of each civil province, no exception to the general rule set out in canon 4 was made in favor of Jerusalem. But then, how should we understand the expression τὴν ἀκολουθίαν τῆς τιμῆς, which literally means "the resulting honor"? In the Middle Ages, when the patriarchal system had long since been established, the ruling about the see of Jerusalem was closely related to the preceding canon which dealt with Rome, Alexandria and Antioch. We can see that canons 6 and 7 of Nicea were completed by canons 3 of Constantinople and 28 of Chalcedon and became the constitution for the patriarchal system. In this regard, it is significant that Balsamon dealt with the question of Jerusalem in his commentary on canon 6 with such a presupposition.[229] The term ἀκολουθία is understood as relating to the hierarchical order of the patriarchal thrones, Jerusalem having the fifth place. Such an interpretation can already be seen sketched out in canon 36 of Trullo. It is very evident that this was not at all the original meaning of canon 7 of Nicea. The ἀκολουθία τῆς τιμῆς is to be understood in relation to what comes before in the text: the bishop of Aelia is to be honored (τιμᾶσθαι), and this honor carries with it certain legitimate consequences. The fathers of Nicea did not believe it was necessary to be precise about what that entitled; they intended to ratify the *status quo*. While the historical data do not permit us to clarify this point very much, one thing is certain: the bishop of Aelia had a precedence over his provincial colleagues, not including, however, the metropolitan of Caesarea. We can establish a certain relation with the stipulation of canon 12 of Chalcedon concerning the canonical status of cities which had received the title of civil capital by imperial decision: "...let these cities, as well as the bishops who govern them, enjoy one single honor, understanding that the right proper to the real capital city remain safeguarded."[230]

Canon 7 with its rather imprecise wording did not really get to the heart of the problem. During the time that followed Nicea, the antagonism between the sees of Caesarea and Aelia grew in intensity, revealing rather sharply the opposition between the principle of apostolicity and that of adaptation to the political geography in determining the importance of bishops and their churches. These factors coming together at this time worked in favor of Jerusalem. At the time of the peace of Constantine, there was a renewed interest in the holy places. In 325, soon after the Council of Nicea, Bishop Macarius received authorization to demolish the principal pagan temple of Aelia; the following year, St. Helen, mother of the emperor, went on a pilgrimage to the holy city. Constantine ordered that a splendid building he constructed around the Holy Sepulchre. At the time of the church's consecration in September 335, numerous bishops came there on the invitation of the emperor.[231] Little by little the name of Aelia faded away, and the city assumed its traditional name of Jerusalem. During the Arian conflict, Jerusalem had been a bastion of orthodoxy; and in 346, Macarius convoked a council there which supported St. Athanasius.[232] St. Cyril of Jerusalem in no way acted as though he were the suffragan of the bishop of Caesarea and justified his position by recalling the apostolicity of his see.[233] At the end of the fourth century, the division of Palestine into three provinces further weakened the position of the see of Caesarea.[234] Nonetheless the situation still remained fluid; the supremacy of Jerusalem was far from being universally accepted. On several occasions we see the bishops of Caesarea exercise their primatial rights.[235] Jerome strongly criticized bishop John of Jerusalem for having called on Theophilus of Alexandria to arbitrate a controversy in Palestine. According to Jerome, who claimed to base himself on the canons of Nicea, John should have called on the bishop of Caesarea and eventually on the bishop of Antioch.[236] Jerome was correct in a formal sense in saying that John should have first spoken to the bishop of Caesarea, but as for his reference to Antioch and his claim that the legislation of Nicea supported such a recourse, this is highly debatable. His interpretation that Jerusalem's ultimate recourse to Antioch was based on canon 6 does not correspond to the intention of the fathers of Nicea. If there was one point, moreover, on which the bishops of Caesarea and Jerusalem were always in agreement, it was that they wanted to prevent the bishops of Antioch from interfering in the affairs of Palestine.

The preeminence of the see of Jerusalem was definitively established during the time of Juvenal, 422-458. As E. Honigmann noted, it is beyond question that this bishop received a decision on this question in his favor from the emperor Theodosius II. Although the text of this decree has not come down to us, the wording of the agreement between Juvenal and Maximus of Antioch, October 23, 451, implied very clearly the existence of such a document.[237] We must assume that the imperial decision was made before the ecumenical council of Ephesus, where Juvenal appeared as one of the leaders of this assembly and the uncontested head of the Palestinian bishops. Juvenal was attempting to extend the influence of his see toward Phoenicia and Arabia to the detriment of Antioch. But the above-mentioned agreement made at the Council of Chalcedon limited the suprametropolitan jurisdiction of Jerusalem to the three provinces of Palestine. Thus we have the formation of the patriarchate of Jerusalem. We note, however, that it was still a little while later that the title of patriarch was officially and exclusively used to designate the bishops of the five principal sees of Christendom.[238]

8

Concerning those who have called themselves "the pure ones," if they ever want to come into the catholic and apostolic Church *en masse*, it seems right and proper to the holy

and great council that they, after having received the imposition of hands, should then remain in the clergy. But first it is important that they promise in writing to accept and to follow the rulings of the catholic Church, that is, they will have communion with those who have been married a second time and with those who renounced the faith during persecution for whom a period (of penance) has been established and a date (of reconciliation) set. It is, therefore, necessary that they follow in full the rulings of the catholic and apostolic Church.

Consequently, when in the cities or villages, there are only clerics ordained by these "pure ones," let them keep their status; on the other hand where there is a bishop or priest of the catholic Church, if certain of these "pure ones" want to be admitted, it is evident that the bishop of the Church should keep the dignity of bishop. As for the person who carries the name of bishop among the so-called "pure ones," he is to have the rank of priest unless the bishop consents to allow him to receive the honor of his title. But if he is not so disposed, let the bishop give him a place as a chorepiscopus or of a priest so that he can appear as being integrated into the clergy. Without this provision, there would be two bishops in the city.

This canon deals with the ways of receiving into the Church clerics coming from the Novatianist sect, which appeared in the middle of the third century in connection with the persecution started by the emperor Decius, 249-251. Novatian, a Roman priest, accused Pope Cornelius of laxity concerning the lapsed Christians, that is, those who had denied the faith during the persecution. Professing an ultra-rigorism, Novatian considered that it was necessary to refuse to reconcile repentant lapsed members to the Christian community even after a time of penance. He broke with the Church and got himself consecrated bishop under fraudulent circumstances.[239] Novatianism attracted adherents nearly everywhere, especially those who favored such rigorism; there were quite a few members in the East. According to Eusebius, the bishop of Antioch may have been predisposed somewhat to this schism.[240] In the fourth century, Novatianism was still powerful. The present canon of Nicea supposes that in certain regions, there were cities and villages where only clerics of this sect were to be found. St. Gregory of Nazianzus, St. Ambrose and Bishop Pacian of Barcelona took strong personal positions against the doctrines of these dissidents.[241] They seem to have maintained themselves until the seventh century, because the Melkite patriarch of Alexandria, Eulogius, 580-607, thought it useful to write against them.[242] After that time, they become lost to history.

On the dogmas of the faith, especially the Trinity, the Novatianists did not differ at all from orthodoxy; moreover, that is why they were very hostile to the Arians. Their differences with the Church only concerned two questions of discipline: the first, which had originally been the only one, was related to the reconciliation of the lapsed Christians. The Novatianists did not accept them even at the moment of death. Later on, probably under the influence of the Montanists, they radically condemned second marriages while the Church, looking on them with a certain disfavor and clearly indicating this in canon law and in the liturgical tradition, nevertheless accepted them, following the teaching of Holy Scripture.[243] The fathers of Nicea thought that this schism could be healed, at least in part; and trying to make that possibility easier, they offered honorable conditions to the Novatianist clergy. This was done, however, without infringing on the rights of the legitimate catholic hierarchy. We know that one Novatianist bishop named Acesius was called to Nicea by the emperor Constantine in the hope of convincing him to return. Acesius declared that he did not see any difficulty in accepting the symbol of faith issued by the council, as well as the decision about Pascha. He underlined that the difference between the two groups was really a question of discipline.[244] It was precisely because there was no difference on trinitarian doctrine that the council did not require rebaptism, as was the case for the Paulianists.[245] The object of the present canon was to determine the means of integrating the Novatianist clergy and not the more general problem of how to receive members of this sect into the catholic Church. These dissidents, according to canon 7 of the Council of Laodicea, were to be anointed with holy chrism.[245] This ruling was to be repeated in later canonical documents relating to the reception of dissidents.[247]

Concerning the Greek text of this canon, there are no really significant redactional variants. At the most, it is proper to mention a clarification introduced by the term κοινῇ *(en masse);* although absent from several ancient manuscripts, it is most probably the wording of the original text.[248] In addition, it seems preferable to link the adverb ποτέ to what follows rather than to the phrase that precedes it. We have thus translated in the following way: "Concerning those who have called themselves 'the pure ones,' if they ever want to come into the catholic and apostolic Church..."; and not in the following way: "Concerning those who have formerly called themselves 'the pure ones,' if they want to come into the catholic and apostolic Church..." It is moreover the first translation which is reflected in the ancient Latin translations, whenever they took into account the Greek adverb in question.[249]

The only real difficulty posed by the canon has to do with the meaning which it is proper to give to χειροθετουμένους (literally "having received the imposition of hands"). What significance did this rite have for the fathers of Nicea who required it for the reconciliation of Novatianist clergy? At the time of the first session of the seventh ecumenical council, Patriarch Tarasius, confronted by the problem of the admission of repentant iconoclastic bishops, made reference to this canon and maintained that this imposition of hands did not mean reordination but was a blessing marking their reconciliation.[250] The *Synopsis* in its abbreviated redaction of this canon says οἱ εὑρισκόμενοι κεχειροτονημένοι,[251] meaning simply that in this case "those who had received ordination" (in the Novatianist group). This is also the interpretation given by Zonaras and Balsamon.[252] On the purely grammatical level, this interpretation is difficult to accept, for if such were the meaning, we would expect to find an aorist or a perfect form of the verb. As for the interpretation of Patriarch Tarasius, even if it were theoretically possible, it runs into some grave difficulties.[253]

Questioned by Aphyngius on the manner of receiving Novatianist clerics, Theophilus, Archbishop of Alexandria, 385-412, answered him by referring expressly to the canon of Nicea saying that they must be re-ordained.[254] This was by no means, in the present case, a question of a personal opinion but of a witness to the practice of the time. The relative proximity in time to the Council of Nicea gives to this testimony an exceptional value. It is equally interesting to make a link between the decision on the Novatianists and that adopted by the same council concerning the Meletians, seeing that the two groups were quite similar. Now the conditions set out for the integration into the catholic Church of Meletian clerics presents some obvious common points with those adopted for the reception of Novatianist clerics.[255] The council stipulated in particular that those who had been ordained by Meletius should be admitted into the orthodox clergy "after having been confirmed by a more holy ordination" (μυστικωτέρᾳ χειροτονίᾳ βεβαιωθέντας).[256] If we recall that the Church has always condemned all repetitions of authentic ordinations,[257] it is evident that what they had in mind was a true ordination and not just any complementary rite of rehabilitation to the ministry. That the term χειροθετουμένους referring to the integration of clerics of the Novatianist group means "after having been ordained" is corroborated by the fact that the fathers of Nicea elsewhere used the verb χειροθετεῖν as a synonym for χειροτονεῖν.[258] Let us add that several ancient Latin versions of the canon of Nicea have rendered χειροθετουμένους in a way that allows no ambiguity, as ordination.[259] The refusal to recognize the ordination conferred in the Novatianist group ought not to surprise us at all. It was in conformity with the tendency of that era, in which the Church generally considered as null all ordinations done against the canonical norms. Only somewhat later did a new concept appear in the West, under the influence of Augustinian theology, and a great deal of time passed before it replaced the older idea.[260] The orthodox East, sometimes departing from absolute rigor, nonetheless placed the recognition of irregular ordinations in the category of οἰκονομία.[261] Beyond this attitude of principle, it is proper to notice that the origin of the Novatianist hierarchy was tainted by a very specific and serious fault; the episcopal consecrations of Novatian had been procured in a fraudulant way. On this subject, Pope Cornelius, in a letter to Fabius of Antioch, spoke of "an imposition of hands that was counterfeit and vain."[262]

The fathers of Nicea, after having ordered that the Novatianist clerics had above all to repudiate their errors and then to receive an imposition of hands which we have indicated was of a sacramental nature, were precise about the means of integrating these clerics into the orthodox clergy. The major difficulty concerned the case of former bishops of the sect where there was already a bishop of the Church. Where there was no orthodox bishop already installed, the solution was easy. The canon offered to the orthodox bishop several possibilities: either to integrate the Novatianist cleric into his college of presbyters[263] or to accept him with the dignity of bishop but without any jurisdictional powers[264] or to take him as a chorepiscopus, a country bishop, that is, make him an auxiliary for a rural area administratively dependent on the city.[265] The fathers of Nicea wanted absolutely to avoid having two bishops in the same city leading the Christian community (ἵνα μὴ ἐν τῇ πόλει δύο ἐπίσκοποι ὦσιν). They had no intention at all of setting out a new principle but only of recalling the traditional discipline. St. Cyprian considered this principle as an obvious truth.[266] From his point of view, Pope Cornelius had already properly stated the case about Novatian: "This avenger of the gospel, did not he know that there must be only one bishop in a catholic church?"[267] Nonetheless, this reminder of the traditional discipline by the Council of Nicea reinforced the importance of this norm because of the exceptional authority which Nicea's decisions acquired in the Church. When the emperor Constantius in 357 proposed to the Christians of Rome that they split up the office of bishop between Liberius and Felix, they answered: "Only one God, only one Christ, only one bishop."[268] This answer clearly showed that the basis of this principle was not simply of a practical order, but had a veritable theological meaning. St. Augustine even had some doubts as to whether the canon of Nicea allowed the election of a coadjutor bishop.[269] This scruple was certainly excessive because the only thing that this canon required absolutely, along with general church legislation, was that there be only one ruling bishop. Consequently the existence of vicar bishops was in no way incompatible with this ruling; moreover there were at that time chorepiscopi, country bishops, who had unquestionably received episcopal consecration.[270] If the territorial principle as such is a permanent given of orthodox ecclesiology, its expression in this canon is nonetheless an expression of the politico-cultural environment of the era: the Roman Empire was constituted by a federation of cities upon which depended a surrounding rural area.[271] Originally bishops had been established in the country towns as well as in the major cities; this situation is attested to in the letter of St. Clement of Rome to the Corinthians,[272] but as church organization rather rapidly copied the structure of the empire, the Christian communities of country areas began to enter into the spheres of influence of the neighboring large cities; and the country bishops, in the same way, found themselves subordinated to those of the cities. As. P. Nautin correctly observes, the use of the term chorepiscopus "is the best proof that already for some time 'country bishops' did not mean the same thing as just the term 'bishop.'"[273] Although it is difficult to follow exactly the unfolding in time of this process, we can estimate that generally it was completed by the middle of the third century.

In relation to the greater importance of cities, we note that the fathers of Nicea expressed the principle of one ruling bishop in one place by stating that there could be but one single bishop "in the city." Moreover, we do not find in the ancient canonical documents one single term to designate the territory over which each bishop exercised his authority; they have to resort to a paraphrase: "the (urban) community and the countryside that is tied to it."[274] Such an organization, perfectly adapted to the administrative geography of the empire, was obviously not always transferable elsewhere. Thus, for example, in ancient Ireland, where there had been no urban organization nor civil districts with well-defined limits, the bishop was rather like the spiritual pastor of a tribe than the religious leader of a territory.[275] Equally, we can cite the case of medieval Serbia; because there were few cities, almost all of the first bishops lived in monasteries.[276]

The territorial principle is inherent in Orthodox ecclesiology, and it is effectively respected in the geographical limits of the various patriarchates and autocephalous churches. On the other hand, in our time and beyond the limits of these territorial churches, we witness a certain failure to observe this principle. It is proper to recognize that this constitutes a serious attack on strict canonical observance. It is certain that these existing abnormalities will progressively have to be eliminated. Taking into account the complexity of the concrete problems, such a rectification of canonical order cannot happen overnight everywhere and all at once. An agreement among the mother churches concerned is indispensable. In a parallel way, it is necessary for the clerics and Orthodox faithful in any one place to become more and more conscious of the canonical implications of the fact that they all belong to one single Church.[277]

9

If certain men have been made priests without inquiry, or if having been examined, they acknowledged the sins committed by them and despite this confession, some other men acting against the canon impose hands on such people, the canon does not admit them because the catholic Church requires unquestionable conduct and character.

The fathers of Nicea were only calling attention in this canon to a ruling which goes back to the very beginnings of Christianity itself; we find it expressly formulated in the New Testament.[278] Although the present ruling concerns the priesthood, at least according to the original Greek,[279] the canonical tradition requires an examination beforehand of anyone entering the clergy. St. Basil severely admonished some country bishops who were neglecting this obligation. He wrote the following on this subject:

> The servants of the Church are not to be admitted until after they have gone through a rigorous test and all their conduct has been thoroughly examined, and this according to custom which has been always the practice of the churches of God...[280]

The general meaning of this canon is that we must proceed with priestly ordination without previous inquiry, nonetheless there still exist some questions about the text itself: did the fathers of Nicea mean that just the fact of having ordained someone without injury beforehand entailed, by that very fact, that the person should be deposed, or that this sanction should apply only if something was discovered after the fact which should have been an impediment to ordination in the first place? This second interpretation is founded moreover on a textual variant very well attested to in the manuscript tradition: instead of ἤ, we find εἶτα.[281] In this case, the meaning is the following: "If certain men have been made priests without inquiry and afterwards, having been examined, they acknowledge sins committed by them..." Such a reading is supposed by several ancient Latin translations.[282] It is nonetheless hardly likely that such was the original text. How, in effect, would it be possible to say that "despite this confession" such men would be ordained? Another reading says εἴτε.[283] Logically there is a strong probability that this conjunction was in the initial text. If we admit this hypothesis, we can explain the appearance of the two variants mentioned above, ἤ and εἶτα, by taking into account the morphologic closeness.

Whatever it may have been, the intention of the fathers of the council is clear: whoever has been raised to the priesthood despite grave faults must be excluded from the ranks of the clergy. The expression τὰ ἡμαρτημένα αὐτοῖς is not related to sins in general "because there is no man living who does not sin," but only to serious offences which are considered as impediments to ordination. From the origins of Christianity, there has been consensus on the fact that serious sin, such as apostasy, murder, fornication and adultery, constituted insurmountable obstacles to becoming a cleric. Moreover, strict conditions of irreproachable conduct were required in relation to marriage. Subsequent jurisprudence was only to make certain points more explicit.[284]

10

If anyone who has renounced the faith has been promoted to the clergy, whether because the bishops did not know about

the apostasy or because they did not take it into account, the church canon is not lessened by either reason; for as soon as these men are discovered, they are to be deposed.

This canon is related, on the one hand, to the preceding one since it deals with an impediment to ordination; it is linked, on the other, to canons 11, 12 and 14 in that it concerns the question of those who have renounced the faith during persecution, the lapsed Christians (παραπεπτωκότες). These disciplinary rules were very timely because the great persecution begun in 303 did not completely end until the defeat of Licinius in 324.

To weaken during a persecution and therefore to give up the faith assuredly constituted a grave sin, so that clerics in that situation were liable to deposition from their church functions.[285] As for laymen, they were submitted to a long penance proportional to the degree of the guilt.[286] In any case, such an apostasy is considered as an impediment to ordination, and that is what the fathers of Nicea believed good and proper to make clear in this present canon. In contrast, catechumens who had renounced the faith could be promoted to the clergy after baptism if they were otherwise worthy; in effect sins committed before baptism were not taken into consideration.[287] It is to be noted that there was a sin, and therefore an impediment to ordination, only if the apostasy was seen as a voluntary act. This is what canon 3 of the Council of Ancyra stipulates expressly:

Those who ran away, but who were arrested or turned in by their own relatives, who suffered the loss of their property, who suffered torture, who have been put in prison on stating that they were Christians, but who have been constrained either by forcing them to take incense in their hands or by forcing them to eat food offered to idols, and who despite this continued to say that they were Christians and have shown their suffering in all that happened to them by their bearing and in their attitude and in their life filled with humility; these people having not committed any sin, must not be deprived of communion. If they have been so deprived by too great a severity or by lack of information on the part of some, they must be immediately readmitted. This should follow for laymen as well as for clerics. In the same way, we have examined the case of laymen who have been forced to sacrifice to see if they can be promoted to orders, and it has therefore been decided that they too, not having committed any sin, could be promoted if their previous honest life allows it.[288]

11

About those who have renounced the faith during the tyranny of Licinius without having been forced, without having lost their property, without having faced dangers or anything of the sort, it has been decided by the holy council that although not being worthy of mercy, nonetheless, we will make use of gentleness in their cases. Consequently, those among them who were baptized and manifest a real repentance must remain three years among "hearers" and during seven years, they must pray prostrate and then during two years they will participate in the prayers of the people but without participating in the offering.

Although it may be a question of gentleness, this canon is more rigorous than the one set out in 306 by St. Peter of Alexandria, who, referring to the gospel parable of the fig tree, prescribed a period of four years of penance.[289] But we must recall that St. Peter of Alexandria had issued this ruling in the middle of a period of persecution, so that those who repented were exposing themselves to a great danger. In contrast, the decision of the fathers of Nicea is less severe than those of St. Basil and St. Gregory of Nyssa, for whom apostates could be reconciled only at death's door.[290] We can assume that since there was no persecution, renunciation of the faith was even more serious. The canon of Nicea has a place, therefore, in the middle ground when it comes to severity.

In this text we find mentioned the degrees which a penitent had to pass through before he was fully reintegrated into the Church. He had first of all to stand with the "hearers" (ἀκροώμενοι), that is, with the first-level catechumens in the narthex, who were required to leave when all the catechumens were dismissed. During the second period of their penance, they had the right to enter into the church proper and to be prostrate near the ambo,[291] but they still had to leave with the catechumens. In the third stage, they were present at the whole liturgy, but without receiving communion. On the different categories of penitents at this time, two canonical texts give us very valuable information. The first is canon 11 attributed to St. Gregory of Neocaesarea (+c. 270), which in reality dates from the fourth century. The text is as follows:

The place of the weepers is in front of the entrance door of the church, where the sinner must be and ask the faithful who enter to pray for him. The place of the hearers is inside the entrance door in the narthex, where the sinner must be until the prayer of the catechumens, and then he must leave; for, having heard the reading of the Scriptures and the preaching, let him leave and not listen to the prayer of the faithful. To be an attender is to be with the faithful and not leave with the catechumens. Finally comes the participation in the holy gifts.[292]

The second text is canon 75 of St. Basil:

To him who had made himself unclean with his sister born from the same father or mother, we forbid him access to the house of prayer until such time that he has renounced his iniquitous and criminal conduct. After he has become aware of his terrible sin, let him spend three years as a weeper standing at the door of the houses of prayer and asking the people who enter to pray for him, so that each one may have pity on him and beseech the Lord for him with fervent supplications. After this period, let him be admitted during another period of three years as a hearer only: let him listen to the reading of the Scriptures and the preaching, and then let him leave judging him unworthy of the prayer of the faithful. Then if he has sought the Lord with tears and prostrated himself before him with a contrite heart and deep humility, let him be a prostrater during three more years. And thus when he has shown fruit worthy of his penance, let him be admitted at the tenth year to the prayer of the faithful without participation in the offering; and after he has attended with the faithful during two years at the prayer, he will be judged finally worthy of communion.[293]

Let us note that the fathers of Nicea, by issuing their canon concerning the apostates, did not want to set an unchangeable norm but only a particular ruling in relation to the persecution of Licinius, whose government was qualified as a "tyranny." Licinius had initially followed the same religious policy as Constantine. After the defeat of Maximinus Daia in 313, he published a decree at Nicomedia which offered to everyone "the freedom to follow the religion of his choice." In this decree, it was clearly stated that the cultic centers that had been confiscated must be restored in the shortest possible delay.[294] The victory of Licinius, therefore, seemed to usher in a policy of wide tolerance for the Church. A little while after 313, the Council of Ancyra was held along with the Councils of Caesarea and Neocaesarea. Licinius at first continued in the line of the above-mentioned decree but contrary to Constantine, he did not grant special favors to the Church. After the deterioration of his relations with Constantine, he took a harder, more hostile line toward Christianity. He seems to have found the influence of Christianity to be dangerous.[294] He forbade the holding of councils and purged the army and the administration of Christians. Here and there, following on the zealousness of certain civil servants, probably going beyond the intentions of Licinius himself, there were bloody persecutions.[296] Constantine definitively defeated Licinius on September 18, 324, near Chrysopolis. All the anti-Christian measures issued by Licinius were set aside by Constantine, then master of the whole Roman Empire. He therefore extended to the East the type of relations already existing in the West between the Church and state.

12

Those who, being called by grace and being obedient to its first movement, have laid aside their sword belts who have later on, like dogs returning to their vomit, even gone so far as to pay money and give gifts to be reinstated in the military service, all those persons must remain among the prostraters during ten years, after a period of three years as hearers. But it is good and proper to examine their attitudes and their way of being penitent. In effect, those among them who with fear, tears, submission and good works show that their change of mind was real and not simply on the surface, when they have passed the prescribed time among the hearers then they can participate in the prayers (of the faithful); it is even up to the bishop to treat them with more leniency. As for those who endure their penance with indifference and judge that the procedure set out for being readmitted into the Church is sufficient for expiation, those persons are to be required to do penance for the full time required.

This canon is closely connected to the preceding one; this is clearly marked by the grammatical construction.[297] Once he had come into open conflict with Constantine, Licinius made the war into a contest between the old religion and Christianity. Military men under orders were forced to sacrifice to idols in order to show their attachment to the pagan divinities.[298] Christians obviously refused and were excluded from the army. Some men regretted having followed their first feelings by becoming Christian and asked to be reintegrated into the army. In these cases, the men were truly apostates.

The term τὰς ζώνας means the sword belt of a soldier, and this is how the ancient Latin versions have properly translated it;[299] it is therefore a figure of speech for military service. We note that from the point of view of the text, it is not necessary to make a correction by adding the negative μὴ before the verb εἰσιέναι. The meaning would then be as follows: "...those who regard not being allowed into the Church as sufficient";[300] this reading is not attested to in any ancient Greek manuscript.

The fathers of Nicea allowed to each bishop the right to soften the sentence, taking into account the contrition of the penitent. Here is the constant position of pastoral care in such questions.[301] There had been a recent precedent concerning this attitude. Canon 5 of the Council of Ancyra stated the following:

> The bishops have the power, after having examined the conduct of each person, to be lenient (φιλανθρωπεύεσθαι) or to prolong the time of penitence; but above all, they must look into the life of each person before and after (the fall) and adjust the leniency accordingly.[302]

However, it is to be observed that the fathers of Nicea set a minimal limit to this leniency. In any case, the guilty persons must spend three years in the category of hearers. The willingness to be lenient should not be confused with laxism.

13

We must now observe the ancient and canonical law with regard to those who are about to die, so that if someone is about to die, he must not be deprived of the last and very necessary sacrament. If, after being in a hopeless state, having received communion and participated in the oblation, he gets well, let him be placed with those who only participate in prayer.

As a general rule, for all persons about to die and who ask to receive the eucharist, let the bishop, after inquiry, allow them to participate in the offering.

This canon is composed of two parts: the first, closely related to the preceding canons, is aimed at the lapsed Christians who are in danger of dying during their time of penance. The fathers of Nicea recalled "the ancient and canonical law" according to which they must not be refused reintegration into the Church's communion by receiving the eucharist. Such was the position of numerous churches, especially Rome and Alexandria, in the preceding century.[303] But then the following question arose: in case of a cure, was it necessary to consider the reconciliation that had taken place to be irreversible, or would it be proper for the dying person, once his health had been reestablished, to resume his place among the penitents?[304] Dionysius of Alexandria had firmly sanctioned the first solution.[305] However, this point of view did not universally win out, and it was the second which received the sanction in the present canon of the fathers of Nicea.[306] They no doubt judged it unnecessary to be precise about the length of penance still to be served since that had already been set out in the two preceding canons. John the Scholastic, or more probably the editor of the text he had in hand when he compiled his *Synagoge,* thought it useful, however, to be precise about the matter by inserting in the text of the canon the following phrase: "until the completing of the time fixed by the great ecumenical council."[307] It is very likely that we have here a scholion; this addition, moreover, was omitted in the redaction of the *Syntagma in XIV Titles.* We are of the opinion that this scholion is very ancient because the *Interpretatio Caeciliani* contains a formula which, with the exception of the adjective "ecumenical," seems to be a calque of the Greek text of this scholion.[308]

At the time of this clarification about the lapsed Christians, the fathers of Nicea set out, in the second part of the canon, a more general rule that communion must not be refused to a Christian in danger of death because of an illness, even if he is under an ecclesiastical sanction. The reason for the mention of the inquiry beforehand did not introduce, properly speaking, a restriction to this principle. The reason for the inquiry was to determine if the person had in fact been baptized and if he really manifested the desire to receive holy communion.

14

As for catechumens who renounce the faith, the holy and great council has decided that during three years, they should be only hearers and that after that they may pray with the catechumens.

This canon ends the series of rulings of the council about the lapsed Christians. As Bishop Nicodemus Milash noted, since in the case of the catechumens, they did not fully belong to the Church, their apostasy was not judged as serious as that of those already baptized.[309] The hearers constituted a category inferior to that of the catechumens properly speaking; this is clearly stated by canon 5 of the Council of Ancyra. To become hearers again was therefore a step backwards.[310] According to the first meaning of the term, pagans and Jews interested in Christian doctrine were called hearers. They attended the teaching part of the liturgy in the narthex without taking part in the prayer. As certain penitents had to stay in their ranks and leave the church at the same time as they did, there was a tendency in the canonical terminology to assimilate these penitents to the hearers. But we should not go so far as did J. Mayer in affirming that hearers exclusively designated the aforementioned category of penitents.[311]

15

Because of the great agitation and troubles which have recently occurred, it has been decided to abolish completely the custom which, contrary to the rule, has been introduced in certain places, so that it is forbidden for a bishop, priest or deacon to go from one city to another. If anyone, after the decree of the holy and great council, dares to attempt such a thing or busies himself in actually doing it, his scheme will be struck with absolute nullity, and he will be reinstalled in the church for which he was ordained bishop, priest or deacon.

The difficulties posed by this canon are not of a philological order; in the manuscripts we do not find any variants affecting the meaning. Certain Greek editions as well as some ancient Latin versions omit the mention of the deacon at the end of the text.[312] The mention of deacon, however, goes without saying since deacons are included earlier in the text. As for the adjective "apostolic" as a modifier of the noun "rule," it does not figure in the ancient manuscripts of the *Synagoge* or in the *Syntagma in XIV Titles.*[313]

The fathers of Nicea felt the need to formulate the principle of stability for the clergy because for some time the infractions of this rule had become frequent, at least "in certain places." Let us note that in the text the two terms κανών and συνήθεια are clearly opposed. The first does not refer to a canon of written law which has been previously issued, but it indicates the traditional Church norm. As for the second, it does not always have a pejorative sense. For example, it is the term used in canons to designate the legitimate custom of according certain honorary prerogatives to the bishops of Jerusalem; but here it means an abusive practice. The very fact that it was necessary to issue such an ordinance reveals a certain change in ecclesiological ideas. For Christianity during the first centuries, the local church was a structured, stable entity. Each bishop directed his community, advised by his presbyters and assisted by his deacons.[314] The organic solidarity of the local church is well expressed in the famous formula of St. Cyprian: *plebs sacerdoti adunata et pastori suo grex adhaerens*.[315] In this stable framework, the movement of a cleric from one church to another could only have a completely exceptional character. The same St. Cyprian announced the admission of the presbyter Numidicus into the clergy of Carthage as an extraordinary event.[316] As for the link between the bishop and his church, it was considered as permanent; it was common to compare this relation with that between a husband and wife in marriage. The orthodox bishops participating in the Council of Alexandria in 338-9, after having recalled the words of St. Paul, "Are you tied to a wife? Do not try to break the relation,"[317] added the following: "If this is said about a wife, how much more is it to be said about a church and its bishop. When someone is tied to a church, he must not seek to find another, so as not to be found to be an adulterer, according to the Holy Scriptures."[318]

The easing of the traditional discipline can be explained this way: the increase in the number of Christians had as a consequence the multiplication of churches. The priests were more and more called on to fulfill functions previously reserved for the bishop, and this entailed a dissolution of the presbyterate as a college. At first, the priests were the counselors of the bishop; then they became his delegates. Simultaneously, the greater frequency of council meetings made the bishops more aware of their mutual solidarity and made them less aware of their relation with their own communities.[319] The Council of Arles in 314 had condemned the transfer of lower clerics as well as that of priests and deacons.[320] It was not at all a question of bishops, no doubt because the situation had never yet presented itself in the West.

How should we understand canon 15 of Nicea? In other words, what was aimed at by the fathers of the first ecumenical council in this decree? Did they want radically to forbid all transfers of churchmen, bishops in particular, from one church to another, or did they want only to forbid arbitrary transfers, that is, those done without regular procedure? The reasoning set out at the beginning of the canon which says "because of the great agitation and troubles which have recently occurred..." could constitute an argument in favor of the second interpretation. Moreover, Eustathius, an important person in the council, had himself been transferred not long before from the see of Boerrhea to that of Antioch, with the approval of the bishops at the Council of Nicea. Were they contradicting themselves in this case?[321] The question needs to be asked differently. First of all, let us not forget that written church law was only in its beginning stage; consequently, we must not expect to find answers for all sorts of questions. Much later, Balsamon introduced distinctions which Matthew Blastares would pick up and which would become from then on classic:[322] (1) the word μετάθεσις (*translatio*) was used to mean the transfer, decreed by an authoritative synod, of a bishop from one see to another which was canonically vacant. Balsamon justified this kind of transfer on the basis of canon 15 of the Holy Apostles, which says the following:

> No bishop should be permitted to abandon his own community (παροικίαν) to take possession of another even if he is constrained by many people, unless he has a serious reason which forces him to do so, for example, if he can be more useful in this other community for the interest of religion (λόγῳ εὐσεβείας). In this case, he cannot make the decision himself; he can only agree with the judgment and the fervent imploring of many bishops.[323]

(2) The word μετάβασις (*transitio*) was used when a bishop for reasons other than his own desire, finds himself available, for example, if he cannot go to the place where he has been named bishop because of foreign occupation; this bishop can be elected by an authoritative synod to a vacant see. Such a "displacement" is not illegitimate and can be based on canon 18 of Antioch. (3) The word ἐπίβασις (*invasio*) was used to mean the arbitrary occupation of a bishop's see. This offense is condemned with the greatest severity; canon 1 of the Council of Sardica sets out complete excommunication for a guilty bishop. But returning to the canon of Nicea, it would be an anachronism to think that the fathers of the council envisioned such distinctions. Their intention seems only to have been to stop the practice of transfers, without striking down retroactively those transfers that had been made before. This prohibition was not without effect: near 330, Eusebius of Caesarea, asked to occupy the see of Antioch, refused by referring to the principle set out by the fathers of Nicea.[324] However, the ruling was very far from being scrupulously respected even though it was to be repeated many times.[325]

Not only did the Arians not observe this ruling, but even the orthodox sometimes did not observe it. As much of a stickler for strictness as was St. Basil, he warmly approved the transfer of Euphronius from the see of Colonia to that of Nicopolis, in the interest of the faith.[326] As for St. Gregory the Theologian, who was criticized for his transfer to the see of Constantinople, he considered that he was attacked on the basis of laws long since out of date.[327] He was not wrong in saying that his case was examined "with more anger than reason," but he exaggerated when he spoke of "laws long since dead." Even much later, transfers were never regarded as a normal thing. Balsamon, somewhat prone to admit infractions of the rule in this matter, never dared claim that stability in a church was not the general norm. He affirmed on the contrary that the transfer of a cleric was acceptable only for a very serious cause and on the pleading of many bishops.[328] In the West, the rule was on the whole well respected in antiquity and in the earlier Middle Ages, not only for bishops but also for other clerics.[329] In the East the rule was never very rigorously observed for priests, deacons and lower clerics;[330] but, by constrast, it was better respected for bishops, no doubt for ecclesiological motivations. For a long time, the translations of bishops, without being as exceptional a phenomenon as in the first three centuries of Christianity, remained nonetheless rare.[331] From the twelfth century on, translations and displacements of bishops were to become more frequent following the political upheavals caused by the invasions of the Turks and the Franks; and all this was accentuated as the later Middle Ages advanced. It is to be noticed, however, that the synodal acts referring to transfers most often carry justifications for the decisions on the basis of *οἰκονομία*.[332] In modern and more contemporary times, practice varies notably among the various patriarchates and autocephalous churches. In Russia, transfers were very rare until the second half of the sixteenth century;[333] even for a long time after that, they were not frequent. This situation changed with the *Oberprokurator* N.A. Protasov (1836-55). K.P. Pobedonostsev, (1880-1905), imposed the practice of multiple and systematic translations.[334] In February 1918, the local council of the Russian Church reestablished the principle of stability, not allowing any infractions except under exceptional circumstances;[335] nonetheless translations are made quite frequently. Since the last century, translations of bishops have been rather frequent in the patriarchate of Constantinople.[336] In the Church of Greece, where the subject has been the subject of lively controversy, attempts to impose strict stability of bishops has been a vain effort.[337] The Bulgarian Church no doubt has observed this rule the best: residential bishops with the title of metropolitan are not mobile; the only exception is a promotion to the rank of patriarch.[338]

As for priests and deacons, we have already stated that the rule has never really been observed, although canon 5 of Chalcedon repeated the prohibition against transfers not only for bishops but also for other clerics. However, a cleric cannot be installed in another diocese without the written permission of the bishop from whose diocese he is coming.

16

Priests and deacons or, in general, any member of the clergy who have the audacity, not considering the fear of God and not knowing the Church's rule, to abandon their churches, must not under any circumstances be received in another church but by all means must be forced to return to their proper communities, and if they refuse, they are to be properly excommunicated.

In addition, if anyone dares to take someone who is under the authority of another bishop and to ordain him in his own church without the consent of the bishop in whose clergy he was enrolled, let the ordination be regarded as null.

This canon follows logically from the preceding one. It envisions first of all the case of clerics who obstinately refuse, notwithstanding the ruling of canon 15, to return to their own local church. In the second half, canon 16 renders null an illicit promotion of a cleric in a local church other than his own. No cleric can leave his own church and install himself elsewhere without the express written consent of his bishop (dismissory letters). The cleric who does not respond to this requirement cannot be received in another church, and if he is obstinate, he is properly to be excommunicated. Later canonists, notably Zonaras and Balsamon, have sought to clarify the meaning of the term ἀκοινωνήτους in the text, relating it to canon 15 of the Holy Apostles which says the following:

If a priest or a deacon or in general anyone of the clergy abandons his community (παροικίαν) and goes into another, completely separating himself from his former charge, and lives in this new community against the warning of his own bishop, we order that he no longer be allowed to celebrate the liturgy, especially if he refuses to obey the call of his former bishop and persists in disorder. However, he should be allowed to receive communion as a layman in the new community.

Basing themselves on this canon of the Holy Apostles, Zonaras and Balsamon considered that the excommunication spoken of by the fathers of Nicea consisted in a suspension of liturgical functions.[339] This interpretation was taken up again in the *Pedalion*[340] and is rather probable, because it does not appear that excommunication here refers to a complete exclusion from the church community. If this was the intention of the canon, such a serious sanction would have been made more explicit.[341] The ancient Latin versions as well as the Old Slavonic *Kormchaya* do not shed new light; they are in this instance a copy, pure and simple, of the Greek text.[342] As for the authors of the *Kniga Pravil*, they adopted the maximalist interpretation.[343] Canon 16 of Nicea does not set out any sanctions against the bishop who accepts a cleric under these irregular conditions, although canon 16 of the Holy Apostles declares that such a bishop must be excommunicated (ἀφοριζέσθω) "as a master of disorder."[344] On the other hand, the canon of Nicea strikes down as null the promotion to a higher order of a cleric accepted illegitimately into another church. Unfortunately this rule has been and still is often broken. At the time of the Council of Carthage, August 28, 397, Bishop Epigonius complained about one of his fellow bishops who had ordained a reader of his diocese to be a deacon. The affair was roundly condemned, and it was decided that the guilty bishop, if he did not repent, would be regarded as excommunicated. On this occasion, the council reaffirmed the universal scope of this violated rule.[345]

17

Seeing that many of those enrolled in the clergy, being full of greed and of a shameful money-grubbing spirit, have forgotten the sacred word which says that "he did not give his money out for interest" and who in lending out their money require a certain percentage in return, the holy and great council has judged it just that if anyone, after the publication of this decree, takes interest for a loan or, for whatever reason, holds back half of the loan or invents another thing with the mind to realize a shameful profit, he shall be deposed from the clergy and taken off the clergy list.

At this time in history, there was no distinction made between a loan at interest and usury properly speaking, which is defined as an excessive rate of interest. As J. Gaudemet has written, "according to the economic ideas of antiquity, interest could not be considered anything but a dishonest advance deduction against the debtor; a sum of money loaned out could not grow only by the simple passing of time."[346] However, Roman civil law did allow a loan at interest and established rulings fixing the authorized rate of interest.[347] The Old Testament forbade loans at interest between Jews, but permitted Jews to have them with non-Jews.[348] From a universalist perspective, the ancient Christian tradition considered the forbidding of usury as absolute.[349] That is understandable so much the more because in the Roman Empire of the time, the interest rate was very high.[350]

It is to be noted that the fathers of Nicea did not issue their ruling only as a preventive measure but because many (πολλοὶ) clerics were loaning money at usurious rates. This was not a recent evil; already in the preceding century, St. Cyprian accused certain bishops of this scandalous practice.[351] Canon 20 of the Council of Elvira says that the cleric who accepts usurious interest must be deposed.[352] Canon 13 of the Council of Arles set out excommunication for this offence.[353] Canon 44 of the Holy Apostles stipulates that "the bishop, priest or deacon who requires interest from those to whom he loans money must cease or be deposed."[354] It does not appear that these canons eradicated this corrupt practice. The canon had to be repeated by the Council of Laodicea.[355] We find it also in the *codex canonum* of the African Church.[356] Again at the end of the seventh century, it was reaffirmed by the fathers of the Synod in Trullo.[357]

We notice the expression at the end of the canon: καθαιρεθήσεται τοῦ κλήρου καὶ ἀλλότριος τοῦ κανόνος ἔσται. Clerics of each local church were enrolled on a list. By ceasing to be part of the clergy following their deposition, they automatically ceased to be on this list.

18

It has come to the knowledge of the holy and great council that in certain places and in certain cities, deacons distribute communion to priests although it is contrary to the rule and custom to allow the Body of Christ to be given to one who has the power to offer it by someone who does not; it has equally been learned that certain deacons take communion even before bishops. Therefore, let all this come to an end, and let deacons stay within the limits of their assigned roles

remembering that, on the one hand, they are the servers of the bishops, and on the other, they are inferior to priests. Consequently, let them receive the eucharist according to their order after the priests, whether it be the bishop or the priest who gives it to them. Deacons are likewise not permitted to sit among the priests, because that is contrary to the rule and order. If someone after these decisions does not want to submit to them, let him be suspended from the diaconate.

By this ruling, the fathers of Nicea wanted to eradicate abuses in the conduct of certain deacons. They are, therefore, formally forbidden to give communion to priests; nor are they allowed to sit among the priests in the sanctuary. On the occasion of the issuing of this canon, the doctrinal reasons that underlie it were called to mind. It is abnormal that those who have the power to consecrate the eucharist[358] should receive communion from those who do not possess this power.[359] The deacons serve bishops and are lower in the ecclesiastical hierarchy than priests. How can we explain this overstepping of their limits by some deacons? In the primitive Church, priests formed a college presided over by the bishop, and they were his counselors. But with the advance of Christianity, the communities in the large cities took on such proportions that it was impossible to have all the faithful meet together in one place for worship. The Church, therefore, had to create other centers and the bishop delegated to the priests his authority to preach the word and celebrate the sacraments. The number of priests grew considerably. We know, for example, that at Rome, under the pontificate of Cornelius, 251-253, there were forty-six priests.[360] This dispersion of the priests made the collegial character of the presbyterate less evident.[361] As for the deacons, they helped the bishop in the administration of the church, particularly in taking care of the charitable and material needs of the church. But their number remained unchanged at seven in conformity with what had existed in the Jerusalem Church at the time of the apostles.[362] Because they were close collaborators of the bishop, enjoying his confidence,[363] certain deacons in the important cities had a tendency to see themselves as above priests. This was particularily the case in Rome; thus the thesis has been put forward that this canon may have been suggested by the priests who represented Pope Sylvester. According to what we know about the council, we cannot categorically affirm this theory; however, it is not altogether unlikely.[364] Whatever was the case, this ruling had little effect in Rome if we judge by what St. Jerome wrote about some Roman deacons in his time.[365] In the East near the end of the fourth century, canon 20 of the Council of Laodicea reminded everyone that "the deacon must not sit in the presence of the priest but can only do so on the invitation of the priest."[366]

The prohibition of the Council of Neocaesarea limiting to seven the number of deacons in each local church does not seem to have been universally recognized as normative. We know, for example, that in the middle of the sixth century, the Great Church of Constantinople counted one hundred deacons; this number, though it was considerable, increased rapidly and a decree of the emperor Heraclius in 612 set the number of deacons at one hundred and fifty.[367] The Synod in Trullo by its canon 16 annulled the ruling of the fathers of Neocaesarea, expressly questioning its scriptural basis of limiting the number of deacons to seven.[368]

We have said that the deacons were the close collaborators of the bishops; as such, some of them occupied very important functions in the metropolitan churches and especially in the patriarchal chanceries.[369] The fathers of the Synod in Trullo had to make the following clarification:

> As we have learned that in certain churches there are deacons in positions of authority in the church's administration (ὀφφίκια ἐκκλησιαστικὰ) who, having become thereby arrogant and pretentious, and who take a position ahead of priests, we order that a deacon, whatever his dignity or job in the church, must not sit before the priest unless, representing the person of his own patriarch or metropolitan, he arrives in another city to carry out some official business...[370]

Commenting on this canon of the Quinisext Council (Trullo), Nicodemus Milash noted that in our own time the problem is no longer with us because now priests, and not deacons, fill important functions in the dioceses.[371] Let us note, however, that even in our time in Constantinople the archdeacon has a rather wide responsibility in the administration of the church on the local level.[372]

19

Concerning the Paulianists who return to the catholic Church, a decree has been adopted according to which they must absolutely be rebaptized. If some of them were before members of their clergy, they may, after being rebaptized, be

> ordained by the bishop of the catholic Church on condition,
> however, that they appear without stain and blameless. But if
> an inquiry shows that they are unacceptable, they are to be
> properly deposed. The same principle is to be observed for the
> deaconesses and in general for all the members of the clergy.
> We have mentioned the deaconesses serving in this condition
> although they have not received the imposition of hands, and
> they must absolutely be counted among the laity.

We do not know who proposed the canons issued by the Council of Nicea or how they were worked out. This canon deals with a problem analogous to that of the Novatianists, and it would have been logical that it precede or follow it. We are, therefore, led to think that the canons were edited immediately each time that propositions were made and accepted. This procedure would also explain the somewhat jumbled character of some of the statements.[373] Another difficulty comes from the fact that the fathers of Nicea evidently had the situation of their own time in mind and did not feel the need to furnish precise details, which makes it very difficult for us to understand the meaning and scope of this or that formulation. In this instance, the observation applies particularly to the second half of the canon concerning the deaconesses.

The ruling envisions the case of the Paulianists who wanted to be received into the catholic Church.[374] It concerned the disciples of a third-century bishop of Antioch named Paul. Born in Samosata, he became bishop of Antioch around 260. His becoming bishop was quite in line with his close political relations with the court of Palmyra. At this time, in effect, the Palmyrian state had broken away from Roman rule.[375] The worldly attitude of this bishop, his pomp and his ill-gotten fortune were not long in scandalizing the pious faithful,[375A] but he is remembered more for his heretical doctrine. In 264 a council was held at Antioch, to which Firmilian of Caesarea in Cappadocia, Gregory of Neocaesarea and Hymenius of Jerusalem came. This first council accomplished nothing because "the supporters of Paul of Samosata tried very hard to hide and cloak what was heterodox."[376] A second council met in 268, and it was made up of seventy to eighty members. Paul was condemned by it, deposed and replaced by Domnos, son of Demetrianus, the predecessor of Paul as bishop of Antioch.[377] Though canonically deposed, the heretic did not want to retire. He had many strong supporters at Antioch, no doubt among Syrian elements who were favorable to the government of Palmyra. He was successful in retaining his position for some time with the protection of Queen Zenobia. This monarch "seems to have dreamed of engineering the triumph of a wide syncretism and absorbing and conciliating all the religions which people were arguing about. Paul was in line with these views, and his theology agreed with her policy."[378] After the Roman army had taken control of the region in 272, the orthodox Christians of Antioch called on the emperor Aurelian, and he ordered that the Church "was to be given to those who held the same Christian doctrine as the bishops in Italy and in Rome."[379] Recourse to the civil authority had nothing shocking about it because it was a question of civil law; it is nonetheless interesting when we consider the historical period. What is also significant is the legal basis for the emperor's decision: communion with the bishops of Italy and in particular with the bishop of Rome. In the third century, the state authorities knew perfectly well what were the principles of church organization. It is difficult to know exactly what was the teaching of Paul of Samosata. In our own time, certain historians of dogma have thought that his adversaries, who were much influenced by the ideas of Origen, misinterpreted his doctrine.[380] The heterodoxy of Paul, whatever was its source, was undeniable: he professed a strict monarchianism which meant for him that there was only one divine person, the Father. His christology was of an adoptionist type, and Jesus was a mere man to whom God gave a very high degree of his grace. The Word and the Spirit were not substantive realities but only words describing divine action. Paul and his disciples used the trinitarian formula officially sanctioned by all, but they completely denied the meaning behind it.

The Paulianists never constituted a widespread group. It does not seem that they ever moved beyond Antioch and its surrounding areas. At the time of the Council of Nicea, they were in rapid decline. Very soon after that, they were no longer spoken of except as a past historical reality.[381] However, the same cannot be said for his ideas. The doctrine of Paul of Samosata seems notably to have influenced that of Photinus, bishop of Sirmium in the middle of the fourth century.[382] As Photinus was condemned not only in the East but also at Milan, the westerners knew about this teaching. That explains the fact that some ancient Latin versions of the canons of Nicea contain an insertion in the text of this canon mentioning the Photinians.[383]

In the eastern confines of the Byzantine Empire, there appeared during the seventh century a dualistic sect whose followers were called by the Armenians *Pavlikeank*, which translates in Greek as Παυλικι-ανοί.[384] This Armenian term was a derogatory name meaning "the miserable followers of Paul." It was not long before these heretics were confused with the Paulianists. Several reasons explain the assimilation: first of all, the similarity between the two words "Paulicians" and "Paulianists"; then the appearance of a story, no doubt legendary, that said that one of the founders of this dualistic sect was named Paul and was the son of a Manichean from Samosata. Finally the confusion was aided by the similarity between the Syrian city of Samosata and the Armenian city of Arsamosata, the real center of the Paulician sect. Zonaras and Balsamon admitted without hesitation that the Paulicians were the same thing as the Paulianists.[385] According to the canon of Nicea, the Paulianists who wanted to enter the catholic Church had absolutely (ἐξάπαντος) to be rebaptized, although in their group baptism was conferred according to a proper rite. But their trinitarian doctrine was completely heretical. As St. Athanasius of Alexandria and St. Innocent of Rome explained very clearly, that is why the Church required rebaptism.[386]

What did the fathers of Nicea mean by the expression "a decree has been adopted" (ὅρος ἐκτέθειται)? Did they want to say that at the council they had made a decision which they were making public by the present canon, or were they making reference to a previous ruling? This second hypothesis is by far the most likely. In effect, when it was a question of a decision of the council, the fathers of Nicea used the simple past tense (aorist) while here the verb is in the perfect tense.[387] Who decreed that the Paulianists had to be rebaptized? Hefele thought that it was a reference to canon 9 of the Council of Arles.[388] This is highly improbable because the canon of Arles, which itself, moreover, is not free from ambiguity, seems especially to take into consideration the use of a correct trinitarian formula as the criterion for a valid sacrament.[389] Besides, this ruling had a very general character while the fathers of Nicea made reference to a decree specifically concerning the Paulianists. We do not know either by whom or when such a decree was adopted. Taking into account the authority of the Council of Nicea, it was only the canon issued by this prestigious assembly that was henceforth to be remembered.[390] Personally, we believe that the decree that the fathers of Nicea were referring to was the one issued by the Council of Antioch of 268, which condemned Paul and his doctrine.

Since the Paulianists were received in the Church by baptism, the validation of ordinations conferred in their sect was not an issue. However, the fathers of Nicea did not exclude *a priori* the possibility that repentant Paulianist clerics, once baptized, might be ordained and thereby integrated into the orthodox clergy. For that to happen, they had, of course, to satisfy the requirements of the inquiry that all candidates for ordination had to go through. The only exception, implicitly admitted, was that according to the norm explicitly formulated in canon 2 of Nicea, it was forbidden to ordain neophytes; now in the case of the Paulianist clerics, they could be ordained right after their reception by baptism into the catholic Church. As for those judged ineligible, they must be deposed ($\kappa\alpha\theta\alpha\iota\rho\epsilon\tilde{\iota}\sigma\theta\alpha\iota$). Zonaras and Balsamon noted that the term was used here improperly ($\kappa\alpha\tau\alpha\chi\rho\eta\sigma\tau\iota\kappa\tilde{\omega}\varsigma$) because to be deposed, it is necessary to have previously received a valid ordination.[391]

It is extremely difficult to understand what the fathers of Nicea meant in the second half of the canon concerning the deaconesses. The formulation lacks clarity. Even if we accepted the reading found in the *Church History* of Gelasius as well as in two ancient Latin versions, where the first mention of deaconesses is replaced by that of deacons, we would not overcome the difficulty.[391] In this case, the expression "We have mentioned the deaconesses..." becomes completely unintelligible. Moreover, there is no logical place to break in the reading since the double mention of deaconesses is sufficiently attested to in the manuscript tradition that we can take it as authentic and sure.[393]

Why did the fathers of Nicea make this insistence concerning deaconesses in a canon about the Paulianists when they did not say a word about them in the canon about the Novatianists? Let us try to answer that question. The existence of a female diaconate goes back even to the origins of Christianity.[394] This institution was maintained until the early Middle Ages.[395] The functions of the deaconesses are well known: they consisted of visiting sick women and teaching women and children and looking after good order during the liturgical services in that part of the church reserved for women. The deaconesses helped the bishop and priest at the time of the baptism and chrismation of adult women. The functions of deaconesses seemed to be particularily wide in the eastern Syrian areas. Now bishop Paul was from Samosata, and we know that he introduced eastern Syrian usages in Antioch.[396] We can guess that among other innovations, he gave an important role to the deaconesses, a custom which was carried on by the Paulianists. This may explain why there is a mention of deaconesses in the canon about the clergy of this sect. If the existence of deaconesses is very well attested from the very beginning of Christianity, we have, in contrast, no testimony prior to the last twenty years of the fourth century regarding the rite of becoming a deaconess.[397] In this regard, the silence of the *Apostolic Tradition*, a work composed in the third century—at least in the form we have it now—is very meaningful.[398] It is, therefore, not at all certain that already at the time of the Council of Nicea, candidates for the female diaconate received an imposition of hands. Consequently, we cannot affirm that the phrase "We have mentioned the deaconesses..." is uniquely related to the Paulianists. If this phrase concerns deaconesses in general, maybe the fathers of Nicea wanted to remind people that this type of ministry did not have a priestly character properly speaking; this is what St. Epiphanius rightly underlines.[399] This reminder could have appeared very opportune to the members of the council because the Paulianist deaconesses received into the catholic Church would probably have wanted to keep the prerogatives previously acquired but which were not accepted by the orthodox. Obviously, considering the ambiguity of the text of this canon, we set out the above explanation only as a hypothesis.

20

Seeing that certain people kneel on Sunday and during the Pentecost season, so that there might be the same practice in all the communities, it has been decided by the holy council that prayers should be addressed to the Lord standing up.

The last of the twenty canons issued by the fathers of Nicea deals with a liturgical question. Although it does not have the same importance as the decision on the date of Pascha, this ruling nonetheless shows the desire of the members of the council to see that certain points of liturgical discipline judged important be universally observed. We met the same preoccupation in canon 18 about deacons.

The text of this ruling presents no variants in the manuscript tradition that affect the meaning. It is proper to consider the primitive reading of τῷ κυρίῳ. Besides the fact that it is given in the best manuscripts of the *Synagoge*, it is also corroborated by all ancient Latin versions of this canon.[400] The *textus receptus* based on the *Syntagma in XIV Titles* reads τῷ Θεῷ.[401]

Here, as elsewhere, we have translated ἐν πάσῃ παροικίᾳ as "in all the communities." It is the term which we find in patristic literature to designate the territory over which each bishop exercised his jurisdiction.[402] It is, therefore, a synonym for "local church." In the Russo-Slavonic version of the *Kniga Pravil*, we read *vo vsekh eparkiiakh*.[403] This is certainly the modern form of expressing the same idea. However, we prefer to avoid the use of the terms "eparchy" or "diocese" with this meaning since in earlier times, these words had an altogether different definition.

The practice of standing during prayer on Sunday and during the time between Pascha and Pentecost goes back in the Church to very great antiquity. This custom is clearly attested to by Tertullian.[404] St. Hilary of Poitiers saw it as coming from the apostles.[405] St. Peter, bishop of Alexandria martyred in 311, explained the reason for it as follows: "...on Sunday we celebrate a day of joy because of him who was raised from the dead on that day, during which time we no longer kneel according to the received tradition."[406] St. Basil stated the reason this way:

> And we say our prayers standing on the first day of the week, but everybody does not know why; since we are resurrected with Christ and obliged to aspire toward the higher realities, we not only remind ourselves, by standing during prayer, of the grace that was given to us on this day of resurrection, but also that the first day of the week seems to be somehow the image of the eternity to come.[407]

> In the same way, during all the fifty days after Pascha we are reminded of the anticipated resurrection...; during this time, the customs and orientation of the Church have taught us to prefer the standing position in prayer, thus transposing our minds from the present to the future by this outward physical reminder.[408]

This ruling has never been abolished; on the contrary, the fathers of the Synod in Trullo expressly repeated the prohibition of praying kneeling on Sunday.[409] It is, therefore, regrettable that in our own times this ruling is sometimes transgressed by the laity, indeed by clerics. In contrast, the office of kneeling prayers on the day of Pentecost is only a violation of this rule on the surface, because liturgically it is the vespers of Monday.[410] This remains true even if, in practice, this rite is generally anticipated and celebrated immediately after the liturgy of Pentecost.[411]

CHAPTER I FOOTNOTES

[1]Gal 6:16.

[2]G.L. Prestige, *God in Patristic Thought*, 2nd ed. (London, 1952), p. 76.

[3]J. Lebreton, "Le desaccord de la foi populaire et de la theologie savante dans l'Eglise chretienne du IIIe siécle," *RHE* 19 (1923), pp. 501-6, and 20 (1924), pp. 16-23. This distinction, however, must not be absolutized, first of all because it would be necessary to agree on the notions of "cultured" and "uncultured"; and then even for learned theologians of this time, we often encounter a naive realism. On this matter, see B. Lonergan, *The Way to Nicea* (Philadelphia, 1976), pp. 105-118.

[4]G. Bardy, *Recherches sur Lucien d'Antioche et son école* (Paris, 1936).

[5]On the usage of the term Συλλουκιανίσται, see G. Bardy, *op. cit.*, pp. 201-204. In the framework of this work we could not give even a summary bibiliography on the dogmatic aspects of the Arian controversy. We will have to be content, therefore, with mentioning, beside the works cited in the preceding notes, the pages consecrated to this problem in the work of V.V. Bolotov, *Lektsii po istorii drevnei tserkvi*, IV: *Istoriia tserkvi v period vselenskikh soborov*, 3rd part, *Istoriia bogoslovskoi mysli* (posthumous edition put together by A. Brilliantov [Petrograd, 1918], pp. 1-134). We mention also H.M. Gwatkin, *Studies of Arianism*, 2nd edition (Cambridge, 1900).

[6]On the probable date of the beginning of the Arian controversy, see Ch. Kannengiesser, "La date de l'apologie d'Athanase 'contre les paiens' et 'sur l'incarnation du Verbe'," *RSR* 58 (1970), pp. 383-428, particularly 404-414.

[7]We can get a rather clear idea of the doctrine of Arius by this profession of faith (see G. Bardy, *op. cit.*, pp. 235-238) and by the excerpts that have come down to us of his *Thalia*: G. Bardy in *La Revue de Philologie, de Littérature et d'Histoire Anciennes* (Paris, 1927), pp. 211-33 and (1930), pp. 253-268.

[8]See A. Lieske, *Die Theologie der Logosmystik bei Origenes* (Munster, 1938). See also T.E. Pollard, "The Origins of Arianism," *JTS* n.s. 9 (1958), pp. 103-111. This scholar underlines the Alexandrian elements in the synthesis of Arius. The soteriological aspects of the Arian controversy are emphasized in the work by R.C. Gregg and D.E. Groh, *Early Arianism* (Philadelphia, 1981).

[9]On this first phase, see E. Schwartz, "Zur Geschichte des Athanasius," *Gesammelte Schriften* III (Berlin, 1959), *passim*. Also, "Zur Geschichte der alten Kirche und ihres Rechts," *ibid.* IV (Berlin, 1960), more especially, pp. 155-275. Also see, D.L. Holland, "Die Synode von Antiochien (324/5) und ihre Bedeutung für Eusebius von Caesarea und das Konzil von Nizäa," *ZK* 81 (1970), pp. 163-181.

[10]On the city of Nicea, see the article of H. Leclercq, "Nicée," *DACL* XII, 1, col. 1179-1232. See also A.M. Schneider, "Die römischen und byzantinischen Denkmäler von Iznik-Nicaea," *Istanbuler Forschungen* 16 (Berlin, 1943).

[11]Eusebius, *De Vita Const.* III, 8, *PG* 20, col. 1061C. Eustathius, *ap.* Theodoret, *HE,* I, 9, PG 67, col. 85B. Hilary, *Contra Constantium* 27, *PL,* 10, col. 602B. Athanasius, *Hist. arian. ad monachos* 66, *PG,* 25, col. 772B; *Apol. contra arianos,* 23 and 25, *PG* 25, col. 285D and 389B; *De Synodis,* 43, *PG* 26, col. 768D; *Epist. ad Afros episc.* 2, PG 26, col. 1032B. In this last letter, written around 369, we find the symbolic number which has generally been accepted by subsequent history: 318 fathers. The list of bishops, not without its own uncertainties, has been transmitted in some Latin, Greek, Coptic, Syriac, Arabic and Armenian recensions. On this subject, see the edition of H. Gelzer, H. Hilgenfeld and O. Cuntz, *Patrum Nicaenorum nomina...*(Leipzig, 1898), cap. XI, pp. LX-LXIV. This work must be completed by that of E. Honigmann, "Une liste inédite des Pères de Nicée," *Byzantion* 20 (1950), pp. 63-71. See also L. Voronov, *Dokumenty i akty vkhodiashchie v sostav "Deianii pervogo vselenskogo sobora 325 goda,"* BTr 11 (1973), pp. 90-111, especially pp. 107-110.

[12]Concerning this symbolic number, see V.V. Bolotov, *op. cit.* p. 24.

[13]Let us mention as a certainty the presence of Cecilian of Carthage, of a bishop of Calabria, of Bishop Nicasius of Die in Gaul. On the identification of the see of bishop Nicasius, see G. Morin, "D'où etait Nicasius, l'unique représentant des Gaules au concile de Nicée," *Revue Benedictine* 16 (1899), p. 72-75. To these bishops, we must add Ossius of Cordova and the two Roman priests who represented Pope Sylvester.

[14]See V.C. de Clercq, *Ossius of Cordova: A contribution to the History of the Constantinian Period* (Washington, 1954).

¹⁵*De Vita Const.* III, 7, *PG* 20, col. 1061 AB. The first legate is often called "Victor" in the Latin documents; see *EOMIA* fasc. I, pars prior, pp. 36-37.

¹⁶*Op. cit.* p. 24.

¹⁷Can. 8, 14, 15, 17, 18. *Letter to the Churches of Egypt,* Socrates, *HE* I, 9, *PG* 67, col. 77B.

¹⁸*COD*, pp. 4-5; cf. J.N.D. Kelly, *Early Christian Creeds* (London, 1950), pp. 215-216. In this same work, see pp. 217-230 for the analysis of this creed. See also J. Ortiz de Urbina, *Nicée et Constantinople* (Paris, 1963), pp. 69-92.

¹⁹*De Vita Const.* III, 6, *PG* 20, col. 1060B.

²⁰Thus the fathers gathered at Constantinople in 382 understood the term "ecumenical council" to mean a "synod going beyond the border of a civil diocese." See *Syntagma* p. 100. Very exceptionally do we find this expression with this non-technical meaning in what follows, but in this case, it is a question of a literal translation of a Latin text in which we read: "ad concilia...universalia": *Letter of the Council of Carthage (424-425) to Pope Celestine, loc. cit. CCL* 259, p. 171. Cf. for the Greek translation: *Synt.,* p. 453: εἰς οἰκουμενικὴν σύνοδον. The Greek singular is explained by an alteration in the Latin text and not by a mistake of the translator.

²¹*HL,* I¹, pp. 416-419; cf. *CCO,* p. 21.

²²Theodoret, *Historia ecclesiastica* I, 7, *GCS,* p. 32.

²³*De Vita Const.* III, 13, *PG* 20, col. 1069B.

²⁴The context naturally suggests this meaning: *ibid.* III, 13, col. 1069B. Cf. St. John Chrysostom, *In Matt. hom.* LXXXV, 4, *PG* 57-58, col. 763. Theodoret uses the word προεδρία to designate the function of a bishop: *Historia Ecclesiastica* I, 7, *GCS,* p. 32.

²⁵Gelasius of Cyzicus, *Historia ecclesiastica* II, 5, *GCS,* p. 44. In our time this opinion is held by J. Ortiz de Urbina, *op. cit.* p. 54. It is based first of all on the testimony of Gelasius, but it is unanimously recognized by specialists that the account of Gelasius must be read with extreme care: this is admitted moreover by J. Ortiz de Urbina himself, *ibid.* p. 296. He advances, however, the following argument: Ossius is always named first in the lists of bishops; moreover, the delegation sent from Rome was composed only of two priests whereas in previous councils the first of the Roman legates was a bishop. If in fact Ossius appears as first in the most ancient lists of signatories (by being the most ancient lists, they are therefore the most trustworthy), he is not mentioned as a representative of the Roman see. See for example, EOMIA, fasc. I, pars prior, p.36. On the contrary, we can suppose that it is later custom which leads us to think that the first signature must necessarily have been the representative of the pope.

²⁶On the role of Eustathius, see Theodoret, *Historia ecclesiastica* I, 7, *GCS,* p. 32. On the role of Alexander, *ibid.* I, 9, p. 41. V. Phidas has proved in a convincing way that the bishop who held the first position was Eustathios of Antioch: " Ἡ προεδρία τῆς Α´ ἐν Νικαίᾳ Οἰκουμενικῆς Συνόδου," *Ekklesiastikos Pharos* 57 (1975), pp. 218-68 and 401-446.

²⁷On this matter, see the works cited in n. 5. Also see G.L. Prestige, *op. cit.* pp. 197-218; B. de Margerie, *La Trinité chretienne dans l'Histoire* (Paris, 1975), pp. 91-172.

²⁸St. Athanasius, *Epist. ad Afros episc.* 2, *PG* 26, col. 1032C.

²⁹Eusebius, *H.E.* V, XXIII-XXV, *SC,* 41, pp. 66-72. On this question, see A. Strobel, *Ursprung und Geschichte des frühchristlichen Osterkalendars, TU* 121 (Berlin, 1977), pp. 17-69. According to J. Jeremias: "La celebration pascale de la communauté primitive a survecu dans la celebration des Quartodecimans," *La dernière cène, Les paroles de Jésus,* French edition (Paris, 1972), p. 139.

³⁰Council of Laodicea, canon 7; pseudo-canon 7 of the 2nd ecumenical council.

³¹Exodus 12:1-3; Leviticus 23:9-14; Numbers 27:16. After the Exile, the month of Abib, that is the month of corn, was called Nisan. See the article "Pâque" by H. Haag, *Dictionnaire de la Bible,* suppl., t. 6 (Paris, 1960), col. 1120-1149.

³²V. Grumel, "Le problème de la date pascale au IIIᵉ et IVᵉ siècles," *REB* XVII (1960), pp. 165-166.

³³This theme was to be particularly developed in a sermon by an unknown author at the end of the 4th century: *Homelies pascales,* III, "Une homelie anatolienne sur la date de Pâques en l'an 387"; the study, editing, and translating were done by F. Floeri and P. Nautin, *SC* 47 (Paris, 1957).

³⁴V. Grumel, *La chronologie* (Paris, 1958), pp. 6-8. A. Strobel, *op. cit.,* pp. 122-137.

³⁵Eusebius, *Historia ecclesiastica* VII, XXII, 13-19, pp. 225-227. See the article "Meton" in *RA* XV², col. 1458-1466.

³⁶V. Grumel, *art. cit.,* pp. 174-176.

[37]St. Epiphanius, *Haereses* LXX, *PG* 42, col. 356C and 357B. On the relation between this text and the *Didascalia*, see F.X. Funk, *Didascalia et Constitutiones Apostolorum* (Paderborn, 1905), Testimonia Veterum, p. 7. See also A. Strobel, *op. cit.*, pp. 347-352. An analogous position was taken by a certain Trekentios, a contemporary of Peter of Alexandria (301-311); *Chronicon Paschale, PG* 92, col 73-76.

[38]V. Grumel, *art. cit.*, p. 168.

[39]Canon 1: "Primo in loco de observatione Paschae dominicae: ut uno die, et uno tempore per omnem orbem a nobis observaretur, ut juxta consuetudinem litteras ad omnes tu dirigas," *SC* 241, p. 46. It does not seem that the fathers gathered at Arles really grasped the complexity of the problem as it was presented in the East.

[40]*Historia ecclesiastica* I, 16, *PG* 67, col. 912A.

[41]Professor Archpriest Livery Voronov, *op. cit.*; also see J. Ortiz de Urbina, *op. cit.*, pp. 295-297.

[42]J. Schmid, *Die Osterfestgabe auf dem ersten allgemeinen Konzil von Nicäa* (Vienna, 1905), p. 66.

[43]VI. Beneševič, *Ioannis Scholastici Synagoga L Titulorum* (Munich, 1937), p. 156.

[44]Canon 1, *Syntagma*, p. 252.

[45]*De synodis*, 5, *PG* 26, col. 688C.

[46]On this subject, see Ed. Schwartz, *Zur Geschichte des Athanasius, Gesammelte Schriften*, 3 (Berlin, 1959), pp. 216-226.

[47]*Haereses*, LXIX, *PG* 42, col. 220A.

[48]Theodoret, *Historia ecclesiastica* I, 9, Parmentier edition, p. 41.

[49]Eusebius, *Vita Constant.*, III, 18-19, *PG* 20, col. 1073-1077.

[50]*De synodis*, 5, *PG* 26, col. 688BC.

[51]*HE*, I, 18, *PG* 67, col. 60D.

[52]*CA* V, XVIII, Funk edition, p. 287.

[53]*Syntagma* p. 63.

[54]*Haer.* LXX, *PG* 42, col. 360A.

[55]"Kanonicheskie normy pravoslavnoi paskhalii i problema datirovki paskhi v usloviiakh nashego vremeni," *BTr* 7 (Moscow, 1971), *loc. cit.*, p. 205.

[56]Epist., XXIII, 1, *PL* 16, col. 1026-1027.

[57]*Liber de Paschate*, Praef., *PL* 67, col. 485A.

[58]*PG* 92 col. 85A. On this matter see the excellent study published by J. Beaucamp, R. Bondoux, J. Lefort, M.-Fr. Rouan, and J. Sorlin, "Le prologue de la Chronique pascale," *Travaux et Mémoires*, 7 (Paris, 1979) pp. 223-301. In the middle of the sixth century, Cosmas Indicopleustes wrote: "Quel peuple de l'orient et de l'occident du sud et du nord, ayant crue Christ, ne prédit, partant de méthodes de calcul diverses, les fêtes pascales pour de nombreuses années?," *Topographiene chretienne*, III, 68, *SC* 141, pp. 508-509. We would like to have more details on this subject.

[59]D.P. Ogitsky, *art. cit.*, pp. 205-207.

[60]"...τῷ καίρῳ ἐν ᾧ ποιοῦσυν οἱ Ἰουδαῖοι." He adds that we finally arrived at an accord; *Epist. ad Afros episc.*, 2, *PG* 26, 1032CD.

[61]*Rhalles-Potles* II, p. 10.

[62]Syntagma alphabetique, lettre P, chapter 7, *ibid,* VI, p. 420.

[63]*Hist. religios.* III, 7, *PG* 82, col. 1336D.

[64]Epiphanius, *Haereses* LXX, *PG* 42, col. 353BC.

[65]*PG* 48, col. 861-872, *loc. cit.,* col. 870-871.

[66]"Une homélie anatolienne sur la date de Pâques en l'an 387," the study, editing and translating done by F. Floeri and P. Nautin, *SC* 47 (Paris, 1957).

[67]*Loc. cit.,* pp. 170-171.

[68]*CT* XVI, 6, 6 and 10, 24, p. 883 and 904.

[69]F.H. Kettler, "Der meletianische streit in Ägypten," *Zeitschrift für neutestamentliche Wissenschaft* 35 (1936), pp. 155-193. E. Amann, "Melece de Lycopolis," *DTC* 10², col. 531-536. It is to be noted that the correct form of this bishop's name is "Melitios" and not "Meletios"; on this matter see Chrysostome Papadopoulos, Ἱστορία τῆς Ἐκκλησίας Ἀλεξανδρείας (Alexandria, 1935), p. 151, note 2.

[70]See the chronological data of the first part of the Meletian schism in the book of S.L. Greenslade, *Schism in the Early Church* (London, 1953), p. 54.

[71]*Epist. ad Meletium Lycopolitanum, PG* 10, col. 1565-1568.

[72]P. Batiffol, "Le Synodikon de S. Athanase," *BZ* 10 (1901).

[73]*CPG*, pp. 33-57.

[74]Socrates, *Historia ecclesiastica* I, 6, *PG* 67, col. 53A; Athanasius, *Apol. contra arianos*, 59, *PG* 25, col. 356B.

[75]A. Martin, "Athanase et les Mélitiens," in *Politique et théologie chez Athanase d'Alexandrie* (Paris, 1974) pp. 32-33.

[76]J. Meyendorff, *Orthodoxie et Catholicité* (Paris, 1965), pp. 53-54, sees in Meletios the champion of the provincial system in the face of Alexandrian centralism.

[77]The account of St. Epiphanius, *Haereses* LXVII, *PG* 42, col. 184-201, gives a sympathetic image of Meletios. It is certain that the bishop of Constantia had been influenced in his youth in Palestine by the words of Meletios.

[78]Cf. *infra* our analysis of canon 6.

[79]Socrates, *HE* I, 9, *PG* 67, col. 77-84 Letter: Ἐπειδὴ τῆς τοῦ Θεοῦ χάριτος.

[80]*Ibid.*, col. 77D-81B.

[81]S.L. Greenslade, *op.cit.*, p. 151, note 16.

[82]H.J. Bell, *Jews and Christians in Egypt* (London, 1924), pp. 41-42.

[83]Professor Archpriest L. Voronov, "Dokumenty i akty vkhodiashchie v sostav Deianii pervogo sobora 325 goda," *BTr* 11 (Moscow, 1973) pp. 90-111, more especially, pp. 93-94.

[84]H. Hess, *The Canons of the Council of Sardica* (Oxford, 1958) p. 52. W. Plöchl, *Geschichte des Kirchenrechts, I: Das Recht des ersten christlichen Jahrtausends,* 2nd edition (Vienna, 1959), p. 277. The same confusion about the origin of the canons of Sardica is found in the "Prisca," W. Plöchl, *op. cit.,* p. 278. In the "Versio Isidoriana" prior to the previous one, we find the following remark at the beginning of the canons of Sardica: "Incipit concilium nichenum XX episcoporum quae in greco non habentur sed in latino inueniuntur ita," EOMIA, t. I, fasc. II, pars III, p. 540. On the "Versio Isidoriana," see Plöchl, *op.cit.,* pp. 277-278.

[85]*Hefele-Leclercq* I[1], pp. 511-527

[86]The ancient title given in the "Recensio Photio prototypa" of the Nomocanon in XIV Titles, V.N. Beneševič, *Kanonicheskii sbornik XIV titulov* (St. Petersburg, 1905) p. 152; cf. *CCO,* p. 23.

[87]For example, see Plutarque, *Pompée,* 14.

[88]*PGL,* art. "kliros," p. 157.

[89]*Rhalles-Potles* II, p. 115.

[90]Cf. I Nicea, canon 2; Ancyra, canons 10 and 14; Basil, canon 69; Trullo, canon 20; *Syntagma,* pp. 84, 233, 234, 501, and 159.

[91]*Syntagma,* p. 66. It is clear, therefore, that the canonical texts are uniquely aimed at those that Roman law called the eunuchs (*eunuchi, castrati*) and not the "spandones" whose impotence resulted from a natural deficiency.

[92]Eusebius, *HE* IV, VIII, 1-5, *SC* 41, pp. 95-96.

[93]*SP* II, pp. 44-45.

[94]Cf. infra, our commentary on canon 3 of Nicea.

[95]On this person, see Chrysostome Papadopoulos, Ἱστορία τῆς Ἐκκλησίας Ἀντιοχείας (Alexandria, 1951), p. 184.

[96]*Haereses* XXXVIII, *PG* 41, col. 1012A,B.

[97]L. Bréhier, *La civilisation byzantine* (Paris, 1950), p. 14.

[98]Canon 8, *Rhalles-Potles,* pp. 676-677.

[99]I Timothy 3:6.

[100]This appears in the explanations proposed by Zonaras and Balsamon, *Rhalles-Potles* II, pp. 117-120. Cf. the scholia on this canon, V.N. Beneševič, *Kanonicheskii Sbornik, Prilozheniia,* p. 10.

[101]EOMIA, fasc. I, pars altera, pp. 114-115 and p. 185.

[102]*Hefele-Leclercq* I[1], p. 536.

[103]For Rudolf Sohm, the emphasis put on divine initiative in the election of bishops constitutes a fundamental aspect of what he calls "the sacramental law." On this subject, see the article of Yves Congar, "Rudolf Sohm nous interroge encore," *RSPT,* tome 57, #2, 1973, pp. 263-94. A good panorama of Church practice in this era is given in the article of R. Gryson, "Les elections ecclesiastiques au IIIe siècle," *RHE,* vol. LXVIII, #2, 1973, pp. 353-404. Apostolic Canon 80, *Syntagma,* p. 79.

[104]*Syntagma,* p. 267.

[105]See the article "Catéchumenat," P. de Puniet, *DACL,* t. 112, col. 2579-2620.

[106]Although this canon is written in clear terms, it does not seem that the Byzantine Church from this time on excluded all possibility of exceptions. We must not forget that this canon was issued in order to cut short recriminations by the Roman Church concerning the rapid promotion of Photios from layman to patriarch. For the canons mentioned, see *Rhalles-Potles* III, pp. 256-257 and *ibid.* II, p. 701.

[107]*Synagoge*, p. 90, note 11. This restrictive interpretation is not corroborated by any ancient Latin versions; EOMIA, fasc. I, pars altera, pp. 116-117 and 186-187; Str., p. 25.

[108]*CJC*, 3, Nov. CXXIII, c. 29, pp. 615-616.

[109]*Synagoge*, p. 90. This reading is missing in several manuscripts of the *Synagoge*.

[110]See the article "Συνείσακτος," *PGL*, pp. 1317-1318.

[111]See the article "Agapètes," E. Magnin, *DDC*, t. I, pp. 311-315. *Epeisaktos* is the form attested in novella CXXIII, c. 29, *op. cit.,* p. 615. In novella VI, c. 6, *ibid.,*p. 44, it is a question of "τῶν καλουμένων ἀγαπητῶν."

[112]For the first time in the Latin translation of canon 3, it is the Interpretatio Attici which gives us the term "subintroducta." EOMIA, fasc. I, pars altera, p. 116; we find it in Dionysius, *ibid.*, p. 257.

[113]I Corinthians 7:29 and especially 9:5: "Μὴ οὐκ ἔχομεν ἐξουσίαν ἀδελφὴν γυναῖκα περιαγεῖν."

[114]Epist. IV, *CSEL*, pp. 472-478.

[115]Eusebius, *Historia ecclesiastica* VII, XXX #12, 41, p. 217.

[116]*Syntagma*, p. 236.

[117]*Syntagma*, pp. 515-516, *loc. cit.,* p. 515.

[118]Epist. XXII, 14, edition (Paris: Les Belles Lettres, 1949) t. I, p. 123.

[119]"Πρὸς τοὺς ἔχοντας παρθένους συνείσακτους," *PG* 47-8, col. 495-514.

[120]*CT,* XVI, 2, 44 edition of Mommsen (Berlin, 1905), p. 851.

[121]In Trullo, canon 5, *Syntagma,* pp. 147-8; II Nicea, canons 18 and 22, *ibid.,* pp. 223-4 and 227-228.

[122]In its most ancient form, the anecdote is found in Socrates, *HE* I, 11, *PG* 67, col. 104A. On the dependence of the accounts of Sozomen and Gelasius vis-à-vis Socrates, see R. Gryson, *Les origines du célibat ecclésiastique* (Gembloux, 1970) pp. 88-90. We may consider the anecdote legendary not only because of the silence of the sources of the time but also because of the confusion of persons: Paphnutius was a confessor of the dissident Meletian group and was not even a bishop. Tradition has transferred certain traits belonging to Potamon, orthodox bishop of Heraclius in Upper Egypt. On this subject, see Fr. Winkelmann, *Paphnutius der Bekenner und Bischof. Probleme der Koptischen Literatur* (Halle, 1968), pp. 145-153. R. Gryson, in an article subsequently published, fully recognizes the inauthenticity of the anecdote reported by Socrates: "Dix ans de recherches sur les origines du célibat ecclésiastique," *Revue théologique de Louvain* 11 (1980), pp. 157-185. As for when Rome began to want to impose the new rule of celibacy, R. Gryson, in this same article, hesitates between Pope Damasus (366-384) and Pope Siricius (384-399).

[123]M. Meigne, "Concile ou collection d'Elvire?," *RHE* LXX (1975), pp. 361-87, has shown that it was a question of a collection with elements added as time went on. This opinion is largely accepted by the specialists. One point, however, is contested; it concerns the meaning to be given to the prohibition formulated in canon 33: "Placuit in totum prohibere episcopis, presbyteris et diaconibus vel omnibus clericis positis in ministerio abstinere se a coniugibus suis et non generare filios: quicumque vero fecerit, ab honore clericatus exterminatur," *Hefele-Leclercq* I[1], pp. 238-239. A literal translation suggests that it is permanent continence that is prohibited. M. Meigne, following this interpretation, sees in it a reflection of the eastern legislation. But it is not in literary Latin. S. Leuchli, *Power and Sexuality, The Emergence of Canon Law at the Synod of Elvira* (Philadelphia, 1972), p. 19, observes properly that "...the language of these canons remained primitive and simple." R. Gryson, in his article "Dix ans de recherches...," shows that it was in effect popular Latin (pp. 161-162). Therefore, it is unquestionable that the canon wants to express a prohibition of marital relations for the clerics "positis in ministerio," that is for bishops, priests, and deacons.

[124]Acts 8:10

[125]Acts 6:3; Titus 1:5. *Lettre de Clément Romain*, 42:4, edition of H. Hemmer (Paris, 1926), p. 86; 43:1, p. 88; 44:2 and 3, p. 90; 54:2, p. 110

[126]*Syntagma*, pp. 84-85; *Pravila,* I, p. 181. On this problem of translation, see N. Milash, *Pravila* I, p. 47.

[127]XV, 1, edition of J.P. Audet (Paris, 1958), p. 240.

[128]See Cyrille Vogel, "L' imposition des mains dans les rites d'ordination en Orient et en Occident," *La Maison-Dieu* 102 (Paris, 1970), pp. 57-72. See also P. Van Beneden, *Aux Origines d'une terminologie sacramentelle, Ordo, Ordinare, ordinatio dans la littérature chretienne avant* 313 (Louvain, 1974).

[129]Acts 6:6 and 13:3; I Timothy 4:14 and 5:22; II Timothy 1:6; Hebrews 6:2.

[130]See E. Lohse, *Die Ordination im Spätjudentum und im Neuen Testament* (Göttingen, 1951), pp. 28-66. Also K. Hruby, "La notion d'ordination dans la tradition juive," *La Maison-Dieu* 102 (1970), pp. 30-56.

[131]"Rapport des Pères du concile d'Ephèse aux Empereurs," *ACO*, I I, 3, p. 3: "...τοὺς θεοφιλεστάτους μητροπολίτας ἐπισκόπους," St. Leo, Epist. CVI, 2: "metropolitani episcopi," "τοὺς μητροπολίτας ἐπισκόπους," *PL*, 54, col. 1003B and 1004B.

[132]See for example: Antioch, canon 9, *Syntagma, p.* 256; Proclus, *Letter to Domnus*, PG 65, col. 884A.

[133]EOMIA, fasc. I, pars altera, pp. 116 and 258.

[134]*Ibid.,* p. 189.

[135]The version called "Gallica": "qui in metropoli sit constitutus," *ibid.,* p. 188. This paraphrase is to be related to the one found in canon 20 of Antioch: "τῶν πεπιστευμένων τὰς μητροπόλεις."

[136]OEMIA, *ibid.,* Versions of Cecilian and Atticus, p. 117; Prisca, *ibid.,* p. 117; Isidoriana, *ibid.,* p. 189. Here is the most archaic Latin paraphrase in the Codex Ingilrami: "eum qui in ampliori ciuitate provinciae...id est in metropolim," *ibid.,* p. 117.

[137]Cf. *infra* our analysis of the canon in question.

[138]See our article: "La pluralité des consécrateurs dans les chirotonies épiscopales," *Messager* 42-3 (1963), pp. 97-111.

[139]Epist. LXVII, *CSEL* p. 739.

[140]*SC* 241, p. 56.

[141]See Fr. Dvornik, *The idea of apostolicity in Byzantium and the Legend of the Apostle Andrew* (Cambridge, Mass., 1958), pp. 6-7.

[142]*Ibid.,* pp. 4-5.

[143]On the organization of the Church in the provincial framework before Nicea, see P. Ghidoulianov, *Mitropolity v pervye tri veka Khristianstva* (Moscow, 1905), pp. 181-261.

[144]A.H.M. Jones, *The Later Roman Empire*, Vol. I (Oxford, 1964), pp. 42-43.

[145]*Ibid.,* II, pp. 881-883.

[146]Antioch, canon 9: Laodicea, canon 12, *Syntagma,* pp. 256 and 269

[147]J. Gaudemet, *L'Eglise dans l'Empire romain* (Paris, 1958), pp. 382-383.

[148]See J.B. Chabot, *Synodicon orientale* (Paris, 1902), pp. 263-75.

[149]See Letters XLVII, XLVIII, XLIX, L: Collection Les Belles Lettres, t. I (Paris, 1964), pp. 60-66. Also, *ibid.,* the introduction by P. Gallay, pp. xi-xiii.

[150]Ep. XXIV, chapter II, *PL* 20, col. 548B-549A.

[151]J. Gaudemet, *op. cit.,* pp. 333-4. *Pravila,* I, pp. 183-190.

[152]Socrates, *Historia ecclesiastica,* I, 9, *PG* 67, col. 81AB. Theodoret, *Historia ecclesiastica* I, 9, *GCS,* pp. 40-41.

[152a]See our article "Quelques remarques à propos des élections épiscopales dans l'orient byzantin," *REB* XXV, 1967, pp. 101-105.

[153]*Syntagma,* pp. 235-6; pp. 260-1; p. 69.

[154]Orat. XVIII, c. XXXV, PG 35, col. 1072B.

[155]Justinian, Nov. CXXIII, c. 1 and CXXXVII, c. 2, *CJC,* 3, pp. 594 and 696-7. These stipulations only sanctioned the customary law. In effect, this practice is mentioned in the explanation of the motion adopted at the Council of Chalcedon concerning the see of Constantinople, *ACO* II, I, 3, pp. 99 (458).

[156]See for example the scholia for chapter XXIII of title I in the Nomocanon in XIV Titles, *PP* I, p. 60.

[157]The participation of the laity generally took the form of a primary election. The final decision was in the competence of the episcopal synod. See the present *Statute of the Orthodox Church in America,* article 6, section 10.

[158]On this variant found in Gelasius, see *GCS,* p. 113. It is attested to in the following Latin versions: Caeciliani, EOMIA, fasc., I, *pars altera,* p. 118; Attici, *ibid.,* p. 118; Codex Ingilrami,

ibid., p. 119; Gallica, *ibid.*, p. 194; Gallo-Hispana, *ibid.*, p. 194; Isidori, *ibid.*, p. 195; the two Dionysian versions, *ibid.*, p. 260. For the Syriac text, see F. Schulthess, "Die syrischen Kanones der Synoden von Nizäa bis Chalcedon," *Abhandlungen der Gesellschaft der Wissenschaften zu Göttingen,* 10, 2 (1908), p. 17.

[159]*Syntagma,* p. 255.

[160]S. Salaville, "La τεσσαρακοστή du Ve canon de Nicée (325)," *EO* XIII (1910), pp. 65-72.

[161]Canon 20 of Antioch, *Syntagma,* p. 262. Other canons of Antioch that clarify the decisions of Nicea: 13, 19, *ibid.,* pp. 252-3, pp. 253-54, p. 261.

[162]Cf. *infra* our analysis of canon 1 of Chalcedon.

[163]Apostolic Canon 37: *Syntagma,* p. 71.

[164]In Trullo, canon 8; II Nicea, canon 6: *Syntagma,* p. 150 and pp. 213-214.

[165]See S. Salaville, *art. cit.*

[166]Elvira, canon 54, *Hefele-Leclercq* I[1], p. 250.

[167]Apost., can. 12, 13, 32; Antioch, can. 2 and 6, *Syntagma,* pp. 64, 68, 253, 255.

[168]See our article, "La législation du concile de Sardique sur le droit d'appel dans la tradition canonique byzantine," *Messager* 80 (1972), pp. 201-230.

[169]"...it is obvious that the council of the province will direct the affairs of each province according to what was decided at Nicea," canon 2, *loc. cit., Syntagma,* p. 97.

[170]*Ibid.,* p. 262.

[171]*Ibid.,* p. 69

[172]See Othmar Heggelbacher, *Geschichte des frühchristlichen Kirchenrechts bis zum Konzil von Nizäa 325* (Fribourg, Switzerland, 1974), pp. 105-21.

[173]M. Goguel, *L'Eglise primitive* (Paris, 1947), p. 183.

[174]C. Lübeck, *Reichseinteilung und kirchliche Hierarchie bis zum Ausgange des vierten Jahrhunderts* (Munster, Westphalia, 1901), p. 34.

[175]Acts 15:1-35. See H. Conzelmann, *History of Primitive Christianity* (Nashville, 1973), pp. 82-90. C. Vogel shows that it is nonetheless very difficult to see in the assembly of Jerusalem the origin of the synodal system in the church: *Primatialité et synodalité dans l'Eglise locale durant la période anté-nicéene, Aspect de l'Orthodoxie* (Paris, 1981), pp. 53-66.

[176]*Syntagma,* p. 121.

[177]*Ibid.,* pp. 150-151.

[178]*Ibid.,* pp. 213-214.

[179]This already appears in the rubric under which figures the first half of the canon in the *Synagoge,* E. Beneševič, p. 32. This is also the interpretation of Zonaras and Balsamon, *Rhalles-Potles* II, pp. 128-131.

[180]*Synagoge,* p. 32; Rufini, EOMIA, t. I, pars altera, pp. 197 and 199.

[181]E. Schwartz, *Der sechste nicaenische Kanon auf der Synode von Chalkedon, Sitzungsberichte der Preuss. Akademie der Wissenschaften,* Phil.-hist. Klasse (Berlin, 1930). H. Chadwick, "Faith and Order at the Council of Nicaea: A Note on the Background of the Sixth Canon," *HTR* vol. LIII LIII (1960), pp. 171-195. M.R. Cataudella, "Intorno al VI canone del Concilio di Nicea," *Atti della Accademia delle Scienze di Torino, Classe di Science Morali, Storiche e Filologiche,* 103, (1969), pp. 397-421. Fr. Dvornik, op. cit., pp. 3-39. Bl. Phidas, Προϋπόθεσεις διαμορφώσεως τοῦ θεσμοῦ τῆς πενταρχίας τῶν πατριαρχῶν (Athens, 1969), pp. 51-95.

[182]Such is Hefele's interpretation, *Hefele-Leclerca* I[2]. pp. 558-9.

[183]The principal testimony called on is taken from the correspondence of Synesios: Siderios was transferred from the diocese of Palebisca to the metropolitan Church of Ptolimais, Ep. LXVII, *PG* 66, col. 1417A. But this testimony comes about one century after the council of Nicea. We also refer to the fact that St. Epiphanius calls Meletios "archbishop" of the Thebaid, *Haer.* LXIX, 3, *PG* 42, col. 208A.

[184]Bl. Phidas, *op. cit.,* pp. 59-60.

[185]*Epist. ad Meletium Lycoholitanum, PG* 10, col. 1565-8.

[186]*Apud* Athanas., *Apol.,* 69, *GP* 25, col. 1372.

[187]J. Gaudemet, *op. cit.,* pp. 445-446.

[188]The version of Cecilian: "suburbicaria loca," EOMIA, fasc. I, pars altera, p. 120; Prisca: "suburbicaria loca et omnem provinciam," *ibid.,* p. 121; Gallo-Hispana: "uicinas...provincias," *ibid.,* p. 196; Rufini: "suburbicarium ecclesiarum," *ibid.,* p. 197.

[189]We know of the placement of the dioceses of this schismatic group by the official notice

(βρέβιον) that Meletius had to furnish to Alexander of Alexandria, *apud* Athan., *Apol.,* 71, *PG* 25, col. 376-7.

[190]J. Marquardt, *Organisation de l'Empire romain,* II (Paris, 1892), pp. 431-435.

[191]This is what St. Jerome already thought; *Liber ad Pammachium,* 37, *PL* 23, col. 407A. Pope Innocent I also understood canon 6 of Nicea in this sense; Epist. XXIV, *PL* 20, col. 547-551.

[192]H. Chadwick, *art. cit.*

[193]M.R. Cataudella (article cited in note 112) thinks that it is proper to make a clear distinction between "the ancient customs" concerning Rome and Alexandria, on the one hand, and "the prerogatives" recognized in Antioch and other metropolitan cities on the other. He considers, therefore, that is is necessary to relate "ὁμοίως" to what follows in the text. This seems to us arbitrary: to disassociate so radically the case of Antioch from that of Rome and Alexandria. Why then mention Antioch at all? Besides, if we admit this interpretation, we will misunderstand the use of the adverb "ὁμοίως." As for maintaining, as Cataudella does, that canon 2 of the Council of Constantinople in 381 corroborates his point of view, this seems really paradoxical.

[194]EOMIA, fasc. I, pars altera, p. 196.

[195]J. Marquardt, *op. cit.,* pp. 337-378.

[196]See a Syriac version of the canon, *Analecta Sacra,* t. IV (Paris, 1883), p. 455.

[197]Cf. Const., canons 2 and 3; Chalcedon, canon 27; Trullo, canon 36: *Syntagma,* pp. 96-7, 125, 168.

[198]See K. Lübeck, *Reichseinteilung und kirchliche Hierarchie des Orients bis zum Ausgange des vierten Jahrhuderts* (Munster, Westphalia, 1901), pp. 140-148. See also *Pravila* I, pp. 203-204.

[199]*Op. cit.,* pp. 633-640.

[200]For the version of the Codex Ingilrami, EOMIA, I, pars altera, p. 121. For the Interpretatio caeciliani, *ibid.,* p. 120.

[201]*Ibid.,* p. 120. We find the same formulation in the "Prisca translatio," *ibid.,* p. 121; but this testimony in itself is not conclusive because as F.B.C. Maassen has shown *(Geschichte der Quellen und der Literatur des canonischen Rechts im Abendlande bis zum Ausgange des Mittelalters* [Graz, 1870], pp. 30-32) we are dealing with a redactional combination of the Interpretatio Attici and the version given in the Codex Ingilrami.

[202]This hypothesis proposed by E. Schwartz has been accepted by Fr. Dvornik (*op. cit.,* p. 17). It is contested by Bl. Phidas (*op. cit.,* p. 92). According to the Greek "Acts of the Council of Chalcedon," after Paschasinus had read canon 6 of Nicea in its Roman form, Aetios, archdeacon of patriarch Anatolius, had this same canon read without the term "τῶν μητροπόλεων" (*ACO* t. II, vol. 1, 3, p. 95/454/). This would imply that the Antiochian text had been substituted for the one previously used at Constantinople and which archbishop Attikos (406-425) had sent to the African bishops. But the majority of historians think that the corrective re-reading of canon 6 never took place. Most likely, it is an insertion made by a copyist. On this subject, see our article, "Problèmes primatiaux au temps du concile de Chalcédoine," *Messager* 77 (1972), pp. 35-62, especially p. 55.

[203]See the article, "Jean III le Scholastique," by E. Herman, *DDC,* t. VI, col. 118-120.

[204]Fr. Schulthess, *op. cit.,* p. 18.

[205]Gallica, EOMIA, I, pars altera, p. 196; Isidoriana, *ibid.,* p. 197. Dionys. I and II, *ibid.,* p. 260. We can verify this omission also in the Gallo-Hispana, *ibid.,* p. 196 and in the version of Rufinus, *ibid.,* p. 197; we mention these two versions apart because they are in fact paraphrases.

[206]See *CCO* pp. 8-10.

[207]*Synagoge,* p. 44, note 45. *Syntagma,* p. 86, note 4, Greek text. Latin versions based on a Greek text show "μὴ δεῖν," Caeciliani, *op. cit.,* p. 20; Attici, *ibid.,* p. 120; Gallica, *ibid.,* p. 198; Isidoriana, *ibid.,* p. 199; Dionys, I-II, *ibid.,* p. 261. This is also what is supposed in the translation of the *Kniga pravil* (*Pravila* I, p. 195).

[208]This formulation, or other analogous ones (cf., for example, Constantinople, canon 4; Chalcedon, canon 6), are often wrongly regarded as imprecise, being related to a rudimentary stage of sacramental theology. In reality, this corresponded to an axiomatic conception in Christian orthodoxy: what the Church decides in a legitimate way is an expression of the will of God. Therefore, whatever goes against that decision is without value. Such an idea does not exclude an eventual recourse to "Economy" in very precise circumstances. Even if in our time, we often prefer to use a more nuanced terminology, it is very obvious that fundamentally the orthodox position has remained unchanged.

[209]*Apud* Athan. *Apol. contra Arianos,* 69, *PG* 25, col. 372C.

[210]The importance of the Meletian question during this period is well clarified by Annik Martin, "Athanase et les Mélitiens (325-335)," an article published in the collection, *Politique et théologie chez Athanase d'Alexandrie* (Paris, 1974), pp. 41-61.

[211]Canon 19, *Syntagma,* p. 261.

[212]It was favored by the constitution of Church districts, above metropolitan areas, which corresponded to civil dioceses. Cf. *infra* our commentary on canons 2 and 6 of the Council of Constantinople.

[213]*Cf. supra,* note 91.

[214]First title: "Περὶ τῆς ὁρισθείσης τοῖς πατριάρχαις ἐκ τῶν κανόνων τιμῆς," *Synagoge* p. 32.

[215]*Ralles-Potles* II, pp. 128-131.

[216]EOMIA, I, pars altera, p. 121. According to the version of the "Acts of Chalcedon" established by Rusticus, we have an accusative singular "primatum" (*ACO,* t. II., vol. III, pars tertia, p. 109/548/). It is however, very probable that Paschasinus used the plural "primatus" which is a form found in the Codex Ingilrami and which is supposed by the translation of Paschasinus' intervention in the Acta Graeca: " Ἡ ἐκκλησία Ῥώμης πάντοτε ἔσχεν τὰ πρωτεῖα" (*ibid.,* vol. I, 3, p. 95/454/).

[217]See *Pravila* I, p. 197, note 1. In a Coptic version of canon 6, this idea is clearly expressed: the jurisdiction exercised by the bishop of Alexandria over several provinces is legitimate "since it is a law established by the bishops of Rome," *Hefele-Leclercq* I[1], pp. 553-554 and I[2], appendix VIII, p. 1184.

[218]See E. Schwartz, "Die Kanonessamlungen der alten Reichskirche," *Gesammelte Schriften,* t. IV (Berlin, 1960), pp. 159-275, especially pp. 211-212. See also V.V. Gervase Jalland, *The Church and the Papacy* (London, 1949), p. 309.

[219]About the see of Milan, see J. Gaudemet, *op. cit.,* pp. 384-385. On the papacy at the time of Liberius and Damasus, see *Histoire de l'Eglise* (Fliche-Martin), t. 3 (Paris, 1947), chapter V, edited by J.R. Palanque, 4, pp. 228-236. E. Caspar (*Geschichte des Papsttums* I [Tübingen, 1930], p. 523) established a link between this initial addition and canon 3 of the council of Sardica.

[220]EOMIA, t. I, pars altera, p. 167.

[221]*Ibid.,* p. 121.

[222]Hans Zucker, *Studien zur jüdischen Selbstverwaltung im Altertum* (Berlin, 1936), p. 150. M. Simon, *Verus Israel* (Paris, 1948), p. 235.

[223]Eusebius, *Historia ecclesiastica* IV, VI, 2-4, *SC* 31, pp. 165-6. On the revolt of Bar-Kochba, see M. Noth, *Histoire d'Israel* (Paris, 1954), pp. 448-453.

[224]Eusebius, *Historia ecclesiastica* IV, V, 3, *SC* 31, p. 164.

[225]Eusebius, *Historia ecclesiastica* VII, XIX, *SC* 41, p. 193.

[226]It is to be noted that Eusebius, while always calling attention to Church continuity, prefers to use the name Jerusalem in connection with the bishop's see: *Historia ecclesiastica* V, XII, 1, *SC* 41, p. 41; VII, XXVIII, 1, p. 212 and XXXII, 29, p. 230. It is really about Mazabanius, bishop of Aelia (VII, V, 1, pp. 168-169), but the quote is taken from a letter of Dionysius of Alexandria.

[227]*Historia ecclesiastica* VII, XXII, 29, p. 230.

[228]See the examples given by E. Honigmann, "Juvenal of Jerusalem," *DOP* 5 (1950), pp. 209-279, especially p. 212.

[229]*Rhalles-Potles* II, pp. 129-131.

[230]*Syntagma,* p. 118

[231]*Hefele-Leclercq* I[3], pp. 666-667.

[232]E. Honigmann, *op. cit.,* p. 215; *Hefele-Leclercq,* I[3], p. 836.

[233]Sozomen, *Historia ecclesiastica* IV, 25, *PG* 67, col. 1196A. Theodoret regrets this conflict about the primacy, *Historia ecclesiastica* II, 26, 5-11, *GCS,* pp. 157-8.

[234]This division is officially mentioned in 409; *CT* VII, 4, 30, p. 322. However, it is attested to during the course of the preceding century; see E. Honigmann, *op. cit.* p. 213, note 20.

[235]E. Honigmann, *op. cit.,* p. 215-217.

[236]*Cf. supra,* note 191.

[237]*ACO,* t. II, vol. I, pars tertia, p. 7 (366).

[238]H. Fuhrmann, "Studien zur geschichte mittelalterlicher Patriarchate," *Zeitschrift der Savigny Stiftung,* 70, Canonistische Abteilung, 39 (1953), pp. 112-176. Bl. Phidas, Ἱστορικοκανονικὰ προβλήματα περὶ τὴν λειτουργίαν τοῦ θεσμοῦ τῆς πενταρχίας τῶν πατριαρχῶν (Athens, 1970).

[239]See the article "Novatien et Novatianisme," E. Amann, *DTC*, t. 11, 1st part, col. 816-849.

[240]*Historia ecclesiastica*, VI, XLIV, 1, *SC* 41, p. 159.

[241]St. Gregory of Nazianzus, Orat. XXXIX, 19, *PG* 36, col. 357BC. St. Ambrose of Milan, *De paenitentia, passim, CSEL*, vol. LXXIII, pp. 119-206. Pacian of Barcelona, Epist. III, *passim*, edition of Ph. H. Peyrot (Nimegue, 1896), pp. 44-99.

[242]A work analyzed by Photios, *Library*, codex 182, *PG* 103, col. 532-535; codex 208, *ibid.*, col. 677BC; codex 280, *PG* 104, col. 325-356.

[243]I Corinthians 8:8-9 and I Timothy 5:14. Canons 1 of Laodicea, 4 and 24 of St. Basil, *Syntagma*, pp. 267, 467-8, 486. On the liturgical blessing of second marriages, see K. Ritzer, *Le mariage dans les Eglises chrétiennes*, French edition (Paris, 1970), pp. 163-170.

[244]Socrates, *Historia ecclesiastica* I, 10, *PG* 67, col. 100-101; cf. Sozomen, *Historia ecclesiastica* I, 22, *ibid.*, col. 924-925. Socrates' sympathy for the rigorist position of the Novatianists is not in doubt. On this matter, see Glenn F. Chesnut, *The First Christian Histories: Eusebius, Socrates, Sozomen, Theodoret, and Evagrius* (Paris, 1977), p. 177.

[245]Cf. *infra* our analysis of canon 19 of Nicea.

[246]There is no reason to take notice of the fact that the canon of Laodicea *(Syntagma*, p. 268) considers the Novatianists as heretics. They were then considered as such as well as all members of sects separated for a long time from the communion of the catholic Church. Very explicit in this regard is the decision adopted by the fathers of Constantinople in 382 (canon 6 of the second ecumenical council, *Syntagma*, pp. 97-100).

[247]"Canon 7" of the second ecumenical council, *Syntagma*, pp. 100-1. Timothy, priest at Hagia Sophia in Constantinople, "Treatise on the reception of dissidents," *ibid.*, pp. 724-726. Aristenus, commentary on canon 8 of Nicea, *Rhalles-Potles* II, p. 136. On the origin of canon 7 mentioned above, see our commentary in the following section.

[248]*Synagoge*, p. 113. The term "κοινῆ" is attested to in the quotation of the canon made at the second council of Nicea, Mansi, t. 12, col. 1022A. On the other hand, we do not find a trace of it in the ancient Syriac version; see Schulthess, *op. cit.*, p. 19.

[249]Attici, EOMIA, I, pars altera, p. 122; Rufini, *ibid.*, p. 203; Dionysii Ia and IIa, *ibid.*, p. 262.

[250]Mansi, 12, col. 1022D.

[251]*Rhalles-Potles* II, p. 136.

[252]*Ibid.*, pp. 134-136.

[253]We must not forget that the Novatianists no longer existed at this time; the exegesis of patriarch Tarasius was therefore not based on the contemporary Church practice. Moreover, he presents this interpretation himself as only probable: "μήπως ἐπ' εὐλογίας ἐνταῦθα τὴν χειροτονίαν λέγει καὶ οὐχὶ χειροτονίας," cf. *supra*, note 249.

[254]Canon 12 of Theophilus of Alexandria, *Syntagma*, p. 538.

[255]Letter of the council of the Church of Alexandria, Socrates, *Historia ecclesiastica* I, 9, *PG* 67, col. 77-84; Theodoret, *Historia ecclesiastica* I, 9, *GCS*, pp. 37-42.

[256]*Ibid.*, col. 80A and p. 40.

[257]Apostolic Canon 68; Carthage, canon 47, *Syntagma*, p. 68; *CC* p. 187. On this question see the work of L. Saltet, *Les réordinations* (Paris, 1907).

[258]The council decided that Meletius did not have the right "to ordain or to make promotions" (μήτε χειροτονεῖν, μήτε προχειρίζεσθαι), *loc. cit.*, col. 80A. On the Meletian schism, see E. Amann, "Mélèce de Lycopolis," *DTC*, 10, first part, col. 531-536. See also the article by Annik Martin mentioned above.

[259]Version of Atticus, EOMIA, I, pars altera, p. 122; Rufini, *ibid.*, p. 203, Isidoriana, *ibid.*, p. 203.

[260]See P. Pourrat, *La théologie sacramentaire* (Paris, 1910). It seems that this author is too eager to consider the doctrine of St. Augustine purely and simply, on this matter, as coming uniquely from a reflection on Church practice. The weak points of the Augustinian argument are well set out by S.L. Greenslade, *Schism in the Early Church* (London, 1953), pp. 174-179.

[261]A.S. Alivizatos, Ἡ Οἰκονομία (Athens, 1949), pp. 72-82.

[262]Eusebius, *Historia ecclesiastica* VI, XLIII 9, *SC* 41, p. 156.

[263]The expression "τὴν τοῦ πρεσβυτέρου τιμήν" is used in the canon. The term "τιμή" designates here both the function and the honor which are attached to him. A bit further on in the same canon, to express the idea of honor without the exercise of any function, the expression "τῆς τιμῆς τοῦ ὀνόματος" is used.

²⁶⁴Cf. canon 18 of the council of Antioch; see also *The Letter of the Council of Ephesus to the Synod of Pamphylia; Syntagma,* pp. 260-261 and pp. 108-111.

²⁶⁵See the work of F. Gillmann, *Das Institut der Chorbischöfe im Orient* (Munich, 1903).

²⁶⁶Epist. LIX, 5, *CSEL,* p. 672 and LXVI, 5 *ibid.,* p. 730.

²⁶⁷Eusebius, *Historia ecclesiastica* VI, XLIII, 11, *SC* 41, p. 156.

²⁶⁸Theodoret, *Historia ecclesiastica* II, 17, GCS, p. 376.

²⁶⁹Epist. CCXIII, 4; *CSEL,* vol. LVII, p. 376.

²⁷⁰This is what canon 10 the council of Antioch expressly affirms: "...τοὺς καλουμένους χωρεπισκόπους, εἰ καὶ χειροθεσίαν εἰ ἐν ἐπισκόπου εἰληφότες," *Syntagma,* p. 257.

²⁷¹See J. Marquardt, *Organisation de l'Empire romain,* t. I (French edition, Paris, 1889), pp. 3-27.

²⁷²XLII, 4, edition of Hippolytus (Hemmer, Paris, 1926), p. 86.

²⁷³"L'évolution des ministères au IIᵉ et au IIIᵉ siècles," *RDC* XXIII, 1-4 (1973), pp. 47-58, *loc. cit.,* p. 53.

²⁷⁴Apostolic Canon 34; Antioch, canon 9, *Syntagma,* pp. 68-69 and 256.

²⁷⁵H. Leclercq, article "Irlande," *DACL,* t. VII², col. 1461-1552, especially col. 1496-1497.

²⁷⁶C. Jireček, *La civilisation serbe au moyen-age* (French translation, Paris, 1920), p. 16.

²⁷⁷See J. Meyendorff, "Contemporary Problems of Orthodox Canon Law," *Living Tradition* (Crestwood, 1978), pp. 99-114, especially p. 107, where we find the proposed text of a canon on this subject.

²⁷⁸I Timothy 3:2-5 and 5:22; Titus 1:6-9.

²⁷⁹Several ancient Latin versions also mention the episcopate: Cecilian, EOMIA, I, pars altera, p. 126; Atticus, *ibid.;* Prisca, *ibid.,* p. 127. Interpretatio Rufini reads "ad sacerdotium," *ibid.,* p. 209; this phrase is related as much to the priesthood as to the episcopate according to the terminology of the time.

²⁸⁰Canon 89 (Lettre á des chorevêques), Synt., pp. 512-514, loc. cit. p. 512.

²⁸¹*Synagoge,* p. 84.

²⁸²Interpr. Caeciliani, *op. cit.,* p. 126; Attici, *ibid.,* p. 126; Prisca, *ibid.,* p. 127; Rufini, *ibid.,* p. 209; Isidori, *ibid.,* p. 209.

²⁸³*CCO,* p. 31. In the introduction to this work, P. Joannou indicates the manuscripts that he used for the correction of the standard text, pp. 1-11. Unfortunately, he is not precise in this instance from which manuscript he got this variant.

²⁸⁴All the orthodox treatises on canon law mention in a more or less complete fashion the impediments to ordination. This subject has been studied in great detail in the work by John Papaloukas-Evtaxias, *Τοῦ κανονικοῦ Δικαίου τῆς ὀρθοδόξου ἀνατολικῆς ἐκκλησίας τὸ περὶ ἱερατικῆς ἐξουσίας* (Athens, 1872), pp. 39-251. On the examination beforehand, see Elias Patsavos, *Ἡ εἴσοδος εἰς τὸν κλῆρον κατὰ τοὺς πέντε πρώτους αἰῶνας* (Athens, 1973), pp. 178-184.

²⁸⁵Apostolic Canon 62; Ancyra, canons 1 and 2; Peter of Alexandria, canon 10, *Syntagma,* pp. 75, 229, 588-589.

²⁸⁶Ancyra, canons 4, 5, 6, 7, 8, 9; Peter of Alexandria, canons 1, 2, 3, 4, 5, 6, 7, 8, *Syntagma,* pp. 230-233, 578-585.

²⁸⁷Ancyra, canon 12, *Syntagma,* p. 233.

²⁸⁸*Syntagma,* p. 230.

²⁸⁹Canon 3, *Syntagma,* p. 580.

²⁹⁰Basil, canon 73; Gregory of Nyssa, canon 2, *Syntagma,* pp. 502, 617. In fact these two canons mark a return to the practice adopted by the Church in the third century after the persecution of Decius. See Cyprian, Ep., 55, 6, and 17, *CSEL,* III², pp. 627-628 and 635-636.

²⁹¹See the *Pedalion* for a layout of a church with the indications for the diverse implacements, pp. 764-765.

²⁹²*Rhalles-Potles* III, p. 66.

²⁹³*Syntagma,* pp. 202-203.

²⁹⁴Lactantius, *De mort. persec.,* 472-12, *CSEL,* XXVII, pp. 228-233. Eusebius, *Historia ecclesiastica* X, V, 2-14, *SC* 55, pp. 104-107.

²⁹⁵See E. Stein, *Histoire du Bas-Empire,* t. I (Paris, 1959), pp. 103-5. According to this author, it is impossible to determine if this change of religious policy was the cause or the consequence of the rupture between Licinius and Constantine. In any case, the Christians of the East were sympathetic with Constantine, which explains in part the increasingly severe measures taken by Licinius.

²⁹⁶It is at this time that the martyrdom of the Forty Martyrs of Sebaste in Little Armenia took

place.

[297]"Οἱ δὲ προσκληθέντες. . ." The particle δὲ is attested to in most of the manuscripts (*Synagoge*, p. 101, note 3; *Syntagma*, p. 89). We must consider it as belonging to the primitive text; its omission in the manuscripts of the *Synagoge* can easily be explained by the fact that canon 12 is not quoted following canon 11.

[298]Eusebius, *Historia ecclesiastica*, X, VIII, 10, *SC* 55, p. 115.

[299]See for example the Interpretatio Attici: "cingulum militiae," EOMIA, vol. I, pars altera, p. 123; Codex Ingilrami: "baltea," *ibid.*, p. 129; Gallo Hispana, "balteos militares," *ibid.*, p. 214.

[300]*Hefele-Leclercq* I¹, p. 593.

[301]See canon 102 of the Council in Trullo, *Syntagma*, pp. 203-204.

[302]*Syntagma*, p. 231.

[303]Dionysius, bishop of Alexandria (264), had given the order "that those who were dying were to be pardoned if they asked to be and especially if they had previously asked to be reconciled so that they might die in hope." Eusebius, *Historia ecclesiastica* VI, XLIV, 4, *SC* 41, p. 160. On the Roman discipline in the middle of the third century see ap. Cyprianum, Epist. VIII, 3, *CSEL*, p. 487.

[304]Ancyra, canon 6, i.f., *Syntagma*, p. 232.

[305]Letter to Colon, *CPG, pp.* 15-6.

[306]This is also what the fathers of Ancyra ordered when they spoke of a re-admission "under conditions" (canon 6). The Council of Nicea having definitively decided the question, it is not surprising that St. Gregory of Nyssa made a pronouncement in the same vein (canon 5, i.f.).

[307]*Synagoge*, p. 70 (title XVIII, 7).

[308]Interpretatio Caecil.: "...donec impleat tempus a magna synodo constitutum," EOMIA I, pars altera, p. 132. This corresponds with the Greek: ". . .ἄχρις ἂν πληρωθῇ ὁ ὁρισθεὶς ὑπὸ τῆς μεγάλης [οἰκουμενικῆς] συνόδου χρόνος." Cf. the Gallo-Hispana version, *ibid.*, p. 218 and the paraphrase of Rufini, *ibid.*, p. 219.

[309]*Pravila* I, p. 223.

[310]This is what Zonaras' commentary on this canon of Nicea underlines very clearly, *Rhalles-Potles* II, p. 144.

[311]*Geschichte des Katechumenats und der Katechese in den ersten sechs Jahrunderten* (Kempten, 1868), p. 54. See Archimandrite Basil Stephanidis, Ἐκκλησιαστικὴ Ἱστορία, 2nd edition (Athens, 1970), pp. 107-9.

[312]*Synagoge*, p. 53, note 18; *Syntagma*, p. 90; EOMIA, I, pars altera: Codex Ingilrami, p. 135; Gallica, p. 224; Gallo-Hispana, p. 222; Isidori, p. 224.

[313]*Synagoge*, p. 53; *Syntagma*, p. 90. This adjective was late to enter into the "standard text"; we find it therefore in the *Pedalion*, p. 143. St. Nicodemus the Hagiorite erroneously believed that there was in it a reference explicitly relating to canon 14 of the Holy Apostles, p. 144. The adjective is found in the *Kniga Pravil* (*Pravila* I, p. 225).

[314]In his Letter to the Ephesians, St. Ignatius of Antioch wrote the following: "Your college of presbyters, of a justly deserved reputation and worthy of God, in tune with the bishop like the strings of a zither" (IV, 1, *SC* 10, pp. 72-73). He exhorts the Magnesians in these terms: "...I implore you about this matter, be of such a mind that you do all things in godly agreement, under the presidency of the bishop who holds the place of God, of the presbyters who hold the place of the senate of the apostles, and of the deacons who, being very dear to me, have received the service of Jesus Christ" (VI, 1, *ibid.*, pp. 98-99).

[315]Epist. LXVI, 8, *CSEL*, p. 733.

[316]Epist. XL, *SEL*, pp. 585-6. To justify this reception into his own diocese, St. Cyprian says that he was "led and directed by the goodness of God," p. 585.

[317]I Corinthians 7:27.

[318]Apud Athanasium, *Apologia contra arianos* 6, *PG* 25, col. 260C.

[319]About the few rare cases of bishops being transferred before the fourth century, see *Historia ecclesiastica* VI, XI, 1-3, *SC* 41, pp. 100-1 and VII, XXXII, p. 227. We are dealing here respectively with Alexander (+250), bishop in Cappadocia who became co-adjutor and then the successor of Narcissius of Jerusalem, and of Anatolius who was ordained by Theotecnius of Caesarea in Palestine to be his co-adjutor but who became bishop of Laodicea in Syria.

[320]Canons 2 and 21, Gallican councils of the fourth century, *SC* 241, pp. 47 and 57.

[321]Charles Munier wrote the following: "The rule of the Council of Nicea concerning the transfer of bishops from one see to another was formal and seems to admit no exceptions. However, the

fathers of Nicea had approved the movement of Eustathios of Boerrhea to the see of Antioch, thus giving the best interpretation of the law they issued. Their design was only to impede factions and maneuvers by people without scruples seeking their own advancement," *Les statuta ecclesiae antiqua* (Paris, 1960), *loc. cit.*, p. 81.

[322]*Rhalles-Potles* II, pp. 146-8; *ibid.*, VI, pp. 84-5, *Pedalion*, p. 16, note 1. *Pravila*, pp. 226-7.

[323]*Syntagma*, p. 64.

[324]*De Vita Constantini* III, 61, *PG* 20, col. 1136A.

[325]Antioch, canon 21; Sardica, canon 1; Carthage, canon 47; Chalcedon, canon 5, *Syntagma*, pp. 262, 280, 343-4 (original Latin text: CC, *op. cit.*, p. 187), p. 115.

[326]*Letter* 227, *PG* 32, col. 852-6.

[327]*Poemata de seipso, PG* 37, col. 1156A.

[328]*Rhalles-Potles*, II, pp. 19-20. Balsamon is the author of a little work "Περὶ μεταθέσεων," *ibid.*, V, pp. 391-4; on this subject, see H.G. Beck, *Kirche und theologishe Literatur im byzantinischen Reich* (Munich, 1959), p. 658.

[329]Pope St. Gregory the Great (590-604) wrote the following: "Quisquis semel in hac ecclesia ordinem sacrum acceperit, egrediendi ex ea ulterius licentiam non habet," Epist. XXXVIII, *PL* 77, col. 762C. To a request to approve a transfer of a bishop given to pope Hilary in 465, by the bishops of Tarraconaisia, the pope answered with a categorical refusal: Epist. II, Ascanio et universis episcopis Tarraconensis provinciae, *PL* 58, col. 17-9. But the Spanish Church did not renounce this practice of transferring bishops. Thus in 693, the 16th council of Toledo decided on a series of transfers; *Hefele-Leclercq*, III[i], p. 585. The first bishop of Rome who had previously occupied another see was Marin (882-884). The novelty of the fact was noticed and condemned by some people; see *Annales Fulgenses* (auctore Meginhardo), A.D. 882, *M.G.H. Scriptores rerum Germanicarum*, p. 99.

[330]See an anonymous scholion on canon 15 of Nicea quoted by V.N. Beneševič, *Kanonicheskii sbornik XIV titulov* (St. Petersburg, 1905), *prilozheniia*, p. 13.

[331]See the interesting number of translations of bishops put together by Socrates, *Historia ecclesiastica*, VII, XXXVI, *PG* 67, col. 817-821.

[332]See for example *PCAS*, document X, pp. 62-3.

[333]E. Golubinsky, *Istoriia Russkoi Tserkvi*, 2nd edition, (Moscow, 1900), I-1, p. 371.

[334]J. Smolitch, *Geschichte der Russischen Kirche*, vol. 1 (Leiden, 1964), pp. 402-3.

[335]*Ochredelenie sviashchenogo sobora pravoslavnoi Rossiiskoi tserkvi ob eparkhialnom upravlennii*, chapter 2, article 18.

[336]Meletios Sakkelaropoulos, Ἐκκλησιαστικὸν Δίκαιον (Athens, 1898), pp. 149-50. There has not been any change in this situation since this time.

[337]A. P. Christophilopoulos, Ἑλληνικὸν Ἐκκλησιαστικὸν Δίκαιον, 2nd edition (Athens, 1965), p. 177; note 12.

[338]Article 54 of the Statute of the Orthodox Church of Bulgaria.

[339]*Rhalles-Potles* II, pp. 149-150. Apostolic Canon 15: *Synt.*, p. 65.

[340]*Op. cit.*, p. 144.

[341]See for example, Antioch, canon 1: "...ἀκοινωνήτους καὶ ἀποβλήτους εἶναι τῆς ἐκκλησίας"; *ibid.*, canon 4: "...ἀποβάλλεσθαι τῆς ἐκκλησίας"; *ibid.*, canon 11: "...ἀπόβλητον γίνεσθαι οὐ μόνον τῆς κοινονίας, ἀλλά καὶ τῆς αξίας," *Syntagma*, pp. 252, 254.

[342]EOMIA, vol. I, pars altera, pp. 136, 137, 225, 226, 227, 269; *Synagoge*, p. 91.

[343]*Pravila*, I, p. 227: "...podobaet im chuzhdym byti obshcheniia."

[344]*Syntagma*, p. 65.

[345]Carthage, canon 54, CC, *op. cit.*, pp. 190-191.

[346]*L'Eglise dans l'Empire romain (IVe-Ve siècles)* (Paris, 1958), p. 579.

[347]Biondo Biondi, *Il diritto romano cristiano*, III (Milan, 1954), pp. 243-250.

[348]Exodus 22:24; Leviticus 25:36-7; Deuteronomy 23:20. The fathers of Nicea quote verse 5 of Psalm 14 in the Septuagint (the masoretic numbering).

[349]See R.P. Maloney, "Early Conciliar Legislation on Usury: A Contribution to the Study of Christian Moral Thought," *Recherches de Théologie ancienne et mediévale* XXXIX (Louvain, 1972), pp. 145-157.

[350]In the canon, the word "ἑκαστοτὴ," is to be noted; it indicates an interest of 12% per month. As for the term "ἡμιολία," it means 1.5 times the amount borrowed.

[351]*De Lapsis*, VI, *CSEL* (Hartel), III, 1, p. 241.

98 THE CHURCH OF THE ANCIENT COUNCILS

[352]*Hefele-Leclercq* I[1], pp. 232-233.

[353]*SC, op. cit.*, p. 52.

[354]*Syntagma*, p. 71.

[355]Canon 4, *ibid.*, p. 268.

[356]Carthage, canons 5 and 16, *CC*, pp. 134 and 138 ("canones in causa Apiarii").

[357]Canon 10, *Syntagma*, p. 151.

[358]The technical significance in Christian Greek of the verb "προσφέρειν" is to be noted; it means to present an offering of the Church community to God. This sacrificial connotation in the term was already found in the Septuagint; from there it naturally passed into the New Testament and especially into the Letter to the Hebrews.

[359]Canon 16 of the council of Arles (*SC, op. cit.*, p. 54) prohibits the abusive custom according to which deacons were unlawfully taking over the right to celebrate the liturgy (*offerre*) during the Diocletian persecution.

[360]Eusebius, *Historia ecclesiastica* VI, XLIII, 11, *SC* 41, p. 156.

[361]See Albano Vilela, *La condition collégiale des prêtres au IIIe siècle* (Paris, 1971).

[362]Canon 14 of the council of Neocaesarea says the following: "in one city, however large it may be, there can only be seven deacons according to the rule; you have proof of the matter in the Acts of the Apostles," *Syntagma*, p. 241.

[363]According to the *Didascalia*, a work written in southern Syria in the first half of the third century, the deacon must be "the ears, the mouth, the heart and the soul of the bishop" (Fr. X. Funk, *Didascalia et Constitutiones Apostolorum*, vol. I [Paderborn, 1905], *loc. cit.*, p. 138).

[364]It was put out by Zeghert Van Espen and reproduced by Nicodemus Milasch, *Pravila* I, p. 232.

[365]Epist. CXLVI, 2: St. Jerome, *Letters*, t. VIII (Paris, Les Belles Lettres, 1963), p. 118. See the article of F. Prat, "Les prétentions des diacres romains au quatrième siècle," *Recherches de Science religieuse* III (1912), pp. 463-475.

[366]*Syntagma*, p. 271.

[367]Justinian, *Novella* III, chapter I (A.D. 535), *CJC* III, p. 21; Heraclius, *Novella* XXII, Z.J.Gr., *Novellae* I, p. 24.

[368]"...We, looking in the apostolic text for the meaning that the fathers gave, have found that they spoke on this matter not of the ministers of the holy mysteries, but of serving tables." After having then quoted the scriptural passage about the institution of the seven (Acts 6:1-6a), the fathers of the Council in Trullo reminded everyone of the interpretation of St. John Chrysotom who supported their point of view (*In act. Ap. hom.*, 14, 3, *PG* 60, col. 116). Quotation of the Council in Trullo: *Syntagma*, pp. 155-157, *loc. cit.*, p. 155.

[369]On the role of deacons at Contantinople at the end of Antiquity and during the Middle Ages, see L. Brehier, *Les institutions de l'Empire byzantin* (Paris, 1949), pp. 496-506.

[370]Canon 7, pp. 148-150, *loc. cit.*, p. 148-9.

[371]*Pravila* I, p. 456.

[372]Stephanos Charalambidis, *Le diaconat* (Paris, 1969), pp. 36-7.

[373]W. Bright, *The Canons of the First Four General Councils*, 2nd edition (Oxford, 1892). On canon 19 of Nicea he wrote the following: "The difficulties which this canon has presented are chiefly due to its lax and, as it were, colloquial wording. It reads somewhat like the first draft of a resolution struck off in debate, and not yet elaborated into form" (*op. cit.*, p. 74).

[374]The original Greek text certainly contained the form "Παυλιανιστῶν"; this is attested to in the best manuscript tradition of the *Synagoge* (edition of V.N. Beneševič, p. 114). This reading is supported by the majority of ancient Latin versions where we find the word "Paulianistis," a pure and simple calque on the Greek: Attici, EOMIA, I, pars altera, p. 140; Prisca, *ibid.*, p. 141; Codex Ingilrami, *ibid.*, p. 141 ("Paulinistas"); Gallica, *ibid.*, p. 234; Rufini, *ibid.*, p. 235 ("Paulianistae"); Isidori, *ibid.*, p. 235; Dionysii I and II, *ibid.*, p. 272. But the form "Παυλιανισάντων " (Paulianis-ants) is nonetheless ancient. We find it in Gelasius of Cyzicus, *Historia ecclesiastica* II, 32, *GCS*, p. 117; it figures in several manuscripts of the *Synagoge, op. cit.*, p. 114, note 16. We also find it in all the manuscripts of the *Syntagma in XIV Titles*, edition of V.N. Beneševič, p. 92. This is why the *Kormchaia* in old Slavonic shows "paulinstvovavshiikh" (*ibid.*, p. 92, line 22).

[375]See M. Besnier, *L'Empire romain de l'avènement des Sévères au concile de Nicée* (Paris, 1937), pp. 212-23. Eusebius, *Historia ecclesiastica* VII, XXX, 6-8, *SC* 41, pp. 215-216.

[375a]*HE* VII, XXX, par. 6-8, *SC* 41, p. 215-216.

[376]*Ibid.*, VII, XXVIII, 2, *op. cit.*, p. 212.

[377]H. de Riedmatten, *Les Actes du procès de Paul de Samosate* (Fribourg, Switzerland, 1952). On the life and the doctrine of Paul of Samosata, see F. Loofs, *Paulus von Samosata* (Leipzig, 1924). See also G. Bardy, *Paul de Samosate*, 2nd edition (Louvain, 1929). Also the article "Paul de Samosate," *DTC* XII, 2, col. 46-51.

[378]M. Besnier, *op. cit.*, p. 220.

[379]Eusebius, *Historia ecclesiastica* VII, XXX, 19, *op. cit.*, p. 219.

[380]See for example, F. Loofs, *op. cit.*, pp. 202-64; J. Danielou, *Nouvelle Histoire de l'Eglise*, t. I (Paris, 1963), p. 253; B. Altaner, *Précis de Patrologie* (Mulhouse, 1961), p. 312.

[381]We are nonetheless still dealing with the Paulianists ("Pauliani") in the law of May 30, 428, directed against the heretical sects, *CT* XVI, 5, 65, pp. 87-88. This text was inserted into the Code of Justinian, I, 5, 5, *CJC* II, p. 51; but that does not mean that the Paulianist group still existed in the sixth century.

[382]See B. Longerman, *The Way to Nicea* (Philadelphia, 1976), p. 78.

[383]Cf. *infra* comm. of Constantinople, canon 1.

[384]See Steven Runciman, *Le Manichéisme medieval* (Paris, 1949), pp. 30-60. Also Nina G. Garsoian, *The Paulician Heresy* (The Hague, 1967). By the same author, "Byzantine Heresy, a Reinterpretation," *DOP* 25, 1971, pp. 85-113. Nina G. Garsoian believes in the "family relationship" between the Paulicians and the disciples of Paul, heretical bishop of Antioch in the third century. She bases her opinion in great part on F.C. Conybeare, *The Key of Truth* (Oxford, 1893). According to Conybeare, an archaic form of Christianity with an adoptionist Christology could have survived for a long time in Armenia. For Garsoian, the evolution toward dualism happened only at the beginning of the ninth century. These assertions seem too hypothetical to be accepted. The insult "Pavlikeank" comes from the well attested devotion of these sectarians for the apostle Paul. See Steven Runciman on this matter, *op. cit.*, pp. 49-50. They simply called themselves Christians, repudiating the Orthodox under the name of Romans, *ibid.*

[385]*Rhalles-Potles* II, pp. 159-160.

[386]Athan., *Oratio II contra arianos*, 42-3, *PG* 26, col. 236-7. Innocent, Epist. XVII, 10, *PL* 20, col. 533B.

[387]F. Loofs, *op. cit.*, pp. 164-201.

[388]*Hefele-Leclercq* I[1], p. 615.

[389]*SC, op. cit.*, p. 50. Hefele talks about canon 8 because the numbering of the canons of Arles is not the same in all the manuscripts. It is true that canon 9(8) of the council had a great scope, but it was about the Africans that the fathers of this assembly were thinking: "De Afris quod propria lege sua utuntur ut rebaptizent..."; this is why we can speak of a certain ambiguity in the statement.

[390]St. Augustine did not know anything else: "Istos sane Paulianos baptizandos esse in Ecclesia catholica Nicaeno concilio constitutum est," *De Haeresibus* XLIV, *PL* 42, col. 34.

[391]*Rhalles-Potles*, II, pp. 159-160.

[392]Gelasius of Cyzicus, *Historia ecclesiastica* II, 32, *GCS*, p. 117; Attici, *EOMIA*, I, pars altera, p. 140; Prisca, *ibid.*, p. 141.

[393]*Synagoge*, p. 114; *Syntagma*, p. 93. This is what is also found in all the ancient Latin versions except the two mentioned in the preceeding note. As for the Gallo-Hispana version, it does not mention deaconesses in what corresponds to the first half of the Greek canon; for this version it only mentions clerics in general (*op. cit.*, p. 236). The ancient Syriac version edited by Schulthess, *op. cit.*, pp. 27-8, contains the double mention of deaconesses like the standard Greek text.

[394]St. Paul in Romans 16:1 wrote as follows: "I recommend to you Phoebe our sister and deaconess of the Church in Cenchreae (οὖσαν διάκονον τῆς ἐκκλησίας τῆς ἐν Κεγχρεαῖς)." Many New Testament exegetes think that deaconesses are being spoken of in I Timothy 3:11. Pliny the Younger, in a letter written from Bithynia to the emperor Trajan around 122, noted that there existed women "quae ministrae dicebantur" among the Christians of his province (Epist. XCVI, 8).

[395]See A. Kalsbach, *Die alte christliche Einrichtungen der Diakonissen* (Fribourg, Germany, 1926). H. Leclercq, "Diaconesses," *DACL*, t. IV-1, col. 725-733. E. Theodorou, "Diakonissa," *TH. ith. E.*, t. IV, col. 1144-1151. Also R. Gryson, *Le ministère des femmes dans l'Eglise ancienne* (Gembloux, 1972).

[396]J. Danielou, *Nouvelle Histoire de l'Eglise*, vol. I (Paris, 1963), pp. 252-253.

[397]*Apostolic Constitutions* XIII, XIX, edition of Funk, p. 524. The rite described in this pseudepigrapha involved an imposition of hands by the bishop accompanied by a prayer. The ceremony took place in the presence of priests, deacons, and deaconesses. (A. Faivre, *Naissance d'une hierar-*

chie [Paris, 1977], pp. 137-8). In Byzantium the ritual was developed so as to conform to the ordination of deacons; J. Goar, *Euchologion sive Rituale Graecorum* (Venice, 1730), pp. 218-219.

³⁹⁸Bernard Botte, *La Tradition apostolique de Saint-Hippolyte* (Munster, Westphalia, 1963).

³⁹⁹"...διακονισσῶν τάγμα ἐστὶν εἰς τὴν ἐκκλησίαν, ἀλλ' οὐχὶ εἰς τὸ ἱερατεύειν," *Haer.* LXXIX, 3, *PG* 42, col. 744D.

⁴⁰⁰*Synagoge*, p. 151, EOMIA, I, pars altera; Caeciliani, p. 142; Attici, p. 142; Prisca, p. 143; Isidoriana, p. 242; Dionysii I and II, p. 273. It is true that the ancient Syriac version reads "Aloho," "God," (Schulthess' edition, p. 28). Another version of the seventh century reads "Moryo," " Lord" (British Museum, Add. 14526, *ibid.*, p. 28). No doubt we have here a correction made from the Greek text.

⁴⁰¹*Syntagma*, p. 93; *Rhalles-Potles*, II, p. 162; *Pedalion*, p. 150.

⁴⁰²*PGL*, p. 1042: "paroikia": community under pastoral jurisdiction of a bishop.

⁴⁰³*Pravila* I, p. 236.

⁴⁰⁴*De orat.*, XXIII, *PL* 1, col. 1191A; *De corona*, III, *PL* 2, col. 79B-80A.

⁴⁰⁵*Prol. in libr. psalm.*, 12, *PL* 9, col. 239C-240A. Cf. Pseudo-Justin (Theodoret of Cyrrhus), *Quaestiones ad orthodoxos*, *PG* 6, col. 1364AB, 1365A.

⁴⁰⁶Canon 15 i.f., *Syntagma*, p. 597 (without numbering).

⁴⁰⁷Canon 91, *ibid.*, p. 427 (equally without numbering).

⁴⁰⁸*Ibid.*, p. 528.

⁴⁰⁹Canon 90, *Syntagma*, pp. 196-197.

⁴¹⁰This is what Matthew Blastares underscores in his alphabetical syntagma, Letter E, chapter 2, *Rhalles-Potles* VI, pp. 241-242. This work was published in 1335. On this subject, see Hans-Georg Beck, *Kirche und theologische Literatur im byzantinischen Reich* (Munich, 1959), p. 786.

⁴¹¹For the Byzantine epoch, see M. Arranz, *Le typicon du Monastere du Saint-Saveur à Messine, Orientalia christiana analecta* 185 (Rome, 1969), p. xxiii and p. 278.

CHAPTER II
THE COUNCIL OF CONSTANTINOPLE

SECTION I: THE BACKGROUND AND PROCEEDINGS

The Council of Nicea did not put an end to the disruptions caused by the doctrine of Arius. The teaching of this heresiarch so flagrantly contradicted Holy Tradition that it was not difficult to get everyone to condemn him. In order to express the dogmatic truth about the relation between the Father and the Son, the emperor Constantine suggested the use of the term *consubstantialis*, no doubt under the influence of his counsellor for religious affairs Ossius, bishop of Cordova. An absolutely literal translation in Greek would have been συνυπόστατον, but this would have been inexact because this adjective had a Sabellian feeling about it; the Latin term had no such connotation.[1] Therefore, the Latin word *consubstantialis* was better translated by ὁμοούσιος, which, when it was introduced into the creed of Nicea, became the keyword of this profession of faith. Even this word, however, was not without its own ambiguities; taking into account its previous meaning in various writings, it could be understood in various ways.[2] The members of the council, though, wanted especially to express their condemnation of the statement of Arius and his followers concerning the Word: "There was a time when He was not."

In the East, many bishops were very sensitive to the dangers of Sabellian modalism, and the partisans of Arian theology adroitly exploited this feeling. The fact that some defenders of the word *homoousios* were tainted with modalistic leanings was a real source of confusion; Marcellus of Ancyra was in this group. There was an important part of the eastern episcopate that did not feel the least bit required to defend a non-scriptural term and so accepted certain formulations which were not intrinsically heretical but whose authors consciously omitted the word *homoousios*.[3] The attitude of the emperor Constantius (337-361) tended to favor dogmatic compromise; this emperor is not remembered well by the orthodox who

reproach him, not without reason, for his caesaropapism, well illus-
trated in his famous declaration reported by St. Athanasius: "What I
want must be regarded as the rule."[4] Still it is proper to note that
this emperor really only followed and did not lead the councils
which were held during his reign and which often issued contradictory decisions. In the middle of the century, an evolution began to
take place. The anti-Nicene party started to break up. Arianism took
on a more radical tone in the form of Anomoeism, and this leftward
movement provoked a deep sense of disapproval. A more moderate
group, though not necessarily orthodox, formed under the name of
Homoeism.[5] As for the eastern bishops close to the Nicene doctrine
but embarrassed by the word *homoousios,* they tried to win the victory for the word *homoiousios,* "of a similar essence." However,
thanks to the inestimable theological contribution of the Cappadocian fathers, who fought as much against subordinationism as
against modalism, many more people began to return to orthodoxy.
The Council of Antioch in 379, gathering together 153 bishops, can
be considered as the turning point in the turning of the tide toward
orthodoxy.[6]

Up until about 360, the continual theological debates about the
definitions of Nicea only concerned the status of the Word. The
creed of Nicea ended with an anathema aimed at those who said
that "there was a time when He was not," "before being begotten, He
was not," "He was made from what was not or from another person
or nature," or "the Son of God was created unchangeable or mutable."
The symbol of faith issued by Nicea said only that the fathers
believed "in the Holy Spirit," nothing more. Controversy about the
divinity of the Holy Spirit broke out when certain people who
accepted the full divinity of the Son began to affirm that the Holy
Spirit was only a superior creature.[7] They were called "Macedonians" after Macedonius, who was the homoeousian bishop of Constantinople deposed by the Arians in 360. No doubt he professed this
opinion, but the three principal promoters of this heresy were Eustathius of Sebaste, Eleusius of Cyzicus, and Marathonius. They were
also called "Pneumatomachians" because they "fought against the
Spirit"; this was how they were referred to by the fathers of the Council of Constantinople, 381. Orthodox teachers quickly came to the
defense of the faith but did not quote any of the texts of these heretics,
and since none of their works have come down to us, it is very difficult to know just what was the argumentation of the "Spirit-fighters."

The orthodox answer was quick and decisive, and this heterodox opinion promptly withered, but it gave the fathers of the Church the chance to clarify Christian doctrine on this subject. St. Gregory the Theologian had this to say:

> The Old Testament clearly showed the Father, but only dimly showed the Son. The New Testament revealed the Son and hinted at the divinity of the Spirit. Today the Spirit lives among us, and is making himself more clearly known. As long as the divinity of the Father had not been recognized, it was dangerous to preach openly the Son; in the same way, as long as the divinity of the Son was not admitted, it was dangerous to impose, if we dare to use such words, the belief in the divinity of the Spirit as an added burden. You see the order in which God is revealed, an order that we must respect in our own turn: not revealing everything in a rush and without discernment but also not keeping anything hidden until the end of time. The one tendency risked injuring those who were outside and the other one would have separated us from our own brothers.[8]

We can say that from this period on, the dogma of the Trinity had found its definitive expression in Holy Tradition.

Badly counseled by his ministers and no doubt impressed by the diversity of theological currents then dividing the Christian East, the emperor Valens (364-378) thought he was taking the best course by backing the homoean party, which he felt had the best chances of rallying the largest number of adherents. In reality, orthodoxy was slowly but surely consolidating its position. Was the emperor aware of this near the end of his life? Whether he was or not, just before his death he revoked the sentence of exile which he had pronounced against certain orthodox bishops.[9] Thus Meletius was able to return to Antioch, and Peter, the brother and successor of St. Athanasius, to Alexandria.

Since the exile of Paul in 342, the see of Constantinople had been continuously occupied by heretics. When the emperor Gratian confirmed in 378 the decision taken by Valens before his death to allow the return of pro-Nicene bishops to their sees, the little group of orthodox in Constantinople saw their chance to overturn the situation in the capital. They approached Gregory the Theologian; this action was supported by, maybe even suggested by, several orthodox bishops in the East, among whom was St. Basil. Gregory was the son of Gregory the Elder, bishop of Nazianzus. When Basil created some new dioceses to consolidate his influence as metropolitan, which had been weakened by the division of Cappadocia into two provinces,[10] he consecrated Gregory the Theologian to be the bishop of an insignificant little town called Sasima (372), but Gregory ran away and never exercised his office there. He helped his father at Nazianzus and after the death of the Elder, Gregory replaced him for some time in the administration of the diocese. In 375, he left for the monastery of St. Thecla in Seleucia of Isauria to lead a contemplative life. There in 379 he was asked to come and lead the catholic community in Constantinople. Although Gregory had never really exercised his office of bishop at Sasima, this request constituted a formal transgression of the canonical norm recalled by the fathers of Nicea which prohibited the transfer of bishops.[11] In fact this rule had already suffered many infractions in the East, and the interest of the faith could justify such a transgression in this case.[12]

On January 19, 379, the emperor Gratian raised Theodosius to the rank of emperor and gave him charge of the eastern half of the empire. Theodosius was a general from Spain and a convinced partisan of Nicene orthodoxy. He did not wait long to show his colors. On February 28, 380, Theodosius issued an edict saying that anyone who did not follow the faith of Damasus of Rome and Peter of Alexandria[13] was a heretic. Theodosius entered Constantinople on November 24, 380, and two days later, Demophilus, the Arian bishop, was expelled from the capital and the next day Gregory took possession of the Church of the Holy Apostles. Before this event, however, a very strange thing happened: Peter of Alexandria had been for some time very disturbed by the rise of Gregory and his influence over the orthodox community of Constantinople. In effect, as long as the see of the capital had been occupied by heretics, Peter had the first place in the Christian catholic East. The turn-around in Constantinople could possibly put the primordial position of the bishop of Alexandria in question. Thus Peter tried to take control of the church of Constantinople by interposing his own candidate. Some Egyptian bishops accompanied by a squadron of marines were able to enter the Church of the Resurrection, which was the sanctuary of the orthodox in Constantinople—the Arians then still held the large churches, and there they consecrated a certain Maximus. However, Maximus was driven out by the emperor, who considered Gregory as the legitimate pastor.[14]

On January 10, 381, an imperial decree was issued by which the meetings of the Photinians, the Arians and the Eunomians were forbidden; their churches had to be given back to orthodox bishops.[15] This change brought about by the catholic Church in the West as well as in the East required that certain pending problems be solved. It would have been preferable that a general council of the two great parts of Christianity be convoked, but that was difficult to bring about because in the previous fifty years, a climate of mistrust had grown between the orthodox of the East and of the West.[16] As W. de Vries has written, one thing stands out clearly: "...the East had then decided to settle its own affairs by itself and in complete independence, allowing no input from the West at all, be it from the bishop of Rome or any other western bishops."[17] It is quite true that there was absolutely no question of deciding dogmatic questions; the Council of Nicea had done that, and it therefore seemed sufficient in this regard solemnly to confirm attachment to the symbol of faith set out by this council. It was equally necessary to sanction the installation of Gregory in the see of Constantinople as well as the eviction of Maximus.[18] The Antiochian question did not figure in the official agenda since in the East, Egypt excepted, Meletius was seen as the legitimate bishop. However, it would have been difficult to neglect this subject completely since in this case Paulinus, the leader of the minority group, was in communion with Alexandria and Rome.[19]

The council was called together on the initiative of the emperor Theodosius.[20] If they ever existed, the acts of this assembly have not come down to us, nor do we have the *tomos* written by the fathers of the council, a document that would have condemned the christological and trinitarian heresies of the time.[21] We do possess, however, the synodal letter addressed to Theodosius,[22] the list of the members of the council,[23] and the canons which were issued. The other sources of information are found in the ancient church historians,[24] the letter to Pope Damasus written by the fathers of the council of Constantinople in 382,[25] and the autobiographical references in the writings of St. Gregory the Theologian.[26] There is a tradition attested to from the time of the Council of Chalcedon which attributes to the fathers of Constantinople in 381 the creed later accepted by the whole Christian world.[27] Because it incorporates a great number of the elements found in the symbol of faith issued by Nicea, we often call it the Niceno-Constantinopolitan Creed, following the example of J.B. Carpzov.[28] Several hypotheses have been put forward concerning its origin and connection with the second ecumenical council.[29] It is not within the framework of this work to treat this problem, which really concerns the history of dogma. We will, therefore, simply say this: its origin goes back beyond this council. In fact, a practically identical symbol of faith appears in the conclusion of the *Ancoratus*, a dogmatic treatise written by St. Epiphanius in 374. At the same time, we cannot deny all links between our present creed and the Council of Constantinople; in this regard, we have the witness of Theodore of Mopsuestia (428) who was the disciple of Diodorus of Tarsus and an influential member of the council.[30] The most likely hypothesis is that it was the profession of faith pronounced by Nectarius before his baptism and his consecration as bishop. Probably it was on this occasion that the council gave its approval to this creed.

From the moment that this Council of Constantinople was received as ecumenical, the text of its creed was considered untouchable. Such was and is the firm conviction of the Orthodox; it was still the position of Rome in the ninth century.[31] At an uncertain date, probably around the sixth century, in the Latin version used in the Spanish liturgy, improperly called the Mozarabic, the *filioque* was inserted into the Niceno-Constantinopolitan creed. Little by little this addition spread throughout the whole West and was accepted in Rome itself at the beginning of the eleventh century.[32] The Orthodox have always contested the doctrine of the procession of the Holy Spirit *ab utroque* and have denied to any particular local church the right to modify this common symbol of the faith.[33]

The council opened in May, 381, and closed on July 9 of the same year; there were about 150 members,[34] and from the fifth century on this number has often served to designate the council itself. The members came from the civil dioceses of the East, Pontus, Asia and Thrace. Timothy of Alexandria and Dorotheus of Oxyrhincus arrived later because they had not been invited at the same time as the others.[35] At about the same time Ascolius of Thessalonica also arrived even though he was not in the emperor Theodosius' territory, since Gratian, the western emperor, had taken over the provinces of the eastern part of Illyricum in September, 380.[36] Ascolius had baptized the emperor Theodosius and was invited by him because of their personal relationship.[37] Although Ascolius was also the personal confidant of Pope Damasus, it was not as papal legate that he attended the council. Moreover, his name does not appear at all in the list of signatories of the council. The emperor had also invited bishops of a "semi-

Arian" bent in the hope that they could be brought to an orthodox point of view. Efforts were made to convince them, but they did not change their positions. These 36 bishops left the capital even before the opening of the council.[38]

In the thought of the emperor Theodosius who convoked it, as well as in its composition, the Council of Constantinople of 381 was exclusively an inter-diocesan synod of the eastern church. In order to gather together a really ecumenical council, it would have been necessary for both emperors, Gratian and Theodosius, to call it. Moreover, it was only Theodosius that the fathers of the council asked to ratify the decisions they had taken.[39] We must not misinterpret the meaning of this action: in no way did the fathers want to beg the approval of the emperor, but they wanted to have the force of law given to their decisions. Theodosius agreed to their request knowing beforehand what they were going to do. In order to make things very clear, the imperial edict of July 30, 381, listed the bishops in each civil diocese that everyone had to be in communion with if they were to be considered orthodox. Naturally this decree concerned only the eastern half of the empire. These bishops were the following: Nectarius of Constantinople,[40] Timothy of Alexandria for Egypt; Pelagius of Laodocea and Diodorus of Tarsus for the East; Amphilochius of Iconium and Optimus of Antioch-in-Pisidia for Asia; Helladius of Caesarea, Otreius of Melitene, and Gregory of Nyssa for Pontus; Terennius of Scythia and Martyrius of Marcianopolis for Thrace.[41] There was no question of the bishop of Ephesus since he was a semi-Arian, or of the bishop of Antioch since the successor of Meletius had not yet been elected.

The fathers of the council sent the dogmatic decree to the western episcopate as a point of information,[42] but they did not think it was necessary officially to notify western bishops of the disciplinary canons they had issued.[43] Certain bishops of the West, especially Ambrose of Milan, were very displeased by the fact that they had not been associated with the decisions made in Constantinople.[44] In this light some churchmen and scholars have often wondered how the synod of Constantinople of 381 could have been considered by later periods as ecumenical. The fathers of Constantinople in 382 were already calling the previous year's council, 381, ecumenical,[45] but it is nonetheless certain that they did not give to this adjective the technical and precise meaning that it acquired later on. We have a proof of this in the canon that the fathers issued where the term "ecumenical council" denotes an episcopal assembly that is composed of bishops from more

than one civil diocese.[46] The notion that ecumenical councils constituted a unique category of synod having well defined characteristics
did not yet exist in the fourth century.[47]

The validation of the council of 381 was made seventy years later
by the fathers of Chalcedon. In effect, they put the creeds of Nicea
and Constantinople, 381, on the same level.[48] In addition, the ruling
on the privileges of the see of New Rome adopted by a small number
of fathers, October 29, 451, is presented as an explication of canon 3
of the council of 381.[49]

The initiative for citing the creed of Constantinople at Chalcedon
was taken by the imperial commissioners, no doubt with a hidden
motive. The emperor Marcian was persuaded that, in order to put an
end to the christological debates, it was necessary for the Council of
Chalcedon to issue a dogmatic decree on the spot, but the majority of
the members of this assembly wanted to stand by the symbol of faith
of Nicea. Besides, at Ephesus in 431, had not the fathers decided that
it was forbidden to compose any other profession of faith then that of
Nicea?[50] In calling attention to the creed of Constantinople, the imperial representatives wanted to show that in the face of new doctrinal
deviations, nothing excluded the necessity of issuing an appropriate
definition, as the 150 fathers in 381 did, to refute the pneumatomachian heresy. As to the second point, the confirmation and clarification
of the privileges of the see of Constantinople, the emperor Marcian was
able to count on the total support of Archbishop Anatolius and of the
clergy of the capital. But it was necessary to show that this was not an
innovation. Thus such a declaration would only be a re-affirmation and
clarification of the decision adopted by the council of 381. This would
imply that Constantinople, 381, was really ecumenical.

The West was not at all ready so easily to accept such a position
even though no one contested the perfect orthodoxy of the creed of
Constantinople. In the decree of Pope Gelasius (492-496) entitled *De
recipiendis et non recipiendis libris*,[51] the Council of Constantinople is
not mentioned. However, it is admitted by Pope Hormisdas (514-
523).[52] St. Gregory the Great (590-604) made clear that this recognition only applied to the definition against Macedonius.[53] Nonetheless,
the canons of the Council of Constantinople have for a long time been
a part of the Latin canonical collections.[54]

The council was first presided over by Meletius of Antioch, who
was the most outstanding person at the council. The fathers quickly
moved to the solemn sanctioning of the promotion of St. Gregory the

Theologian to the see of the capital, after declaring invalid the consecration of Maximus the Cynic. Before the end of May, Meletius died unexpectedly; his death brought again to the fore the thorny question about Antioch. Had there been an agreement between Meletius and Paulinus to the effect that the first one to die would not have a successor? This is what Socrates affirms, but according to Theodoret this proposal of Meletius was not agreed to by Paulinus.[55] Which one should we believe? We are inclined to believe Theodoret. The backers of Paulinus showed a very strong sectarian spirit; and, in addition, if the claim of Socrates were exact, how could we explain the fact that the bishops of the diocese of the East present in the council were so unanimously opposed to the recognition of Paulinus? This is even more of a problem, seeing that Gregory the Theologian suggested the solution. He greatly resented the rejection of his proposal and let the fathers of the council know so in no uncertain terms.[56] Once the bishops of the East had returned from Constantinople, they chose the priest Flavian as bishop of Antioch. After the death of Meletius, Gregory assumed the chair of the council. Since his accession to the see of Constantinople had been ratified, this position naturally fell to him as the bishop of the place where the council was sitting.

After the arrival in the capital of Ascolius of Thessalonica, Timothy of Alexandria, and Dorotheus of Oxyrhincus, things began to go sour for Gregory. Ascolius had received instructions from Pope Damasus not to recognize any bishop transferred from one church to another; these instructions, without expressly mentioning it, obviously had Gregory in mind.[57] On the same pretext, Timothy, who could not forget the affront caused by the eviction of Maximus, claimed that Gregory was not the legitimate bishop of Constantinople.[58] Faced with this double objection, Gregory—who after all did not have the aptitude or taste for practical activities —sought to avoid a fight. He resigned and after giving a beautiful and moving farewell homily,[59] he retired to Nazianzus where he was born.

The rejection of Maximus and then the resignation of Gregory led everyone to look for a candidate acceptable to all. It was under these conditions that the senator Nectarius was chosen; he had been recommended by Diodorus of Tarsus. The council presented his candidacy along with others to the emperor Theodosius, who chose Nectarius. The fathers then realized that he was not even baptized. Cyriacus, bishop of Adana, took it upon himself to teach the new bishop-elect his duties as a pastor; he was baptized and then consecrated bishop of Constantinople.[60] It is strange to note that the fathers cited a canon of Nicea to contest the promotion of St. Gregory the Theologian on the grounds that he was being transferred from one see to another, while another canon forbade the ordination of a neophyte; however, there was no opposition, and the matter went forward. Nectarius then presided over the council until it closed July 9, 381.

Before leaving, the fathers issued a canonical document which starts by a confirmation of the faith of Nicea accompanied by a condemnation of the trinitarian and christological heresies of the time. Then came the rulings for maintenance of good order among the churches, with an appendix stating the prerogatives of the bishop of Constantinople. This document ends with an affirmation of the nullity of the election of Maximus the Cynic as well as the ordinations which he carried out.

From the redactional point of view, this text presents the syntactic peculiarity of being one whole sentence: there is one main clause which introduces a series of subordinate clauses. Although in their *Address* to the emperor Theodosius the fathers speak in the plural about "rulings" (κανόνας) that they issued,[61] the division of the text into separated and numbered canons is not very old. The document was added as a whole to the canonical collection of Constantinople and Antioch at the end of the canons of Laodicea.[62] This is why at the Council of Chalcedon at the time of the discussion about the rights of the see of Constantinople, a secretary read this text from its beginning up to the passage concerning the question,[63] while at this same council other synodical canons were mentioned with the numbers they had in the document being read.[64] The division into separate canons of the document issued by Constantinople, 381, is therefore from a later time. This also explains the variants that we find in ancient Latin versions.[65] Finally, at the beginning of the sixth century, a division into four canons spread throughout the East. Since then, this division has remained stable in the collections which give the canons according to their origin as well as in systematic collections.

In 382 a council was held in Constantinople which included most of the bishops who had been present at the previous year's council. The question on the agenda was as follows: the westerners hardly appreciated the fact that they had been kept out of decisions about church affairs in the East, and they insisted that a real ecumenical council be held. The fathers of Constantinople politely but firmly maintained their point of view that they had the authority to regulate their own affairs, but to show their good will, they sent three delegates to the Council of Rome.[66] They also adopted two decrees. The first directly concerned the question of Antioch and declared that they accepted all those in Antioch who confessed the unique divinity of the Father, the Son and the Holy Spirit. The second, which was also probably related to the situation in Antioch, dealt very precisely with the right to bring complaints and charges within the Church. These two decrees were later joined to these of the council of 381 in eastern collections.[67] Thus in the *Synagoge* of John the Scholastic, we find six canons placed under the authority of the second ecumenical council.[68] However, the two canons of the council of 382 have never been accepted in the Latin collections.[69]

In the *Syntagma in XIV Titles,* there is a canon 7 attributed to the second ecumenical council; it deals with various methods of receiving heretics into the Church. It was long believed that it came initially from a letter written in Constantinople around 460 to Martyrius of Antioch. In fact this document is older. It is an excerpt from a letter sent from Ephesus to Nestorius of Constantinople in 428. After the condemnation of Nestorius by the third ecumenical council, it is thought that the dishonorable name of Nestorius was erased.[70] Why was this text from the *kanonikon* of the church of Ephesus placed along with the canons issued in 381-82? Perhaps because it seemed to constitute a complementary statement to canon 1 of Constantinople.

SECTION 2: THE CANONS OF THE COUNCIL

The Canons of the 150 Holy Fathers gathered together in Constantinople during the consulship of the most illustrious Flavius Eucherius and Flavius Evagrius, the 7th of the Ides of July.[71]

Here is what we have decided, we the bishops of different provinces gathered together in Constantinople by the grace of God and on the invitation of the pious emperor Theodosius.

1

Let no one undermine the faith of the 318 fathers gathered at

Nicea in Bithynia, but let it remain firm and untouched, and let every heresy be anathamatized; in particular, that of the Eunomians or Anomeans, that of the Arians or Eudoxians, that of the Semi-Arians or Pneumatomachoi, that of the Sabellians, that of the Marcellians, that of the Photinians, and that of the Apollinarians.

In the standard text as is found in the *Pedalion,* in the collection of Rhalles and Potles and in the Russo-Slavonic *Kniga Pravil,* the preamble is integrated into the first canon; in addition, it is abridged, and the first person plural is replaced by the third person, which gives the following text: "The holy fathers gathered together in Constantinople have decided."[72] The Latin version called Prisca is even briefer: "sancta synodus dixit."[73] In Dionysius, the preamble is purely and simply omitted.[74] We should not be surprised at its absence in the *Synagoge* since this work is a systematic collection in which the canons are divided according to subject matter. In contrast, however, in the *Syntagma in XIV Titles*, the preamble is found in a form very close to that read during the seventeenth session of the Council of Chalcedon.[75]

The text of this first canon contains some differences depending on the recension consulted; the differences concern the list of heretical groups. The best reading is certainly that given by V.N. Beneševič in his edition of the *Syntagma in XIV Titles*.[76] It agrees substantially with the Dionysian translation.[77] This edition is found in the *Kniga Pravil*, with just a tiny difference: the Eunomians are considered to be a distinct group from the Anomeans.[78] In the *Synagoge,* as in the *synodikon* read at the Council of Chalcedon, moreover, the Marcionites are mentioned.[79] It is very probable that this is a very ancient interpolation. It seems difficult to believe that this mention of the Marcionites was in the original text; it is, in fact, completely out of place in the middle of a list in which the other heresies mentioned have to do with trinitarian and christological matters. The canon starts with a solemn affirmation about the untouchable nature of "the faith" of Nicea. By this term "faith," we must understand both the doctrine of the council as well as the creed itself.[80]

Most properly, the fathers of Constantinople systematically condemned the subordinationist and modalistic deviations. Anomoeism was a development of the doctrine of Arius. The name comes from the followers of this heresy who said that the Son was different in everything from the Father (κατὰ πάντα ἀνόμοιος τοῦ πατρός). The leaders of this tendency were the sophist Aetius and his disciple, bishop Eunomius of

Cyzicus. They proclaimed that God was a unique and simple essence characterized by ἀγεννησία; thus the Son, being begotten, cannot be of the same essence as the Father or even of a similar essence. The Eunomians, who made great use of Aristotelian dialectic, affirmed that since God was an absolutely simple being, he was perfectly comprehensible. The Cappadocian fathers vigorously refuted their opinions.[81] We find an echo of the orthodox reaction against this heresy in the anaphoras of St. Basil and St. John Chrysostom in which they affirm that God is "incomprehensible" (ἀκατάληπτος).

The canon then goes on to condemn "the Arians or Eudoxians"; the equating of these two requires an explanation. Eudoxius had successively been bishop of Germanicius and Antioch. At that time, he professed Anomoeism, but after the Council of Seleucia in 359, he rallied to homoeism, which was favored by Constantius and was considered to be the official doctrine of the *"Reichskirche."* In fact, the theological evolution of Eudoxius, brought about by purely opportunistic motives, was more apparent than real, because homoeism was marked by its deliberately concocted imprecision: if the Son was held to be similar (ὅμοιος) to the Father, it was only a moral similarity. The homoeans, in fact, rejected not only the orthodox teaching on consubstantiality but even the very idea of a similarity of essence (homoioussianism). This is why the catholics properly saw in the homoeans nothing but Arians and called them that.[82] This was the heretical form of Christianity which was to become the national religion of most of the Germanic peoples, in whom it was to persist for a long time.[83]

Then comes the condemnation of the semi-Arians or the pneumatomachoi. Those who categorically rejected the teaching of Arius yet who had a strong feeling against the word ὁμοούσιος and who were suspicious of certain of this word's defenders were often called semi-Arians. Open opponents of the divinity of the Holy Spirit were often found among this group. The fathers of Constantinople, however, used the term "semi-Arian" in a restricted sense as a synonym for "pneumatomachoi." We note that in the translation of Dionysius Exiguus the word "semi-Arians" was replaced by "Macedonians."[84]

With the Sabellians, we are confronted with a completely different type of heresy. Sabellius, probably from Libya, came to Rome near the end of the time of Pope Zephyrinus (199–218); he taught a modalistic doctrine, that is, he denied the real distinction between the divine persons. The Sabellians never formed an organized sect, but rather they represented a diffused current of thought whose advocates had nothing else in common with Sabellius except their modalistic doctrines. This is what St. Basil states in his writings to the citizens of Neocaesarea about those who were spreading such opinions: "The evil of Sabellius, which was spread about in former times and which had been extinguished by the fathers, they are trying to reestablish."[85]

In reality, at this time, modalism was especially promoted by the Marcellians and the Photinians, mentioned after the Sabellians in the text of the canon. The bishop of Ancyra, Marcellus (+c. 374) was an enthusiastic defender of the Nicene definition, but he gave it an erroneous interpretation, and this fact provoked misunderstandings which were adroitly exploited by the Arians. For Marcellus, God is a unique person whose pre-existing Word has no distinct existence. The exteriorization of the Word is purely functional, an "active energy" of God in creation and in redemption; this energy will cease to exist at the end of time.[86] Perhaps because of the still rather rudimentary state of Latin theology at that time, the westerners were not able to see the heresy of Marcellus and, despite the rebukes of St. Basil, they refused to condemn the bishop of Ancyra.[87] Photinus was the disciple of Marcellus, but, in addition, he combined trinitarian modalism with a christology that reproduced the adoptionist theories of Paul of Samosata, bishop of Antioch, who had been condemned in the third century.[88] More clear-sighted than in the case of Marcellus, some western bishops gathered together in council in Milan condemned Photinus in 345, and they renewed their verdict two years later. They sent their decision to the eastern bishops assembled in Sirmium, who did not miss the chance to remind the westerners of the links between the heresy of Photinus and that of Marcellus.[89]

The last heterodox group mentioned is the Apollinarians. They take their name from Apollinaris;[90] this heretic was from Laodicea, today Lattaqia in Syria. He was a zealous defender of the Nicene creed and in 360 was chosen bishop of his native city by its orthodox believers. It did not take long to see that his christological doctrine was tainted with serious errors: conceiving the unity of Christ in the Word-flesh framework, he drew some rather extreme conclusions. He refused to recognize a non-divine principle of animation for the person of Christ, for according to him, to admit that Christ had a reason-able soul (νοῦς) would compromise his personal unity; Christ, in this case, could not have been exempt from the inherent sinfulness of free will. Consequently, according to Apollinaris, the Word was directly united to a fleshly body without a soul.

The orthodox first showed their suspicion about the opinions of Apollinaris in 362 at the Council of Alexandria. However, a forceful reaction only developed a bit later. In 377, Apollinaris was condemned in Rome, the following year in Alexandria, then in 379 in Antioch and finally in Constantinople in 381. He had enthusiastic disciples who formed a sect which was to disappear only between 420-430. But before their demise, they were cleverly able to falsify the writings of the great Athanasius. Thus, in all good faith, St. Cyril of Alexandria used the celebrated formula "one incarnate nature of the Word of God" (μία φύσις τοῦ Θεοῦ Λόγου σεσαρκωμένη) thinking it was authentically from St. Athanasius.[91] Obviously, Cyril did not give it the same meaning as Apollinaris, because by "flesh" he understood human nature in its integrity, including a rational soul.[92]

2

Let the bishops refrain from interfering in churches outside the limits of a diocese and from causing trouble in the churches; but, in conformity to the canons, let the bishop of Alexandria take care of just the affairs of Egypt; let the bishops of the East only govern the East, the prerogatives recognized by the canons of Nicea for the church of the Antiochians being preserved; let the bishops of the diocese of Asia take care of just the affairs of Asia; the bishops of Pontus, only the affairs of Pontus; the bishops of Thrace, only the affairs of Thrace. If they are not invited, let the bishops refrain from going outside a diocese for an ordination or for any other ecclesiastical act. The above-mentioned rule about the dioceses being observed, it is obvious that the council of the province will direct the affairs of each province according to what was decided at Nicea. Concerning the Church of God among the barbarian nations, it is important that they be administered by the custom established in the time of the fathers.

The text of the canon, in the manuscript tradition, has no variants which seriously alter its meaning. We note that in the beginning of the canon the verb ἐπιβαίνειν was replaced by ἐπιέναι in later redactions; this change gives an archaic flavor to the text but does not change the meaning at all.[93] Also at the end of the text, ἐπὶ τῶν πατέρων was replaced by παρὰ τῶν πατέρων meaning "by the fathers." One manuscript reading which has passed into the standard text simply omits the preposition in this place so that "fathers" becomes a determinative complement of "custom."[94]

In this canon, the "dioceses" ($\delta\iota\omega\iota\kappa\dot{\eta}\sigma\varepsilon\iota\varsigma$) are mentioned; this was a novelty in church law for, up to that time, dioceses had not even been referred to, not at Nicea or Antioch or even at Sardica. This innovation marked the growing tendency to model the jurisdictions of the Church on the civil boundaries of the Roman state. Ever since the administrative reforms of the emperor Diocletian, the dioceses had formed territorial entities made up of several provinces. It did not take long for some of these groupings to be considered too large and to be broken up. Thus, under Constantine, Moesia was divided into two dioceses: Dacia and Macedonia; about 380, Egypt was separated from the East.[95] We have already said that the council of 381 was made up of bishops from only the eastern part of the empire; that is why in this canon, the western dioceses were not mentioned.

We cannot say that this canon brought about changes in the government of the Church, since it did not introduce or sanction a uniform hierarchical structure for the dioceses; on the contrary, it respected the *status quo*. We notice that for Egypt only the bishop of Alexandria is mentioned; this fact takes into account the hegemony that he exercised over all the bishops in his jurisdictional area. For the East, the canon speaks of bishops in the plural with reference, however, to the prerogatives recognized by canon 6 of Nicea concerning the bishop of Antioch. It is doubtful that at this time the bishop of Antioch had effective control of the elections of all the metropolitans of this territory, even more so since the internal divisions of the church of Antioch hardly favored such an extension of power. As for Asia, Pontus and Thrace, there is no reference to the bishops of their chief cities. If the see of Ephesus in Asia could pride itself on its apostolic origins and its importance as a city, its bishops played no determining role in the life of the Church. The story was to be different in the following century, though, when Constantinople ran up against heavy resistance.[96] During the first half of the fourth century, the see of Caesarea in Cappadocia was so much in the background that, as V. Phidas notes, we do not even know who were the bishops of this church.[97] St. Basil gave to this see a great reputation, but after his death in 379, Caesarea lost much of its importance. As for the see of Heraclea in Thrace, its star faded even before it had consolidated its position; it was too close to Constantinople.

Dionysius Exiguus translated the beginning of the canon, $\tau o\dot{\nu}\varsigma\ \dot{\nu}\pi\grave{\varepsilon}\rho$

διοίκησιν ἐπισκόπους, in the following way: *Qui sunt super dioecesin episcopi*,[98] and this shows that he understood this expression to mean "the bishops who head a diocese."[99] This interpretation is erroneous, because the preposition ὑπὲρ followed by the accusative means "beyond" and not "at the head of, on top of"; this is the correct meaning when it is followed by the genitive. Moreover, in the text of the canon, we again meet the expression ὑπὲρ διοίκησιν, but no double meaning is possible due to the context. It is ironic to note that the Prisca, which Dionysius openly disdained,[100] gives a better translation here than does Dionysius himself.[101]

If the fathers of the Council of Constantinople in 381 did not try to establish a pyramidal, hierarchical structure of the dioceses, neither did they conceive of them as simple geographical groupings; they saw in them coherent entities in which the bishops ought to assume common responsibilities. In this regard, it is proper to draw a parallel with the stipulations of canon 6. Although this canon was in reality issued by the council of 382, the parallel is not arbitrary since the participants in these two synods were, for the most part, the same bishops. We will see when we analyze canon 6 that the diocese was envisioned as forming a higher jurisdiction of ecclesiastical justice.

As church institutions developed, the stage of diocesan organization did not last long, due to various factors. The case of Egypt is an exception only in appearance, because the extent of jurisdictional authority of the bishop of Alexandria had always been independent of the civil boundaries, and the Council of Nicea had confirmed this situation based on "ancient customs."[102] In contrast, the bishops of Antioch never succeeded in extending their effective control over the whole diocese of the East. In this regard, Louis Bréhier very correctly wrote the following:

> The patriarchate of Antioch compared to that of Alexandria offered the same contrast in antiquity that the Seleucid state offered to the Lagidic state. On the one side, a compact and clearly marked territory, an ethnic unity, a thousand-year-old administrative organization, and a people accustomed to obedience; on the other side, an immense territorial spread without precise boundaries on the north and east, a mosaic of races, languages, diverse customs...[103]

Thus despite the attempted interventions of the bishops of Antioch, Cyprus succeeded in maintaining its autocephaly, a status which was confirmed at the Council of Ephesus in 431.[104] In addition, the see of

Jerusalem, whose honorific status had been recognized by canon 7 of the Council of Nicea, not only freed itself, little by little, from the metropolitan jurisdiction of Caesarea, but even before 431 it had assured itself a metropolitan jurisdiction over Palestine and tried even to extend it farther.[105] As for the dioceses of Asia, Pontus and Thrace, they gradually entered into Constantinople's sphere of influence. Socrates thought that the fathers of the council of 381 had established the division into patriarchates,[106] but in that he fell into an anachronism.

All historians are agreed that this ruling of the council of 381 mainly aims at the see of Alexandria; this see was supporting a minority group in Antioch and had gotten scandalously mixed up in the internal affairs of the diocese of Thrace with the ordination of Maximus. On this matter, we wonder how Timothy of Alexandria was able to endure the affront that the adoption of canons, 2, 3 and 4 represented for this church. Thus, some have suggested that they were issued either before the arrival of Timothy at the council or after his departure.[107] These are only unverifiable hypotheses. In any case, these decisions having been made with the full agreement of the emperor Theodosius, it would have been very difficult for the bishop of Alexandria to oppose them openly. But history clearly shows that following the council the successors of Timothy, Theophilus, Cyril and Dioscorus, acted as if these canons were null and void. We must not however, reduce the scope and the importance of canon 2 to a circumstantial measure directed against the pretentions of the bishops of Alexandria to authority outside their areas. The fathers of Constantinople, having observed many anomalies and especially the inopportune and anti-canonical interventions which had taken place all during the Arian crisis, tried to set out very clearly the principle of non-interference. Thereby they also implicitly denied, to the West in general and to Rome in particular, the right to get mixed up in the affairs of the eastern church.[108]

After having set out the ruling which forbade the bishops of one diocese to intervene in the church life of another, the fathers of Constantinople took very special care to recall the validity of the decisions of Nicea on the competence of the provincial council. On this matter, Balsamon notes most properly that at this time each metropolitan district enjoyed autocephaly.[109] It is not by accident that the status of the churches "among the barbarian nations" was mentioned immediately after the reminder of the competence of the provincial council. The problem concerning these churches was related to the modalities of the synodal system in territories where there were few bishops. According to the interpretation, certainly correct, that Zonaras and Balsamon give, this reference to established custom means that the bishops of these countries could join bishops in council for church administration without strictly applying the rule that separates the competence of different regions.[110] But obviously, such a thing was not to happen arbitrarily; it was necessary that custom be respected, especially in reference to this or that church and this or that major city. Canon 28 of Chalcedon was to introduce a partial modification to this rule.

3

As for the bishop of Constantinople, let him have the prerogatives of honor after the bishop of Rome, seeing that this city is the new Rome.

This canon is closely connected with the preceding one; in very early texts, they were not even separated. This close relation is marked by the adverb μεντοί which indicates here not an opposition but a correlation with an emphatic insistence on what follows the statement. The author of the Prisca translated it by *autem*[111] and Dionysius by *verumtamen*.[112] The Isidorian version omits the linking particle,[113] as do subsequent translations, including the *Kniga Pravil*.[114]

The text of the canon has been very stable in the manuscript tradition. There is one reading that omits the word ἐπίσκοπον after Κωνσταντινουπόλεως,[115] but this no doubt is due to the distraction of the copyist. It does not change the meaning at all, for such abbreviations are quite common in Greek even now.[116]

This canon sanctions in law an established situation which had been developing for some time. The center of gravity of the empire had been moving east ever since the third century. Constantine decided to concretize this evolution by the choice of a new capital. Very quickly after his victory over Licinius at Chrysopolis (September 18, 324), he chose the site of Byzantium, ancient colony of Megara on the European coast of the Bosphorus.[117] The construction work began immediately in the fall of 324; the dedication was solemnly celebrated on May 11, 330. Construction was finally finished around 335-36.[118] Constantine's judicious choice of a site has been underlined many times, judicious from every point of view: strategic, economic and cultural.[119] As a new city, Constantinople was not attached in any juridical way to the earlier city of Byzantium. G. Dagron has observed on this point that "there is an historical discontinuity."[120] Moreover, as the imperial capital, it was from its foundation exempt from all dependence on Heraclea; Constantinople was therefore not considered to be administratively tied to the province of Europe.[121] We have every reason to believe that this exceptional situation had its repercussions on church organization.

We have no sure historical data on the origins of Christianity in Byzantium. The fact that the heretic Theodotus the Tanner came from this city to Rome around 150 allows us to suppose that a Christian community existed in Byzantium around the second half of the second century. However, the claims that the church there was founded by the apostle Andrew and that his disciple Stachys was bishop after him is a late legend.[122] The traditional list of bishops of Byzantium for the period before the episcopate of Metrophanes (306-14) no longer has any credibility.[123] It was during the time of Bishop Alexander (314-37) that the great change took place that gave birth to Constantinople. From then on, Alexander was called "bishop of New Rome."[124]

Seeing that the city of Constantinople was not part of the civil province of Europe, canon 4 of Nicea relating to the election of bishops in the provincial framework was not applicable. In addition, as bishops continually came to the capital for various reasons, the custom was established that these bishops should take part in the election and consecration of the bishop of Constantinople. This is what happened for Paul, the successor of Alexander.[125] The secular power could not let such an event take place unnoticed; the government had a vital interest in the choice, and it did not take long for this interest to show itself. In 338 or 339, in conformity with the emperor Constantius' wishes, the orthodox Paul was deposed and replaced by the schemer Eusebius;[126] as H. Lietzmann notes, this nomination marked the great importance for Christianity of the see of Constantinople, the rival of Alexandria.[127] The transfer of Eusebius from Nicomedia to Constantinople was to show, if that were needed, that the see of the imperial capital did not depend on Heraclea. The ambitious prelate would certainly not have abandoned his metropolitan church to become the suffragan bishop of Heraclea.[128] The only trace of the ancient subordination of the bishops of Byzantium to Heraclea was the privilege which allowed them to consecrate the patriarchs of Constantinople; this privilege continued up to the end of the Middle Ages.[129]

The fathers of the council of 381 did nothing more than sanction the weighty position of Constantinople in the East and recognize its role among the major sees of the universal church. This is what the expression τὰ πρεσβεῖα τῆς τιμῆς means. In the order of ecclesiastical precedence, the bishop of Constantinople came "after" (μετὰ) the Roman bishop. In the Middle Ages, certain writers tried to interpret this preposition in a chronological sense, that is as saying that the primacy of Constantinople was later in time.[130] This interpretation was taken up by Aristenus;[131] Zonaras rejected it, and he underlined that the preposition indicates the inferiority in rank.[132] To support his refutation, Zonaras referred to Novella 131 of Justinian and to canon 36 of the Synod in Trullo.[133] The decision of the fathers of the council of 381 was a transposition onto the ecclesiastical plane of the political position of Constantinople; the new imperial city was considered a "Second Rome" from the time of its foundation and was officially called that.[134] On the politico-administrative level, Constantinople was outside the system of dioceses and provinces; it was the same situation for the Church's organization. If Constantinople saw itself confirmed in its position among the major sees of the Church, its bishop had no "ancient customs," and for good reasons, in contrast with the bishops of Rome, Alexandria and Antioch, which would allow him to exercise a metropolitan jurisdiction over a vast territory. Such a centralizing tendency was, however, bound to develop rapidly; this process was all the more encouraged by the lack of centralism in Thrace, Pontus and to a certain extent even in Asia. It was in the time of St. John Chrysostom (398-404) that the church of Constantinople really began to intervene in these three dioceses, for up to then Nectarius had been very prudent. Only two interventions were made and these on the request of the parties involved.[135]

Did canon 3 of the Council of Constantinople elicit any hostile reactions in the West when it was promulgated? An affirmative answer is given by those who attribute the passage in the *Decretum Gelasianum* about the patriarchal sees to the Council of Rome in 382.[136] But this hypothesis does not seem very likely to us, although it has been accepted by numerous scholars.[137] There was certainly no explicit reception of the canon, but rather a tacit one; this is what certain indications allow us to think: St. Ambrose addressed Nectarius as the first hierarch in the East.[138] Pope Leo listened without protest to the reading of this canon by Eusebius of Doryleum.[139] At the beginning of the Council of Chalcedon, the Roman legates not only did not question the ranking of Anatolius among the bishops of the major sees but agreed with the indignation of most of the fathers toward Dioscorus, who had given only the fifth place to Flavian at the "robber council" of Ephesus. Paschasinus of Lilybaeum, the head of the papal delegation, made a specific and unambiguous statement on this subject which then provoked Diogenes of Cyzicus to remark that the representative of Rome knew the canons, thus making reference to the decision of the council of 381.[140] Opposition to canon 3 flared up when a group of fathers at Chalcedon put forth a motion, later on called canon 28 of that council, which claimed to be based on the decision of the council of 381.[141] Such an interpretation effectively corresponds to the custom which had grown up during several preceding decades; but we cannot thereby attribute this extensive interpretation to the fathers of the council of 381.[142]

Let us note how the ancient Latin versions have rendered the Greek expression τὰ πρεσβεῖα τῆς τιμῆς. In the Prisca we find *primatum honoris* and in the Isidoriana *primatus honorem*.[143] The first Dionysian recension says *honorem primatum*. This is probably a copyist's error, as Turner suggests. The second recension says *honoris primatum,* which gives a proper meaning.[143a] These translations all have a metonymous character, for the "prerogatives" (πρεσβεῖα) are in fact the consequences of the "primacy" (πρωτεῖον).

4

Concerning Maximus the Cynic and the disorder that he caused in Constantinople, we have decided that Maximus has never been and is not now a bishop, nor are those that he ordained, no matter what order of the clergy they were ordained to; everything that was done in his name or done by him is declared null and void.

The last of the decisions adopted by the council of 381 deals with the adventure of Maximus the Cynic in Constantinople. We have already noted how Peter II of Alexandria had used Maximus to try to take control of the church of Constantinople. This attempt miserably failed. St. Gregory the Theologian has vividly recounted this very strange story, which was extremely unpleasant for him personally.[144] It is quite possible that this scandalous intrusion of Alexandria into the affairs of another church was one of the causes that pushed the members of the council to issue the canon about the bishop of New Rome.[145]

Nullity was pronounced on the ordination of Maximus and, therefore, on all ordinations performed by him; this decision was quite within the spirit of ecclesiastical tradition. In the same way, canon 6 of Nicea considered as null any promotion of a bishop without the approval of the metropolitan. The fathers of Constantinople used a formula similar to that of the fathers of Nicea: "He is not a bishop." It was no accidental matter that two similar terms were used.[146] The Greek term ἀκυρωθέντων was correctly translated in Latin, at least in the ancient versions, by *irritum* or by *infirmata*.[147]

Although this decision is related to a particular case, it must be considered important in canon law because it establishes a precedent by expressing a fundamental norm: the Orthodox Church does not recognize ordinations carried out in an irregular manner, even if the consecrators are "canonical" bishops such as were the Egyptian bishops sent by Peter of Alexandria to consecrate Maximus.

Maximus never accepted his eviction and continued his intrigues in the West. The bishops gathered in Aquilea in September, 381, under the authority of Ambrose of Milan, believed what Maximus told them and thus considered him to be the legitimate bishop of Constantinople.[148] But the council which was held in Rome, 382, did not go along with this decision; morever, Pope Damasus never did want to recognize Maximus.[149] Thus it seems that the question of the see of Constantinople was not even brought up at this council. In addition, the eastern bishops had made known the irrevocable nature of their decision on this matter.[150] Nectarius was recognized by Pope Damasus,[151] and from then on Maximus completely disappears from history.

Finally, we note that the slight variations in the text of this canon in the manuscript tradition only concern unimportant details and in no way affect its meaning.[152]

5

Concerning the tome of the westerners, we have also received those who in Antioch confess one single divinity of the Father, Son and Holy Spirit.

This declaration coming from the council which was held in Constantinople in 382 is very difficult to interpret. The difficulty does not come from a textual problem; the manuscript tradition does not present any significant variants.[153] On the one hand, we cannot say with any certainty just what was the document identified as the "the tome of the westerners." On the other hand, due to the concise and allusive formulation of this canon, it is difficult to determine what the mentioned reception is aimed at when read in the context of the schism in Antioch.

The tome in question was a dogmatic treatise of some kind. We find the term "tome" often used with this meaning in the fourth and fifth centuries; thus, for example, "the tome to the Antiochians" of the Council of Alexandria in 362, the "tome of the Council of Constantinople" in 381, the "tome to the Armenians" of Proclus in 435, and the most famous of all, the "tome to Flavian" of Pope Leo in 449. Is the document alluded to in this canon the same one mentioned in the synodical letter? This is possible, although according to this letter, it was issued in Antioch.[154] In this case, that would mean that a treatise composed in the West and sent to the easterners was approved by the Council of Antioch in 379. One thing is certain; this tome of the westerners had nothing to do with the Council of Sardica in 343, as Zonaras and Balsamon both thought.[155] It dates from the time of Pope Damasus (366-384) and is related to the misunderstandings generated by differences in trinitarian terminology between easterners and westerners of the time.[156] We also know that the bishops of Italy had written to the easterners about the schism in Antioch.[157] The Council of Antioch in 375 had accepted a series of Roman documents as a sign of good will toward the West; this is formally attested to.[158] According to G. Bardy, this interpretation concerns three texts.[159] The first (*Ea gratia*) seems to have been edited in 374;[160] it was an answer to Letter 243 of St. Basil that the priest Dorotheus had carried to Rome.[161] The second (*Illud sane miratur*) deals entirely with the refutation of Apollinarianism;[162] it was certainly edited at the closing of the council held in Rome in 377. The third text (*Non nobis quidquam*) contains a condemnation of the Pneumatomachoi and the Apollinarians; it is presented as a simple commentary on the creed of Nicea.[163]

The fathers of the Council of Constantinople of 382, by accepting the tome already approved in Antioch, wanted to show their identity of faith with the West, but we must not see in canon 5 any opening toward Paulinus and his group, contrary to what some scholars think.[164] For the fathers of the council of 381, the regularity of Flavian's position was beyond question, as is eminently clear from their synodical letter.[165] For them, the intervention of the westerners in this affair was totally out of place. It was not, however, until 398 that Rome decided to recognize Flavian.[166] Balsamon describes this canon as "particular" (*ἰδικὸς*).[167] Actually, it has only an historical interest, and its interpretation remains in part conjectural.[168]

In the *kanonikon* of Bishop Palladius of Amasea, 21 supplementary canons are attributed to the fathers of Constantinople.[169] All these canons, except two, coincide with canons 56-74 of St. Basil. One of these two, 18, appears to be nothing other than a particular manner of interpreting our canon 5. This is how it is set out: "We must call Pneumatomachoi all those who do not accept in theology the consubstantial Trinity according to the tome set out in Antioch."[170] In the *Synagoge,* immediately after the text of canon 5, we find the following addition: "Here are the bishops gathered together: Nectarius, bishop of Constantinople, Timothy of Alexandria, and the 150 other bishops."[171] Without doubt, this phrase was found in the source used by John the Scholastic.

6

Because many people are seeking to sow trouble and confusion in church ranks, being motivated by a hateful and slanderous spirit, they invent accusations against the orthodox bishops who administer the churches; their only intention is to impugn the reputations of the priests and to provoke troubles among peoples living in peace. It has, therefore, seemed right and proper to the holy council of bishops assembled in Constantinople that accusers no longer be accepted without previous inquiry; neither should just anybody be allowed to present himself as an accuser of those who administer the churches. This ruling does not, however, exclude everyone from making accusations. But if someone issues a personal complaint against a bishop, that is, of a private nature, whether the person suffered injury from the bishop or suffered from an illegal action of the bishop, the religion of the complaining person should not be taken into account in matters of this kind. It is absolutely necessary that the conscience of the bishop be clear, and whoever claims to have been injured, regardless of his religion, must be able to obtain justice. But, if the complaint against the bishop is about a churchly matter, then the religion of the accusers must be examined, first of all since heretics are not permitted to accuse orthodox bishops in matters that concern the Church. (We mean by heretics those who have already been excluded from the Church for a long time, those who even after such exclusion have been anathematized by us, and those who pretend to profess the true faith but who have separated themselves from the bishops in communion with us and who hold separate assemblies.) In addition, if certain people have been condemned and excluded from the Church or excommunicated, whether they be clerics or laymen, they will not be allowed to accuse a bishop before they been cleared of the things they have been reproached for. In the same way, those who have been accused cannot turn around and accuse a bishop or other clerics before having shown their innocence as to their alleged misconduct. On the other hand, if some persons who are neither heretics nor excommunicated, who have not received any condemnation and have not been accused in any way, if any of these persons claim to have a complaint against the bishop in a churchly matter, the holy council requires them first to submit their complaint to all the bishops of the province and in their presence to prove their accusations. If, however, the other bishops of the province cannot redress the wrongs imputed to the bishop, let them then appeal to the greater council of bishops of the diocese, convoked just for this reason. These bishops should not, however, present their complaint until they have agreed in writing to accept for themselves the sentence handed down if it is shown that they have slandered the accused bishop.

If anyone, not abiding by these decisions mentioned above, dares to weary the ears of the emperor or to disturb the law courts of the civil authorities or an ecumenical council, thus scorning all the bishops of the diocese, that person should not be allowed to make such an accusation since he disregards the canons and injures the good order of the Church.

This canon is extremely important from the point of view of church judicial procedure.[172] By issuing it, the fathers of Constantinople wanted to avoid any reoccurrence in the future of the numerous abuses of the preceding period. First of all, some remarks on the text itself: we must note that, contrary to what E. Schwartz thought, the canon has nothing in common with canon 21 of the *kanonikon* of Amasea. Schwartz was led into error, no doubt, by the title of this *kanonikon* in certain manuscripts.[173]

The text of canon 6 has some variants, but only one slightly affects the meaning: besides τοῖς κοινωνικοῖς ἡμῶν ἐπισκόποις, there exists this reading: τοῖς κανονικοῖς ἡμῶν ἐπισκόποις.[174] In the first case, the meaning is "...of the bishops in communion with us"; in the second case, the meaning is "of our canonical bishops." The first reading is certainly preferable, as Beveridge has already noted.[175] However, it is the second which we find in the *Pedalion* and in the edition of Rhalles and Potles.[176] It is also on the second reading that the Russo-Slavonic translation of the *Kniga Pravil* is based.[177] Certain manuscripts have the following first-line title: Ἔτι δὲ καὶ τάδε προσδιώρισεν ἡ σύνοδος,[178] that is, "Here again is what the council decreed." We note that the term ἱερεὺς is used in its ancient meaning to designate a bishop; this usage was maintained for quite a long time.[179] Also to be noted is the expression τούς τε πάλαι τῆς ἐκκλησίας ἀποκηρυχθέντας, which means "those who have been excluded for a long time from the Church." We are dealing here with the most severe form of excommunication.[180] As for the expression "weary the ears of the emperor," it seems like a reminiscence of canon 11 of Antioch.

Three fundamental elements hold our attention in this canon:
1) Who can be an accuser of a bishop and under what conditions can the complaints be received?
2) Who is defined in canon law by the term "heretic"?
3) What are the normal tribunals for judging a bishop?

Relating to this last point, there is a subsidiary question which asks what the authors of the canon precisely understood by the terms μείζων σύνοδος and οἰκουμενικὴ σύνοδος. The canon makes distinctions about the receivability of different kinds of complaints, based on their nature. Those complaints about *res privatae* are declared acceptable whatever the religion of the person making the complaint. If, in this case, the church courts are able to judge, it is because of the ecclesiastical status of the accused bishop. In fact, an imperial law of September 23, 355, stipulated that bishops were exempt from the jurisdiction of civil courts and that they could be judged only by their equals.[181] Consequently, to reject systematically all complaints from a heterodox or a pagan against a bishop would be an implicit authorization of the bishops to violate the civil laws. This would be a scandalous attack on the elementary rules of morality and law. On the other hand, in trials concerning church matters, the problem was posed differently. The religious status of the accuser was to be taken into consideration. We are obviously not dealing with pagans in this case; and they are not even mentioned since they have no reason to get involved in the internal matters of the Christian community.

These are the people who cannot be accusers: those who have themselves been accused of some misconduct and have not been discipiined;
those who have been previously condemned; those who are excommunicated. Heretics in general are equally excluded from being accusers,
and here the canon makes clear who is designated by that term. There
are three categories. First all those who advocate any of the ancient
heresies; we know which sects are being referred to by going back to
the canons of this era which name them.[182] Then there are the heretics
who were anathematized at the council of 381.[183] The fathers in council at Constantinople in 382, being for the most part the same bishops
who had made up the council of the previous year, spoke of "those
who have been excommunicated by us" (τοὺς. . .ὑφ᾿ ὑμῶν ἀναθεματι-
σθέντας). Then they added as heretics "those who pretend to profess
the true faith but who separate themselves from the bishops in communion with us and hold separate assemblies." It is not difficult to
understand who is being aimed at here: Paulinus and his group. However, we must not see in this assertion of the fathers of the council of
382 only one isolated opinion, motivated by the circumstances and the
passions aroused in connection with the schism in Antioch. The tendency to assimilate, up to a certain point, persistent schisms to heresies
was at the time a point of view widely held among the orthodox, and
St. Jerome gave the reason for it: "...there is no schism that does not
fabricate some heresy so as to seem to have a good reason for separating itself from the Church."[184] It is proper not to forget that this
canon deals with a precise and therefore limited problem: the receivability of accusations against orthodox bishops. All those who in one
way or another found themselves in an irregular situation were not
allowed to be accusers when church matters were concerned. When it
was a question of the means of integrating dissidents, however, there
was a completely different approach to the question; distinctions were
established between different categories of dissidents, as St. Basil the
Great sets out very well in his first canonical letter to Amphilochius of
Iconium. Basing himself on ancient tradition, St. Basil distinguishes
between heresies, schisms and parasynagogues. "Heresies" applies to
whose who "are completely separated from and who are total
strangers to the very faith." "Schism" is spoken of when "those who
have gone away for certain ecclesiastical reasons or for some problems
that should have been resolved by mutual agreement." The "parasynagogues" are "the factions which rebellious priests or bishops and
undisciplined people have formed."[185]

Indeed the differences between these categories do not always appear very clear. Does the distinction between parasynagogue and schism rest only on the extent of the separatist movement or on the existence of serious divergences about church discipline? In addition, as St. Jerome has noted, if schisms perpetuate themselves, they have a tendency to justify their break by doctrinal considerations. St. Basil himself was not absolutely consistent, however; he admitted that the baptism of schismatics, as distinct from that of heretics, was receivable, but he declared that objections exist about the baptism of the "pure ones," that is, the Novatians,[186] who were certainly schismatics and not heretics; this was implicitly recognized by the fathers of Nicea.[187]

Let us look now at the question of the courts capable of judging a bishop accused by someone whose respectability and orthodoxy are not in question.[188] Normally, the provincial council has this power, in conformity with the general principle set out in canon 2 concerning the competence of this church organ. But the fathers of Constantinople envisioned the case where bishops of a province would not be able to make a judgment. They described this possibility in the following terms: "if the other bishops of the province cannot redress the wrongs imputed to the bishop..." (εἰ δὲ συμβῇ ἀδυνατῆσαι τοὺς ἐπαρχεώτας πρὸς διόρθωσιν τῶν ἐπιφερομένων ἐγκλημάτων τῷ ἐπισκόπῳ...). Such a difficulty can certainly result from the complexity of a case. That expression appears to suggest rather another explanation: the practical impossibility can come from the personality of the accused, for example, if it is the metropolitan of the province. Then an appeal to "a higher council" made up of bishops from the civil diocese is envisioned. To avoid abuses, it is stipulated that the accusers must agree in writing to accept for themselves the sentence which would be handed down if during the trial the accusation is shown to be trumped up.

Is this "higher council" (μείζων σύνοδος) a full assembly of all the bishops of a diocese, or is it an organ of appeal like the one foreseen in canons 12 and 14 of Antioch, that is, the provincial council but enlarged by the presence of some other neighboring bishops? The first interpretation was held by Zonaras, Balsamon and, more recently, by Nicodemus Milash,[189] but Karl Müller preferred the second interpretation.[190] Here is his argument: We must question the identity of the terminology about the μείζων σύνοδος; in addition, the gathering together of a full council of bishops was already difficult for small dioceses and completely unthinkable (*"undenkbar"*) for large ones like the East, for example.[191] This argument does not seem too convincing. First of all, the cases where the provincial councils were supposed not to be capable of making a judgment must have been very exceptional and, therefore, rare; this was all the more so since the canon contained a dissuasive clause. It is therefore clearly an exaggeration to consider the holding of such diocesan councils as practically impossible. The great number of episcopal councils of the time shows that the bishops got around quite a bit and travelled very far. Moreover, the similarity in terminology concerning the μείζων σύνοδος in the legislation of the Council of Antioch and the Council of Constantinople in 382 does not at all imply a strict equivalency of meaning. This equivalency would only be possible if at the time of the Council of Antioch, around 330, the diocese was already used as a jurisdictional framework for church administration. This was not the case. Finally, the text of canon 6 itself surely indicates very clearly that we are dealing with a full council of the diocesan bishops, since it says that anyone who might want to have recourse to a higher court would thereby show his scorn for all the bishops of the diocese.

The fathers of the Council of Constantinople did not want any interference from the secular authorities, even from the highest such authority, in the proceedings against accused bishops; this was also the attitude, at least in principle, of the state.[192] But what is the meaning of the prohibition of recourse to an "ecumenical council"? As we have already said, this term had not yet acquired the technical meaning it would later receive; it could designate either a truly general council or a wider council than the episcopal assemblies of one diocese. In any case, this prohibition, whose goal was to avoid the poisoning effect of conflicts, was not always respected. We must recognize that it was difficult to apply when the primate of a diocese was involved. Thus, St. John Chrysostom wanted to defend himself before an "ecumenical council,"[193] no doubt understanding that term to mean a council of the whole eastern empire.[194] If we relate canons 2, 3 and 6 of the double council of 381-2, we see the tendency to consider the dioceses as wider church districts; the bishops of these areas were supposed to regulate their own affairs together and without any exterior intervention. These groupings—ornamented by the authority of certain sees, which first tacitly and then explicitly received a supra-metropolitan jurisdiction—were rather rapidly to develop into the constitutions of the patriarchates. However, these patriarchal jurisdictions were not defined strictly on the basis of the geography of civil dioceses. Canons

7 of Nicea, 8 of Ephesus, and 28 of Chalcedon deal with this matter, and it will be studied at a later time.

7

Those heretics who come over to orthodoxy and to the society of those who are saved we receive according to the prescribed rite and custom: Arians, Macedonians, Novatianists who call themselves "pure and better," Quartodecimans or Tetradites as well as Apollinarians. We receive them on condition that they present a written document and that they anathematize every heresy which is not in accord with the thinking of the holy, catholic and apostolic Church of God, and then they should be marked with the seal, that is, anointed with chrism on the forehead, eyes, nostrils, mouth and ears. And as they are marked with the seal, we say "seal of the gift of the Holy Spirit."

As for Eunomians who are baptized with only one single immersion, Montanists here called Phrygians, Sabellians who teach the doctrine of "Father-Son" and commit other abominable things, and all the other heresies — for there are many of them here especially among the people coming from the country of the Galatians — all those among them that want to come over to orthodoxy we receive as pagans: the first day, we make them Christians, the second catechumens, then the third we exorcize them by blowing three times on their faces and ears; then we teach them, and we make them come to the church for a long time and to hear the scriptures. After that, we baptize them.

We have already said that this text, which is found in the *Syntagma in XIV Titles* as canon 7 of the second ecumenical council, is only a copy of another document which claims to be a letter addressed to Martyrius, bishop of Antioch (459-471), from Constantinople. The content of the letter and that of the canon are substantially identical except for two differences. In the canon, the expressions related to letter writing are omitted. In addition, a passage of the letter that deals with the ordination of heretics received into the Church after their chrismation is missing from the canon.[195]

As Schwartz and Honigmann have clearly shown, this document is to be dated well before the time of Patriarch Gennadius (458-471) because it does not mention the Nestorians or the Monophysites.[196] No doubt it is related to the anti-heretical campaign that Nestorius led at the beginning of his time as patriarch in 428. We must, therefore, link it with the imperial law of May 30, 428, which was directed against all dissidents.[197] Nestorius had inquired about the manner of receiving heretics in the diocese of Asia, and the letter is probably the official response which was sent to him. This is why the document is not presented as an official order but as a description of existing practice in the capital.[198] Why was this text later attributed to the representative of the bishop of Antioch in Constantinople or to Gennadius? Perhaps Martyrius wanted to find out how heretics were received in the church at Constantinople. It was probably in this second redaction that the letter was preserved.[199] This is, however, only a very plausible hypothesis; it is very obvious, moreover, that in the thinking of the time, any mention of the name of Nestorius had to disappear from any orthodox document.

This canon is important since it was accepted as normative in the East. It is not interesting for purely historical reasons, since even the sects enumerated in it have long ago disappeared; it is important for us because we find in it a permanent criterion concerning the ways of receiving heterodox. This criterion is founded on the proximity or distance of the doctrine of the dissident groups from the doctrine of the Church. On the basis of this data, different methods of reception into the Church were set out. First of all, there were the heretics whose trinitarian doctrine, even if it contained errors, was not so far from orthodoxy as to vitiate baptism. Repentant followers of these sects were not be rebaptized; they had, however, to renounce their errors and then be united to the catholic Church by chrismation. The second category of heretics was made up of those sects whose baptism could not be recognized even by extreme condescesion.[200]

The document does not introduce any innovations into the practice of the Church by not requiring the rebaptism of all dissidents; at the most, this canon establishes a codification. We know that this question provoked violent controversy in the third century; each side in the controversy stuck to its guns without really resolving the problem.[201] But the Council of Nicea implicitly decided the question by admitting the Novatianists and the Meletians into the Church without rebaptism. The legislation of Laodicea continued in the same direction,[202] and this council's decrees had a direct influence on our present document.[203] St. Basil personally leaned toward rigor but recognized the good sense of the distinctions about the reception of dissidents.[204] Apostolic canon 46, despite its general character, cannot be taken as absolutely normative.[205] The Council of Carthage of 256 required the rebaptism of all heretics regardless of their beliefs, and this decision is well established in the oldest redaction of the *Syntagma in XIV Titles.*[206] According to the fathers of the Synod in Trullo, however, this had only a limited relevance, being the expression of a local custom (ἔθος).[207]

Among the sectarians received without rebaptism, the Arians are mentioned first. We may find this indulgence a bit surprising since it seems to be in complete contradiction with the position of St. Athanasius,[208] but, as we have already said, from the end of the fourth century distinctions were made among the "Arians": there were the Homoeans who professed a trinitarian doctrine much less radical than did Arius and his disciples.

We have spoken of the Macedonians in the commentary on canon 1 of the Council of Constantinople. By economy, they too were to be received into the Church without rebaptism. The Macedonians, on the whole, accepted the divinity of the Word without restriction; they had, on the other hand, an imprecise doctrine about the Holy Spirit but did not go so far as denying his being as a distinct person. It is proper to quote here the comment of B. de Margérie in order to understand the indulgence of the orthodox in this matter: "The conscious, explicit and thought-out recognition of the divinity of the Holy Spirit and its affirmation by the New Testament is a relatively late development in the Church..."[209]

The Sabbatians received their name from the founder of their sect, one Sabbatius, a Jew who converted to Novatianism but later withdrew from this group to form his own distinct sect.[210] These partisans called themselves "Protopaschites," that is, the observers of the primitive Pascha. In fact, they did not differ from the Novatianists except that they celebrated this feast according to the calculation of the Jews.

Concerning the Novatianists, our document only follows the regulation clearly set out by canons 8 of Nicea and 7 of Laodicea, even though St. Basil seems to indicate that these sectarians had other opinions.[211] Ἀριστερoὺς is no doubt a copyist's bad reading of ἀρίστους; this correction is also behind the translation of the *Kniga Pravil.*[212]

Those who celebrated Pascha on the fourteenth day of the spring moon, whatever day that might be, were designated under the name of "Quartodecimans" (*Τέσσαρεσκαιδεκατῖται, Quattuordecimani*). This question had greatly shaken the Church in the second century because the Christians of Asia did not want to adopt the general practice.[213]

The number of people who refused to adapt gradually diminished, but there still remained some diehards in the fifth century. They were also the target of Nestorius' attacks.[214] If the name "Quartodecimans" is perfectly clear, this is by no means so for "Tetradites," by which the Quartodecimans were also designated and which according to etymology seems to be related to Wednesday.[214a] According to Theodoret of Cyrrhus, these dissidents shared the rigorist position of the Novatianists on penitence.[215] Canon 7 of Laodicea anticipated the same modalities for receiving Quartodecimans and Novatianists into the Church. These rulings are taken up again in this present document.

Finally, in this category the Apollinarians are mentioned. We have already said what the error of Apollinaris was in our analysis of canon 1 of Constantinople.

The document declares that the members of all the other sects are to be received in the manner of pagans, that is, by passing through all the degrees of Christian initiation.[216] Three heretical groups are expressly named. The Eunomians professed the total dissimilarity between the Father and the Son. They had replaced the triple immersion in baptism by just one; this is underlined in the document. They also had deliberately changed the sacramental formula.[217] In these conditions, the recognition by economy of the baptism conferred in this sect would have been unthinkable.

Montanism had grown up in Phrygia between 156 and 172 as a prophetic and charismatic movement ending up in illuminism.[218] It built itself into an exclusive sect. The Montanists believed in millenarianism, and they exalted abstinence from sexual activity to an exaggerated degree. To what degree did they diverge from orthodox trinitarian doctrine? On this point, the opinions of the fathers do not agree: St. Epiphanius categorically affirmed that "concerning the Father, the Son and the Holy Spirit they have the same feelings as the holy catholic Church."[219] St. Jerome, on the other hand, accused them of Sabellianism.[220] As for St. Basil, he maintained "that they were obviously heretics because they blasphemed against the Holy Spirit by attributing the name of the Paraclete in an improper and shameful way to Montanus and Priscilla." For the bishop of Caesarea, the nullity of their baptism was beyond question.[221] This was also the opinion of the fathers of Laodicea.[222] The reason for rejecting the baptism of the Sabellians was obvious: they did not admit the real distinction between the divine persons; they could not, therefore, really baptize in the name of the Father, the Son and the Holy Spirit.

We note finally that in Aristenus' annotated *Synopsis,* this present document is divided into two canons: the one on the dissidents received into the Church by chrismation and the other on those who had to be rebaptized. Thus, in those collections which follow the *Synopsis,* eight canons are attributed to the Council of Constantinople.[223]

CHAPTER II FOOTNOTES

[1]P.P. Joannou, "La législation impériale et la christianisation de l'Empire romain (311-476)," *OCA* 152 (Rome, 1972), p. 39. G. Christopher Stead ("'Homoousios' dans la pensée de saint Athanase," *Politique et théologie chez Athanase d'Alexandrie* [Paris, 1974], pp. 231-253) rejects any western influence concerning the introduction of the term "consubstantial" into the symbol of Nicea. The argumentation of this scholar does not contain any decisive elements supporting his thesis.

[2]J.N.D. Kelly, *Early Christian Creeds* (London, 1950), pp. 242-254.

[3]This is the case for the four symbols in connection with the council of the Dedication (341). See V.V. Bolotov, *Lektsii po istorii drevnei Tserkvi, IV: Istoriia Tserkvi v period vselenskikh soborov,* 3rd part, *Istoriia bogoslovskoi mysli* (Petrograd, 1918), pp. 55-64. See also Kelly, pp. 55-64.

[4]"...ὅπερ ἐγὼ βούλομαι, τοῦτο καινὸν...νομιξέσθω," *Hist. Arian.* 33, *PG* 25, col. 732C. This was only an application to religious affairs of the saying of Roman law: "quod principi placuit legis habet vigorem." On this formula, see J. Gaudemet, *Le formation du droit séculier et du droit de l'Eglise aux IV*[e] *et V*[e] *siècles,* 2nd edition (Paris, 1979), p. 11. On the relations between the Church and the Roman state at this time, see W. Schneemelcher, "Kirche und Staat im 4. Jahrhundert," *Bonner Akademische Reden,* 37 (Bonn, 1970).

[5]See the commentary on canon 1 of the council of Nicea, above.

[6]*Héfele-Leclercq* I[2], p. 985.

[7]On this heresy, see J. Kelly, *Early Christian Doctrines,* 5th ed. (New York, 1978), pp. 258-269. Also B. de Margerie, *La Trinité chrétienne dans l'Histoire* (Paris, 1975), pp. 146-152.

[8]Orat. XXXI (Theologica V), 26-27; *PG* 36, col. 161C-164B.

[9]The emperor made this decision in November, 377: Joannou, p. 79.

[10]Cf. *supra:* 2nd part, our analysis of canon 4 of Nicea.

[11]The transgression was aggravated by the fact that in this case it was a question of going from one civil diocese to another.

[12]Cf. *supra,* our analysis of canon 15 of Nicea.

[13]*CT* XVI, 1, 2, p. 853.

[14]Theodoret affirmed twice that Maximus was an Apollanarian: *HE* V, 8, 3 and 15; *GCS,* pp. 287-288. No other source corroborates this claim.

[15]*CT* XVI, 5, 6, pp. 856-857.

[16]See E. Amand de Mendieta, "Basile de Césarée et Damase de Rome: Les causes de l'échec de leurs négotiations," *Biblical and Patristic Studies in Memory of Robert Pierce Casey* (Freiburg ïm Breisgau, 1963), pp. 122-166.

[17]*Orient et Occident, les structures ecclésiales vues dans l'histoire des sept premiers conciles oecuméniques* (Paris, 1974), p. 46.

[18]Socrates, *HE* V, 8, *PG* 67, col. 576B; Sozomen, *HE* VII, 7, *ibid.,* col. 1429B; Dionysius Exiguus, *Str.,* p. 60.

[19]See F. Cavallera, *Le schisme d'Antioch* (Paris, 1905), *passim.*

[20]"...they came to Constantinople following your Piety's letter": this is how the fathers of the council wrote to the emperor in their address, *Syntagma,* p. 94 and further on: "...you have honored the Church by your letters of invitation," *ibid.,* p. 95.

[21]The existence of such a document is expressly attested by the letter of the fathers of the council of Constantinople of 382; see Theodoret, *HE* V, 9, 13, *GCS,* p. 293. The anathemas of this tome have

been preserved in an Arabic translation in the nomocanon of Michael of Damietta; see W. Riedel, *Die Kirchenrechtsquellen des Patriarchats Alexandrien* (Leipzig, 1900), pp. 94-97. A brief anti-Appolinarian passage of the tome is reproduced in a Nestorian document of the 7th century; see Oscar Braun, *Das Buch der Synhados oder Synodicon orientale* (Stuttgart-Vienna, 1900), p. 326.

[22]*Syntagma*, pp. 94-95.

[23]V.N. Beneševič, *Kanonicheskii sbornik XIV titulov, prilozheniia* (St. Petersburg, 1905), pp. 87-89. This list, somewhat touched up, is not at all exhaustive; on this matter see *Héfele-Leclercq* I², p. 6, note 1. See the list published since then by Turner, EOMIA, II, 3rd part, pp. 434-464.

[24]Socrates, *HE* V, 8, *PG* 67, col. 576-581; Sozomen, *HE* VII, 7-9, *ibid.*, col. 1429-1440; Theodoret, *HE* V, 7-8, *GCS*, pp. 286-288.

[25]Theodoret, *HE* V, 9, pp. 289-294. This letter is addressed to Damasus, Ambrose, Britton, Valerian, Ascolies, Anemios, Basil and all the other bishops gathered in Rome.

[26]*Poemata de seipso*, verses 1506-1904, *PG* 37, col. 1133-1162.

[27]This symbol of faith was quoted for the first time at the third session of the council of Chalcedon, *ACO* II, I, p. 276.

[28]On this subject see Kelly, *Early Christian Creeds*, 3rd ed. (New York, 1972), p. 296.

[29]*Regestes*, n. 1.

[30]R. Tonneau and R. Devreesse, "Les homélies catéchétiques de Theodore de Mopsueste," *Studi e Testi* (Rome, 1949). See hom. IX, 1-3, pp. 215-217; hom. X, 7, pp. 255-257; 11, p. 263, p. 269; 20-21, p. 277.

[31]*Acta collationis romanae descripta a Smaragdo, PL* 102, col. 971-976. Pope Leo III (795-816) had the unaltered text of the symbol engraved in Greek and Latin on a silver tablet; L. Duchesne, *Liber pontificalis,* vol. II (Paris, 1892), p. 26.

[32]On the history of the controversy, see A. Palmieri, "Filioque," *DTC* V, 2, col. 2309-2343.

[33]This is what Mark of Ephesus strongly underlined during the discussion which took place in Ferrara, October 8, 1438, *Concilium Florentinum, Acta Graeca*, part I-a, vol. V, fasc. I (Rome, 1953), pp. 52, 56 and 57.

[34]A certain number of bishops were represented by priests; one bishop from Pontus sent a reader.

[35]W. Ensslin, *Die Religionspolitik des Kaisers Theodosius des Grossen, Sitzunghberichte der Bayerischen Akademie der Wissenschaften,* philosophisch-historische Klassen (Munich, 1953), pp. 31-32. On the council in its whole, see A.M. Ritter, *Das Konzil von Konstantinopel und sein Symbol* (Göttingen, 1965).

[36]Fr. Dvornik, *The Idea of Apostolicity in Byzantium* (Cambridge, Massachusetts, 1958), p. 25.

[37]According to W. Ensslin, p. 21, it was in the fall of 380 that Ascolius baptized the very sick emperor. Because of the plural used by St. Gregory "Μακεδόνες," it seems clear that the bishop of Thessalonica did not come alone, *Poemata de seipso,* vers. 1800, *PG* 37, col. 1155A.

[38]Socrates, *HE* V, 8, col. 576-577. These were "pneumatomachian" bishops.

[39]*Syntagma,* p. 95. The term used is "ἐπικυρωθῆναι."

[40]The mention of Nectarius, at the beginning of the edition of the text, shows the importance of the see of Constantinople, as a center of communion of the Church in the eastern part of the empire.

[41]*CT* XVI, 1, 3, p. 834.

[42]Cf. *supra,* note 21.

[43]This is what pope Leo affirms in a letter to archbishop Anatolius of Constantinople, *ACO,* II, IV, p. 61. At the time of the debate on the rights of the see of New Rome, the papal legate Lucensius observed that the disciplinary decisions of the council of 381 did not figure "in synodicis canonibus," *ibid,* II, III, p. 548. This absence of official notification did not mean that the existence of these canons was unknown in Rome in the fifth century. They were known in the West no doubt from the fall of 381 on; on this subject, see Dvornik, *Byzance et la primauté romaine* (Paris, 1964), p. 38.

[44]Letters "Quamlibet," *PL* 16, col. 947-949 and "Sanctum," *PL* 16, col. 950-953.

[45]Theodoret, *HE* V, 9, 13, p. 293.

[46]Cf. *infra,* our commentary on canon 6.

[47]On this subject, see our article, "Le concile oecuménique comme autorité suprême dans l'Eglise," *Jahrbuch der Gesellschaft für das Recht der Ostkirchen*, Band II (1974), pp. 128-142, especially p. 132.

[48]3rd session, *ACO,* II, I, p. 276 and 5th session, *ibid.*, p. 324.

[49]17th session, *ibid.*, pp. 447-448.

[50]Canon 7.

[51]E. von Dobschutz, *Das Decretum Gelasianum De libris recipiendis et non recipiendis in kritischen*

The Council of Constantinople

Text *(Texte und Untersuchungen*, 38 [Leipzig, 1912]), p. 8.
[52]*PL* 69, col. 166.
[53]Ep. 34, *PL* 77, col. 893.
[54]Gaudemet, pp. 167-168. Cf. *infra* our analysis of canon 1 of Chalcedon.
[55]Socrates, *HE* V, 5, PG 67, col. 572A; Theodoret, *HE* V, 3, 9-16, *GCS*, pp. 280-282.
[56]*Poemata de seipso*, vv. 1572-1796, *PG* 37, col. 1138A-1155A.
[57]For the passage concerning this question, see Damasus, letter 5, *PL* 13, col. 367-369.
[58]*Poemata...*,vv. 1800-1815, *PG* 37, col. 1155A-1156A.
[59]Homily "Supremum vale," *PG* 36, col. 481-489.
[60]Sozomen, *HE* VII, 8, *PG* 67, col. 1433-1436.
[61]*Syntagma*, p. 95.
[62]See our analysis of canon 1 of Chalcedon.
[63]*ACO*, II, I, 3, p. 96 [455].
[64]See our analysis of canon 1 of Chalcedon.
[65]See *Regestes*, no. 2.
[66]Cf. *supra* note 25.
[67]In the old Syriac collection attested to by the manuscript of the British Museum, *Add. 14528* (A.D. 500/1), the introduction of the canons of the council of 382 did not count as a canon when the translation was made. The collections only formed one single canon, as in the work of Dionysius. In addition, the decision about Maximus the Cynic was put together with the decree about "the Tome of Westerners," issued by the council of 382. This four part division was taken up into the ancient Arabic collection of the Melkites. See F. Schulthess, *Die syrischen Kanones der Synoden von Nicaea bis Chalcedon* (Göttingen, 1908), pp. 109-110. See also E. Jarawan, *La collection canonique arabe des Melkites et sa physionomie propre* (Rome, 1969), pp. 72-77.
[68]*Synagoge*, p. 6. Such a case of combining is not at all uncommon in dealing with canons. The canons of a council held in Caesarea were added to those of Ancyra and attributed to the council held there. In addition, very early on at Rome, the canons of Sardica were written at the end of those of Nicea to form a *corpus nicaenum*.
[69]About canon 6, pope Nicholas I (858-867) wrote to emperor Michael: "...quod tamen non apud nos inventum, sed apud vos haberi perhibetur," Epist. VIII, Mansi, XV, col. 192D. We can recognize the hand of Anastasius the Librarian in this clarification.
[70]See the commentary on the canon.
[71]*Syntagma*, p. 94. We find the following preamble in the first recension of Dionysius: "Incipit (sic!) canones Constantinopolitani Concilii, qui ab episcopis centum quinquaginta prolati sunt, quos inclytae recordationi Theodosius imperator, pater Archadii et Honorii principum conuocauit, quando beatus Nectarius Constantinopolitanae ecclesiae damnato Maximo sortitus est pontificatus officium," *Str.*, p. 60. In the second recension, the preamble is a bit more concise: "Sub Theodosio piissimo imperatore apud Constantinopolim expositi sunt canones tres. Hae definitiones expositae sunt ab episcopis CL, qui in idipsum apud Constantinopolim conuenerunt, quando beatus Nectarius est ordinatus," Fr. Maassen, *Geschichte der Quellen und der Literatur des canonischen Rechts im Abendlande* (Graz, 1870), p. 120 (=*PL* 67, col. 169D).
[72]*Pedalion*, p. 155; *Rhalles-Potles* II, p. 165; *Pravila* I, p. 237.
[73]*PL* 56, col. 808B (=EOMIA, II, 3rd part, p. 408).
[74]In the second Dionysian recension, the text of canon 1 comes immediately after the preamble: "Non rescindendam fidem..."; "Fidem non violendam...," EOMIA, *ibid.*, p. 405.
[75]*ACO*, II, I, 3, p. 455. It is to be noted that in the text now in use, there is also a mention of the canons of Nicea: "Μὴ ἀθετεῖσθαι τὴν πίστιν μηδὲ τοὺς κανόνας... ."
[76]*Syntagma*, p. 76.
[77]EOMIA II, 3rd part, p. 405. See *ibid.*, pp. 464a-464b, the reconstructed list of Turner.
[78]*Pravila* I, p. 237.
[79]*Synagoge*, p. 116; *ACO*, II, I, 3, p. 455. Many manuscripts of the *Synagoge* do not contain this mention of the Marcionites, p. 116, note 33. The Marcellians were not named in the text read at Chalcedon. The Marcionites "Μαρκιανιστῶν" are perhaps quoted as a result of a copyist's error due to the similarity of names.
[80]For example, see St. Athanasius, *De Synodis*, 10, *PG* 26, col. 697A. The term is used with this double meaning in canon 7 of the council of Ephesus. Elsewhere, this was to engender polemics in the context of controversies about the exact meaning of this ruling of the fathers of the third ecumenical

138 THE CHURCH OF THE ANCIENT COUNCILS

council. See *infra* our commentary on this canon of Ephesus.

[81]Elena Cavalcanti, "Studi eunomiani, " *OCA* 202 (Rome, 1976).

[82]H. Marrou wrote that "...the homoean credo of 360 defined what we can call the historical Arianism such that it would henceforth be professed by the communities or peoples hostile to catholic orthodoxy and to the symbol of Nicea," *Nouvelle Histoire de l'Eglise,* t. I (Paris, 1963), p. 303.

[83]X. Le Bachelet, "Arianisme," IV, i-viii, *DTC,* I, 2, col. 1849-1859.

[84]*Str.* p. 60: "Machedonianorum." Toward the end of the 4th century, Macedonius, homoeousian bishop of Constantinople (342-346 and 351-360), was considered to have been the initiator of the pneumatomachian faction. From then on, the advocates of this heresy were called "Macedonians." In 383, the Macedonians were distinguished from the Pneumatomachians as we can see from the law of July 25, 383: *CT* XVI, 5, p. 859. On the "Semi-Arians," see the article of E. Amann, *DTC* XIV, 2, col. 1790-1796.

[85]Letter 210, 3, *PG.* On Sabellianism, see B. de Margerie, *op. cit.,* pp. 111-113.

[86]V. de Fondeville, *Ideas trinitiarias y cristologicas de Marcelo de Ancyra* (Madrid, 1953).

[87]J. Ortiz de Urbina, *Nicée et Constantinople* (Paris, 1963), pp. 209-210.

[88]Cf. our commentary of canon 19 of Nicea.

[89]*Histoire de l'Eglise,* publiée sous la direction de Fliche et de Martin, t. 3 (Paris, 1947), chapter 3, by G. Bardy, pp. 133-135.

[90]H. Lietzmann, *Apollinaris von Laodicea und seine Schule* (Tübingen, 1904). A. Grillmeier, *Le Christ dans la Tradition chrétienne,* (Paris, 1973), pp. 257-272.

[91]*Ad Jovianum,* H. Leitzmann, p. 251.

[92]Grillmeier, pp. 461-467 and 474.

[93]*Synagoge,* p. 32, note 42; *Syntagma,* p. 96; "ἐπιβαίνειν" is surely the primitive reading; it is the one found in the text read at Chalcedon, *ACO* II, I, p. 455.

[94]*Synagoge,* p. 33, note 28; *Syntagma,* p. 97. For the omission of the preposition, see *ibid.,* p. 97, note 2. Standard text: *Pedalion,* p. 156; *Rhalles-Potles* II, p. 170. The text read at Chalcedon contained "ἐπὶ," *ACO,* II, I, p. 455.

[95]A.H.M. Jones, *The Later Roman Empire,* Vol. I (Oxford, 1964), pp. 46-7 and 373-375. For the date of the detachment of Egypt, see Th. E. Mommsen, *Verzeichnis der römischen Provizen aufgesetzt um 297, Abhanlungen der K. Preuss. Akad. der Wiss.,* Ph.-hist. Kl. (Berlin, 1863), pp. 494-496. But according to Jones, p. 373, the detachment of Egypt took place under the reign of Valens (364-378).

[96]See our article, "Problèmes primatiaux au temps du concile de Chalcédoine," *Messager,* no. 77 (1972), pp. 35-62. It is also to be noted that Memnon of Ephesus played an important role as ally of St. Cyril at the third ecumenical council.

[97]Προϋποθέσεις διαμορφώσεως τοῦ θεσμοῦ τῆς πενταρχίας τῶν πατριαρχῶν (Athens, 1969), p. 143.

[98]EOMIA II, part 3a, p. 411.

[99]See what bishop Nicodemus Milash wrote, *Pravila* I, pp. 248-249.

[100]"...imperitia...priscae translationis," *Strewe,* p. 1.

[101]"Ut extra terminos non ingredere alienos...," EOMIA, *op. cit.,* p. 411.

[102]Canon 6.

[103]*Les institutions de l'Empire byzantin* (Paris, 1949), p. 451.

[104]Canon 8.

[105]Cf. *supra* our commentary on canon 7 of Nicea.

[106]*Historia Ecclesiastica* V, 8, *PG* 67, col. 577C-580A.

[107]A. Ritter believes that these rules were formulated before the arrival of the bishops from Egypt and Macedonia in Constantinople, *Das Konzil von Konstantinopel und sein Symbol* (Göttingen, 1965), p. 96. V. Monachino thinks that Timothy had already left Constantinople at that time. "Genesi storica del canone 28 di Calcedonia," *Gregorianum* 33 (1952), p. 267.

[108]Ritter, *pp.* 90-91.

[109]*Rhalles-Potles* II, p. 171.

[110]*Ibid.,* pp. 170-171.

[111]EOMIA, *op. cit.,* p. 418. It is the same adverb that we find in the "Versio a Rustico edita" of the acts of the council of Chalcedon: *ACO,* II, III, 3, p. 549. An ancient Latin version quoted by Maassen, *op. cit.,* p. 944, reads "tamen."

[112]EOMIA, *ibid.,* p. 419.

[113]*Ibid.,* p. 418.

¹¹⁴*Pravila* I, p. 253. The old Slavonic version of the *Kormchaya* contains the particle "zhe," *Syntagma* p. 97.

¹¹⁵*Syntagma*, p. 97.

¹¹⁶Hubert Pernot and Camille Polack, *Grammaire du grec moderne* (2nd part) (Paris, 1921), section 345, p. 185.

¹¹⁷On the history of this city in antiquity, see V.P. Nevskaia, *Vizantiia v klassicheskuiu i ellinicheskuiu epokhi (Moscow,* 1953).

¹¹⁸G. Dagron, *Naissance d'une capitale, Constantinople et ses institutions de 330 à 451* (Paris, 1974).

¹¹⁹For example, see what F.J. Ouspensky wrote, *Istoriia Vizantiiskoi imperii,* t. I (Petrograd, 1913), pp. 60-62.

¹²⁰Dagron, p. 13.

¹²¹John Malalas, *Chronographie,* Bonn edition, p. 323; cf. *Chronicon paschale,* Bonn edition, p. 530.

¹²²F. Dvornik, *The Idea of Apostolicity in Byzantium and the Legend of the Apostle Andrew* (Cambridge, Mass., 1958).

¹²³Simeon Vailhé, "Origines de l'Eglise de Constantinople," *EO* X (17), pp. 287-295.

¹²⁴Ed. Schwartz, "Zur Greschichte des Athanasius," *Gesammelte Schriften,* Band 3 (Berlin, 1959), p. 136.

¹²⁵Sozomen, *Historia ecclesiastica* III, 7, *PG* 67, col. 1037C.

¹²⁶Socrates, *Historia ecclesiastica* II, 7, *PG* 67, col. 193C.

¹²⁷*Historie de l'Eglise ancienne*, French edition (Paris, 1941), p. 191.

¹²⁸Bl. Phidas, Ἐνδημοῦσα σύνοδος (Athens, 1971), p. 28.

¹²⁹Symeon of Thessalonica, *De sacris ordinationibus,* 225-226, *PG* 155, col. 440.

¹³⁰V.N. Benešević, *Prilozheniia,* p. 21, no. 147.

¹³¹*Rhalles-Potles* II, p. 176.

¹³²"...ὑποβιβασμὸν δηλοῦσα καὶ ἐλλάτωσιν," *ibid.,* p. 173.

¹³³Novella CXXXI, c. II: "Ideoque sancimus secundum earum definitiones [that is, those of the first four ecumenical councils] sanctissimum senioris Romae papam primum esse onmium sacerdotum, beatissimum autem archiepiscopum Constantinopoleos Novae Romae secundum habere locum post sanctam apostolicam sedem senioris Romae, aliis autem omnibus sedibus praeponatur"; *CJC* 3, p. 655. Canon 36 of the council in Trullo: "...ὁριζόμεν ὥστε τὸν Κωνσταντινουπόλεως θρόνον τῶν ἴσων ἀπολαύειν πρεσβείων τοῦ τῆς πρεσβυτέρας Ῥώμης θρόνου, καὶ ἐν τοῖς ἐκκλεσιαστικοῖς ὡς ἐκεῖνον μεγαλύνεσθαι πράγμασι δεύτερον μετ'ἐκεῖνον ὑπάρχοντα." *Syntagma,* p. 168.

¹³⁴Socrates, *Historia ecclesiastica* I. 17, *PG,* 67, col. 116BC. In a poem addressed to the emperor Constantine by Porphyrius, Constantinople was called "altera Roma," Dagron, p. 46.

¹³⁵St. Gregory the Theologian asked Nectarios for his support in favor of Bosporios, bishop of Colonia in Cappadocia (Letter 185, *Les Belles Lettres,* vol. II [Paris, 1957], pp. 75-76). Dagron properly notes that this intervention was not based on a right of jurisdiction in Cappadocia. It was explained by the fact that Nectarios was in a position to intervene for good effect with the imperial administration into whose hands the affair could have fallen. Sozomen mentions the case of an intervention by Nectarios in Pontus: A certain Gerontios, former deacon of the Church of Milan, but suspended by Ambrose, had come from the East and had been consecrated bishop in Nicomedia by Helladios of Caesarea; Ambrose protested to Nectarios (*Historia ecclesiastica* VIII, 6, *PG* 67, col. 1529-1532). We can think that the bishop of Milan addressed himself to the first hierarch of the Eastern Church so that he might transmit the complaint to the competent authorities. For the interventions of St. John Chrysostom who assumed a veritable power of jurisdiction, see *Regestes,* nos. 16-20, 22-24, 29.

¹³⁶Cf. *supra* note 51.

¹³⁷Among others, we mention C.H. Turner, Ed. Schwartz, E. Caspar, H. Marot, T.V. Jalland, B.J. Kidd, W. Ullmann, W. de Vries. It is rejected on the other hand by Fr. Dvornik, *Byzantium...* , p. 44. Dagron, from his point of view, writes that "neither the West nor the East in 381 feared what seems to us today like the first consecration of the grandeur of Constantinople. Thus, there was no protest against canon 3 before the council of Chalcedon..." (p. 460). Ch. Pietri defends the date of 382 and affirms that "this text fits quite well into the context of the ecclesiastical relations of Rome with the Christian East in 382" (*Roma Christiana* [Rome, 1976], pp. 866-72, especially 868).

¹³⁸Cf. *supra,* note 135.

¹³⁹*ACO,* II, I, p. 456.

¹⁴⁰*Ibid.,* p. 53.

¹⁴¹*Ibid.,* p. 447-448. Cf. *infra,* the analysis and commentary of this famous text.

[142]It is noteworthy to observe that Theodoret of Cyrrhus in his *Church History*, written in 449-450, assumed that St. John Chrysostom already exercised a legitimate jurisdiction over Thrace, Asia, and Pontus (V, 28, 2, *GCS*, 329). He projected into the past a factual situation widely accepted in his own time.

[143]EOMIA, II, 3rd part, p. 418.

[144]*Poemata de seipso*, vv. 728-1029, *PG* 37, col. 1079-1100.

[145]Such is the opinion of V. Monachino, "Genesi storica del canone 28 de Calcedonia," *Gregorium*, 33 (1952), p. 267.

[146]*Pravila*, I, pp. 257-258.

[147]Dionysius, EOMIA, II, 3rd part, p. 419: "..in inritum deducta esse." Isidoriana, *ibid.*, p. 420: "...in inritum devocavitis." Prisca, *ibid.*, p. 420: "infirmata esse."

[148]Synodale "Sanctum," Ambrose, Epist. XIII, 3-5, *PL* 16, col. 950C-953A.

[149]Epist. V, "Decursis litteris," *PL* 13, col. 365-369. Epist. VI, "Ad meritum," *PL* 13, col. 369-370.

[150]Theodoret, *Historia ecclesiastica* V, 9, 15, *GCS*, p. 293.

[151]This recognition was attested to by Pope Boniface (418-423), Epist. XV, §6, *PL* 20, col. 783A.

[152]*Synagoge*, p. 11, notes 32-43. *Syntagma*, p. 97, notes 6 and 7.

[153]*Synagoge*, p. 108. *Syntagma*, p. 97.

[154]"...τῷ τε ἐν Ἀντοχείαι τόμῳ παρὰ τῆς ἐκεῖ συνελθούσης συνόδῳ γεγενημένῳ," Theodoret, *Historia ecclesiastica* V, 9 §13, *GCS*, p. 293.

[155]*Rhalles-Potles* II, p. 178-180.

[156]Bolotov, pp. 101-104.

[157]"Scripseramus dudum..." is what we read in the synodale "sanctum," *PL* 16, col. 950B.

[158]"Explicit haec epistola vel expositio synodi romanae habitae sub Damaso papa et transmissa ad Orientem; in qua omnis orientalis ecclesia facta synodo apud antiochiam, consona fide credentes et omnes ita consentientes eidem superexpositae fidei singuli sua subscriptione confirmant," Mansi, 3, col. 461.

[159]"Le concile d'Antioche (379)," *Revue benedictine* XLV (1933), pp. 196-213. On this subject, see also Schwartz, pp. 36-55.

[160]Mansi, 3, col. 460.

[161]*PG* 62, col. 901C-912A.

[162]Mansi, 3, col. 461.

[163]*Ibid.*, col. 461.

[164]For example, Cavallera, *Le schisme d'Antioche* (Paris, 1905), p. 248, note 2, and Bardy, article cited above. Bardy, moreover, is very nuanced on this subject for he recognized that the easterners were not ready to make any concession on the legitimacy of Meletius. He understood this canon in the sense that people were disposed to accept the Paulinians who came over to the majority. This does not appear to us to be the direct meaning of the canon.

[165]Theodoret, *Historia ecclesiastica* V, 9, 16, *GCS*, pp. 293-294.

[166]On the stages that led to this recognition, see S.L. Greenslade, *Schism in the Early Church* (London, 1953), pp. 165-167.

[167]*Rhalles-Potles* II, p. 179.

[168]As William Bright noted, *The Canons of the First Four General Councils*, 2nd edition (Oxford, 1892), p. 113: "The sentence is too concise to be self-explanatory."

[169]On these 21 canons, see E. Honigmann, "Trois mémoires posthumes d'histoire et de géographie de l'Orient chrétien," *Subsidia Hagiographica* 35 (Brussels, 1961), pp. 57-62.

[170]M. Gedeon, Ἀρχεῖον ἐκκλησιαστικῆς ἱστορίας, vol. I (Constantinople, 1911), pp. 372-373.

[171]Title XXXVI, §14, p. 108.

[172]On the practical level of course, it must be related to the whole of the canonical rulings on this subject: Apostolic canons 7-14; Chalcedon, 9, 17, 21; Antioch, 11, 13, 14, 15; Sardica, 3, 4, 5, 7, 8, 9, 14; Carthage, 8, 12, 15, 19, 28, 87, 96, 125, 128-131, Letter to bishop Boniface of Rome.

[173]"Ἐκ τῶν κανόνων τῶν ἁγίων πατέρων περὶ ψευδοκατηγόρων," *Syntagma* p. 61. Ed. Schwartz, "Die Kanonessamlungen der alten Reichskirche," *Gesammelte Schriften*, Band 4 (Berlin, 1960), p. 184. Text of canon 21 in Gedeon, pp. 373-374.

[174]*Syntagma*, p. 66, note 48.

[175]*Synodikon sive Pandectae* (Oxford, 1672), vol. Ii, Annotationes, p. 99.

[176]*Pedalion*, p. 160; *Rhalles-Potles*, II, p. 181.

[177]*Pravila* I, p. 263.

[178]*Synagoge*, p. 66, note 4.

[179]St. Gregory of Nazianzus called St. Basil, bishop of Caesarea, "ἄνδρα ἱερέα," Epist. XVI §8, *PG* 37, col. 52A. Canon 39 of Carthage forbids the primate to call himself "princeps sacerdotum," in the Greek translation "ἔξαρχον τῶν ἱερέων," that is, "chief of the bishops," *CC*, p. 85. Justinian declared that the pope of Rome is at the head "παντῶν τῶν ἁγιωτάτων τοῦ Θεοῦ ἱερέων," *CJ*, I, 1, 7, CJC, II, p. 8; Cf. Novella CXXXI, c. 2, *ibid.*, III, p. 655.

[180]Thus Alexander of Alexandria wrote about Arius and this first followers: "'Απεκήρυχθαν ἀπὸ τῆς ἐκκλησίας," Socrates, *Historia ecclesiastica* I, 6 *PG* 67, col. 49B.

[181]*CT* XVI, 2, 12, p. 838. This exemption, which was abolished by the emperor Julian, was reestablished by Valentinian I; see Ambrose, Epist. XXI, 2, *PL* 16, col. 1003AB. On this law, see the article of K1. M. Martin, "Constance II, Athanase, et l'Edit d'Arles," in the collection *Politique et theologie chez Athanase d'Alexandrie* (Paris, 1974), pp. 63-91.

[182]Laodicea, canons 7 and 8; Basil, 1 and 47; Constantinople, 7. *Syntagma*, pp. 268-269, 461-465, 492-493, 100-1.

[183]Canon 1 of Constantinople. *Syntagma*, p. 96.

[184]"...nullum schisma non sibi aliquam confingit haeresim, ut recte ab Ecclesia recessisse videatur," *Commentariorum in epistolam ad Titum liber*, III, *PL* 26, col. 598A.

[185]Canon 1 of St. Basil, cf. *supra* note 181.

[186]*Ibid.* See our article, "Les sources canoniques de saint Basile," *Messager* no. 44 (1963), pp. 210-217, especially p. 212.

[187]Cf. *supra* our analysis of canon 8 of Nicea.

[188]Cf. Canon 21 of Chalcedon. *Syntagma*, p. 122. The requirement of an inquiry into the personalities of the accusers of bishops is repeated there. See also Apostolic canon 74, *Syntagma*, pp. 77-78; Carthage, 8, 19, 128-130. *CC*, pp. 103, 106-107, 230-231.

[189]*Rhalles-Potles* II, pp. 182-6; *Pravila* I, p. 269.

[190]"Kanon 2 und 6 von Konstantinopel 381 und 382," *Festabe für Adolf Jülicher* (Tübingen, 1927), pp. 190-202.

[191]*Ibid.*, p. 202.

[192]Cf. *supra* note 180.

[193]Socrates, *Historia ecclesiastica* VI, 15, *PG* 67, col. 709C-711A.

[194]This is what caused H.E. Symonds to note in *The Church Universal and the See of Rome*: "But with the Emperor against him, there was no hope that such a council would do him justice so he turned to the West..." (London, 1939), pp. 94-95.

[195]For the text in its canonical form, see *Syntagma*, pp. 100-111. Text of the letter, *PG* 119, col. 900B-1A. Syriac recension in the work of Fr. Schulthess, *Die syrischen Kanones...*, p. 145.

[196]Schwartz, *Kanonessammlungen*, pp. 159-275; on this question, pp. 164-6. Honigmann, pp. 74-82. In the second edition of the *Regestes* (Paris, 1972) §145, V. Grumel takes the opinion of Schwartz and Honigmann. According to Schwartz, it is a question of a letter written by Theophanes of Philadelphia in Lydia while according to Honigmann, it is the work of the metropolitan of Ephesus. This second opinion seems more probable.

[197]CT XVI, 5, 65, pp. 878-9. On the intervention of Nestorius with the emperor Theodosius II, see Socrates, *Historia ecclesiastica* VII, 29, *PG* 67, col. 804-5.

[198]This nuance is not brought out in the French translation of this text done by P.P. Joannou, *CCE*, p. 53.

[199]This is what L. Ligier suggests: *La confirmation* (Paris, 1973), pp. 151-2.

[200]Insisting on the expression "all the other heresies," A.P. Christophilopoulos maintains that only the members of the sects mentioned in the first part of the canon are dispensed from rebaptism. He refuses, therefore, all extensive application of economy by analogy: "Ἡ εἰς τὴν ὀρθοδοξίαν προσέλευσις τῶν ἀλλοθρήσκων καὶ ἑτεροδόξων," an article reproduced in the collection, *Δίκαιον καὶ ἱστορία* (Athens, 1973), pp. 206-23. This is one opinion which reflects a widespread position in the Orthodox Greek world.

[201]L. Villette, *Foi et sacrement* (Paris, 1959), pp. 106-38.

[202]Canons 7 and 8, *Syntagma* pp. 268-9.

[203]Ligier, pp. 129-135.

[204]Canons 1 and 47; cf. *supra* note 181.

[205]See the commentary of bishop Nicodemus on this canon, *Pravila*, I, pp. 116-7.

[206]See V.N. Beneševič, *Kanonicheskii sbornik XIV titulov* (St Petersburg, 1905), pp. 238-239.

[207]Canon 2, i.f., *Syntagma*, p. 144.

[208]*Oratio II contra Arianos*, §42, *PG* 26, col. 236-237.

[209]de Margerie, p. 146.

[210]This is why a law of Theodosius II considered the members of this sect to be deserters of Novatianism, *CT* XVI, VI, 6 (March 21, 413), p. 883. On Sabbatios, see Socrates, *Historia ecclesiastica* V, 21, *PG* 67, col. 621-625.

[211]Canons 1 and 47. In this last text of St. Basil, the expression "περὶ μὲν ἐκείνων κανὼν ἐξεφωνήθη εἰ καὶ διάφορος..." is rather difficult to interpret. *Syntagma*, p. 493. On the Novatians, see our commentary on canon 8 of Nicea.

[212]"Luchshmi," *Pravila*, I, p. 271. The word is simply omitted in the old translation of the *Kormchaya* edited by V.N. Beneševič, *Syntagma*, p. 100. Balsamon gives a fanciful explanation to this name, *Rhalles-Potles* II, p. 190.

[213]Eusebius, *Historia ecclesiastica* V, XXIII, XXV, *SC* 41, pp. 66-72. See M. Goguel, *L'Eglise primitive* (Paris, 1947), pp. 411-440.

[214]At the council of Ephesus, this affair was dealt with on July 23, 431, in relation with the symbol that had been accepted by those dissidents who wanted to be united to the Church, *ACO*, I, I, 7, pp. 95-106.

[214a]Neither the explanation of Balsamon, *Rhalles-Potles* II, p. 190, nor that of Leclercq, *Héfele-Leclercq*, II², p. 36, is convincing.

[215]*Haer.*, III, 4, *PG* 83, col. 406B.

[216]The expression "ποιοῦμεν αὐτοὺς χριστιανούς" was a normal expression in antiquity to designate the beginning stage of the process of joining the Church. On this subject, see *Pravila*, I, p. 284.

[217]According to St. Epiphanius, they baptized "in the name of the uncreated Father, the created Son, and the sanctifying Spirit created by the Son," *Haereses*, LXXVI, 6, *PG* 42, col. 637B. The one immersion practiced by these heretics is mentioned also by Didymus, *De Trinitate, liber secundus*, XV, *PG* 39, col. 720A. Canon 50 of the Holy Apostles declares that, "if a bishop or a priest does not do three immersions in one single initiation (τρία βαπτίσματα μίας μυήσεως), but only one single immersion given for the death of the Lord, let him be deposed...," *Syntagma*, p. 73.

[218]Eusebius, *Historia ecclesiastica* V, XIV and XVI-XIX, *SC* 41, pp. 45 and 46-60. See K. Land, *Kirchengeschichte Enfürte* (Gutersloh, 1960), pp. 105-149 and P. de Labriolle, *La crise montaniste* (Paris, 1913).

[219]*Haereses* XLVII, 1, *PG* 41, col. 856B.

[220]Epist. XLI, 3, *PL* 22, col. 475.

[221]Canon 1, *Syntagma*, p. 463. "...τίνα οὖν λόγον ἔχει τὸ τούτων βάπτισμα ἐγκριθῆναι... ."

[222]Canon 8, *Syntagma*, pp. 268-269.

[223]Text of the Synopsis with the commentary of Aristenus in *Rhalles-Potles* II, p. 191. All the printed editions of the *Kormchaya Kniga* contain the divisions into 8 canons in chapter 11, following the "Epitome canonum."

CHAPTER III

THE COUNCIL OF EPHESUS

SECTION 1: THE BACKGROUND AND PROCEEDINGS

The fourth century had been dominated in large part by the trinitarian controversy. The christological problem in itself (the relation between the humanity and divinity of Christ) had not really been touched on much before 352, when the heretical opinions of Apollinaris, bishop of Laodicea in Syria, began to be known. The reaction to this new error led theologians to think about the christological question. The opposition to Apollinarianism was particularly strong in the Antiochian milieu, where there was a proper desire to show the full integrity of the human nature of Christ; but then there was the risk of minimizing the perfect unity of the person of Christ by insisting too strongly on this point. As for the Alexandrians, they put the accent on this unity, underlining that the Word is the unique subject of the divine as well as of the human experiences of Christ. The contrast between these two theological approaches was complicated by a serious misunderstanding about the meaning of the word "nature" (φύσις). While the Alexandrians understood it to mean a concrete individual, a being existing in an independent manner, the Antiochians used it to designate either the divinity or the humanity seen together as a package of characteristics or attributes.[1] The violence of human passions and the rivalry of the great sees to gain the upper hand in the East gave to the christological controversies a considerable magnitude.

The conflict broke out shortly after Nestorius, a priest of Antioch known for his eloquence, was called by the court in Constantinople to succeed Bishop Sisinnius, who had just died. He was consecrated on April 4, 428. We know very little about his personality before he became a bishop unless we give credence to the legends which were later concocted by Monophysite writers; maybe he had been the student of Theodore of Mopsuestia.[2] Right after his installation, he

began a ferocious campaign against heretical sects. In this repressive
action, he sought and obtained support from the secular authorities.[3]
When the last advocates of Pelagianism were expelled from the West
and took refuge in Constantinople, Nestorius showed a certain indulgence toward them; still, he wrote to Pope Celestine on this question.
He took advantage of the occasion to expose to his Roman colleague
some of his own thoughts on christology, criticizing those who called
the Virgin Mary "Theotokos." He saw in this term the sign of a confusion between the divinity and the humanity of Christ. This first letter did not receive an answer, so he wrote a second one in the same
line of thought.[4] It was not answered either, at least not right away.
We must certainly see in this silence a mark of prudence rather than
of negligence on the part of the pope.[5] In Rome, the authorities tried
to find out as much as they could about Nestorius, especially when
they shortly began to hear echoes of the troubles he and his friends
were causing in all the East because of their publicly expressed opinions;[6] the commotion had even gotten as far as Egypt. Thus toward
the end of 423, Cyril of Alexandria made a very clear theological
statement to the monks under his authority, but without mentioning
the name Nestorius.[7] When Nestorius heard of the affair, he was
greatly irritated. Cyril answered that he had only been expressing traditional doctrine, and he wanted to warn Nestorius of the troublesome
rumors that were running wild in Egypt and at Rome about his teaching.[8] Nestorius briefly answered by complaining of what he judged to
be a most unbrotherly attitude.[9] At the beginning of 430, Cyril wrote
again to Nestorius;[10] this letter is extremely important for christology
since it was to be approved by the Council of Ephesus as an expression of the orthodox faith. Nestorius answered it by a direct attack on
the doctrinal positions of St. Cyril.[11] The rupture was complete. Cyril
tried in vain to obtain the support of Theodosius II and the imperial
family, but faced with this defeat, the bishop of Alexandria thought of
turning toward Rome. Thus, he wrote an extremely deferential letter
to Pope Celestine in which he asked what attitude should be adopted
toward Nestorius.[12] The relations which had formerly been very close
between Rome and Alexandria had gone into decline due to the proceedings against St. John Chrysostom carried on by Theophilus, the
uncle and predecessor of Cyril as bishop of Alexandria. When Cyril
became bishop in 412, he perpetuated the same cool relations with
Rome. We can safely assume that he did not accept the addition of St.
John Chrysostom's name to the diptychs of the church of Alexandria

until 420, if not later and perhaps under imperial pressure.[13] In any case, faced with Nestorius, the Rome-Alexandria axis was once again reforged. On behalf of Cyril, Deacon Poseidonius carried a whole dossier about Nestorius to Pope Celestine. Leo, archdeacon of Rome and future pope, asked John Cassian to give his considered opinion on the doctrine of the bishop of Constantinople. The conclusion of Cassian's investigation was clear: Nestorius' opinions were related to the heresy of Paul of Samosata and Pelagius.[14] The verdict of Rome was not long in coming. A synod presided over by Pope Celestine was held in August, 430, and condemned Nestorius, who was required to retract his opinions within ten days under pain of excommunication. Cyril was the one charged with executing this decision.[15] Even more, he received all the letters giving the sentence pronounced by the Roman synod.[16] He himself called together the bishops of his jurisdiction for a council in November, 430, and four of them were designated to go to Constantinople and to present the Roman demands. The bishop of Alexandria, going beyond the instructions of the pope, composed twelve anathemas in which christological doctrine was formulated according to the purest Alexandrian terminology; Cyril wanted to force Nestorius to subscribe even to his terminology.[17] This demand was not only to bring about a refusal on the part of Nestorius but also to affront many bishops especially in the diocese of the East; this is exactly what happened. In any case, at Nestorius' instigation, the emperor decided to call a general council to re-establish peace in the Church. A letter of Theodosius II to Cyril on this subject clearly shows that in the thinking of the emperor it was the bishop of Alexandria who was the accused in this affair.[18] On November 19, 430, the invitations were sent out. All the metropolitans with some of their suffragans were to come to Ephesus for Pentecost of the following year.[19] Although the bishops delegated by Cyril met Nestorius only on December 6, it is highly probable that the sentence of the Roman synod was already known in Constantinople,[20] but the imperial decision to convoke a general council clearly meant that the Roman sentence was not held to be irrevocable.

What was the reaction of Pope Celestine to this imperial invitation? He did not raise any objection; on the contrary, he congratulated Theodosius II for his zeal for the faith. The pope announced to him that he would send two bishops, Arcadius and Projectus, as his representatives as well as the priest Philip, but he would not retract the judgment already given. Nestorius must change his opinions or else the sentence recently pronounced against him would come into full effect.[21] In addition, the pope gave his delegates instructions to act in concert with Cyril and to go along with everything he decided.[22] As for the emperor, he considered that nothing had already been decided; it was up to the council to decide everything, in complete independence. To assure this liberty, he dispatched Count Candidian to Ephesus as commander of the guard; he was to maintain order in the meetings and to keep out any laymen and monks who might try to cause trouble.[23]

In comparison with what we know about the deliberations of the councils of Nicea and Constantinople, our knowledge of the happenings at Ephesus is incomparably better, but it is far from complete. The proceedings are set out in documents gathered together after the fact with clear apologetical intentions; they contain many blank spots, some of which are intentional.[24] The critical edition of the diverse collections of these documents has been the work of the celebrated philologist Edward Schwartz.[25]

The emperor had wished for a balanced representation of all regions among the bishops, but this was not the case. Cyril brought fifty or so bishops with him. He also had an imposing number of important clerics and monks at his side; among these was to be found the famous Shenoudi, abbot of the White Monastery of Atripius in the Thebaid. The Egyptians arrived in Ephesus some days before Pentecost. Nestorius was already there with his suite, especially Count Irenaeus.[26] On June 12, Juvenal of Jerusalem arrived with fifteen bishops from Palestine. The civil diocese of Asia was, if we leave out Africa, the area of the empire with the largest number of bishops, nearly 300. Without being able to say that the primatial authority of Ephesus was effective over the whole of the diocese, the prestige of this apostolic see was incontestable, and the increasing number of interventions by the bishops of Constantinople was greatly resented. Memnon of Ephesus, and with him the 100 bishops who were supposed to be at the council, were going to be extremely valuable allies of St. Cyril. The western contingent was numerically very weak, even if we include the bishops from the Illyricum who were under the jurisdiction of Rome while being the civil subjects of Theodosius II.[27] The see of Constantinople, with the support of the civil authority, had been trying for some time to extend its influence over this vast territory.[28] The African Church was only invited at the last moment and was disorganized anyway by the Vandal invasions. However, the African primate, Capreolus of Carthage, sent his deacon Bessula to be his representative.[29] St. Augustine was personally invited; the news of his death (August 28, 430) had not yet reached the East. There were, of course, the three Roman delegates who, like the Syrian bishops as we will see, arrived late.

It is to be noted that although Cyril and Nestorius were in Ephesus well before the opening of the council, they did not try to meet, each considering the other to be accused and just waiting for the conciliar condemnation. As for Memnon, he made his position quite clear by refusing to allow Nestorius and his adherents into the churches of the city.

The debates of the council did not begin until fifteen days after the date fixed for its opening. John of Antioch had let it be known that he and his bishops would be a bit late for the council, and he asked that the opening be put off for a little while. But Cyril, in agreement with Juvenal and Memnon, decided to speed things up. He wanted to take advantage of the situation, knowing that John and his bishops wanted to put him on trial for his anathemas. The absence of the Roman delegates was no problem for St. Cyril because he saw himself as having received a commission from Pope Celestine the preceding year, and so he signed the decisions of the council in his own name and that of the bishop of Rome also.[30] Was this juridically correct? It is doubtful, seeing that the pope had designated his own representatives; Cyril did not, however, fear being repudiated because the pope considered the sentence handed down in Rome to be fundamentally valid. In any case, neither the delegates after their arrival in Ephesus nor the pope himself later on disavowed St. Cyril.

Thus Cyril convoked the council for June 22; however, he made this decision only the day before. On the evening of June 21, Cyril received a protest from 68 bishops, numbering 21 metropolitans among them.[31] Whether it was too late to postpone the meeting or whether Cyril thought such an action untimely, the decision stood, and on Monday June, 22, nearly 160 bishops gathered in the cathedral of Ephesus, dedicated to Mary.[32] The proceedings began immediately despite the protest of Count Candidian, who decided to write to the emperor without delay informing him of what had happened. Who presided at the meetings of the council? It is not certain that there was one single president, but it appears that a group of bishops, Cyril, Memnon and Juvenal among them, took a decisive role.[33]

Here is how we can reconstruct the proceedings of the meeting on

June 22:[34] Nestorius was absent, since he did not consider the general convocation sent out by Cyril and his followers to be valid. He was sent a second invitation but without any result. Nestorius was summoned a third time, but, of course, it had no effect either. In the meantime, the fathers of the council began to examine the points in question and adopted Juvenal's proposition: contradictory doctrines should be judged by the criteria of the symbol of Nicea, which was then read. After that, Acacius of Melitene read the second letter of Cyril to Nestorius (καταφλυαροῦσι μέν). Cyril then asked that the council make a declaration on the content of this letter; it was probably approved unanimously. Palladius of Amasea asked that the answer of Nestorius be read, and it was declared contrary to the faith of Nicea. After these votes, the meeting went on for a long time. Many texts were read, notably the anathemas of St. Cyril. Theodotus of Ancyra and Acacius of Melitene were heard from; they called attention to some recent statements of Nestorius. A florilegium of patristic statements was read which had been composed by Cyril, as well as a collection of Nestorius' writings; then the letter of Capreolus of Carthage was also read. Flavian of Philippi asked that all this material be included in the dossier of the acts of the council, and finally the sentence was pronounced. After having verified the impious character of the doctrine professed by Nestorius, the fathers of the council declared the following:

> Necessarily being constrained by the canons and by the letter of our very holy father and concelebrant Celestine, bishop of the church of the Romans, with many tears we have made this following sad decision against him [Nestorius]: Therefore, He against whom he has blasphemed, our Lord Jesus Christ, has decreed by the present and very holy council that Nestorius be excluded from the episcopal dignity as well as the whole priestly college.[35]

We note the mention of the sentence already pronounced in Rome; however, the fathers of the council were not content to sanction it automatically. It was only after having conducted their own proper investigations, as they wrote to the emperor, that the fathers gathered in Ephesus decided the case against Nestorius.[36] In the acts of council, the decree is followed by 190 signatures, implying that some were added later on. In fact, 154 members of the council took part in this session, as well as the deacon Bessula.[37]

The sentence issued against Nestorius was made known to him by a rather graceless letter:

> The holy council, gathered together in the great city of the Ephesians by the grace of God, on the convocation of the very pious sovereigns and friends of Christ, to Nestorius, the new Judas: Be informed that, by reason of your impious preachings and of your disobedience to the canons, this present day, June 22, in conformity with church rules, you have been deposed by the holy council, and you are excluded from all rank in the Church.[38]

According to the report of the events immediately given by St. Cyril to the clergy and faithful of Alexandria, this conciliar decision was welcomed in Ephesus by great demonstrations of popular joy.[39]

The fathers of the Council of Ephesus did not promulgate a new dogmatic definition, but rather they solemnly declared that the second letter of Cyril to Nestorius was in conformity with the faith of Nicea; they also condemned Nestorius' answering letter. All this implied the belief of the Church in the personal unity of Christ. In addition, the custom of calling the Virgin Mary "Theotokos" was confirmed.[40]

At the end of this first meeting, many questions remained unanswered. Nestorius complained of the summary procedures used against him.[41] As for Count Candidian, the emperor's representative, he let it be known that he considered the meeting irregular and had so communicated his opinion to Theodosius.[42] The reaction of the emperor was not long in coming. On June 29, an imperial bull annulled everything that had been decided seven days before; in addition, all the bishops were to stay in Ephesus until a new imperial representative, Count John, arrived, who was to inquire into the events and prevent any new disorder.[43]

In the meantime, on June 26, John of Antioch and the Syrian bishops with him arrived in Ephesus. Count Ireneus, being a friend of Nestorius, went to John and his suite to inform them of what had happened. Thus having arrived in Ephesus, the Antiochians dismissed the representatives of Cyril on being officially informed of Nestorius' deposition; Cyril's representatives required the Antiochians to have no relations with the ex-bishop of Constantinople. Immediately, with the support of Count Candidian, John and his group held a meeting; it was attended by those bishops who had not wanted to go to Cyril's meeting of June 22. How many members were there in this counter-council? According to the acts of the council, which were produced by Cyril's men, there were 43; there were 53 according to the synodikon of Rusticus.[44] One motion was adopted that summed up the complaints of the opponents: Cyril and Memnon were held mainly responsible for the happenings of June 22, and they were deposed and excommunicated until they and their followers came back to their senses.[45] We note that John of Antioch and his followers held back from openly supporting Nestorius; they had for the most part not approved of his campaign against the term "Theotokos," but they considered the twelve anathemas of St. Cyril as tainted with Apollinarianism.

On July 9, the representatives of the Roman Church arrived. In conformity with the instructions of the pope, they contacted Cyril. The next day, a new meeting of the council was held in Bishop Memnon's residence. All who attended the first session were there. They read the letter of Celestine which the Roman delegates were carrying; the delegates then asked to hear the minutes of the June 22 meeting. The following day, July 11, the Romans expressed their agreement with what had been done before their arrival, and they ratified the deposition of Nestorius. One of the delegates of Rome took advantage of the occasion to exalt the authority of the pope as the successor of St. Peter.[46] Even though this intervention certainly did not reflect the thinking of the majority of the fathers of the council, it did not provoke any protests. Thus as E. Symonds observed: "It is not the custom of Eastern bishops, or perhaps of bishops in any part of the world, to protest against the claims of Rome, when Rome is on their side."[47] The support of the Roman delegates, who were supposed to represent the whole of the West, allowed the Cyrillian majority henceforth to consider the council as ecumenical,[48] while the council held by John of Antioch was called "a conventicle of apostasy" (τὸ τῆς ἀποστασίας συνέδριον).[49] On July 16, the council sent two summonses to John ordering him to appear, obviously without result; a third one on the following day had no more success. As a result, the council excommunicated John and his followers, but, perhaps due to the moderating influence of the Roman delegates, they were not deposed. A series of measures were adopted against all who held any shade of opinion similar to the errors of Nestorius and the Pelagian Celestius. We will speak about this later on in the analysis of the canons.[50]

A letter to Pope Celestine informed him of what had taken place at the council.[51] In fact, it gave a somewhat deformed image of reality; the importance of the number of bishops with John of Antioch was minimized, and it declared that several of them were irregular. The pope was informed that the council had confirmed the condemnation given by the see of Rome against the Pelagian leaders. There is no trace in the acts of the council of any examination of this problem, but it must be recalled that these acts are in no way integral minutes. Thus, there is no reason to put this assertion in doubt. It is nonetheless true, as several historians have noted, that the artifical linking of Nestorius, the followers of John of Antioch, and the Pelagians had an ulterior motive: the Cyrillians wanted to please Pope Celestine.[52] There is no mention in this letter of any anathemas which had been the dogmatic cause of the determined opposition of the Antiochians. There is no allusion either to the protests that brought about the premature opening of the council. A letter addressed to the emperor put great stress on the ecumenicity of the council.[53] A sixth session was held on July 22, and a profession of faith was read which had been denounced by Charisius, priest and treasurer of the church of Philadelphia in Lydia.[54] We will speak about this in our commentary on canon 7. On July 31, there was a debate on the election of the metropolitan of Cyprus.[55] We will also study this question in our commentary on canon 8.

The council brought up other questions also, but we do not know at just what time. There was a condemnation of the Messalians;[56] a decision on the bishops of the province of Europe confirmed the *status quo*;[57] a request presented by a former bishop of Pamphylia was also examined.[58] The letter sent by the Council of Ephesus to the synod of this province was put into the *Syntagma in XIV Titles,* and we will comment on it later on.

In the first days of August, a person of very high rank in Constantinople, John *comes sacrarum largitionum,* arrived in Ephesus.[59] He was the bearer of a letter from the emperor. Having drawn some conclusions, in his own fashion, from what the majority of the council had decided as well as from what the opposition has decided, Theodosius declared his approval of the deposition of Nestorius, Cyril and Memnon! He affirmed that it was necessary to stand by the faith of Nicea; John of Antioch and the bishops on his side interpreted this statement as a rebuff of Cyril's anathemas. Finally the leaders of the two rival assemblies were invited to return home.[60] The events that followed formally belong to the period after the council, but since in reality they constitute an extension of what happened at Ephesus, we must mention them briefly. Nestorius accepted to return to his monastery in Antioch and was replaced in Constantinople by an aged monk named Maximian. Cyril and Memnon were first held as prisoners in

Ephesus, but Cyril managed to escape and returned to Alexandria. Very soon, however, an imperial edict allowed him and Memnon to take up again their duties as bishops,[61] but this action did not resolve the basic problem. The schism continued between the majority of the episcopate and the minority composed especially, but not exclusively, of the bishops of the diocese of the East. Cyril went to great lengths to get back into the good graces of Constantinople. He gave rich gifts to those persons he considered to be influential.[62] The effect of such largesse was not long in making itself felt. During his detention in Ephesus, Cyril also sent a secret message to Dalmatius, a monk famous in Constantinople for his ascetic life; this monk had always been hostile to Nestorius and his teaching. Dalmatius organized a powerful demonstration in front of the imperial palace and even obtained an audience with Theodosius.[63]

The pope had expressed his joy at Nestorius' replacement by Maximian, but at the same time he hoped that relations could be reestablished with John of Antioch and his followers.[64] Celestine died in July, 432, and his successor, Sixtus III followed the same policy. From his side, Cyril was satisfied by the condemnation of Nestorius and wanted to restore relations with the bishops of the diocese of the East. The emperor was also greatly preoccupied by the question; thus he took decisive initiatives to bring about a reconciliation. He charged a civil servant by the name of Aristolaos to undertake the necessary steps. Finally, an accord was arrived at in the spring of 433: John of Antioch recognized the deposition of Nestorius and the condemnation of his doctrine. As for Cyril, he remained silent about his anathemas and accepted a formula probably composed by Theodoret of Cyrus. The word "Theotokos" was found in it but was explained in a manner that satisfied the theologians of Antioch. The word συνάφεια used to indicate the relation of the divinity and the humanity in Christ was put aside; the term ἕνωσις was used, and the doctrine of the communication of idioms was made explicit.[65] This important document, often called the Formula of Union, dissipated for a time the misunderstandings between the Antiochians and the Alexandrians; it was properly considered as an official dogmatic definition of the Church and thus the final act of the third ecumenical council.[66] Nestorianism was henceforth relentlessly pursued and harassed in the Roman-Byzantine empire. A law of August 8, 435, even prohibited the adherents of Nestorianism to call themselves Christians; they were also forbidden to hold meetings.[67] Banished from the empire, the Nestorian theologians took refuge in Persia, where they managed to have their doctrine accepted among the Christians of that country.[68] The fathers of the Council of Ephesus did not issue any canons bearing on general church discipline, but they did pass certain rulings required by the local circumstances of the times. In addition, they gave some answers to concrete cases and problems that were submitted to them. From this very diverse material, Byzantine canonists have drawn some texts that were inserted into the canonical collections toward the end of the sixth century.

The first six canons which are found in the eastern collections dating from after Chalcedon are extracts from the letter which the fathers sent around to make known their decisions at the July 17 session. They were approved at the time of the second session on July 31. After these six canons, we find the διαλαλία, that is, the resolution adopted by acclamation at the meeting of July 22; it states that there is to be no other symbol of faith except that of Nicea. Later on, this decree was counted as canon 7. When the council met on July 31, there was a vote on a motion (ψῆφος) about the bishops on Cyprus. It was later on numbered as canon 8 of the Council of Ephesus.

We add to these texts a letter of the Council of Ephesus to the synod of Pamphylia concerning bishop Eustathius. This insertion, posterior to the compilation of John the Scholastic, is found in the *Syntagma in XIV Titles* and in the *Synopsis* of Stephen of Ephesus. In the printed editions of the *Kormchaya Kniga,* the letter is considered as canon 9 of the council.[69] This numbering comes from the *Epitome canonum* of Symeon "Magister and Logothete."[70] The ancient eastern canonical collection with continuous numbering was used by the fathers of Chalcedon and did not contain the canons of Ephesus. Regardless of what E. Revillout thought, there is no reason to see in this omission a sign that the church of Constantinople refused to admit the canons of a council that had been marked by the triumph of its Alexandrian rival.[71] The ancient Latin canonical collections do not contain these canons either, and Dionysius Exiguus did not put them into his work at all. This omission in the collections of this era is simply explained by the fact that what were later on called by the name "canons of Ephesus" were only disciplinary decisions related to specific cases and did not have any necessary universal application. Nonetheless, these canons, especially the eighth as well as the letter to the synod of Pamphylia, present a certain interest which goes considerably beyond the limits of the concrete cases which motivated their promulgation. Undoubtedly, it is for this reason that they were later on introduced into all canonical collections.[72]

SECTION 2: THE CANONS OF THE COUNCIL

The canons of the 200 holy fathers gathered together in Ephesus after the 13th consulship of Flavius Theodosius and the 3rd of Flavius Valentinian, the august eternal ones, the 10th of the kalends of July.[73]

1

Since it was necessary that those who did not at all attend the holy council for a churchly reason or by reason of physical infirmity—whether they live in an urban or a rural area—should not be ignorant of what was decided concerning them, we hereby make known to your Holiness and Love that if the metropolitan of the province, being separated from the holy ecumenical council, joined the assembly of apostasy or joined it later on, or even if he only shared the opinions of Celestius, he can undertake no action against the bishops of the province, seeing that he has already been excluded from all churchly communion by the council, and thus is suspended. What is more, it is the responsibility of the bishops of the province and of the neighboring metropolitans who are of orthodox opinion to exclude him completely from the rank of bishop.

In order to fully understand the meaning of this canon, we must not lose sight of the fact that it is an excerpt from an encyclical letter; in its preamble, allusion is made to the counter-council presided over by John of Antioch and whose members were considered to be followers of Nestorius and Celestius and thus excommunicated.[74] The *Syntagma in XIV Titles* and the *Kormchaya Kniga,* in a slightly abridged form, give the preamble of the letter.[75] The preamble is not found in the *Synagoge* at all, and the text of the canon has consequently been altered somewhat: the expression "concerning them" (περὶ αὐτῶν) was omitted. We note also that the name of Celestius has been replaced by that of Nestorius. The mention of Celestius is found, however, in the original text of the letter, as the most ancient Greek recensions of the document prove; the Latin translation of Rusticus follows the Greek.[76] Because he had taken refuge in the East, Celestius was the best known of the Pelagians, and besides, Marius Mercator had drawn the attention of church circles in Constantinople to the heretical nature of the doctrine advocated by this western visitor. The encyclical letter suggests the possibility of a rapprochement between the opinions of Celestius and those of John of Antioch's followers, themselves already suspected of Nestorianism. This association, made with the intention of smearing the members of the counter-council, seems rather artificial. As Dom H. Leclercq has noted, "the two heresies had very little in common."[77]

According to the requirement of this canon, if a metropolitan had taken or was taking the side of the counter-council, by that very fact he was excommunicated and suspended; he thereby lost all his jurisdictional power over his suffragans. Concretely, this decision was no doubt made on the request of two bishops of the province of Europe in the diocese of Thrace, Euprepius and Cyril, who feared reprisals from their metropolitan Phritilas of Heraclea, a follower of John of Antioch.[78] The canon even went farther: it required the bishops who were in this situation to agree with the orthodox metropolitans of the area (τοῖς πέρι μητροπολίτας) and to proceed to the deposition of their dissident metropolitan. The participation of the surrounding metropolitans in the process of deposition and election signifies, according to Nicodemus Milash, that the church tribunal the fathers had in mind was the council of the diocese (ἡ σύνοδος τῆς διοικήσεως).[79] This interpretation is possible, but the wording of the canon does not allow us to be absolutely sure, at least in our opinion.

2

If certain bishops of a province have abandoned the holy council and have gone over to apostasy, or were trying to find ways of getting around the council, or after having signed Nestorius' deposition, later on turned to the assembly of apostasy, those bishops, following the judgment of the holy council, are completely separated from the priesthood and deprived of their rank.

The preceding canon envisioned the case of dissident metropolitans which put the problem of jurisdictional power on the shoulders of their suffragans. Here it is a question of simple bishops (ἐπαρχιῶται ἐπίσκοποι).[80] It is implicitly supposed that their metropolitans have remaind faithful to orthodoxy. There is, therefore, no indication what procedure ought to be followed for their deposition since, at this time, that procedure had been well established in the canonical tradition. It is true that the wording of the canon seems to suppose a deposition *latae sententiae*: ἀλλοτρίον εἶναι τῆς ἱερωσύνης καὶ τοῦ βαθμοῦ ἐκπίπτοντα,[81] but this is totally unthinkable. What the fathers of Ephesus wanted to say was that the offense in question had to be punished in this way. It belonged to the competent judicial organ, the provincial synod in this case, to begin the trial and pronounce the sentence.

3

If, in any city or rural area, certain clerics have been restrained from exercizing their priesthood by Nestorius and his followers because of the rectitude of their opinions, we have deemed it right and proper that they be reintegrated into their rank. As a general rule, we ordain that the clerics who are in agreement with the orthodox and ecumenical council should in no way be submissive to bishops who have gone over to apostasy or will do so.

Such is the text that we find in the *Syntagma in XIV Titles;* it corresponds very closely to the recension of the *Collectio Vaticana* of the conciliar acts. The Latin version of Rusticus' *Synodikon (Collectio Casinensis)* is nearly a literal translation.[82] In the *Synagoge,* the wording of the canon is substantially the same: the text differs on some points from the concordant recensions mentioned above, but it is basically simply more wordy.[83]

The canon contains two parts. First of all, it rehabilitates and reintegrates into their former functions those clerics that Nestorius and sympathetic bishops had deposed because these clerics refused to go along with their erroneous christology. The second part is in the logical flow of the two preceding canons. Dissident hierarchs lost their jurisdictional power: consequently, those who found themselves under the authority of such bishops were freed from obedience to them. This ruling was issued so as to respond to very precise historical circumstances, but it has a great value for jurisprudence because it is an application to a particular case of a universal norm of canon law. It is no doubt because of this line of thinking that the second half of the canon was expanded by John the Scholastic or by the author of the recension he used. Here is the text:

As a general rule, we ordain that the clerics who are in

agreement with or about to submit to the ecumenical and orthodox council, now or later on, should never and in no way be submissive to bishops who have gone over to apostasy or who will go over or to those who transgress the holy canons and the orthodox faith.

4

If any clerics should apostasize and, in private or in public, dare to take the side of Nestorius' or Celestius' ideas, the holy council has thought it good and proper that they be deposed.

Here again, we find some textual differences between the *Synagoge* and the *Syntagma in XIV Titles;* we leave aside, however, the purely grammatical differences in order to take up those affecting the meaning. The *Synagoge* eliminates the mention of Celestius here as elsewhere, probably because the memory of this western heretic did not last long in the mind of eastern Christianity.[84]

Here is the end of the canon in the *Synagoge:* ...καὶ τούτους εἶναι καθηρημένους ὑπό τῆς ἁγίας συνόδου. This is the Greek reading that is assumed by Rusticus' translation: ...*et hos a sancta synodo esse depositos,*[85] but we cannot consider it to be the best because the recension of the *Syntagma* corresponds exactly to that of the *Collectio Vaticana.*[86]

After having regulated the cases of metropolitans and simple bishops accused of sharing the heretical opinions of Nestorius and Celestius, the fathers of the council made a ruling against other members of the clergy (priests, deacons and lower ministers) who held heretical ideas: they should also be deposed. The translation of the *Kniga Pravil* seems to assume that the term "cleric" applies only to those who have received holy orders. Here is its reading: "...pravednym priznal sviatyĭ sobor izverzhennym byti i sim iz sviashchennago china";[87] this translation, however, is not exactly correct.

5

Those who have been condemned by the holy council or by their own bishops for culpable actions and those whom Nestorius (contradicting the canons with the indifference that characterizes him) or his followers sought out or may seek out to return to communion or to their rank, we have judged that these persons should in no way profit from these actions and should remain deposed.

In the text of the *Collectio Vaticana* and in the *Recensio Trullana* of the *Syntagma in XIV Titles* found in the Codex of Patmos 172, we

read ὑπὸ τῆς Ἁγίας Συνόδου.[88] In this case, we are obviously dealing
with the Council of Ephesus itself; this is how Rusticus understood it
as well, and his tranlation reads like this: *...ab hoc sancto conventu.*[89]
But the article τῆς is omitted in the *Synagoge* and the *Syntagma in
XIV Titles* as well as in the recension of the conciliar acts found in the
Collectio Seguieriana.[90] If we adopt this second reading, the meaning
of the canon is greatly extended: it deals then with a sanction made by
any legitimate synod. However, the presence of the adjective ἁγία, universally attested to in the manuscript tradition, makes us lean toward
the first reading.

The *Recensio Tarasiana* reads ἀκοινωνήτως in the place of ἀκα-
νονίστως; this copyist's error was spread throughout all the old Slavonic versions of the *Kormchaya Kniga,* where we find the word "bezpriobshchenie".[91] On the other hand, the *Kniga Pravil,* based on the
correct Greek text, reads, *vopreki pravilam.*[92]

The fathers of the Council of Ephesus accused Nestorius of ἀδια-
φορία, which literally means "indifference." We should understand this
term to mean, however, a lack of discernment, as the Latin translation
of Rusticus suggests; there we find the word *indiscretio.*[93] This is also
the interpretation that Zonaras gives to the word.[94] We do not know
what were the concrete cases the fathers of the council had in mind
when they issued this canon; the present state of our historical information is too incomplete to give an answer to this question.

6

**Similarly, if, in whatever manner, anyone should want to
set aside what was done in each case at the holy council of
Ephesus, the holy council has decided that, if they are
bishops or clerics, they should be completely deposed from
their rank, and, if they are laymen, they should be excommunicated.**

The *epistula tractoria* of the Council of Ephesus ends with this canon,
which is a kind of conclusion to the whole corpus. The text of the
Synagoge indicates that this text is a canon of the Council of Ephesus
before quoting it; no doubt, this is why the expression τῇ ἐν Ἐφέσῳ in
the text itself of this canon is omitted. This wording is, however, well
attested to in the other recensions.[95]

We have translated περὶ ἑκάστου by "in each case," that is, according to all the decisions made by the council. From the genitive ending,
we cannot know whether it is a masculine or a neuter noun; the same

question exists for the ablative plural in the Latin version of Rusticus: *de singulis.*[96] This difficulty, though, does not affect the meaning of this ruling in any significant way; if we consider it to be neuter, at most, the scope of the canon becomes more general.

A resolution adopted by the same holy council after having read the statement of the 318 holy fathers of Nicea and of the impious symbol altered by Theodore of Mopsuestia and presented by Charisius, priest of Philadelphia, to this same holy council of Ephesus.

7

Therefore, after their reading of these things, the holy council decreed that no one is permitted to produce, to edit, or to compose another faith than that set out by the holy fathers gathered in Nicea with the Holy Spirit.

As for those who would dare to compose another faith, present it, or propose it to those who might want to be converted to the knowledge of the truth (whether coming from Hellenism, Judaism, or from any other heresy) these persons, if they are bishops or clerics, will be set aside; the bishops separated from the episcopate and the clerics from the clergy; if they are laymen, they are to be excommunicated. In the same way, if any bishops, clerics or laymen are found to admit or to teach the doctrines contained in the statement presented by the priest Charisius on the subject of the incarnation of the only-begotten Son of God, or, what is more, to admit or to teach the impious and perverse dogmas of Nestorius which are joined to the statement, let them fall under the sentence of this holy and ecumenical council: that is, a bishop should be separated from his episcopate and deposed, a cleric equally deposed from the clergy, and a layman excommunicated, as was said above.

In order to understand this decree correctly, we must first of all be conscious of its historical context. The text was adopted on July 22, during the session held at the residence of Bishop Memnon of Ephesus. The official minutes of this sixth session do not give us a complete account of what happened that day; they were written up sometime afterwards, and they contain additions and omissions.[97] Here are the documents that are found in the acts concerning this session: (1) a list of those present which is a reproduction of the list of the inaugural meeting with the names of the Roman representatives added; (2) the symbol of Nicea read by the notary Peter; (3) the same patristic florilegium which had been read on June 22, with some additions; (4) the statement of Charisius; (5) the conciliar decision, that is, our canon; (6) the same florilegium of Nestorius' writings read at the first session; and (7) a list of the signatories.

This meeting was brought about when the priest Charisius, steward of the church of Philadelphia, wanted to submit a question to the council for its judgment. Two priests of Constantinople, Anastasius and Photius, gave letters of recommendation for the bishops of Lydia to two of their fellow priests, Anthony and James. James went to Philadelphia where he converted a certain number of Quartodecimans and Novatianists. This mission was set in the context of Nestorius' anti-heretical campaign which he started at the beginning of his epis-copate.[98] As these dissidents came over to the Church, they were required to sign a formal renunciation of their former heretical beliefs; they were then given a symbol of faith, but the text they received expressed an Antiochian christology, that is, the relation between the divinity and humanity of Christ was expressed by the word συνάφεια.[99] Because Charisius voiced his disapproval, he was excommunicated; this is understandable when we realize that bishop Theophanes of Philadelphia was in favor of the Antiochian position and that at Ephesus, he was in the anti-Cyrillian group.[100]

Who was the author of the tainted symbol? The preamble of the conciliar decree in the *Syntagma in XIV Titles* indicates that Theodore of Mopsuestia wrote it.[101] According to St. Cyril, we know that Theo-dore's name was mentioned on this occasion.[102] It is true that in the acts of the council there is no mention of his name, but this is because Cyril had it taken out when later official minutes were written up; he did not want to give new life to the controversy with the Antiochians. Marius Mercator did not doubt at all that Theodore was, in fact, its author,[103] and we can therefore say that such an attribution is highly likely.

Because of the action taken against him by his bishop, Charisius appeared to be a victim of the Nestorians, and he asked the council for justice. To demonstrate his orthodoxy, he gave his profession of faith to the council in the form of a creed very close to the wording of Nicea but a little different in form.[104] Then, the council adopted a resolution (διαλαλία) by acclamation which was later on inserted in the canonical collections.[105]

The *Synagoge* gives only the text of the decree itself,[106] while the *Syntagma in XIV Titles* contains a preamble, as we have already noted. In the *Pedalion* as well as in the work of Rhalles and Potles, this preamble is not found, but the introductory formula is there under the form of a genitive absolute: τούτων ἀναγνωσθέντων.[107] This anomaly spread throughout the translation of the *Kniga Pravil,* where we find this wording: *Po prochtenii sego.*[108]

The text of the decree contains no significant variants in the manuscript tradition; we note only that the *Recensio Tarasiana* of the *Syntagma* and consequently the Old Slavonic version omit the expression "as was said above."[109]

How are we to understand the expression "...the impious and perverse dogmas of Nestorius which are joined to the statement...(ἅ καὶ ὑποτέτακται)"? At this same meeting, excerpts from Nestorius' works were read; these were added to the dossier. We find them in the acts of the council right after the text of the decree.[110] Thus, we have the explanation of this expression.

This canon has been the cause of many controversies in subsequent centuries. It has been widely used for questionable polemical purposes because people have not sufficiently taken into account its historical context and therefore what the fathers had in mind when they issued the ruling. The text contains two parts: the first consists of a general prohibition against substituting another creed for the faith of Nicea, that is, for the dogmatic definition of the first ecumenical council. The second part is a condemnation of those who might profess the doctrine contained in the heretical symbol which the fathers of Ephesus learned about through Charisius; this condemnation was extended to those who maintained similar christological errors. This second part of the canon is not really problematic; such is not the case for the first part, however. Did the fathers of the third ecumenical council want to close the door forever to all development in the formulation of dogmas, indeed to all doctrinal investigation which might go beyond the definition of Nicea? This interpretation was that of Dioscorus, who based himself on this decree when he asked the robber council of Ephesus in 449 to condemn Flavian of Constantinople and Eusebius of Doryleum, whom he judged to be guilty not even of having composed a new symbol of faith but only of having raised new theological questions.[111] The Monophysites also used this argument against the definition of Chalcedon, although the fathers of that council, anticipating the objections, refuted the complaint in advance.[112]

If we again place the decree of Ephesus in the context of the affair brought up at the sixth session, we can reasonably doubt that its

authors wanted to give it such a wide range. Their goal was to stop
the composition and diffusion in the Church of symbols of faith that
contained errors, such as the one attributed to Theodore of Mopsuestia or simply like the one of Charisius; the objectionable part in these
rewrites was that they took unacceptable liberties with the Nicean text.
That the fathers of Ephesus did not want to forbid completely the
composition of other dogmatic formulas, if that seemed necessary, is
clearly brought out by the declaration of St. Cyril about the Formula
of Union of 433. In a letter to Acacius of Melitene, he wrote the
following:

> The holy council held in Ephesus took the measure of pro-
> hibiting the introduction into the churches of God of any
> other statement of faith than that which exists: the one which
> the thrice-blessed holy fathers defined as they spoke in the
> Holy Spirit. But the bishops of the diocese of the East
> who—I do not know how—maintained an equivocal atti-
> tude toward the definition of Nicea and attracted to them-
> selves the suspicion of not thinking properly and of being in
> contradiction with the doctrines of the gospel and the apos-
> tles, could those bishops quiet these infamous rumors by
> keeping silent? Rather, was it not necessary that they justify
> themselves by letting everyone know their real thoughts? Did
> not the illustrious disciple of Christ write the following: "Be
> always ready to give a reasoned defense of your hope to
> anyone who asks you questions?"[113] Whoever follows this
> advice does not act like an innovator, he does not invent a
> new statement of faith, but he only shows to those who ques-
> tion him what faith he has concerning Christ.[114]

The fathers of Chalcedon in their dogmatic decree quoted not only
the symbol of Nicea but also that of Constantinople, which thus made
its official entrance onto the historical scene.[115] At the end of the
decree, they essentially summarized the wording of the prohibition set
out by the Council of Ephesus, without any express reference, however, to Nicea.[116] The same formula was taken up with slight modifications in the dogmatic decree of the sixth ecumenical council.[117]

The Council of Constantinople in 879-80 did the same thing, but its
more precise formulation of the dogmatic decree was aimed at the
addition of the *filioque* clause, though without mentioning it specifically.[118] The legates of Pope John VIII made no objection since the
Roman Church, in contrast to the rest of the West, continued to keep
the symbol of faith in its unaltered form.[119]

The commentaries of Aristenus, Zonaras, and Balsamon on canon 7 of Ephesus present nothing really outstanding; they establish no link with the contested addition of the *filioque*.[120] In contrast, however, at Ferrara in 1438, the canon of Ephesus was invoked by the Greeks to demonstrate the illegal nature of the addition of the *filioque*. Mark of Ephesus maintained that the prohibition in this canon applied to the symbol of Constantinople, as its content was implicitly expressed in the creed of Nicea.[121] We can certainly deplore the addition introduced into the creed in the West, but it is materially impossible to base this condemnation on canon 7 of Ephesus, which did not directly envision some addition but rather the composition of another formula of faith (ἑτέραν πίστιν) and furthermore concerned the definition of Nicea.

In summary, taking into account the circumstances of the redaction of this decree, we feel that the fathers of Ephesus wanted to prohibit to all individuals (bishops, clerics or laymen) the introduction of individually written formulas of faith. Nothing allows us to think that they wanted to prohibit competent organs of the Church from publishing, if it was felt necessary, new symbols and dogmatic decrees; this is effectively what happened in later history.

A vote of the Holy Council taken following the presentation of a petition to it by the bishops of Cyprus.

8

An innovation contrary to church institutions and the canons of the holy fathers as well as an attack on the liberty of all has been reported to us by Rheginus, the very religious fellow bishop, and by those who were with him, the very reverend bishops of the province of the Cypriots, Zeno and Evagrius. Sicknesses that affect everyone need urgent remedies, all the more so because they can cause such great suffering: therefore, if no ancient custom exists according to which the bishop of the city of the Antiochians performed the ordinations in Cyprus (we have learned by written and verbal reports that this is so), the very reverend men who have had recourse to the holy council, the heads of the holy churches in Cyprus, without being bothered or exposed to violence, will proceed, according to the canons of the holy fathers and ancient usage, to the ordinations of their own very reverend bishops.

The same thing will also be observed in the other dioceses

and everywhere in the provinces, so that none of the bishops beloved of God shall take over another province that, in former times and from the beginning, has not been under his authority or that of his predecessors; and if anyone has thus taken over any province and by force has placed it under his authority, let him give it back so that the canons of the fathers may not be transgressed and so that, under the pretext of holy acts, the pride of worldly power enters and that without our knowing it we may lose little by little the liberty that has been given to us by the blood of our Lord Jesus Christ, the liberator of all men. It has therefore seemed good and proper to the holy ecumenical council that the rights acquired from the beginning and established according to ancient usage from time immemorial be safeguarded intact and inviolate for each province. Each metropolitan has the leisure to take a copy of the acts as a guarantee for himself.

If anyone produces an ordinance contrary to what has now been defined, the holy ecumenical council with one voice declares it to be null.

The primitive redaction of the *Synagoge* only contained seven canons of Ephesus: the six texts from the encyclical letter of the council plus the one about Cyprus. The decree on the definitive character of the faith of Nicea was added some time later, as we have noted above. This resolution was adopted by a vote in good and proper form (ψῆφος) at the end of a discussion that took place during the council's last session. The date indicated in the acts is August 31,[122] but for a long time most scholars have proposed a correction, that is, advancing this session to July 31; in fact, it is impossible that the fathers of the council could still have gathered together after the arrival of Count John at the beginning of August.[123]

The acts tell about the petition presented to the council by the metropolitan of Constantia, Rheginus, and two of his suffragans, the bishops of Kurion and Soli; their goal was to stop the church of Antioch from trying to intervene in the affairs of Cyprus. The acts tell us about the discussion on this petition of the Cypriot bishops and the decision which was made.[124] The text of this decision is what was inserted into the canonical collections.

This question shows that a climate of great tension existed between the Cypriot episcopate and the church of Antioch, which had just come out of a period of relative eclipse as a result of internal divisions.[125] Throughout the civil diocese of the East, the bishops of Antioch tried to put into practical effect the right to control the elections of metropolitans. We have here an application of the principle of accommodating church districts to those of the state; at the time, Cyprus was part of the diocese of the East. The bishops of Antioch also based their claims on canon 6 of Nicea because they then understood this ruling as relating to supra-metropolitan jurisdictions; it originally had a completely different meaning, however.[126] For Alexander of Antioch (408-18), the *de facto* independence of the Cypriot episcopate was only a sequel to the disturbances of the Arian crisis, and he saw the (re)establishment of his authority over the island as a simple return to the *status quo ante.* Alexander had hoped to have his point of view approved by Pope Innocent (402-17), and with a certain prudence, the pope did support Antioch's cause.[127] The successor of Alexander, Theodotus (418-27), supported by his clergy, brought strong pressure to bear on Troilus of Constantia to accept Antiochian hegemony on the island, but in vain. On the eve of the Council of Ephesus, John of Antioch wanted at any price to prevent the bishops of Cyprus from filling their metropolitan see. To that end, he persuaded a highly placed person in the army to intervene officially: Dionysius, *magister utriusque militiae.*

Why did John call on a military leader and not on any civilian officials, in this case, the prefect of the Pretorian guard or the count of the East? Such a recourse would have been more normal. No doubt, as A.H.M. Jones suggests, the reason was that the prefect lived in Constantinople, and John had absolutely no influence over him at all; as for the count, he either did not dare to take such an initiative on his own, or he was not on good terms with the bishop of Antioch.[128] In any case Dionysius did not seem to be troubled by the fact that the governor of Cyprus, *vir clarissimus consularis,* was a civil functionary and not under his authority at all; he sent the governor a written order (*praeceptum,* πρόσταγμα), dated May 21, 431, which ordered him to oppose the election of a metropolitan.[129] Another written order was addressed to the clergy of Constantia asking them not to choose a candidate for the vacant see.[130] In reality, Dionysius did not deal with the fundamental question; he merely wanted to postpone the election until the forthcoming general council could make a decision. But the Cypriot bishops and the clergy of Constantia were not intimidated at all; Rheginus was elected metropolitan. He went to Ephesus with two of his suffragans, and they presented a memorandum to the council hoping it would make a declaration on the legitimacy of the autocephaly of Cyprus. In this document, they maintained that the interference of Antioch went "against the apostolic rulings and the decrees of the very holy council of Nicea."[131] Assuredly, the petition of the Cypriots was presented in a very favorable context: John of Antioch and the eastern bishops with him were, for the moment, considered to be schismatics by the Cyrillian majority. In addition, Rheginus presented himself as a determined opponent of Nestorius.[132] But, on the other side, it was a very delicate matter for the fathers of the council to decide this question without hearing the arguments of John of Antioch.

Thus, without refusing to study the affair, they proceeded with circumspection. After having heard the declaration of the Cypriot bishops and received two letters from the *magister utriusque militiae,* they asked for more explanations. Zeno of Kurion affirmed that Dionysius had acted at the instigation of John of Antioch and his clergy; this is by no means doubtful. Evagrius of Soli declared that John of Antioch wanted to subjugate the island by claiming the right to ordain bishops, contrary to the canons and long standing custom. The council took great pains to make sure that the Church of Antioch had never intervened in the ordinations of Cyprus. In passing we note that in all this debate the word *cheirotonia* referred to the election as well as the ordination of a bishop; this is in line with the ancient Greek meaning as used in the Church. Zeno emphatically maintained that from apostolic times the bishops of Antioch had never been involved in the ordinations in Cyprus. But the fathers of the council insisted on recalling the existence of the prerogatives of Antioch according to canon 6 of Nicea. Zeno made a new denial to the effect that episcopal elections in Cyprus had always been carried out by the synod of the province. The fathers of the council wanted to know specifically who had elected Troilus and his two predecessors, Sabinus and Epiphanius: Zeno affirmed that they had been elected by the synod of the province. After these inquiries, the vote was taken. It is certain that if John of Antioch had been able to give an opposing point of view, he would have taken up the position expressed sometime before in a letter of Alexander to Pope Innocent, but where is the truth? It is not easy to give a categorical answer. Moreover, as the official text of the council shows, a slight doubt lingered in the minds of the council members.

The Christianization of Cyprus goes back to the apostolic age.[133] From that time on, can it be shown that there was any dependence on the see of Antioch? Perhaps John, the bishop of that great city, would have furnished irrefutable proofs of such a dependence; the witness of Nicephorus Callistus is, however, much too late to be given any credence.[134] It is more probable that, since it was protected by its isolation, Cyprus was able to escape from being absorbed into a greater church entity that was modeling itself on the civil diocese of the East during the fourth century. The hierarchical organization on the island even during the following century managed to retain archaic features. We learn about this from Sozomen: there were bishops not only in the cities but also in the villages.[135] This went against the general trend in the East, which had been approved by canonical legislation.[136] We have here a sign of the Cypriot tendency to be different.

The bishops of Cyprus were thinking of Nicea's canon 4 when they spoke of the rulings established by this council; the fathers of Ephesus made allusion to canon 6 when they presented it as a possible objection. This canon 6, however, only indicates the exceptions to the general rule formulated in canon 4; it only incidentally makes reference to the rights of Antioch and does not specify the geographical extent of this see's jurisdiction. Again, in its original wording and with the three exceptions aside, the canon recalls the prerogatives of the metropolitan churches.[137]

Let us come back to the text itself of canon 8 of Ephesus. The preamble is the one found in the *Syntagma in XIV Titles.* We have retained the reading ἐκ προσελεύσεως given by two of the most ancient manuscripts, the *Codex Vallicellianus F. 10* and the *Codex Patmensis 173.*[138] This is a technical expression referring in juridical language to a petition or a request.[139]

The text of the canon itself, such as we find it in the critical edition of the *Syntagma in XIV Titles* differs only in insignificant details from that of the *Collectio Atheniensis.*[140] In contrast, that of the *Synagoge* departs on several points from this consensus without, however, altering the meaning of the canon. In only one place is it ambiguous: while the other recensions say that each metropolitan has the leisure to take a copy of the acts (a reading which is moreover confirmed by the Latin translation of the *Collectio Winteriana*[141]), that of the *Synagoge* speaks of the metropolitan in a less clear fashion.[142] The standard text of the canon is very close to the *Syntagma in XIV Titles* in its critical edition;[143] the same thing goes for the Russo-Slavonic translations of the *Kniga Pravil.*[144] The only difference is at the beginning of the canon: instead of "holy fathers," it reads "holy apostles." This variant, completely absent from the ancient manuscript tradition, comes from a codex of Trebizond dated 1131.

The canon is made up of two parts. In the first part, the council recognized the autocephaly of Cyprus. However, this recognition was conditional and only effective if there had never existed any ancient custom (ἦθος ἀρχαῖον) by which the bishops of Antioch controlled the ordinations on the island. This restrictive formulation shows that the somewhat categorical declarations of the Cypriots had not removed all the doubts among the members of the council. The second part has a general scope. It requires that the autocephaly of the metropolitan districts be maintained everywhere, except where a different usage was in effect for a long time. They were recalling the legislation of Nicea. We must note that this ruling went against the current of concentration, then very strong, and which was to produce the constitutions of the patriarchates. By nullifying in advance any ruling against their own decision, the fathers of Ephesus were certainly thinking of an eventual imperial edict.

The attempt by a metropolitan illegally to establish his authority over another province constituted in the eyes of the members of the council an act which "shows the pride of worldy power" (ἐξουσίας τύφος κοσμικῆς). This formula greatly resembles the one we find in the letter that the Council of Carthage sent to Pope Celestine, 425-6. The African bishops asked the pope not to let the "heady pride of the world" (*fumosum tyfum saeculi*) be introduced into the Church of Christ.[145] This similarity is all the more striking because it is highly unlikely that the fathers of Ephesus knew the text, indeed of the existence of the letter of the African bishops; the papal representatives, of course, most likely knew about it, but they were not very likely to speak of a document that spoke unflatteringly about the Roman see. In the two cases, the meddling of one church in the affairs of another was felt to be foreign to the Christian spirit.

Stephen of Ephesus, in his *Synopsis*, retained but only summarized the second half of the canon in a very general way;[146] thus, since the *Kormchaya* is directly dependent on Stephen's work, it also has a summarized version of the canon.[147]

The Council of Ephesus prudently decided that Cyprus would in the future enjoy the status that it had formerly; in other words, it was to enjoy its independence as an established fact if it were established that

Cyprus had never been formerly under the authority of Antioch in the election of its bishops. About 50 years later, in 488 or so, the Monophysite patriarch of Antioch, Peter the Fuller, profiting from the support of the emperor Zeno, wanted to include Cyprus in his jurisdictional sphere. He based his claims on the fact that the island had received Christianity from Antioch. But then the discovery of the relics of St. Barnabas by Anthemius of Constantia put an end to the claims of Peter; since the church in Cyprus was of apostolic origin, its right to autocephaly was considered well founded by everyone. Such was the opinion of the emperor Zeno who, it is said, gave high honors to the head of the Cypriot church.[148] From then on, there were no other attempts by the patriarchs of Antioch to take over the direction of Cyprus. However, under the reign of Justinian (527-65), the island ceased to be part of the civil diocese of the East; it was incorporated with Scythia, Lower Moesia, Casia, the Cyclades and Rhodes in a new administrative unity having Odessus, presently Varna, as its capital.[149] During the first half of his reign, the emperor Justinian II transplanted the majority of the Cypriots to the Hellespont; he had the Synod in Trullo (691) adopt a decision which provided for the head of the church of Cyprus to live in the new city of Justiniana. This hierarch was to have precedence over all the bishops of the province of the Hellespont, including the metropolitan of Cyzicus.[150] By this temporary measure, the prerogatives (προνόμια) of the see of Constantia were preserved despite its transfer to New Justiniana; the principle of one church jurisdiction on a fixed territory was not undermined either. This situation only lasted seven years, since in 698 the emperor Tiberius III allowed the Cypriots to go back to their island.[151]

At the Synod in Trullo, Bishop John of New Justiniana appeared on the list of signatories right after George of Antioch,[152] but a century later, at the seventh ecumenical council, 787, the signature of Constantine of Constantia appeared after that of the metropolitan of Ephesus.[153] This makes us think that there was an eclipse, *de facto* if not *de jure*, of the Cypriot autocephaly. This situation continued for an undetermined period; it came to an end, however, in the tenth century because a *Notitia episcopatuum* of the reign of Emperor John Tsimiskes (969-76) put the archbishops of Bulgaria and Cyprus ahead of the metropolitans of the patriarchate of Constantinople.[154] The church of the island did not totally escape, however, from the guiding hand of Constantinople. Thus, for example, patriarch Luke Chrysoberges (1157-69/70) and his synod annulled the deposition of a bishop of

Cyprus who had been unjustly set aside.[155] Despite the ups and downs of history, the church of Cyprus has preserved its autocephaly even up to the present time.

Letter of the same Holy Council of Ephesus to the Reverend Synod of Pamphylia concerning Eustathius who had been their metropolitan.

The divinely inspired scriptures say: "Do everything with reflection"; this is all the more true for those who have received the priesthood. They must rigorously manifest discernment in all they do, for those who want to conduct themselves this way will be full of hope and will be carried by a favorable wind in the desired direction. Even though this saying is very true, sometimes a bitter and unbearable affliction is visited on a person, troubling him terribly, derailing him from the path of duty and leading him to consider what by nature is contrary to the law, thinking it advantageous. We have observed something of this kind in the case of the very pious and religious bishop Eustathius. It has, in fact, been verified that he received a regular ordination but, as he says, he was troubled by certain persons and found himself faced with unforeseen circumstances. Then later on, because of too much inertia, he refused to face the troubles which assailed him, even when he was able to turn aside the slanderings of those who were fighting against him. He thus submitted his written resignation—we do not know how. What he should have done rather, once having assumed the weight of the priesthood, was to keep it with spiritual vigor, prepare himself for the labors, and willingly endure the sweat that merits its reward. Since he showed himself, in this case, negligent rather by inertia than by laziness or indolence, your Piety was constrained to ordain our very pious and religious brother and bishop Theodore to take care of the church, for it was not normal that the church should remain widowed or that the sheep of the Lord should remain without someone to guide them. Since Eustathius came in tears not demanding of the above-mentioned very religious bishop Theodore either the city or the church but only the dignity and the title of bishop, we have all felt compassion toward this old man and, having shared his tears, we took pains to find out if the above-mentioned had been legitimately deposed, that is, if he had been found guilty of any wrongdoings which those babbling at his expense were accusing him of; we have truly learned that he committed nothing of the kind, but rather people held his resignation against him. Consequently, we do not blame your Piety for having duly ordained the above-mentioned very pious Bishop Theodore. It was not proper to be too accusatory in regard to the inertia of the old man; it was necessary rather to have pity on him for he thus found himself far from his home city and ancestral dwelling. We, therefore, have deemed it right and proper, and we decree that without any questioning, he should enjoy the name, honor and communion of the episcopate without, however, performing any ordinations or taking over a church and officiating in it at his own will. Let him celebrate only if a brother and bishop invites him or allows him according to his disposition and love in Christ. Moreover, in case you would like to show yet more kindness to him, now or later, that would also equally please the council.

The text of this letter such as we find it in the *Syntagma in XIV Titles* is the same as in the *Collectio Atheniensis* of the acts of the Council of Ephesus.[156] However the compiler of the *Syntagma* did not think it useful to reproduce the whole beginning of the letter either because it is of no interest from the canonical point of view or because it simply repeats the title, author, and addressee of the writing.[157] Besides that, we notice that in the manuscript tradition, the text is presented with a great homogeneity: the variants are minimal, and they do not affect the meaning at all.

The letter is written in a polished style, and it is quite possible that St. Cyril himself was its editor. The initial ethical considerations are expressed in sufficiently difficult language to have given the Latin translator a lot of trouble.[158] The scriptural sentence, "do all with reflection," does not appear exactly in this form anywhere in the Bible; the text nearest to it is found in the Wisdom of Sirach 32:19.[159]

The heading of the letter indicates that it was addressed by the Council of Ephesus to members of the provincial synod of Pamphylia concerning Eustathius, "who was formerly their metropolitan" (τοῦ γενομένου αὐτῶν μητροπολίτου). Although this mention may certainly be ancient, since it appears not only in the manuscript tradition of the *Syntagma* but also in the acts of the council, we cannot consider it to be the original.[160] There were, in fact, at this time two metropolitan cities in Pamphylia: Perga and Side. These sees were occupied respectively by Verinianus and Amphilochius, whose names appear in the acts of the council.[161] On the hand, the name of Theodore appears as bishop of Attalia in Pamphylia.[162] As Zonaras already observed, we are obviously dealing here with the successor of Eustathius.[163] The see of Attalia was not raised to the metropolitan rank until very much later, 1083-4, under the patriarchate of Eustratius;[164] before that, it depended on Perga.[165]

This letter is of great canonical interest because it raises two important and connected questions: the first concerns the legitimacy of the resignation of bishops, and the second deals with the status of resigned bishops. According to this document, Eustathius, after having been elected and consecrated in a canonical way, exercised his episcopal functions during an unspecified length of time. We are therefore not dealing with a case of a bishop whose people refused to receive him, as envisioned by canon 36 of the Holy Apostles and canon 18 of Antioch; it was no doubt by this last canon that the fathers of Ephesus were inspired in making their decision in this case. Certain people were accusing Eustathius of wrongdoing; he was easily able to turn aside the accusations. Very much affected by these slanderous accusations, he sent his written resignation to the provincial synod rather than reacting more forcefully. His passivity and his lack of steadfastness were criticized by the ecumenical council, but he was even more reproached for resigning. This was considered to be an unjustified act and intrinsically culpable, for once anyone freely accepts the charge of the episcopate, he does not have the right to break the link which unites him to his church. The canonical tradition is very firm on this point. In the letter to Domnus II of Antioch written around 442, St. Cyril of Alexandria declared in no uncertain terms:

> ....it is a thing quite in opposition to the institutions of the Church that certain persons who fulfill the sacred functions (τινὰς τῶν ἱερουργῶν) should present letters of resignation; for if they are worthy of exercising the ministry, let them stay there. If, on the contrary, they are unworthy, let them leave it not by resignation but rather because they have been condemned for their acts.[166]

Thus, canon law appears completely to exclude the possiblity of a bishop's resigning. In reality, we need to be a bit more nuanced. What is formally condemned is for a bishop to run away in the face of difficulties. But there can be proper causes for resignation: extreme age or incurable sickness, which can make a bishop incapable of fulfilling the duties of his charge. There can also be objective churchly reasons for resignation: if one part of the episcopate looks on a bishop with suspicion so that his authority is compromised. This was the situation in which St. Gregory the Theologian found himself after his promotion to the see of Constantinople was contested by Pope Damasus and the bishops of Egypt.[167] In addition, if a bishop, or any cleric, commits a grave sin constituting an impediment to the exercise of the priesthood, even if this fault remains hidden and has not given rise to scandal, he is bound by conscience to resign.[168] Canon 16 of the First-Second Council states that a bishop's chair is vacant if the bishop has voluntarily resigned, but in constrast to the interpretation which is sometimes given to this canon, it in no way implies that the fact of resigning has been recognized as normal by the fathers of this council.[169] It is the same for the document that we are dealing with here: the recognition of the canonicity of Theodore as bishop of Attalia does not mean at all that the resignation of Eustathius was morally approved.

According to the strict interpretation of the canons, the fact that a bishop has resigned should mean that he loses his episcopal dignity. We note in passing that Greek does not know the distinction between "resign" and "abdicate." The term παραίτησις designates the two things; however, we must not dig too deeply into this semantic detail for an explanation in canon law of this case. The explanation is in fact based on a fundamental principle which Zonaras explained in his commentary on the letter to the synod of Pamphylia: the episcopal dignity is linked concretely to a function; if a bishop voluntarily abandons this function, he *ipso facto* loses the dignity itself.[170] At the time that Zonaras was writing his work, the question had just become quite relevant because of Nicholas IV Mouzalon, who had been archbishop of Cyprus, but then resigned. Later on, he became patriarch of Constantinople, but this action brought with it much controversy. In 1151, a council declared him deposed, saying that his abdication of the archbishop's chair in Cyprus had deprived him of his pontifical rank. To be patriarch, he should have been reordained, but this is formally prohibited by the canons. The council therefore decided for a sentence of permanent excommunication (ἀκοινώνητον μένειν δι᾿ ὅλης τῆς αὐτοῦ βιοτῆς). There is not much doubt that the commentary of Zonaras was greatly influenced by the controversy surrounding the case of Mouzalon.[171] However, this view corresponds to a wide current of opinion; it is taken up again by Balsamon and Blastares.[172] We find it again later defended by St. Nicodemus the Hagiorite[173] and by Nicodemus Milash.[174] It is stated clearly in the letter that by resigning from a see a bishop might keep the episcopal dignity. Is this sufficient in itself to say that such a thing was really accepted? This is the meaning that has been accepted in our own time. There is no lack of examples in the past either; we can site the case of Martyrius of Antioch in 465.[175] In strict law, it is the competent synod which receives the resignation, and this synod passes judgment on it. Obviously, the desire expressed by the bishop concerned may influence the decision of the synod in the direction of mercy. On the other hand, we do not see how a synod could go against the manifest wish of a bishop without requiring him to renounce the episcopate completely. According to canon 2 of the council of St. Sophia, this is the inevitable consequence of taking the monastic habit after being consecrated bishop.[176]

Why did Eustathius present his request to the Council of Ephesus and not to the synod of his province? Probably, because his province was in an unprecedented state of disarray. The ecumenical council gave its judgment in the direction of condescension, but it took great pains not to question the decision of the provincial synod in any fundamental way. If the fathers of Ephesus stipulated that henceforth Eustathius' right to be called a bishop with the honors that go with that title should be unquestioned ($δίχα$ $πάσης$ $ἀντιλογίας$), they also took great care not to undercut the prerogatives of the bishops of the province concerned.

If, as we have said above, the case of Eustathius cannot be assimilated to that envisioned by canon 18 of the Council of Antioch, where a bishop newly consecrated is prevented from taking up his duties, the stipulations of this canon about the status of such a bishop are fundamentally the same as those of the letter of the fathers of Ephesus: "...he will participate only in the honor and the liturgical celebration without interfering in the affairs of the Church which welcomes him; let him wait until the full synod of the province ($ἡ$ $τῆς$ $ἐπαρχίας$ $τελεία$ $σύνοδος$), after having examined the affair, makes a decision." In the letter of the Council of Ephesus, there is an allusion to an even more favorable decision for Eustathius than that set out; this obviously depended on the synod of Pamphylia. It is not at all out of the question to think, like Aristenus, that this is a reference to an eventual nomination to a vacant see.[177] However, this interpretation cannot be taken for certain.

CHAPTER III FOOTNOTES

¹See V.V. Bolotov, *Lektsii po istorii drevnei tserkvi, IV: Istoriia tserkvi v period vselenskikh soborov,* 3rd part. *Istoriia bogoslovskoi mysli,* Petrograd, 1918, pp. 134-236. R.V. Sellers, *Two Ancient Christologies* (London, 1953), *passim.* A. Grillmeier, *Le Christ dans la Tradition chrétienne* (Paris, 1973), pp. 299-480.

²E. Amann, "Nestorius," *DTC,* XI-1, col. 76-158. P.H. Camelot, *Ephèse et Chalcedoine* (Paris, 1962), pp. 25-26. This author considers it very unlikely that Nestorius was the student of Theodore of Mopsuestia.

³Socrates, *Historia ecclesiastica* VII, 29, PG 67, col. 804AB. Edict of Theodosius of May 30, 428, *CT* XVI, 5, 65, pp. 878-879.

⁴*ACO,* I, II, 3, pp. 12-15.

⁵On the possible reasons for this silence, see T.V. Jalland, *The Church and the Papacy* (London, 1949), pp. 295-296.

⁶*ACO,* I, I, 1, pp. 101-102. On all the agitation that preceded the council of Ephesus, see Camelot, pp. 25-43.

⁷*ACO,* I, I, 1, pp. 10-23.

⁸*Ibid.,* pp. 23-25.

⁹*Ibid.,* p. 25.

¹⁰Letter "καταφλυαροῦσι μέν," *ibid.,* pp. 25-28.

¹¹*Ibid.,* pp. 29-32.

¹²*Ibid.,* vol. I, 5, pp. 10-12.

¹³And even this is not at all certain; we deduce this insertion in the diptychs of the Church of Alexandria from the single fact of the reestablishing of normal relations with Rome and Carthage. See Fliche and Martin, *Histoire de l'Eglise,* t. 4 (Paris, 1945), pp. 157-8, but L. Duchesne remains very skeptical on this subject: *Histoire ancienne de l'Eglise,* t. III, 4th edition (Paris, 1911), p. 302.

¹⁴See Grillmeier, pp. 453-460.

¹⁵*ACO,* I, II, pp. 7-12.

¹⁶*Ibid.,* p. 5-6.

¹⁷*Cyrilli epistula tertia ad Nestorium, ACO,* I, I, 1, pp. 32-42; the anathemas, pp. 40-42.

¹⁸*ACO,* I, II, p. 73-74.

¹⁹*Ibid.,* pp. 114-6.

²⁰This is what W. de Vries thinks: *Orient et Occident* (Paris, 1974), p. 85.

²¹*ACO,* I, II, pp. 25-26.

²²*Ibid.,* p. 25.

²³*Ibid.,* I, I, 1, pp. 120-121.

²⁴Thus in the Acta graeca edited in Alexandria, the protests of count Candidian against the hasty opening of the council are omitted. The position taken by the representative of the emperor is known to us by the Synodicon of Rusticus, *ACO,* I, IV, 2, pp. 31-33.

²⁵W. Devreesse, "Les actes du concile d'Ephèse," *Revue des sciences philosophiques et théologiques* XVIII (1929), pp. 223-242 and 408-231. Also, V. Liebaert, "Ephèse (Concile d')," *DHGE* XV, col. 561-574.

²⁶On this person, see G. Bareille, "Irenee," *DTC,* VII-2, col. 2533-2536.

²⁷Jean Daniélou and Henri Marrou, *La Nouvelle Histoire de l'Eglise* (Paris, 1963), the map on page 390.

²⁸A.H.M. Jones, *The Later Roman Empire,* (Oxford, 1964), vol. I, pp. 211-2 and vol. II, pp. 888-9. Also, J. Gaudemet, *L'Eglise dans l'Empire romain (IVᶜ - Vᶜ siècles)* (Paris, 1958), pp. 403-407.

²⁹*ACO,* I, I, 2, pp. 52-54.

³⁰"Κυρίλλου Ἀλεξανδρείας, διέποντος καὶ τὸν τόπον τοῦ ἁγιωτάτου καὶ ὁσιωτάτου ἀρχιεπισκόπου τῆς Ῥωμαίων ἐκκλησίας Κελεστίνου," *ACO,* I, I, 2, p. 3 (minutes from the first session).

³¹*ACO,* I, IV, pp. 27-30.

³²*Cyriili ad Alexandrinos epistula tertia:* ". . .ἐν τῇ μεγάλῃ ἐκκλησίᾳ τῆς πόλεως ἥτις καλεῖται Μαρία Θεοτόκος," *ibid.,* I, I, 1, p. 117. About this basilica, see the article of M. Restle, "Ephesos," *Reallexikon zur byzantinischen Kunst,* fasc. 10, col. 164-207, and especially col. 166-180: "Marienkirche."

³³Liebaert, col. 566.

³⁴*Ibid.,* col. 565-566.

³⁵*ACO,* I, I, 2, p. 54.

³⁶*Synodi relatio ad Imperatores, ibid.,* I, I, 3, pp. 3-5.

³⁷*Ibid.*, I, I, 2, pp. 3-7: the list of those present; pp. 55-64: the 157 signatures. We add also that other bishops signed later on so that those who approved the deposition of Nestorius were more than 200 ("ὑπὲρ τοὺς διακοσίους").

³⁸*Ibid.*, p. 64.

³⁹*Cyrilli ad Alexandrinos epistula tertia, ibid.*, I, I, 1, pp. 117-118.

⁴⁰Liebaert, *art. cit.*, pp. 556-557.

⁴¹*ACO*, I, I, 5, pp. 13-5. This text was signed by Nestorius and 10 other bishops: Phritilas of Heraclea, Helladios of Tarsus, Dexianos of Seleucia in Isauria, Himerios of Nicomedia, Alexander of Apamea, Eutherios of Tyanes, Basil of Thessalia, Maximos of Anazarbus, Alexander of Hierapolis in Euphratesia, and Dorotheus of Marcianopolis in Mysia.

⁴²*Ibid.*, I, IV, p. 33.

⁴³*Ibid.*, I, I, 3, pp. 9-10.

⁴⁴*Ibid.*, I, I, 5, pp. 123-4 (Collectio Vaticana): 43 signatures. *Ibid.*, I, IV, 2, pp. 37-38 (Collectio Casinensis): 53 signatures; this testimony comes from the Synodicon of Rusticus and is more certain.

⁴⁵*Ibid.*, I, I, 5, pp. 119-24 and I, IV, 2, pp. 33-38.

⁴⁶We are dealing here with the famous statement of the priest Philip: *ibid.*, I, I, 3, p. 58, lines 22-31. Its authenticity has been put in doubt by Archbishop Chrysostomos Papadopoulos, *Τὸ πρωτεῖον τοῦ ἐπισκόπου Ῥώμης*, 2nd edition (Athens, 1964), pp. 59-61. This conjecture seems to be unjustified.

⁴⁷*The Church Universal and the See of Rome* (London, 1939), p. 122.

⁴⁸De Vries, pp. 76-7.

⁴⁹The Encyclical Letter, *passim*, *ACO*, I, I, 3, pp. 26-8.

⁵⁰See *infra* canon 1. The letter of the council to Pope Celestine mentions the condemnation of the Pelagians, *CO*, I, I, 3, pp. 5-9. On this matter, L. Duchesne ironically notes that "de ces choses-là on ne parle qu'au pape avec l'intention évidente de s'en faire bien voir," p. 357.

⁵¹Cf. preceding note.

⁵²Cf. note 50. From his point of view, H.E. Symonds writes that "they (the Cyrillians) announce their confirmation of the Papal condemnation of the Pelagian leaders. No record of this approval is found in the Acta. The statement was possibly inserted with the naive hope of pleasing the Pope," p. 122.

⁵³*ACO*, I, I, 3, pp. 3-5.

⁵⁴*Ibid.*, pp. 84-117.

⁵⁵*Ibid.*, pp. 118-122.

⁵⁶*Ibid.*, pp. 117-118.

⁵⁷*Ibid.*, pp. 122-123.

⁵⁸*Ibid.*, pp. 12-14.

⁵⁹This high functionary administered the imperial treasury which was built up by sumptuous taxes. On this matter, see Jones, vol. I, pp. 105, 369-370, and 427-438.

⁶⁰*ACO*, I, I, 3, pp. 31-32.

⁶¹*Ibid.*, I, I, 7, p. 142.

⁶²*Epistula Epiphanii archidiaconi et syncelli Cyrilli ad Maximianum episcopum Constantinopolim, ibid.*, I, IV, 2, pp. 222-225.

⁶³*Ibid.*, I, I, 2, pp. 66-69. V. Grumel, "Dalmate," *DHGE* XIV, col. 27-28. The manuscript tradition supports two spellings: "Δαλμᾶτος" and "Δαλμάτιος."

⁶⁴The letters of pope Celestine to the emperor Theodosius, Maximian, the clergy, the people of Constantinople, and to the council after the condemnation of Nestorius. *ACO*, I, II, pp. 88-101.

⁶⁵*Ibid.*, I, I, 4, pp. 7-9. The letter of John of Antioch to Cyril of Alexandria. The dogmatic formulation was none other than the profession of faith that the easterners had submitted in Ephesus to the representative of the emperor. *Ibid.*, I, I, 7, p. 70.

⁶⁶J. Karmiris, *Τὰ δογματικὰ καὶ συμβολικὰ μνημεῖα τῆς Ὀρθοδόξου Καθολικῆς Ἐκκλησίας*, t. I, 2nd edition (Athens, 1960), pp. 149-150.

⁶⁷The law of August 3, 435, *CTh* XVI, 5, 66, pp. 879-80. E. Schwartz thinks that this law was passed in 436, *ACO*, I, I, 3, p. 68 and I, IV, p. XI, note 1.

⁶⁸J. Labourt, *Le Christianisme dans l'Empire perse sous la dynastie sassanide* (Paris, 1904). E. Tisserant, "Nestorius, II: L'Eglise nestorienne," *DTC*, XI, 1, col. 157-323. According to the monophysite historian, Michael the Syrian, Barsauma, bishop of Nisibis (second half of the fifth century) may have advised the Persian king to favor Nestorianism in Persia so that the Christians of that country would not have relations with those of the Romano-Byzantine empire. J. B. Chabot, ed.,

Chronique de Michel le Syrien (Paris, 1901!), p. 428.

[69]*Kormchaya kniga*, Moscow edition of 1787, fol. 91.

[70]G. Voelli-H. Justelli, *Bibliotheca juris canonici veteris* (Paris, 1661), t. II, pp. 717-718.

[71]*Le concile de Nicée d'après les textes coptes et les diverses collections canoniques* (Paris, 1881), p. 27.

[72]They already appear in the collection of the LX titles compiled around 534 and the middle of the sixth century, whose existence we know about through John the Scholastic, *Synagoge*, p. 5.

[73]V. N. Beneševič, *Kanonicheskii sbornik XIV titulov* (St Petersburg, 1905), p.155; cf. *Syntagma*, p. 102, note 1 in the Greek text.

[74]*ACO*, I, I, 3, pp. 26-8. The Latin translation in the Synodicon of Rusticus, *ibid.*, I, IV, 2, pp. 242-3.

[75]*Syntagma*, pp. 102-3: the Greek text and the Old Slavonic version. The list of the adversaries is omitted. In the oldest recension of the *Syntagma*, the prologue is not considered at all to be an integral part of canon 1; the canon starts with "Ἐπειδὴ δὲ ἐχρῆν..." ("Since it was necessary..."), *ibid.*, p. 103. It also is to be noted that the preamble, in an abridged form, is found in the printed *Kormchaya Kniga, op. cit.*, fol. 85.

[76]*Synagoge*, pp. 111-2. It is certain that the name of Celestius appeared in the original: *ACO*, I, I, 3, p. 27 and I, IV, 3, p. 243; also *Syntagma*, p. 103.

[77]*Héfele-Leclercq* II-1, p. 338, note 1.

[78]*ACO*, I, I, 7, pp. 112-113.

[79]*Pravila*, I, p. 289.

[80]The philological point of view is to be noted; there is also the adjectival form "ἐπαρχεῶται": *Synagoge*, p. 112.

[81]*ACO*, I, I, 3, p. 28: "'Αποπιπτόντας." On the judicial procedure in the ancient Church, see N. Zaozersky, *Tserkovnii sud v pervye veka Khristianstva* (Kostroma, 1878). Also, our article "Καθαί-ρεσις," *Th. Ith. E.*, τ. 7, col. 151-5.

[82]*ACO*, I, I, 3, p. 28 (Coll. Vaticana); *ibid.*, I, IV, 2, p. 243 (Coll. Casinensis).

[83]*Synagoge*, p. 116. The final part of the canon in the *Synagoge* coincides with that of the Codices of Patmos 172 and 173 which gave the Recensio Trullana of the *Syntagma, Syntagma*, p. 104, note 4.

[84]On this person, see G. Bardy, "Celestius," *DHGE* XII, col. 104-107. He certainly spent time in the East, but the Pelagian controversy hardly had a lasting echo in this part of the Christian world.

[85]*ACO*, I, IV, 2, p. 243.

[86]*Syntagma*, p. 105, *ACO*, I, I, 3, p. 28: "...ὑπὸ τῆς 'Αγίας Συνόδου δεδικαίωται."

[87]*Pravila*, I, p. 299.

[88]*ACO*, I, I, 3, p. 28; *Syntagma*, p. 105, note 1.

[89]*ACO*, I, IV, 2, p. 243.

[90]*Ibid.*, I, I, 3, p. 28, the note for line 11: *Synagoge*, p. 112 (but the article appears in the whole series of manuscripts, note 66); *Syntagma*, p. 105 (here we must note its presence in the codices of Patmos mentioned above, note 1).

[91]*Syntagma*, p. 105: "bezpriobshchenie."

[92]*Pravila*, I, p. 301.

[93]*ACO*, I, IV, 2, p. 243.

[94]*Rhalles-Potles* II, p. 198.

[95]*Synagoge*, p. 147; *ACO*, I, I, 3, p. 28; *ibid.*, I, IV, 2, p. 243; *Syntagma*, p. 105.

[96]*ACO*, I, IV, 2, p. 243.

[97]Liebaert, col. 570.

[98]Cf. *supra* chapter 2, analysis of the supposed canon 7 of the second ecumenical council.

[99]*ACO*, I, I, 7, pp. 97-100.

[100]He is one of the co-signers of the "Contestatio directa beato Cyrillo," *ibid.*, I, IV, 2, p. 28.

[101]*Syntagma*, p. 105.

[102]*PG* 67, col. 345A (Epist. LXXII, ad Proclum).

[103]*ACO*, I, V, 1, p. 23.

[104]*Ibid.*, I, I, 7, p. 97.

[105]The primitive text of the *Synagoge* does not contain this "διαλαλία." There were only seven canons of Ephesus, that is, the six extracts of the encyclical letter plus the resolution on Cyprus; see *Synagoge*, prologue, p. 6. The "διαλαλία" was inserted as an appendix to title XXXVIII, p. 117.

[106]Cf. preceding note.

[107]*Pedalion*, p. 173. *Rhalles-Potles* II, p. 200.

[108]*Pravila*, I, p. 303.

[109]*Syntagma*, p. 106.
[110]*ACO*, I, I, 7, pp. 106-111.
[111]*Ibid.*, II, I, 1, p. 191.
[112]*Ibid.*, II, I, 3, pp. 110-114 (469-473): *Adlocutio ad Marcianum.*
[113]I Peter 3:15.
[114]*ACO*, I, I, 4, p. 24.
[115]See our introduction to the canons of the second ecumenical council.
[116]*ACO*, II, I, 2, p. 130 (326).
[117]Mansi, vol. 11, col. 640.
[118]*Ibid.*, vol. 17A-18A, col. 516-7 and 521-522.
[119]See R. Haugh, *Photius and the Carolingians* (Belmont, 1975), pp. 125-128.
[120]*Rhalles-Potles* II, pp. 201-202.
[121]*Concilium Florentinum*, Series B, vol. V, fasc. 1 (Rome, 1953), pp. 66-224.
[122]*ACO*, I, I, 7, p. 118 and I, V, p. 357.
[123]*Héfele-Leclercq* II-1, pp. 333-334.
[124]*ACO*, I, I, 7, pp. 118-122: Collectio Atheniensis, document 81. We find a Latin translation in the Collectio Winteriana, doc. 6: *ibid.*, I, V, pp. 357-60.
[125]F. Cavallera, *Le schisme d'Antioche* (Paris, 1905).
[126]Cf. *supra* our commentary of canon 6 of Nicea.
[127]Epist. XXIV §3, *PL* 20, col. 549A.
[128]Jones, pp. 376-377.
[129]*ACO*, I, I, 7, pp. 119-120.
[130]*Ibid.*, pp. 120-121. This injunction was avoided in Greek while the "praeceptum" to the governor of Cyprus was issued in Latin, which was still the official language of the imperial administration in the East. On this matter, see E. Stein, *Histoire du Bas-Empire*, t. I, French edition (Paris, 1959), pp. 295-296.
[131]*ACO*, I, I, 7, p. 118.
[132]He gave a very violent speech against the archbishop of Constantinople, whom the council had just deposed: *ibid.*, I, I, 2, pp. 70-71.
[133]Acts 11:19-20; 13:4-12; 25:39.
[134]*Historia ecclesiastica* XVI, 37, *PG* 147, col. 200C.
[135]Sozomen, *Historia ecclesiastica* VII, 19, *PG* 67, col. 1476A.
[136]Sardica, canon 6, i.f.; Laodicea, canon 57, *Syntagma*, pp. 284-285 and 277.
[137]Cf. *supra* our commentary on these two canons.
[138]*Syntagma*, p. 107, note 2.
[139]E. Roussos, *Λεξιλόγιον ἐκκλησιαστικοῦ δικαίου* I (Athens, 1948), p. 375.
[140]*Syntagma*, pp. 107-108; *ACO*, I, I, 7, p. 122.
[141]*ACO*, I, V, p. 360: "...opus habente unoquoque metropolitano ut ad suam securitatem exemplaria actorum excipiat."
[142]*Synagoge*, p. 34: "τοῦ μητροπολίτου"; however, the adjective "ἑκάστου" is given by several manuscripts: *ibid.*, p. 34, note 32.
[143]*Rhalles-Potles* II, pp. 203-204.
[144]*Pravila*, I, pp. 305-306.
[145]*Epist. concilii Africani ad papam Caelestinum, Concilia Africae* (edition of C. Munier) C.C., CXLIX (Turnhout, 1974), p. 172.
[146]G. Voelli-H. Justelli, p. 691 and *Rhalles-Potles* II, p. 206.
[147]Edition cited in note 69, fol. 91.
[148]J. Hackett, *Ἱστορία τῆς ὀρθοδόξου ἐκκλησίας τῆς Κύπρου*, t. I (Athens, 1924), pp. 40-42. The date of this event is difficult to determine; it might have taken place during the fourth patriarchate of Peter the Fuller in 488. The date given by R. Janin, "Chypre," *DHGE* t. XII, col. 795.
[149]Jones, I, pp. 482-483.
[150]Canon 39, *Syntagma*, pp. 170-171 (*CCO*, pp. 173-174). The only correct reading is to be noted also: "...τὸ δικαίον ἔχειν τῆς Κωνσταντιέων πόλεως." The reading that has passed into the standard text is erroneous: "Κωνσταντινουπόλεως."
[151]*De Administrando Imperio*, second edition of Moravcsik and Jenkins, chapter 47, vol. I (Washington, 1967), p. 224 and vol. II (London, 1962, commentary), p. 181. *Regestes*, §261.
[152]Mansi, 11, col. 990.

[153]J. Darrouzès, "Listes épiscopales du concile de Nicée (787)," *REB* 33 (1975) pp. 5-76; for the place of the head of the Cypriot Church, see pp. 31-32 and 62.

[154]Heinrich Gelzer, *Texte der Notitiae episcopatuum* (Munich, 1900), p. 569; G. Konidaris, "Ἡ θέσις τῆς αὐτοκεφάλου Ἐκκλησίας τῆς Κύπρου ἔναντι τοῦ οἰκουμενικοῦ πατριαρχείου κατὰ τὸν Θ΄ καὶ τὸν Ι΄ αἰῶνα," communication published in the *Πρατικὰ τῆς Ἀκαδημίας Ἀθηνῶν* (Athens, 1949), pp. 135-146.

[155]*Regestes*, §1097.

[156]*Syntagma*, pp. 108-111· *ACO*, I, I, 7, pp. 123-124.

[157]"Ἡ ἁγία σύνοδος ἡ κατὰ Θεοῦ χάριν καὶ νεύμασι τῶν Θεοφιλεστάτων Βασιλέων ἐν τῇ Ἐφεσίων συγκροτηθεῖσα τῇ ἁγίᾳ συνόδῳ τῇ κατὰ Παμφιλίαν ἀγαπητοῖς ἀδελφοῖς καὶ συλλει-τουργοῖς, ἐν Κυρίῳ χαίρειν," *op. cit.*, p. 123.

[158]*ACO*, I, V, 2, pp. 356-357 (Collectio Winteriana); especially p. 356, lines 21-24.

[159]Wisdom of Sirach: "Ἄνευ βουλῆς μηδὲν ποιήσῃς," XXXII, 19; letter to the synod: "Μετὰ βουλῆς πάντα ποίει..." It is a free quotation of the text of this deuterocanonical book of the Old Testament.

[160]*Syntagma*, p. 108; *ACO*, I, I, 7, p. 123, lines 25-6; "...περὶ Εὐσταθίου τοῦ γενομένου αὐτῶν μητροπολίτου"; *ibid.*, I, V, 2, p. 356, lines 15-16: "...de Eustathio facto metropolitano."

[161]*ACO*, I, I, 7, p. 85: "Βερινιανοῦ Πέργης τῆς Παμφυλίας"; *ibid.*: "Ἀμφιλοχίου Σίδης." *ibid.*, p. 112: "Βερινιανὸς ἐπίσκοπως τῆς Περγαίων μητροπόλεως ὑπέγραψα."

[162]*Ibid.*, p. 113: "Θεόδορος ἐπίσκοπως πόλεως Ἀτταλείας (ὑπέγραψα)."

[163]*Rhalles-Potles* II, p. 208. This assertion is taken up by Balsamon, *ibid.*, p. 213.

[164]*Regestes* §930.

[165]H. Gelzer, *op. cit.*, p. 541.

[166]St. Cyril, canon 3, *Syntagma*, pp. 564-567.

[167]Socrates, *Historia ecclesiastica* V, 8, *PG* 67, col. 577B; Sozomen, *Historia ecclesiastica* VII, 7, *ibid.*, col. 1432; Gregory of Nazianzus, *Poemata de seipso*, verses 1849-50, *PG* 37, col. 1159A. A little while after having resigned the see of Constantinople, he took charge of the Church of Nazianzus while waiting for it to receive its own bishop Eulalios. This shows that he had not considered his resignation from the see of Constantinople to be an abdication from the episcopate.

[168]*Pedalion*, p. 182, following note 1 on page 179; cf. p. 690, note 2.

[169]Nicetas of Ancyra in the 11th century, justified his resignation by referring to the letter of the council of Ephesus to the synod of Pamphylia and to canon 16 of the First-Second council (*CSP*, pp. 476-478). On this matter, see J. Darrouzès, *Documents inédits d'ecclésiologie byzantine* (Paris, 1966), pp. 250-65.

[170]*Rhalles-Potles* II, pp. 208-13, especially p. 211.

[171]*Regestes* §1035, and Darrouzès, pp. 68-71 and 310-331.

[172]Balsamon, *Syntagma*, II, p. 213-215. The canonist recalls the principle according to which *economia* must not be a substitute for the norm, p. 214. M. Blastares, Σύνταγμα κατὰ στοιχεῖον, Letter E, chapter 28, Rhalles-Potles VI, p. 284.

[173]*Pedalion*, p. 179, note 1.

[174]This famous canonist wrote that "the canons of the Orthodox Church condemn categorically the bishop, metropolitan, or patriarch who presents his abdication (*otrechenie*) of the administration of the Church district which was conferred on him by legal authority; from the moment that he has presented such an abdication, he ceases to be a bishop in the strictest sense of the term," *loc. cit.*, *Pravila*, I, p. 314.

[175]He made this declaration very clearly: "Κλήρῳ ἀνυποτάκτῳ καὶ λαῷ ἀπειθεῖ καὶ ἐκκλησίᾳ ἐρρυπωμένῃ ἀποτάττομαι, φυλάττων ἐμαυτῷ τὸ τῆς ἱερωσύνης ἀξίωμα," Theodore the Reader, *Historia ecclesiastica* I, 21, *PG* 86, col. 176B. On the resignation of bishops, see the very well documented work of C. Rhalles: Περὶ παραιτήσεως ἐπισκόπων κατὰ τὸ δίκαιον τῆς Ὀρθοδόξου Ἀνατολικῆς Ἐκκλησίας (Athens, 1911).

[176]The question asks if a "microscheme" monk who becomes a bishop and later takes the "great habit" can continue to exercise the functions of a bishop. In his commentary on canon 2 of St Sophia, Balsamon answers in the negative, but he recognizes that certain writers have had another opinion; *Rhalles-Potles* II, pp. 709-10. In 1391, the patriarchal synod of Constantinople was required to discuss such a case. This assembly recognized that the rigorist interpretation is not necessarily deduced from the statement of the canon and declared that it was proper to examine each case by itself, *PCAS* XXII, pp. 108-111.

[177]*Rhalles-Potles* II, p. 215.

CHAPTER IV

THE COUNCIL OF CHALCEDON

SECTION 1: THE BACKGROUND AND PROCEEDINGS

The agreement of 433 between Cyril of Alexandria and John of Antioch did not put an end to the christological debates. These discussions were far too passionate on both sides, and new developments could not be avoided. Despite the Formula of Union, the extremists of the two camps had never really disengaged. Many bishops of the diocese of the East would have liked for Cyril expressly to repudiate his "anathemas"; they also considered the deposition of Nestorius to be unjust. On the other side, many friends of St. Cyril saw his acceptance of the Formula of Union as a most regrettable affair.

St. Cyril died in 444 and was succeeded by his archdeacon Dioscorus, an energetic, indeed brutal, prelate; he began his time as bishop by forcing St. Cyril's family to restore the riches that St. Cyril had amassed.[1] Dioscorus also tried to reinforce the hegemony of his see over the whole East, and, in theology, he worked for the complete triumph of the Alexandrian position. In the diocese of the East as well as in the capital of the empire, Dioscorus was able to count on the support of the monks. Those of Syria became his allies when faced with bishops who defended the ideas of the Antiochian school. This is how the people of Edessa were turned against Ibas, their pastor since 435 and one of the pillars of the school of Antioch. Accused of Nestorianism, Ibas' case was examined in Beirut and then in Tyre around 448.[2] In Constantinople, the Alexandrian party had a zealous and influential supporter in the person of Eutyches. Since the death of Dalmatus, this archimandrite had been the moral leader of the monks of the capital.[3] An unshakable supporter of St. Cyril, Eutyches continued, even after the Council of Ephesus, to fight anyone he suspected of being Nestorian. Because of his ascetic life, he was widely known as a very holy man, but his knowledge of theology was quite elementary. St. Leo was to write the following about him: *multum inprudens et nimis inperitus.*[4] Eutyches had the eunuch Chrysaphius as his godchild and spiritual son; this Chrysaphius was the imperial chamberlain and had practically been running the affairs of the empire ever since 441. Dioscorus used Eutyches to make the court believe that the Nestorian heresy was once again raising its head. The emperor Theodosius was thus pushed to get directly involved in church affairs, namely the trial of Ibas and the deposition of Ireneus of Tyre.[5]

In the fall of 448, Bishop Eusebius of Doryleum, who as a layman had stood up against Nestorius, officially accused Eutyches of heresy during a full session of the "permanent synod" (ἐνδημοῦσα σύνοδος) of Constantinople.[6] Flavian, the archbishop of the capital and a peaceful man, would no doubt have preferred not to deal at all with such a question, which risked having very serious consequences. He could not, however, hold back the tide of events. Eutyches tried several delaying tactics to avoid coming before the synod, but he finally appeared on the initiative of Chrysaphius but attended by an imperial commissioner. From the embroiled debates, we know that Eutyches agreed to recognize that Christ is consubstantial with us; this he did reluctantly out of excessive fear that such a recognition could be interpreted in the sense of a humanity, a man, assumed by God, thus a form of adoptionism. On the other hand, he categorically rejected the existence of two natures after the incarnation. Considered as being a Valentinian heretic, a contestable matter,[7] and thus by extension an Apollinarian, a more solidly founded accusation, the old archimandrite was condemned on November 22, deposed from the priesthood, relieved of his functions as head of a monastery, and excommunicated. Those who had any dealings with him were also to suffer excommunication.[8] Eutyches appealed this sentence to the synods of Rome, Alexandria, Jerusalem, and Thessalonica.[9] He also wrote to Peter Chrysologus, Bishop of Ravenna, probably with the hope of obtaining through his mediation the support of the imperial court of the West.[10] Eutyches did not appeal to Domnus of Antioch; he knew he could expect nothing good from him. Domnus had already accused Eutyches of renewing the Apollinarian heresy.[11] From his side, Flavian informed Domnus, Theodoret of Cyrus and Pope Leo.[12] The Roman bishop was not at all happy simply to confirm the decision made in Constantinople; he gave a lengthy exposé of his doctrinal position in a document dated June 13, 449, and known as the "Tome to Flavian." This document was mostly a redaction of Prosper of Aquitaine and affirmed the co-existence of the two natures of Christ in the unity of his person; it indicated the mode of operation of the two natures; and it expressed the doctrine that was later to be called the *communicatio idiomatum (ἀντίδοσις τῶν ἰδιωμάτων).*[13]

Rightly or wrongly, the church of Alexandria felt itself to be the target of the condemnation of Eutyches; thus Dioscorus rejected the condemnation and received the canonically deposed archimandrite into his communion. This act was to be one of the charges against him at Chalcedon.[14] The emperor Theodosius was completely under the influence of Chrysaphius and openly showed his displeasure with the condemnation of Eutyches by even doubting the orthodoxy of Flavian.[15] This whole period was marked by collusion between Chrysaphius, Eutyches, and Dioscorus. According to Liberatus, it was the archbishop of Alexandria who persuaded the emperor to call a new general council.[16] The goals of its promoters were clear; the restoration of Eutyches and the condemnation of Flavian and his followers. For Dioscorus, the council would also assure the definitive preeminence of the see of Alexandria.[17] Theodoret of Cyrus had no illusions about the proposed assembly. He wrote to Domnus that "...there is nothing good to be expected from this council that everyone is talking about unless the Master, in his goodness and showing His usual providence, reduces to nothing the machinations of the devils who are the source of many troubles."[18] Theodosius decided to convoke the council for August, 449, in Ephesus and confer the speaker's chair on Dioscorus. Theodoret was forbidden to attend; on the other hand, Archimandrite Barsauma, who represented the monks of the East,[19] was invited, and he was one of the most ferocious enemies of the bishop of Cyrus. Pope Leo sent three legates: Bishop Julius of Puteoli, the priest Renatus, who died on the way, and Deacon Hilary. They were accompanied by the notary Dulcitius.[19a]

The council opened on August 8 in the church of St. Mary, as in 431. There were about 130 bishops present, the majority in favor of Eutyches.[20] Flavian of Constantinople occupied only the fifth place and appeared as the accused. The Roman legates asked that the letter of the pope be read, that is, the "Tome to Flavian," but this request was not granted.[21] The meeting took place in a very heated atmosphere. After the reading of the acts of the synod of Constantinople of the preceding year, the sentence against Eutyches was set aside, and he was reinstated. Then, basing himself on the decision of the council of 431 concerning the unchangeability of the faith of Nicea, Dioscorus proposed that Flavian and Eusebius be deposed. The bishop of Constantinople immediately protested, and Deacon Hilary then cried out

"*Contradicitur.*"[22] Certain bishops, seeing that things were taking a definite turn for the worse, approached Dioscorus to plead with him not to do anything irregular. Claiming to have been threatened, Dioscorus asked that the doors of the basilica be opened: immediately the church was invaded by soldiers, monks, and laymen, all very excited. Violence, especially against Flavian, resulted.[23] On August 22, there was another meeting that the Roman delegates did not attend, even though they were still in Ephesus. At this session, Ibas of Edessa, Daniel of Charrae, Ireneus of Tyre, and Aquilinus of Byblos were all deposed. The meeting then proceeded to an examination of the case of Theodoret, whom Dioscorus and his followers considered to be their most dangerous adversary; he too was deposed, and anyone who remained in communion with him was threatened with sanctions. Domnus of Antioch, although he showed weakness in retracting his assent to the deposition of Eutyches, did not escape the wrath of the council members and was deposed too. The meeting ended with a very strong approval of St. Cyril's anathemas. Dioscorus was then at the height of his power. Olympius of Evaza even went so far as to call him "the ecumenical archbishop."[24] In fact, it was a fragile and ephemeral success.

Deacon Hilary, who had succeeded in eluding the watchful eye of Dioscorus, on reaching Italy informed the pope of what had happened at Ephesus. St. Leo called the council that had just taken place "a council of robbers" (*latrocinium*) and the name has stuck in history.[25] Hilary carried with him the appeal of Flavian, who suggested to the pope that he call a council of both halves of the Christian world in order to affirm the common faith and set aside what was decided at the irregular assembly of Ephesus.[26] From his side, Eusebius of Doryleum appealed to Pope Leo that he quash the unjust sentence pronounced against him and that he be restored to his episcopal dignity.[27] A third letter of appeal was also carried to Rome; it came from Theodoret, who declared that he was ready to accept the judgment of the pope.[28] We note that these three requests do not refer to the same identical procedure of review: at the time, there was no universally accepted ruling on this question in the East. However, when he received the appeal of Flavian, St. Leo thought that this request should be set in the procedural framework of the Council of Nicea.[29] What was in fact in question here were the canons of Sardica, which in the western collections were found at the end of the canons of Nicea.[30]

On September 29, 449, a synod was held in Rome for the celebration of the anniversary of St. Leo's becoming bishop. At this synod, the pope explained the events that had taken place in Ephesus and associated the "whole council of the West" with his denunciation.[31] He asked Theodosius to convoke a general council and suggested that it be held in Italy.[32] Not having received any response, he appealed to Valentinian III, emperor in the West, to speak to his colleague in the East. This he did, and his mother Galla Placidia also made an appeal.[33] Theodosius answered that he did not see any reason to revoke the decisions made at Ephesus.[34]

Immediately after his deposition, Flavian was sent into exile; he died en route to Hypaepa. Anatolius, Dioscorus' representative in Constantinople, succeeded Flavian in April, 450. The new archbishop notified the pope of his election.[35] St. Leo acted prudently: instead of answering directly, he let the emperor know that he was ready to recognize Anatolius on condition that he accept the second dogmatic letter of St. Cyril and his own Tome to Flavian as adequate expressions of catholic doctrine. The pope then announced the sending of a delegation to Constantinople. If his inquiries received negative answers, he would then insist that the emperor convoke a general council in Italy.[36]

Meanwhile, Theodosius died accidentally on July 28, 450, and his sister Pulcheria took power. She immediately moved to get rid of the chamberlain and eunuch Chrysaphius; next she married a retired officer from Thrace or Illyricum named Marcian, whom she had proclaimed emperor on August 25 of the same year. Pulcheria was hostile to the Monophysite party and disapproved of the robber council of Ephesus.[37] Moreover, in order to have Marcian accepted as emperor of the East, she had to have the official recognition of Valentinian III, who after the death of Theodosius had become the legal emperor of the whole Roman Empire. The new religious policy in Byzantium was therefore going to renew the dialogue with the West and put an end to the interference of the see of Alexandria in the affairs of the East. Those who had been deposed from their functions by the robber council of Ephesus were restored with the exception of Domnus, while Eutyches was exiled to Doliche in Euphratesia. Anatolius adapted himself very well to the new situation. He subscribed to the Tome of Leo and required the bishops under his authority to do the same.[38] The remains of Flavian were brought back to Constantinople and buried in the church of the Holy Apostles. In Antioch also, things had changed: Maximus, who before had been known for his formidable opposition to John and whom Anatolius had consecrated to replace Domnus, now tried to get all the bishops of the East to sign the Tome of Leo.[39]

The emperor Marcian wanted an ecumenical council to be held which would annul the decisions of the Council of Ephesus of 449 and also decide the doctrinal questions. But now the pope was no longer so interested in a council. On the one hand, the invasions of the West made it very difficult for bishops to get around; on the other, he thought that with the new circumstances in the East, the matters that had been held in suspense could be regulated in an easier way. His legates, therefore, in collaboration with Anatolius, officially proceeded with the restoration of the victims of the robber council of Ephesus. The cases of Dioscorus of Alexandria and Juvenal of Jerusalem would be studied by the Roman see; in the meantime, their names were not to be mentioned in the diptychs.[40] Such a procedure was hardly acceptable to the easterners. The action implied a much too direct intervention on the part of the Roman see in their affairs, and above all, it supposed that the Tome of Leo had already regulated the dogmatic problem. Now according to the eastern conception, only a new general council was competent to set aside Ephesus 449. Thus, the emperor Marcian decided to convoke an ecumenical council at Nicea.[41] St. Leo had to accept things as they were, even if he showed very little enthusiasm for the council.[42] So he appointed his legates: Bishops Paschasinus of Lilybaeum and Lucensius of Picenum; Julian of Cos (or Kios) and the priests Boniface and Basil were also added.[43] However, Basil did not participate in the council, perhaps because he became sick or died. According to the instructions of the pope, Paschasinus was given the charge of presiding at the council. In the thought of St. Leo, the goal of the assembly was to regulate the canonical situation of the bishops who had compromised themselves at Ephesus 449, and to reestablish the victims of Dioscorus and his followers in their rights. He considered that the question of faith had already been settled by his Tome; the only thing for the future assembly to do, according to the pope, was to accept his document.[44] The position of the easterners was quite different, and their ideas eventually came out on top.[45]

At the beginning of September, 451, the members of the council began to arrive at Nicea. They were waiting for the emperor, who had expressed the desire to be present at the opening, but the military situation did not allow him to go very far away from the capital. Finally, he asked that the council be held in Chalcedon. This city had the advantage of being close to Constantinople but not so close as to be troubled by the monks of the capital, who were mostly for Eutyches.[46]

On October 9, the first meeting of the council was held in the basilica of the holy martyr Euphemia.[47] How many fathers were at the council? In all probability, the number of bishops who came from far or near, for one reason or for another, must have been close to 510. This corresponds rather closely to the estimate of "around 520" given by the synodal letter sent to Pope Leo. Taking into account the representations by proxy, the real number of participants is around 450. As for the number of 630, it did not appear before the reign of the emperor Constantine Pogonatus (668-685).[48] The representation from the West appears to have been very small in number; if we set aside the Illyrian bishops who formed a separate group, the western presence was reduced to the Roman legates and to a few African bishops who had fled their country because of the invasions of the Vandals.[49]

On the church's chancel, the high dignitaries of the state were seated and exercised a collective presidency, without participating in the votes, of course.[49a] Immediately to their side on the left side of the the nave, the legates of the pope were seated, then Anatolius of Constantinople followed by the bishops of Antioch, Caesarea in Cappadocia, Ephesus, and those of the civil diocese of the East, Pontus, Asia and Thrace. In front of them sat the "opposition," that is, Dioscorus of Alexandria, Juvenal of Jerusalem, and the bishops of Egypt, Illyricum and Palestine. The council lasted until the end of October, and the fathers did not go home until the beginning of November after having written a letter to Pope Leo. How many sessions were there? Fifteen according to the historian Evagrius;[50] nineteen according to the Greek acts, but this number is based on a rather artificial way of numbering. Besides, the order of the sessions (πράξεις, *actiones*) is not always faithful to chronology.[51] On the whole, however, we possess a good record of the proceedings of the council itself, thanks to the minutes that have been preserved; there are, nonetheless, some obscure points due to later reworkings of the text.[52]

From the beginning of the first session, Paschasinus made a rather peremptory request in the following terms:

We have instructions from the blessed and apostolic bishop

of the city of the Romans, head of all the churches; they forbid Dioscorus to sit in the assembly; if he attempts to sit in the council, let him be expelled. These instructions must be respected. Therefore, if it pleases your Greatness, let him depart, or else we will depart.[53]

The imperial commissioners asked the Roman delegation to set out their complaints concerning Dioscorus. Lucensius then declared that Dioscorus had dared to hold a council without having received a mandate from the apostolic see.[54] This is a strange charge, for the Roman legates at Ephesus in 449 had not raised any objection of this kind. What was really reproachable in Dioscorus' behavior was the procedural irregularities and the violence that he tolerated, indeed encouraged, to achieve his ends. The imperial commissioners asked that the accusations against the archbishop of Alexandria be made clear and that the trial proceed in a regular fashion. From then on, Dioscorus was treated as the accused, and the examination of his case was immediately begun. Eusebius of Doryleum set out the charges against the archbishop of Alexandria. It was necessary to read the acts of the synod of Constantinople that condemned Eutyches in 448, also those of the robber council of Ephesus. This prolonged reading was interrupted several times by various agitations. It appeared clear that at Ephesus in 449, the majority of bishops had given their approval under constraint. The council was supposed to decide on Flavian's orthodoxy, though it was not widely doubted. Juvenal of Jerusalem, followed by the bishops of Palestine, passed over to the other side of the assembly, thereby spectacularly showing his agreement with the majority. In the same way, even four Egyptian bishops abandoned Dioscorus, who himself remained obstinately attached to his previous convictions concerning the well-foundedness of the condemnation of Flavian. The imperial commissioners advised that it would be proper to depose those responsible for the robber council of Ephesus, meaning Dioscorus of Alexandria, Juvenal of Jerusalem, Thalassius of Caesarea, Eusebius of Ancyra, Eustathius of Beirut, and Basil of Seleucia. Toward the end of this long session, the imperial commissioners asked that the fathers of the council next examine the basis of the dogmatic problem.[55]

The trial of Dioscorus took place at the second session of the council, Saturday, October 13, in the absence of the imperial commissioners but with Paschasinus as the presiding officer. After having heard the indictment made by Eusebius of Doryleum, the fathers convoked the accused who, despite three calls, refused to appear. Dioscorus was reproached for having on his own initiative arbitrarily readmitted Eutyches to communion and for not having allowed Leo's letter to be read at Ephesus. It was also revealed that he had excommunicated the pope of Rome and that he had persuaded ten other bishops to subscribe to this act. We can assume that this was carried out at Nicea somewhat before the decision to transfer the council to Chalcedon. Some complaints were also heard about the administration of his church. Paschasinus submitted a project of condemnation to the council formulated in the following way:

> ...the very holy and blessed Leo, archbishop of the great and ancient Rome, by us and the present holy council, in union with the thrice-blessed and illustrious apostle Peter, rock and support of the catholic Church, the foundation of the orthodox faith, deposes him and excludes him from every episcopal and priestly dignity.[56]

This text was presented jointly by Bishop Paschasinus and Lucensius as well as the priest Boniface and received the approval of all. The first to express his agreement was Anatolius, who declared that:

> seeing things in the same was as the apostolic see, I vote with it on the deposition of Dioscorus, formerly bishop of the great city of the Alexandrians, having shown himself a stranger to every priestly function because he completely disobeyed the canons of the holy fathers and having been summoned three times, he did not accept to appear.[57]

After Anatolius' explanation of his vote, there were 188 other explanations, all in the same line. Beginning with Maximus of Antioch and Stephen of Ephesus, several bishops mentioned their agreement with Leo and Anatolius. This shows that in the thinking of these bishops, the archbishops of Old Rome and New Rome were associated in a certain form of precedence. The sentence against Dioscorus received the immediate assent of the 252 fathers; others approved it later on so that in the end 308 bishops signed the document.[58] We note that the reasons for the deposition did not directly touch on the dogmatic question; this is why Anatolius could say during the fifth session that "it was not for the faith that Dioscorus was deposed but because he had excommunicated the lord Leo, archbishop, and that summoned three times, he did not come. These are the reasons he was deposed."[59]

The sentence was communicated to Dioscorus in a document with the following wording:

> The holy and great ecumenical assembly by the grace of God,

according to the decree of our very pious emperors, beloved of
God, in the city of the Chalcedonians and in the shrine of the
very holy and victorious martyr Euphemia, to Dioscorus: know
that on October 13, you have been deposed from the episcopate
and made a stranger to every churchly order by the holy
ecumenical council because of your failure to observe the divine
canons, your disobedience toward this holy council, and also
other transgressions for which you have been found guilty; also
because you were called three times by this holy and great
council in conformity with the divine canons to answer your
accusers, but you chose to run away.[60]

Dioscorus was soon exiled first of all to Cyzicus, then to Heraclea,
and finally to Gangra, where he died on September 4, 454.[61]

The third session, according to the enumeration of the Greek acts,
was dated October 10, which supposes that in chronological order, it
was in fact the second session, but E. Chrysos has convincingly shown
that this dating is incorrect and that the session in question must be
dated on October 14.[62] In the name of the emperor, the imperial commissioners asked that the council agree on a new statement of faith. The
Roman legates did not want such a document because, for Pope Leo,
the doctrinal question had already been settled by his Tome to Flavian;
as for the other members of the council, for different reasons, they were
not really in favor of a dogmatic declaration either. They were conscious of the waves that could be caused by such an action. Moreover,
had not the Council of Ephesus in 431 completely forbidden the composition of a new formula? But the emperor Marcian was persuaded
that in order to put an end to the dissensions troubling the state, it was
necessary to promulgate an official definition of the Church which
clarified the christological doctrine of the Church. The bishops asked
for some time to reflect on the question. They read the symbol of Nicea
followed by that of Constantinople (381), which thus made its official
debut on the historical scene.[63] The letters of St. Cyril to Nestorius and
to John of Antioch were read as well as the Tome of Leo. If the
majority of the bishops manifested their approval of this latter document, those of Illyricum and Palestine raised objections about certain
passages. These bishops were reassured when quotations from St. Cyril
were read. It was decided that a commission should be set up, headed
by Anatolius, with the task of working out a text.[64]

The council took up its work again in the plenary session, on Wednesday, October 17. It was properly recognized that the doctrine of
Pope Leo did not differ from that of Cyril or from the fathers of

Nicea or Constantinople. Certain members took advantage of the situation to say that this was also the doctrine professed by Juvenal, Thalassius, Eusebius, Eustathius and Basil; consequently, they asked that these bishops be readmitted to their sees. The commissioners referred the question to Marcian, who gave the question back to the judgment of the council. Indulgence prevailed, and they were accepted. Thirteen Egyptian bishops who had not been seen since the first session of the council came and presented a profession of faith, orthodox in content but not mentioning the name of Eutyches. They were asked to condemn him expressly; and not without some reticence, they finally agreed. In contrast, in spite of the upbraiding of the members of the council, they obstinately refused to make a statement on the Tome of Leo, claiming that they could not do so without the approval of their archbishop. They invoked canon 6 of Nicea in their defense, but such a use of this canon gave it a very wide interpretation. The Egyptian bishops appealed to the witness of Anatolius in this matter, who himself said nothing. Apparently no one was really convinced of the well-foundedness of such a custom. However, on the proposition of the imperial commissioners, the fathers allowed these Egyptian bishops to be present at the election of the future archbishop of Alexandria so that they could sign the necessary documents but on the condition, as Paschasinus asked, that they remain at Chalcedon until that election.[65] The motion presented on this matter by the imperial commissioners with the amendment of Paschasinus was later introduced into the Greek canonical collections and was numbered as canon 30 of Chalcedon.

Later on a group of so-called monks were let into the council; their spokesmen were Dorotheus and Carosus. Among them was the Syrian Barsauma, whose sinister role in the brigandage of Ephesus had not been forgotten, and violent passions were raised among the fathers of the council. The arrogant behavior of these partisans was a prefiguring of what was later on to be the anti-Chalcedonian reaction in eastern monastic circles. Since they claimed that the emperor had promised them a discussion at the council between them and their adversaries, the priest Alexander was sent to the emperor to verify this assertion.[66]

On October 20, the members of the council gathered once again. The priest Alexander gave a complete account of his mission to Marcian, who said that the whole affair was in the competence of the council. The letter of Carosus and his followers to the emperor was reread; canons 83 and 84 of the official canonical collection were quoted, that is, canons 4 and 5 of Antioch.[67] The council gave a delay of thirty days to Carosus and his group to come to their senses. If they did not repent in that time, they would be sanctioned. In the acts of the council, this session is called number 18.[68] This same day, the conflict between Photius of Tyre and Eustathius of Beirut broke out. This affair takes up session 19 in the acts of the council.[69]

Metropolitan Photius of Tyre had first spoken to the emperor, who then sent him to the council. The matter in question was the following: Eustathius of Beirut had stepped on the metropolitan rights of the church of Tyre and performed episcopal ordinations at Byblos, Bostrys, Tripoli, Orthosias, Acca, and Antarades. Eustathius based himself on a decree of the emperor Theodosius II. Photius had paid no attention to it, and for this reason, the standing synod (Ἐνδημοῦσα Σύνοδος) of Constantinople excommunicated him (ἀκοινωνησία) at the beginning of 450. Threatened with deposition, Photius finally gave in after four months, and the sanction against him was lifted. As for the bishops that he had consecrated after the imperial decree, they were reduced to the presbyteral level. The intervention of the standing synod seemed shocking, and even the imperial commissioners raised the question of the nature of this institution: should the name of "synod" be given to the meeting of bishops staying in the capital?[70] People were also surprised that this assembly had decided the question in the absence of Photius.[71] Anatolius tried to justify the existence and competence of the standing synod in these words:

> For a long time, the custom has prevailed that the very holy bishops who are staying occasionally in the city whose name is glorious get together to regulate certain outstanding matters concerning the Church, to examine each one of them, and to make a judgment about the response to be given to those who ask the question. There is, therefore, no innovation on my part, and the most holy bishops on visit to the city who gathered together according to custom have not introduced any new order of things (καινὸν τυπόν). What was done shows the presence of the bishops.[72]

The fathers of Chalcedon who took part in this session gave no answer at all about the well-foundedness or lack thereof of what Anatolius said.[73] Nonetheless, they set aside all the decisions of the standing synod on this matter. Recalling that according to the legislation of Nicea, there could be only one metropolitan in a province, the council recognized that Photius alone had the prerogatives of this office. Eustathius was to be deprived of the jurisdiction which he had usurped in the north of Phoenicia Iᵃ. In his defense, Eustathius made reference to a measure of Theodosius II, but the fathers of Chalcedon categorically affirmed that imperial decrees that go against the canons were null: κατὰ τῶν κανόνων πραγματικὸν μηδὲν ἰσχύσι.⁷⁴ The affair of this session most certainly inspired the promulgation, five days later at session 7, of canon 12. The principle according to which the "pragmatic sanctions" opposed to the canons are without value was admitted by the state, and a law was issued on November 12, 451, quite soon after, which expressly established it in law.⁷⁵ In addition, the council considered the reduction of a bishop to the level of a presbyter to be a sacrilege; this had been done for the bishops ordained by Photius. The excerpt of the minutes of the meeting on this point was later on inserted into the Greek canonical collections as canon 29 of Chalcedon.⁷⁵ᵃ

The fifth session was held on October 22.⁷⁶ There was a reading of the projected formulary worked out during the preceding days in private meetings presided over by Archbishop Anatolius. Unhappily, this important document was not reproduced in the minutes, and we know nothing about its wording. What is certain according to the debates is that it contained the expression ἐκ δύo φύσεων.⁷⁷ This text received great support, but it raised objections on the part of the bishops of the diocese of the East. As for the legates of the pope, they rejected it categorically and threatened to withdraw if it were adopted. Much agitation then swept over the council. The imperial commissioners and the Roman legates maintained that the Tome of Leo should be taken into account, since the council had already received it when Dioscorus was condemned, and he had already accepted the formula ἐκ δύο φύσεων. In other words, it was necessary to choose between Leo and Dioscorus. G. Bardy observes that "in reality, the problem was more complex: it was not between Dioscorus and Leo that they had to choose but between Leo and Cyril, between the Tome to Flavian and the anathemas."⁷⁸ Faced with this dilemma, the bishops declared that they believed as did Leo. We note that an editorial commission was immediately set up; six bishops from the diocese of the East, three from Asia, three from Pontus, three from Illyricum, three from Thrace, and the Roman legates were to come up with a new formulary. The members of the commission withdrew to the oratory of St. Euphemia; their deliberations were secret. After some time, the members of the commission came back into the basilica to

give a reading of their work. This statement was accepted and constituted the dogmatic definition of the fourth ecumenical council.[79] Here
is the text:

> Therefore, following the holy fathers, all of us teach unani-
> mously that everyone must confess that our Lord Jesus
> Christ is one single and same Son, who is perfect according
> to divinity and perfect according to humanity, truly God and
> truly man, composed of a reasonable soul and a body, con-
> substantial with the Father according to divinity and consub-
> stantial with us according to humanity, completely like us
> except for sin; He was begotten by the Father before all ages
> according to His divinity and, in these latter days, He was
> born for us and for our salvation of Mary the Virgin, the
> Mother of God (τῆς Θεοτόκου) according to His humanity;
> one single and same Christ, Son, Lord, only begotten, known
> in two natures, without confusion, without change, without
> division, without separation (ἕνα καὶ τὸν αὐτὸν Χριστόν, Ὑἱόν,
> Κύριον, μονογενῆ, ἐν δύο φύσεσιν ἀσυγχύτως ἀτρέπτως, ἀδιαι-
> ρέτως ἀχωρίστως γνωριζομένον); the difference of natures is
> in no way suppressed by their union, but rather the properties
> of each are retained and united in one single person (πρόσω-
> πον) and single hypostasis; He is neither separated nor divided
> in two persons, but He is a single and same only-begotten
> Son, God the Word, the Lord Jesus Christ, such as He was
> announced formerly by the prophets, such as He Himself,
> the Lord Jesus Christ, taught us about Himself and such as
> the symbol of the fathers has transmitted to us.

The Chalcedonian definition used material from various sources,
principally the second letter of Cyril to Nestorius and his letter to the
Antiochians with the Formula of Union of 433, the Tome of Leo, and
Flavian's profession of faith.[80] Making the point very clearly that the
unity of Christ must not be sought on the level of natures but on the
level of the person or hypostasis, this definition introduced, or rather
officialized, a distinction in terminology which, for those who held
strictly to Alexandrian christology, was difficult to accept. This
explains somewhat the resistance to the reception of the Chalcedonian
dogma later on.

Three days later, the solemn promulgation of the conciliar decree
took place. In the meantime, on October 23, Maximus of Antioch and
Juvenal of Jerusalem were involved in delicate bargaining about the
geographical extent of their respective jurisdictions.[81] Maximus com-

plained about the encroachments of Juvenal in Phoenicia and Arabia. It was decided that the two provinces of Phoenicia and Arabia should belong to Antioch while the three provinces of Palestine should be under Jerusalem. The two primates also pledged to make no new claims in the future. It was made clear that this agreement concluded *in conspectu totius sanctae maioris synodi*, had been *non ex decreto iudiciario sed ex communi consensu.*[82]

On October 25 in the presence of Marcian and Pulcheria, the sixth session took place.[83] The emperor gave a long speech to the fathers in Latin, which was immediately translated into Greek. From the beginning of his reign, Marcian had the purity of the faith very close to his heart. He convoked the present council to eliminate all error and to dissipate all darkness so that from then on, no one would dare to present an opinion or faith different from that which the apostles and the 318 fathers had defended for posterity, different from that which the letter of Leo to Flavian witnessed to.[84] The emperor took himself to be Constantine coming in person to the council to strengthen the faith. After the customary acclamations, Aetius, archdeacon of Constantinople, read the dogmatic decree; it contained an introduction confirming Christian doctrine such as it had been defended by the fathers of Nicea, Constantinople, and Ephesus; then the symbols of Nicea and Constantinople were read. Mention was also made of the reception by the council of the letters of Cyril to Nestorius and to the easterners as well as the letter of Leo to Flavian. Those who admitted "a duality of Sons" were condemned, as were those who confounded and mixed the two natures of Christ. "Those who made up the myth of two natures before the union and of only one after the union" were also excommunicated. Then came the dogmatic definition, properly speaking, that we quoted above. The decree ended with a final section prohibiting the composition or diffusion of a different profession of faith. This was only a slight reworking of the decree of Ephesus issued in relation to the affair of Charisius.[85] There were 452 signatures counting the proxy votes of absent bishops.[86] It is probable that certain signatures were obtained at a later date.

After the prolonged acclamations, Marcian began to speak again and congratulated everyone on having re-established religious unity; this provoked new acclamations with anathemas against Nestorius, Eutyches and Dioscorus. The emperor then announced severe penalties against those who might seek to cause troubles regarding the faith— more acclamations; then the emperor said that "there still exist some points (*capitula*) that, in honor of your Reverences, we have reserved to you, judging it proper that they be regulated canonically by the council rather than imposed by our laws."[87] Three disciplinary decrees were then proposed by Beronician, *secretarius divini consistorii.*[88] The first text intended to put an end to the abuses in the activities of certain monks; it was aimed at the disorders the Eutychian monks had provoked. The second text stipulated that the clergy and monks were not to busy themselves with secular affairs. As for the third text, it recalled the prohibition of the transfer of clerics from one church to another.[89] These imperial suggestions were taken up respectively in canons 4, 3, and 20.

Marcian further proposed that in honor of the holy martyr Euphemia and the council, Chalcedon ought to be honored with the title of metropolitan city without thereby detracting from the prerogatives of the metropolitans of Nicomedia. This imperial decision was also accepted with enthusiasm.[90] At the same time, the bishops asked that they be permitted to leave, but the emperor required them to stay three or four more days in order to examine certain questions.[90a] The acts of the council for the seventh session contain only the text of the 27 canons.[91] Some ancient and concurring witnesses allow us to think that it was actually at this time and not later on that these 27 canons were issued.[92] This session was held on the same day as the preceding one, that is, on October 25.

We have seen that on October 23, the negotiations between Maximus and Juvenal were ended by a friendly accord sanctioned by the council. The question was brought up once more on October 26, at the eighth session. It seems, as E. Honigmann thought, that the preceding negotiations had not been considered official because the emperor's necessary consent had not been obtained.[93] The commissioners therefore raised the question again. The two interested parties made known the terms of their accord so they could be confirmed by the representatives of the emperor and by the members of the council. The Roman legates as well as Anatolius were agreeable. Other bishops gave the same opinion, then the whole council showed its approval by applause. The imperial commissioners congratulated everyone on the conclusion of this agreement.[94]

It seems that Maximus was not slow in regretting the concession he had made to Juvenal when Juvenal found himself faced with a critical situation following an anti-Chalcedonian rising in Palestine. Maximus hoped that St. Leo would disapprove of the accord; this is why in the minutes of the session which he sent to the pope, he added his own comment in the following interpolation: *...si tamen id venerabili pari nostro archiepiscopo Romae maioris Leoni placuerit, qui cupit ubique sanctorum patrum canones infrangibiles permanere.*[95] But Juvenal, with the support of the state, reinstated himself in Jerusalem. As for Maximus, he was deposed in 456 or 457 for some improper act.[96] The constitution of the patriarchate of Jerusalem was never again contested.

Again on October 26, the ninth session took place and mainly dealt with the examination of the case of Theodoret of Cyrus. Deposed by the robber council of Ephesus, he had appealed for justice to Pope Leo, who found him innocent of any crime. Nonetheless, it appeared somewhat suspect to many members of the council. They had not forgotten his friendship with Nestorius and his hostility to St. Cyril, whose anathemas he had refuted. Thus the council categorically required him to make a condemnation of Nestorius in no uncertain terms. He finally reconciled himself to this requirement and stated the following:

> Anathema to Nestorius and to whoever does not call the holy Virgin Mary Theotokos and to anyone who divides the only-begotten Son into two sons. I myself also have subscribed to the definition of faith and to the letter of the very reverend archbishop Leo; this is my opinion. And after all that, may you be saved![97]

The imperial commissioners affirmed that henceforth any doubt about the orthodoxy of Theodoret was put aside and that he should be given back his bishop's chair just as Pope Leo had judged right and proper. This proposition received the assent of the council. Then at the end of the session, Sophronius of Constantina and John of Germanicea, both suspected of Nestorianism, condemned Nestorius and Eutyches. As for Amphilochius of Side, suspected of Monophysitism, he had to anathematize Eutyches, which he did. These three bishops were then restored to their sees.[98]

On October 27, the tenth session took place, during which the case of Ibas was taken up.[99] He presented himself to the council to be restored to his see of Edessa, from which he had been driven by the Monophysites. When he had been priest and director of the theological school of Edessa, he had been an ardent admirer of Theodore of Mopsuestia. Around 434, he wrote a letter to the Persian bishop Mari;[100] in this letter, he accused St. Cyril of Apollinarianism.[101] In 436, he succeeded Rabula as bishop of the metropolitan city of Osrohoene; this Rabula had been a convinced partisan of Alexandrian christology. Ibas ran up against some local opposition which was encouraged by bishop Uranius of Himeria. He was soon accused of irregularity in the administration of his church, and people quoted certain heretical statements which he was supposed to have made: "I do not envy Christ for having become God, for I have become God as much as He."[102] Ibas always energetically denied that he ever said such a thing. His opponents appealed to Domnus of Antioch, but the synod which was held in the capital of the diocese of the East did not decide the question.[103] The accusers were not at all disarmed because they had the support of the court. This was the era when, through the eunuch Chrysaphius, Eutyches was behind the religious policies of Emperor Theodosius II who, by a decree of October 26, 448, ordered that the bishop of Edessa be taken to Phoenicia to appear before a three-member tribunal: Photius of Tyre, Eustathius of Beirut, and Uranius of Himeria.[104] The judicial action opened in Beirut. Daniel of Charrae, nephew of Ibas, and John of Theodosioupolis also found themselves as accused. Certain of the charges formulated against the bishop of Edessa expressed the passionate hatred of his adversaries; others were more serious, especially those touching dogma. Besides the alleged statement of a clearly adoptionist stripe, Ibas was reproached for having treated St. Cyril as a heretic. On this last point, he answered that he did not remember anything more about the matter; he affirmed that in the controversies after the Council of Ephesus, he simply followed his "exarch," John of Antioch.[105] We must also take into account a petition of the clergy of Edessa in favor of Ibas; previously his letter to Mari had been read. The tribunal moved to Tyre on February 25, and the atmosphere in which the examination of the case took place seemed to be greatly improved. Ibas was able to justify himself; he promised, besides, that on his return to Edessa he would anathematize Nestorius. The Monophysite party continued its intrigues against Ibas, who was imprisoned. He then soon learned that a pseudo-council at Edessa had deposed him.

For a better understanding of the unfolding of the events, we have re-established the probable chronological order. In reality, at Chalcedon at the time of the tenth session, the *Gesta Tyri* were read;[106] these presented the cause of Ibas in a rather favorable light. The next day, the eleventh session was held, and the adversaries of Ibas demanded that the *Gesta Beryti* be read; this document contained all the charges then formulated against him.[107] The imperial commissioners suggested that any information about Ibas contained in the acts of the robber council of Ephesus also be made known, but the Roman legates were opposed, claiming that the decisions of this assembly had been annulled by Pope Leo. This objection was accepted. The legates declared that Ibas had been recognized to be innocent and that he ought to be reinstated in his bishop's chair and return to his church from which he had been unjustly expelled. But what should be done with Nonnus, the bishop that followed him? The fathers decided that Nonnus should keep the diginity of bishop and that the case would be examined at a later time by Maximus and the bishops of the diocese of the East.

The members of the council declared in favor of Ibas, but certain bishops added the stipulation that he had to anathematize Nestorius, which he did.[108] Ibas died in 457, and Nonnus took over again the direction of the church of Edessa. By explicitly recognizing the orthodoxy of the letter of Ibas to Mari, Paschasinus had been a bit imprudent, since a century later, the fifth ecumenical council condemned this document because it attacked the doctrine of St. Cyril.[109]

In the evening after the tenth session, the situation of Domnus was briefly examined.[110] His case differed from that of the other victims of the robber council of Ephesus. Through weakness, he had accepted the decisions made by this assembly against the adversaries of Dioscorus; this was not held against him because he too was finally deposed. His successor, Maximus, followed the policy of Anatolius and signed the Tome of Leo. After his deposition, Domnus retired to the monastery of St. Euthymia, close to Jerusalem; he never asked for restoration. At Chalcedon, Maximus suggested that his predecessor ought to enjoy a certain part of the revenue of the church of Antioch for his upkeep. This proposition was submitted to the fathers of the council and they praised the conduct of Maximus and left the decision of the exact amount of the pension up to Maximus.

On Monday, October 29, the twelfth session was held. The fathers took up the conflict about the see of Ephesus.[111] Stephen, the bishop of this great city, had ejected Bassian, who then complained to the emperor Marcian; the emperor in turn sent the case to the council for examination. It seems that this whole affair was very clouded and entangled. Here is how Bassian presented the facts: While he was a priest in Ephesus, Memnon his bishop, who was supposedly jealous of him, forcibly ordained him bishop of Evaza in order to get him out of the city. Basil, the successor of Memnon, recognized the violence done to Bassian and consecrated another bishop for Evaza. After the death of Basil, Bassian was—so he claimed—put into the bishop's chair of Ephesus by several bishops and with the agreement of the clergy and the people of the city. In this way he exercised his episcopal functions for four years. Stephen contested this version of the facts. According to him, Bassian had forcibly taken over the see of Ephesus by a totally irregular action, and later on he was expelled from the city after an ecclesiastical judgment. As for Stephen, forty bishops with the agreement of the clergy and the people regularly installed him as bishop. Concerning the passage of Bassian, who was already bishop of Evaza, the canons 16 and 17 of Antioch were cited; in the collection used at that time, these canons had the numbers 95 and 96.[112]

The imperial commissioners declared that in their opinion neither Bassian nor Stephen was the legitimate bishop and that a new bishop of Ephesus should be chosen. The bishops of the diocese of Asia then insisted that this new bishop be elected and consecrated in the province of Ephesus in conformity with the custom which went back to the origins of Christianity. The clergy of Constantinople intervened from their side to affirm the prerogatives of their church in this matter. The bishops hostile to the intervention of Constantinople in the affairs of the diocese of Asia cried out: "Let the canons be observed!" In their turn, the clergy of Constantinople formulated the claims of their church in the following terms: "Let the decisions of the 150 holy fathers be observed! Let the privileges of Constantinople not be lost! Let the consecration be done here by the archbishop according to custom!"[112a]

The next day during the thirteenth session, the council rendered its judgment on the quarrel between Bassian and Stephen.[113] Both were recognized to be uncanonical; however, they were to keep the dignity of bishop and to receive pensions from the Church of Ephesus. In addition, the council agreed with the request of Bassian that he be given back everything which it could be shown in court that Stephen had taken from him. It is proper to notice that when Archbishop Anatolius declared himself for the installation of a new bishop, he said that the future candidate ought to be elected according to the choice of those that he was going to shepherd (....ἐξ ἐπιλογῆς πάντων τῶν μελλόντων ποιμαίνεσθαι).[114] Metropolitan Maximus of Sardis judiciously observed on this question that

> this opinion of Anatolius was intentionally ambiguous. It maintained that the new bishop was to be elected at Ephesus, which

would give satisfaction to the bishops of Asia, but he did not make clear by what bishop he was to be ordained. This position was exactly in agreement with the opinion of the clerics of his church, who asked that the ordination take place in Constantinople and that it be performed by their own bishops.[115]

On this very day, the council took up the jurisdictional dispute between the metropolitans of Nicea and Nicomedia; this was the fourteenth session.[116] Eunomius, bishop of Nicomedia, had asked the emperor to re-establish the prerogatives of his metropolitan city in the face of the encroachments of Bishop Anastasius of Nicea. This affair had been given over to the council. Anastasius was not content to deny the well-foundedness of the accusation; he also reproached the bishop of Nicomedia for having attacked his right. The principle object of the conflict was the canonical situation of Vasilinoupolis, a market town that once belonged to Nicea and which had been raised to the rank of a city. Anastasius, basing himself on a decree of the emperors Valentinian and Valens who confirmed to Nicea the title of "metropolitan city," had interfered in the church affairs of Vasilinoupolis. But Eunomius had another imperial decree read, more recent, which stipulated that the honor accorded to Nicea was not to slight in any way the rights of Nicomedia. The commissioners noted that in any case these two decrees only dealt with the administrative status of Nicea; according to the rule issued by the fathers of Nicea, there was only to be one metropolitan per province. The members of the Council of Chalcedon stated the opinion that the bishop of Nicomedia was the only true metropolitan in Bithynia. Consequently, Nicea ought only to have an honorary position above the other bishops of the province. Let us recall that the council had already had to decide the conflict in a similar case on Saturday October 20, when the controversy between Eustathius of Beirut and Photius of Tyre was submitted to it. In addition, if we admit that the 27 canons were adopted on October 25, the seventh session, the decision to be made in this conflict between Eunomius and Anastasius was already obvious.[117] After the council made its decision, Aetius, archdeacon of Anatolius, intervened to ask that no abridgment of Constantinople's rights be based on the judgment just given; according to him, it could be proved that Constantinople had rights over Vasilinoupolis. The reaction of the council shows that this intervention aroused feelings of defiance. Cries went up: "Let the canons be observed: Let us hold to the canons!"[118] Despite all this, the commissioners recapitulated the decision on Nicomedia and Nicea and added, taking into account the remark of Aetius, that the competence of the see of Constantinople concerning the consecrations in the provinces would be examined by the council in due course.[119]

The next day, Wednesday, October 31, in its fifteenth session, the council examined another conflict, this one concerning the bishop's see of Perrha in Euphratesia.[120] Sabinian had set out his complaint in an appeal to the emperor. Sabinian had been chosen by the metropolitan of Hierapolis and the other bishops of the province to replace Athanasius, who had been deposed by a council of 28 bishops in Antioch, 445. Accused of wrongdoing by his clergy, Athanasius had refused to appear, a fact confirmed by bishops at Chalcedon who had participated in the council of Antioch. The robber council of Ephesus had arbitrarily reinstated Athanasius and deposed Sabinian. Before the fathers of Chalcedon, and in order to justify his refusal to appear when called three times by the council of Antioch, Athanasius claimed that Domnus had been hostile to him. The commissioners proposed the following decision: having been canonically elected by the synod of the province, Sabinian was the legitimate bishop of Perrha. Athanasius had been justly deposed because he had not obeyed the orders to appear before the council, and therefore he must remain deposed. Maximus of Antioch with his synod should examine this case within eight months to see if the serious accusations against Athanasius were founded or not; if they were, the deposition would be confirmed and the guilty party would suffer the consequences of the civil law (...τοῖς δημοσίοις ὑποπίπτειν νόμοις).[121] On the other hand, if within the prescribed time there were no inquiry or if Athanasius were found innocent, he ought to be reinstated as the bishop of Perrha. In this case, Sabinian was to receive a pension taken from the funds of the church of Perrha; the amount should be fixed by Maximus of Antioch according to the material possibilities of this church. As for Sabinian, he ought, of course, to keep the dignity of bishop. This proposition of the commissioners was accepted by the fathers of the council, who thought it was an excellent idea.

We have seen that, during the discussion concerning the election of a new bishop of Ephesus, there had been a conflict about the place in which the ordination ought to take place. The clerics of Constantinople had loudly claimed this prerogative for their church by invoking the decision of the council of 381. The same day at the end of the following session, the question of the rights of Constantinople in Bithynia were raised in relation to the affair of Vasilinoupolis. The intervention of Aetius, Anatolius' archdeacon, as well as that of the imperial commissioners at the end of the session, proved that a project concerning the privileges of Constantinople had already been prepared for submission to the council fathers. If we refer to the Vasilinoupolis affair, it is not unreasonable to think that this project went even farther than the motion which was finally adopted. It most certainly mentioned a right of control for the archbishop of Constantinople, not only over the ordinations of the metropolitans of Pontus, Asia and Thrace, but also over all the bishops of these dioceses.

The sixteenth session was held on October 31. The minutes of this meeting have not been preserved. In the place where they should be found, the Greek acts contain a letter, dated June 27, 451, written by Pope Leo to the council.[122] As for the *versio correcta* and the *versio a Rustico edita*, they put the text of the 27 canons adopted well before this date in the place of this *actio* which is accounted as the fifteenth session.[123] By what was said at the seventeenth session held the following day, November 1, we know very well that the preceding session had been consecrated to the discussion of the motion on the rights of Constantinople. The elimination of the text of the sixteenth session was done intentionally because the interventions of the opponents of the motion were found in it.[124] It was evidently at Constantinople and at the time of the first redaction of the acts that the minutes of this meeting were omitted. But why was a letter of Pope Leo, which was certainly not read during this session, put in its place? E. Chrysos suggests the following: the content of this letter constituted an indirect refutation of what the Roman legates must have claimed; they could not participate in this meeting because they were not mandated to deal with this subject. The papal letter could be understood, however, as giving the legates complete freedom to discuss this question.[125]

On the other hand, why are the 27 canons inserted in this place in the two above-mentioned Latin versions, while according to the most ancient Roman as well as eastern traditions they are found together with the seventh session? E. Schwartz has presented a most probable hypothesis: the defenders of the "Three Chapters," that is, the authors of these versions, wanted to associate as closely as possible the sessions relating to Theodoret and Ibas with the session which officially adopted the dogmatic decree; they wanted to show the close link between the doctrinal decision and the restoration of these two persons.[126] This theory, however, does not explain why the canons were placed together with the *actio quintadecima*. Perhaps they simply wanted to fill up a space.

On Thursday, November 1, the last conciliar session was held.[127] The discussion was on a motion passed the night before by a small number of fathers concerning the privileges of the archbishop of Constantinople; the discussion continued this time in the presence of the imperial commissioners and with the participation of the Roman legates. The motion was definitively adopted despite the strong opposition of the legates. When we analyse and comment on this famous text, we will speak of this session, the minutes of which have been preserved.

Before the closing of the council, the fathers addressed an *adlocutio* to the emperors; it was very certainly the work of Theodoret.[128] In this document, the fathers justified their acceptance of the Tome of Leo and set out why they felt it was necessary to develop the dogmatic formulation in the face of heretical misinterpretations. We know that the followers of Eutyches and Dioscorus defended the perfect sufficiency of the Nicene creed. As an appendix, the fathers added a florilegium of patristic texts that agreed with the Tome of Leo.[129] They no doubt were looking ahead to the objections that were going to be made to the conciliar definition.

The council also wrote a letter to Pope Leo; it was full of deferential remarks about the Roman see and Leo himself. About this letter, H.E. Symonds has written that "this is perhaps the furthest point ever reached by the Easterners in acknowledging the Papal claims."[130] The fathers of the council informed the pope of the deposition of Dioscorus and their acceptance of the Tome to Flavian. All this was only a preamble, however, because their real purpose was to persuade the pope to accept their decision about the see of Constantinople. The opposition of the Roman legates was only considered a matter of form, and the fathers did not forget to mention that the adoption of the motion was in conformity with the will of the emperor. In a very diplomatic fashion, the authors of the letter expressed their understanding that a papal approbation of the decision would be the proper response to the acceptance of Leo's christological terminology in the dogmatic decree.[131] We know that St. Leo was totally deaf to such a suggestion and categorically rejected the decision on the see of Constantinople. As for the dogmatic decree which in the mind of the emperor Marcian ought to have finally settled the christological question, it only prolonged the controversy for several centuries. The divisions, far from being healed, ended up in a schism which continues to this day. It is moreover undeniable that in Syria, and even more in Egypt, the opposition to the dogma of Chalcedon was a vehicle for a strong nationalist movement. In addition, the decision about the privileges of the see of Constantinople was a lasting bone of contention between the Byzantine East and the Roman Church.

During the session that followed the solemn adoption of the dogmatic decree, in the presence of the emperor, the fathers of Chalcedon issued 27 canons; three of them were responses to the propositions made by Beronician in the name of the emperor.[132] Nonetheless, we notice that the redaction of these three canons differs considerably from the proposed texts. The protocol of the seventh session does not contain the canons; the minutes of the discussion were omitted also. This is particularly regrettable since it makes it more difficult to understand certain canons, especially canons 9 and 17. These 27 canons are the only ones of this council to appear in the *Synagoge* of John the Scholastic as well as in the ancient Latin versions.[133] However, in the *Syntagma in XIV Titles,* whose first redaction was made at the end of the sixth century,[134] the resolution which was voted during session 17 on the prerogatives of the archbishop of Constantinople is found after canon 27. Although this text was never numbered as canon 28, as the ancient manuscript tradition attests, the habit has grown up of mentioning in the the indices that the Council of Chalcedon issued 30 canons.[135] Moreover, it is certain that from the end of the fifth century the motion on the prerogatives of the archbishop of Constantinople appeared in certain Greek collections; this is indirectly attested to by the fact that this text was inserted in two manuscripts of the Prisca.[136] With the obvious intention of putting the motion in a context so as not to give the impression that it was an afterthought, no time was wasted in adding, in a rather clumsy way, excerpts of the protocol of the nineteenth session which stipulated that a bishop must not be reduced to the rank of a presbyter.[137] A little later on, an excerpt from the minutes of the fourth session was added; it was a purely circumstantial text which authorized the bishops of Egypt to defer signing of the Tome of Leo until the election of their new primate.[138]

Finally, as was the case with the stipulations of the council of Ephesus, distinctions have ceased to be made between canons and excerpts, and 30 canons have come to be attributed to the Council of Chalcedon.

SECTION 2:   THE CANONS OF THE COUNCIL

The Canons of the 630 Holy Fathers gathered together in Chalcedon under the consulate of Marcian, the eternally glorious and of him who will be designated consul on the 8th of the Kalends of November.[139]

1

We have decided that the canons issued by the holy fathers in each council up to the present time should remain in force.

Contrary to what its concise wording might lead us to believe, this canon is not a simple statement of general principle which says that the rulings issued by all previous councils should still be observed. The canon refers to a collection which had gradually formed in the East and whose normative authority was already accepted in practice; the Council of Chalcedon simply ratified this ecclesiastical acceptance.[140] However, we must not misinterpret the meaning of such an approval. It is true that this ruling marks a step on the road to an acceptance of a universal *jus scriptum* over customary law of each local church. This tendency to uniformity will crystallize with the legislation of the Synod in Trullo, 691. For the fathers of Chalcedon, the sanction given to the collection which they were using did not imply the rejection of all other canonical sources. At the Council of Constantinople in 381, Nectarius made reference to the "apostolic canons," and E. Honigmann thinks that he was alluding to the 74th of the canons of the Holy Apostles.[141] The collection used at Chalcedon had been built up by successive additions, and it was completed later on by the addition of Chalcedon's own 27 canons.[142]

Several times during the conciliar debates, the bishops made use of a book (βιβλίον) in which the canons were numbered according to a continuous numbering system: at the meeting dealing with the case of Carosus and Dorotheus (the 18th session according to the Greek acts), Aetius, the archdeacon of Archbishop Anatolius, read canons 83 and 84, that is, canons 4 and 5 of Antioch.[143] During the 12th session, which examined the case of the see of Ephesus, canons 16 and 17 of Antioch were read (they were numbered 95 and 96).[144] During the discussion about the privileges of the see of Constantinople, a secretary read the *synodikon* of the council of 381 "in the same book" (ἀπὸ τοῦ αὐτοῦ βιβλίου); he read from the beginning (τάδε ὥρισαν...) up to the passage concerning the prerogatives of the bishop of Constantinople inclusively.[145] It was from this book that the secretary, on the urging of Aetius, had read canon 6 of Nicea.

The Greek text was read to rectify a quotation made earlier by Paschasinus according to a Latin translation that significantly differed from the original.[146] In addition, at the 19th session, concerning the controversy between Photius of Tyre and Eustathius of Beirut, Nicea canon 4 was quoted.[147] It was also read at the 14th session, which dealt with the status of the church in Vasilinoupolis. In the Greek acts, the Nicene canon has the number 6 at this place in the text.[148] It is obvious that this inexact numbering is due to the sloppiness of a copyist whose mistake is explained by the graphic similarity between the cursive writing of δ' and ς'.

Writing to the emperor Leo in 458, the bishops of Pisidia referred to canon 4 of Antioch by the number 83.[149] They were, therefore, using a collection whose numbering was identical with that used by the chancellor's office in Constantinople. This ancient canonical collection has not come down to us in its original Greek form. It was still in use in the sixth century but was quickly eclipsed by the immediate success of the systematic collections that organized the canons by subject. An early work of this kind is only known because it is mentioned by John the Scholastic in the preface of his *Synagoge*.[150] It must have been published a little after 534, the year when the second edition of the *Codex Iustiniani* appeared.[151] This *Collection in LX Titles* was rapidly supplanted by the Συναγωγὴ Κανόνων Ἐκκλησιαστικῶν εἰς Ν´ Τίτλους Διῃρημένη *(Collectio quinquaginta titulorum)*. The *Synagoge* was compiled by John the Scholastic around 550 when he was the representative of patriarch Domnus III of Antioch in Constantinople.[152] Somewhat after the death of John the Scholastic (+577), another systematic collection was made. The canonical material used was more voluminous than that which appeared in the *Synogoge*; in addition, the canons were grouped in a more concentrated manner: this is the *Syntagma in XIV Titles*.[153] Besides these systematic collections, we must mention the appearance in the sixth or seventh century of a Κανονικὴ σύνοψις in which the canons were found in a summary form; the canons of each council were numbered independently.[154]

The old collection with continuous numbering was so totally forgotten that in the ninth century, Photius, one of the most cultured men of his time, when he found a canonical reference in this numbering system in a letter of Patriarch Ephrem of Antioch (527-45), admitted that he knew absolutely nothing about this way of numbering the canons.[155] From that time on, we should not be surprised to find that Zonaras and Balsamon in their commentaries on canon 1 of Chalcedon saw no allusion to a precise collection and understood its wording as a ruling of a general order.[156]

Fortunately, we do not lack solid indications which contribute to our knowledge of the content and ordering of this collection. Up to a certain point, we can even reconstruct the steps in its formation. Let us first note that the order in which the canonical sources are indicated in several subsequent documents shows the influence of the ancient collection's continuous numbering. This is the case with canon 2 of the Council in Trullo: "...We also confirm all the other canons which our holy and blessed fathers issued, that is, the 318 holy fathers at Nicea, those of Ancyra, of Neocaesarea, Gangra, Antioch in Syria, Laodicea in Phrygia, and also the 150 (holy fathers) who assembled in the royal and God-protected city..." We find here the content of the canonical collection used in Chalcedon quoted in exactly the same order. In addition, this collection can also be known through a Syriac translation made at Hierapolis (Mabbug) around 500-501[157] and by a Latin translation of Dionysius Exiguus based on a numbered *Graeca auctoritas*.[158] As for the witnesses of pre-Dionysian Latin collections, they are certainly of an incontestable interest for our knowledge of the ancient Greek corpus; however, we must not jump to any hasty conclusions based on the absence of this or that document in these versions.[159]

The primitive core of the collection used at Chalcedon contained the canons of three previous councils: Ancyra, Caesarea and Neocaesarea. The Council of Ancyra was held between Pascha and Pentecost, 314. A certain number of bishops from Asia Minor and Syria, between 12 and 18, met together under the presidency of Vitalis of Antioch in the capital of the province of Galatia. The purpose of this ecclesiastical assembly was to examine and determine the means for reconciling the lapsed. Some other disciplinary points were also treated. This council issued 19 canons.[160]

During the summer of the same year (314), another council was held in Caesarea; among the 20 bishops present, there were five who had been at Ancyra. This council determined the penances to be imposed on those who had given themselves over to certain forms of immorality. The six canons which are found after canon 19 of Ancyra in the Greek collection and which are attributed to Ancyra were in fact issued at Caesarea. The close chronological and geographical connection between these two councils, as well as the participation of several bishops in both meetings, explain the subsequent confusion. We must also consider two other factors: the insertion into a collection of a continuous numbering system and the similarity in sound and written form between Caesarea and Neocaesarea. However, the ancient Syriac tradition mentioned above along with the ancient Latin versions have kept traces of the existence of the Council of Caesarea; this is clearly substantiated by an ancient Armenian canonical collection.[161]

Following the above-mentioned canons, we have the 14 of the Council of Neocaesarea. We correctly note that this number is universally attested to in the ancient collections. It was only later that the number 15 was accepted by the division of canon 13 in two.[162] This synod was attended by 17 bishops from Galatia, Syria, Palestine and Armenia. Several of these bishops had already taken part in the Council of Ancyra. It is reasonable to think that Vitalis of Antioch also presided over the Council of Neocaesarea.[163] The council's legislation did not deal with the problem of the lapsed; we cannot, therefore, place it too close in time to the Council of Ancyra. In addition, we know that Vitalis of Antioch died in 319, and so that gives us a *terminus ad quem,* if we allow that he presided over this assembly. In any case, it is highly improbable that the synod could have been held after this date because that is when the persecution of Licinius began. If it was held immediately before Nicea, the case of the lapsed would have been touched on, as was to be the case at Nicea. In our opinion, therefore, the council was held near the year 319 and certainly not after.

If the collection had followed a strictly chronological order, the canons of Nicea ought to be found next, but a note reproduced in several later sources and which goes back to the compiling of the *Corpus Antiochenum* makes clear that, due to the authority of the Council of Nicea, its canons were placed at the beginning.[164] We will see later on what can be made of this explanation.

The ancient collection of Pontus ends with 20 canons issued by a council held at Gangra in Paphlagonia probably around 343, with 13 bishops attending.[165] They condemned the Asiatic extremes and the anarchistic tendencies of the followers of a certain Eustathius who was, however, to become bishop of Sebaste in Armenia around 357. No doubt it was in Pontus that a single collection of the above-mentioned canons had already been made. By studying ancient Latin translations, we can see that this block of conciliar canons constituted an autonomous group before being integrated into a larger whole.[166]

   It was at Antioch, probably between 360 and 378, that this collection of Pontus was first enlarged by the addition of 25 canons from a council held in Antioch around 330. From the fifth century on, these 25 canons were erroneously attributed to the council *in encaeniis* of 341.[167] In the middle of the eighteenth century, the Ballerini were the first to cast doubt on this theory of origin.[168] There are few today who think that these canons were issued by the council *in encaeniis*.[169]

   Later on, 59 canons were added from a synod in Laodicea in Pacatian Phrygia. There is no doubt about the existence of such a council in this city because Theodoret in fact mentions a council in Laodicea related to the cult of angels.[170] Actually, this very question is referred to in canon 35. This synod must have been held in the second half of the fourth century; this period is suggested by the state of church discipline described in the canons. We are certainly dealing here with a compilation; according to headings of the canons, we can distinguish two series: the first 19 beginning with the formula $\pi\varepsilon\rho\grave{\iota}$ $\tau o\tilde{\upsilon}$.... The others begin with either $\H{o}\tau\iota$ $o\mathring{\upsilon}$ $\delta\varepsilon\tilde{\iota}$... (canons 20-45 and 49-59) or by $\H{o}\tau\iota$ $\delta\varepsilon\tilde{\iota}$... (canons 46-48). There are some doublets: canons 10 and 31, 9 and 34. Inside the second series, we note a great similarity between canons 22 and 43; we have here the mark of a complex stratification. Several canons are formulated in an extremely concise way. These elements lead us to believe that we are dealing with a resume of the Phrygian church's legislation from the second half of the fourth century.[171]

   Were the bishops who came to Laodicea *"ex diversis regionibus Asiae"*[172] orthodox? Many scholars have their doubts, especially E. Schwartz who relies on the testimony of St. Basil's letter 218.[173] In the present state of our knowledge about this council, and, in addition, due to the lack of information on the relation between the canons transmitted under its name and the synod itself, the question cannot be answered. On the other hand, no one in antiquity ever found anything to criticize about the rectitude of the canons attributed to this council. If the canons of Laodicea do not appear in the *Prisca*, we must not necessarily see in this fact any mark of suspicion. In all probability, they were missing from the original Greek manuscript used by the translator. Moreover, the canons of Antioch were inserted in this version, and here and there, people have had certain doubts about them because, as we have already seen, they were wrongly attributed to the council *in encaeniis*.[174] The church scene was profoundly modified when, at the end of 377, the sentences of exile were revoked against the bishops opposed to homoean Arianism and then in January, 379, by the accession of Theodosius as emperor, a convinced advocate of Nicene orthodoxy. It was then that Meletius, the head of the majority catholic community in Antioch, was able to take up his functions again.[175] In the context of this triumph of orthodoxy and without changing anything, Meletius put the 20 canons of Nicea at the beginning of Antioch's canonical collection. Thus, the canons of the collection used at the Council of Chalcedon were numbered in the following way:

1-20	Nicea	1-20
21-45	Ancyra (+ Caesarea)	1-25
46-59	Neocaesarea	1-14
60-79	Gangra	1-20
80-104	Antioch	1-25
105-163	Laodicea	1-59

Toward the very end of the fourth century or later at the beginning of the fifth century, the *synodikon* of the Council of Constantinople, 381, was inserted at the end of this series of canons. In the early stages, this document was not divided into distinct canons and at the time of the Council of Chalcedon, it was still in block form. This is why, in the 17th session during the discussion of the rights of the see of Constantinople, a secretary read the text from its beginning (τάδε ὥρισαν...) up to the passage dealing with this question.[176]

We have put a question mark by the canons of Laodicea because the presence of this council's canons in the collection used at Chalcedon is not absolutely certain. In fact, outside the above-mentioned *synodikon*, only the canons of Nicea and Antioch were quoted. Taking into account the number of the canons of Antioch, it is obvious that this collection contained the canons of Ancyra, Caesarea, Neocaesarea and Gangra. However, we think it extremely improbable that Laodicea's canons were not also included. At the 17th session, according to the protocol, the secretary read the *synodikon* in the book which he had used previously.[177] Now, if the canons of Laodicea had been added after the Council of Chalcedon, they would equally have been found after the text of the *synodikon* and not before; for when we are talking about this collection of the *syntagma canonum, ordine chrono-*

logica dispositum,[178] we must not misunderstand the meaning of this expression: the chronological ordering in this case is related to the order in which elements were inserted into the collection and not to the chronological order in which the councils were held. The Council of Nicea apart as a special case, this is how the Council of Antioch, which took place before the Council of Gangra, got to be placed after it: Antioch was introduced into the collection at a later date. This Council of Antioch was probably a synod held around 330 and might even be the Council of the Dedication, *in encaeniis*. The argument from silence for the canons of Laodicea is not peremptory.[179]

The canonical codex of the chancery in Constantinople and the one used by the bishops of Pisidia had an exactly identical numbering system. However, a slight difference existed in other recensions. It came from the fusion of canons 4 and 5 of Ancyra (περὶ τῶν βίαν...) and (ὅσοι δὲ ανῆλθον...). This is why we have the following numbering in the work of Dionysius Exiguus as well as in the Syriac version edited in 500-501 at Hierapolis:[180]

21-44	Ancyra (+Caesarea)	1-24 instead of 1-25
45-58	Neocaesarea	1-14
59-78	Gangra	1-20
70-103	Antioch	1-25
104-62	Laodicea	1-59

In the two Dionysian recensions which have come down to us, the *synodikon* of Constantinople, 381, is divided not into four parts but three.[181] The passage on the primatial honor of Constantinople is attached to the part beginning with the words *"Qui sunt super diocesin episcopi...,"* while the third section concerns the intrusion of Maximus the Cynic.[182] The linking of the section on the prerogatives of Constantinople to the second part of the synodal text is also found in the East in the ancient Syriac version made at the very beginning of the sixth century.[183] This no doubt reflected the *Graeca auctoritas* used by Dionysius as well as by the Syriac translator.[184]

We thus had the following numbering in the second verson of the canons:

163 = Constantinople, c. 1 vulg.
164 = Constantinople, cc. 2-3 vulg.
165 = Constantinople, c. 4 vulg.

The division into several canons of the Council of Constantinople's *synodikon* was still recent and not yet fixed. We note that in this continuously numbered collection, certain ancient canons were missing; they were soon put into the new collections, however (*Collectio LX titulorum, Synagoga L titulorum, Syntagma XIV titulorum*).

First of all, we do not find the canons of the Holy Apostles there. We do not think, however, that we need see in this omission any sign of suspicion about this document erroneously attributed to the apostles; it must have received its final form in the same era and in the same region as our continuously numbered collection, that is, in Syria and around 380. The fact that first of all, Dionysius thought it good and proper to insert the first 50 of these "apostolic" canons shows that they were held in great esteem in the Christian East, even though many had doubts about their apostolic origin.[185]

No western document is found in the canonical collection approved at Chalcedon. There were, therefore, no canons from the Council of Sardica. Although the members of this assembly were not exclusively westerners—there existed a Greek recension of the canons issued at Sardica—these canons were not put into the eastern canonical collection after the defeat of Arianism, even though at Rome from the middle of the fourth century on, they were put together with those of Nicea.[186] Perhaps this is the reason why neither Flavian of Constantinople, Eusebius of Doryleum, nor Theodoret of Cyrus mention them in their respective appeals to Pope Leo. At the beginning of the sixth century, Dionysius, who favored the *Graeca auctoritas,* wrote that the legislation of Sardica *"non admisit universitas."*[187] This remark would no longer have been exact somewhat later on when the canons of this council were introduced into the *Collection in LX Titles.*

As for the absence of the Council of Ephesus, we should only be surprised on first glance. In fact, as we have already seen, the third ecumenical council had not, properly speaking, issued any canons.[188] The first six texts that appear as canons in Byzantine collections from the sixth century on are only a numbered division of the conciliar encyclical. As we know, this document only contains *ad hoc* disciplinary statements directly related to the condemnation of Nestorius and Pelagius. Canon 7, added as an afterthought in the *Synagoge* is the text of the resolution approved by acclamation ($\delta\iota\alpha\lambda\alpha\lambda\acute{\iota}\alpha$) during the meeting of July 22, 431, about the unchangeableness of the Nicene Creed. As for canon 8, it is a motion passed ($\psi\tilde{\eta}\varphi o\varsigma$) on July 31 about the autocephaly of Cyprus.

Finally, we note that the *Corpus Antiochenum adauctum* only contained synodal canons. We do not find any rulings written by individual bishops in it. John the Scholastic was the first to introduce into his compilation some rules taken from the correspondence of St. Basil. This was only a beginning because patristic texts in rather large numbers were soon to be inserted into the *Syntagma in XIV Titles* right from its first redaction, and this tendency was only to grow during the Byzantine Middle Ages.

The canonical collection which received the approval of the Council of Chalcedon was completed by the addition of its own canons. The translations of Dionysius reflect an original Greek work in which the canons kept their own numbering,[189] while in the Syriac version made in Hierapolis, they were completely integrated with a numbering system going from 167-193.[190] This canonical collection was eclipsed in the sixth century in the Byzantine East by other collections which took over its content. But thanks to ancient translations in Latin and Syriac, we can reconstitute the birth and development of this corpus which is very properly considered to be *antiquarum collectionum fere omnium quasi principium et fons.*[191]

2

If a bishop sets a price for ordaining someone and sells the grace of God which has no price, and ordains a bishop, a country bishop, a priest, a deacon, or anyone counted among the clergy, or if for money a bishop promotes a treasurer, a defender, a watchman, or anyone else to the service of the Church, such a bishop, being motivated by his own greed in undertaking such a thing, is in danger of losing his position if the deed is uncovered. Let the person not benefit in any way from the ordination or the promotion bought in this fashion, but let him be a stranger to the dignity or the position acquired for a price. Moreover, if any one gets involved in this shameful and illicit business, if he is a cleric, let him be deposed from his position; if he is a layman or a monk, let him be excommunicated.

In its many recensions, the Greek text of this canon has no significant variants. As for the the ancient Latin versions, they reflect the problems presented to a translator by terms which refer to institutions having no parallel in the West. This is particularily evident with regard to the "country bishops"; the oldest mention of this office in a purely western source is found in the Council of Riez, 439, even then it was only to resolve a special case based on canon 8 of Nicea.[192] In the West, the office of country bishop did not really appear until the eighth century.[193] Thus, the author of the *Prisca* created confusion in translating χωρεπίσκοπον by *provincialem episcopum*; Dionysius simply left out the Greek word.[194] The translators also had some hesitation about the way to render the term παραμονάριος in Latin. Here again Dionysius simply did not translate the word at all while, in the *Hispana,* the Greek word is simply written in Latin letters.[195] Rusticus' version relates the paramonary to the *mansionarius.*[196] The interpretation of the *Prisca* is only approximative: it uses the word *ostiarius.*[197] But in fact, the function of a doorkeeper existed in the West as well as in the East and was thought of in the West as one of the minor orders.[198] In contrast, the word οἰκονόμος caused no problem since it was easily understood by the Latins.[199] As for ἔκδικος it presented no problem either because an exactly corresponding term existed in administrative Latin; this is why we find the word *defensor* in all the Latin versions.[200]

The παραμονάριοι were watchmen in the sanctuaries; they also were responsible for maintenance and lamp-lighting. Moreover, this is where the Russian term *ponomar'* comes from.[201] The term is no longer used in modern Greek, but this function is described by the ancient term νεωκόρος. The *Pedalion* gives these words of explanation about this canon: ἤτοι προσμονάριοι. This latter term comes from the verb προσμένω meaning "to wait." The meaning then is that these employees waited for those who came to visit the churches.[202]

The ἔκδικοι (in Latin *defensores*) were at first lawyers, judicial councilors of the churches. At a council held in 407 in Carthage, the fathers decided to ask the emperors to appoint certain *defensores* from among the lawyers who would deal with the civil authorities when necessary.[203] Canon 23 of the Council of Chalcedon shows us that these *defensores* in the East had disciplinary functions; this is confirmed for a later time by the witness of Constantine Porphyrogenetus.[204] In Constantinople, during the Middle Ages, the πρωτέκδικος, that is the chief of the defenders along with two assistants, was responsible for judging minor cases in the name of the patriarch.[205] We will speak later on about the treasurers in the analysis of canon 26.

In canon 2, we note that the verb χειροτονεῖν is used to indicate the accession to all degrees of the clerical state. In other ancient Christian texts, the verb χειροθετεῖν is used as a synonym.[206] Moreover, their meaning is very close etymologically, and it is only by pure convention that later on we see a tendency to establish a distinction between the *cheirothesia,* the rite of installation for minor orders and *cheirotonia,* the sacramental rite for the conferring of the hierarchical orders of bishop, priest and deacon. In this regard, it is proper to recall that in the East, the imposition of hands is used to confer all degrees of the clergy while in the West, this imposition of hands is reserved only for the hierarchical orders.[207]

In his commentary on this canon, Zonaras says that the bishops, priests, deacons and subdeacons receive a cheirotonia (χειροτονοῦνται) while those in minor orders receive a cheirothesia.[208] This last term is not used here by Balsamon; he uses the verb σφραγίζειν, thus designating the cruciform tonsure given to someone entering into the clerical state.[209] Symeon of Thessalonica makes a clear distinction in terminology between the cheirotonia performed inside the altar (ἐντὸς τοῦ βήματος) and the cheirothesia performed outside the sanctuary (ἔξω τοῦ βήματος).[210] Although this distinction between the two words was commonly accepted in canon law and actually corresponds to a difference in the very nature of the orders conferred, we must note that the liturgical terminology does not reflect the precision of the theology.[211] If the fathers of Chalcedon use the verb χειροτονεῖν for the conferring of all clerical orders, they reserve it strictly for that usage. Προβάλλειν means "to promote" and is used by them to indicate the way of acceding to functions which are not in the clerical cursus. In parallel fashion, this distinction is taken up in the body of the text in the nouns χειροτονία and προβολή. The degree conferred in the clergy is designated by the word "dignity" (ἀξία) while the function to which anyone accedes by a promotion is called "charge" (φρόντισμα). Every person in the service of the Church is included in the "canon" (τοῦ κανόνος). The meaning of this term is wider than that given to it by the fathers of Nicea: they only considered clerics to be ἐν τῷ κανόνι ἐξεταζόμενοι.[212]

The misconduct that the council fathers had in mind is the obtaining of clerical dignities or functions in the administration of the Church by the payment of money. Bishops who were found guilty of this wrongdoing were to be deposed. Such is in effect the meaning of the expression κινδυνευέτω περὶ τὸν οἰκεῖον βαθμόν.[213] As for the clerical dignity or the administrative function acquired for a price, it was considered to be annulled by the very fact. Any cleric who got involved in such a shameful transaction was also to be deposed. If the person was a layman or a monk, he was to be excommunicated. The monks are mentioned here with laymen for at that time the majority of them were not in holy orders; moreover, this is still the case in the

East, notably on Mount Athos.

Ordinations and appointments to administrative offices in the Church for money did not exist, no doubt, as long as the Christian communities lived in precarious conditions, even though the first attempt to buy the imposition of hands goes back to the very first years of Christianity. This of course was Simon Magus whom we read about in Acts 19; the word "simony," meaning the buying and selling of holy things comes from his name.[214] Judaism also knew this kind of corruption, and scandalous facts about this practice are reported to us in the Bible.[215]

The plague which these simoniac ordinations constituted became a real epidemic from the fourth century on. St. Athanasius reproached the Arians for this fault.[216] St. Basil also severely criticized bishops in his jurisdiction for this practice.[217] Canon 29 of the Holy Apostles says that "if a bishop has obtained his dignity for money, the same thing goes for a priest or a deacon, let them be deposed, both the ordainer and the one ordained, and let them be completely excluded from communion as I, Peter, did for Simon Magus." St. John Chrysostom intervened in the diocese of Asia where Antoninus of Ephesus had set up a veritable auction of episcopal sees.[218] Among the complaints against Ibas of Edessa at the Council of Beirut, about which we have already spoken, we find this one, that he supposedly took money for ordinations.[219] This canon of Chalcedon reveals to us the extent of the evil since it concerns not only all the degrees of the clergy, but also administrative functions in the Church as well. The council's ruling did not have the hoped-for results. In 458-59, Gennadius of Constantinople and the synod gathered around him made a solemn condemnation of these simoniac ordinations.[220] The civil legislation also forbade this practice,[221] but to no avail! Pope Gregory the Great (590-604) was once heard to say that *"in Orientis Ecclesiis nullum ad sacrum ordinem nisi ex praemiorum datione pervenire."*[222] The Synod in Trullo renewed the condemnation of simoniac ordinations in its canon 22. The reading of canons 4 and 5 of the seventh ecumenical council gives the impression that this traffic was practiced in broad daylight. According to canon 19 of the same council, candidates for the monastic life were also made to pay. Some years later, in 790, Patriarch Tarasius of Constantinople issued an encyclical once again about buying and selling ordinations, and this document was inserted in the canonical corpus of the Byzantine Church.[223] The evil continued to be practiced all through the Middle Ages,[224] however, even into the

Ottoman period and up to the present time.[225]

3

**It has come to the attention of the holy council that some of
those on the list of the clergy, by a shameful money-grubbing
spirit, take on the management of other people's rental properties and become businessmen dealing with temporal matters; they neglect the service of God, visit the homes of
worldly people, and through greed, take on the management
of their material possessions.**

**The holy and great council has therefore decided that from
this time on, no bishop, cleric or monk must manage rental
properties or become the administrators of temporal affairs
unless he is compelled by the law—not being able to get out
of it—to become the guardian of minors or to become
responsible for the affairs of the Church, orphans, helpless
widows, or persons in great need of the Church's help: and
this only if the bishop of the city asks him and in the fear of
the Lord. If anyone from now on goes against these decisions, let him be put under ecclesiastical penalties.**

This canon was issued in response to the desire of the emperor
Marcian expressed during the sixth session. In effect, it takes up the
content of the second of the propositions submitted at this time to the
fathers of the council.[226] They kept the substance of the proposition
and in part the form of the proposed text but introduced some
editorial modifications. They completed the text by introducing a
double exception concerning the care of minors, in the case of legal
obligation, and the protection of certain categories of persons for
whom the Church traditionally had particular concern. In addition,
when the proposed text provided for the deposition of recalcitrants,
the canon as adopted is less precise about the penalties to be given
out. Novella 86 of Leo VI the Wise set out a suspension for a certain
length of time, while only a second conviction brought with it
deposition.[227]

The Church has never categorically been opposed to clerics being
involved in a secular activity when this is necessary. But, of course,
not just any profession or activity is envisioned. Thus, any activity
involving widespread commercial operation or financial speculation
is absolutely prohibited. Before the Council of Chalcedon, the principle had been clearly set out by canons 6 of the Holy Apostles and 16
of Carthage.[228] It is true that this was not something new. Already

in the third century, St. Cyprian chastised bishops who accepted very profitable occupations or got involved in business.[229] Later on, St. Jerome spoke of clerics who became *"procuratores et dispensatores domorum alienarum atque villarum."*[230]

The ruling of the Council of Chalcedon was not very well observed. The same thing is the case for canons 10 of Nicea II and 11 of the First-Second Council. Zonaras notes that despite the formal prohibitions by the canons as well as by the laws of the state, this form of wrongdoing has never been eliminated; after all, there is a certain lack of real will shown by the civil and religious authorities in taking effective measures to suppress this kind of activity.[231]

Finally, we note that there are no variants that affect the meaning of the canon in its many recensions; the same is true for the ancient Latin translations.

4

Let those who truly and sincerely lead a monastic life be honored as is proper! But because certain persons, for whom the monastic life is only a pretext, sow trouble in the affairs of the Church and state by inconsiderately roaming around in the cities trying even to establish monasteries for themselves, it has seemed good and proper that no one be allowed to build or establish a monastery or an oratory anywhere without the consent of the bishop of the city. In each city and country area, let the monks be subject to the bishop; let them seek peace and only apply themselves to fasting and prayer, remaining in the place where they made their profession of renunciation; let them not cause any troubles in the affairs of the Church or state; and let them not get mixed up in such affairs by leaving their monasteries, except if eventually they are permitted to do so by the bishop of the city for some grave necessity. In addition, let no slave be admitted into the monasteries with the intention of becoming a monk without the consent of his own master.

We have decided that whoever goes against the present ruling will be excommunicated, so that the name of God will not be blasphemed.

As for the bishop of the city, he must exercise oversight in the monasteries, as is proper.

This canon, as well as the preceding one, was issued in response to a proposed decree made by the emperor Marcian at the sixth session.

It was actually the first of the texts presented to the fathers of the council. The canon substantially reproduces the wording of the imperial document and in part does so literally.[232] However, the fathers did not go along completely with the emperor's request; in his proposal, not only slaves but also *adscripticii (ἐναπόγραφοι)* were mentioned, that is, farmers who were not slaves but were treated as such by their masters with the only exception being that they could not be moved elsewhere.[233] The civil law, however, did not take into account this omission and so forbade the *adscripticii* from taking the monastic habit without the permission of their masters.[234]

Considered in its whole, this canon constituted the first official definition of the status of monks in the framework of the institutional Church. The glaring abuses which had been apparent for some time, notably at Ephesus in 449, required this juridical clarification.[235] The preamble of the canon underlines the fact that the council felt no antipathy toward monasticism in general. The fathers wisely set out the principle of the jurisdiction of each bishop over the monks that were located on the territory under his authority. It is not permitted to set up a monastery or an oratory without his authorization. The monks must respect their vow of stability and consequently stay in the monastery where they took the habit.[236] Canon 21 of the seventh ecumenical council recalls this principle but lessens its rigor somewhat, allowing a monk to go to another monastery if he receives the permission of his own abbot. Canon 4 the First-Second Council repeats the rule of stability as the norm, but it envisions the case where the bishop, for the good of a monastery, might transfer some monks elsewhere or give some monks work outside their own monastery, and this is permitted.[237] Among the canons attributed to St. Nicephorus, patriarch of Constantinople (806-815), there is one which sets out three cases in which a monk can abandon his monastery: if the abbot is a heretic; if women come into the monastery; if children live in the community to receive a secular education.[238] Thus, although stability is the canonical norm, it cannot be considered as a constituent element of monastic life on the same level as chastity and poverty. Stability is linked to obedience which does not exclude, in certain circumstances, going beyond the rule.[239]

It is clear that the intention of the legislators in issuing this canon was to affirm the superior, and therefore decisive, authority of the bishop in the case of a conflict between the obedience due to the abbot and that due to the bishop. A century later, the legislation of the emperor Justinian will make clear that it is right of the bishop to confirm the election of abbots.[240] From the ninth century on and after the victory of Orthodoxy over iconoclasm, the phenemenon of "patriarchal stauropegia" developed in the Byzantine Empire, that is, the exemption of certain monasteries vis-à-vis the jurisdiction of the local bishop.[241] We must certainly note that such an exemption does not at all signify the independence of the stauropegial monastery but its submission to the titular authority of the patriarch which, in this case, is substituted for that of the bishop of the locality. It is true that some monasteries claimed to have a freedom from all episcopal juris- diction, but that was a serious distortion of the canons which was corrected toward the end of the Middle Ages.[242] Let us note that from the fifth century on, in order to control the monks and to inspect the monasteries under their authority, many bishops appointed exarchs.[243]

The present canon prohibits monks from getting involved in any way in church affairs. The fathers of the council were no doubt think- ing about the troubles caused by the Eutychian monks. This ruling was to have little effect, however, because many monks considered it their duty to fight for their doctrinal opinions or to fight against what seemed to them to be attacks on church discipline or Christian moral- ity. In the realm of dogma, the conduct of the monks was often bene- ficial for orthodoxy, as was the case when they fought against the iconoclastic heresy in great numbers. The enlisting of many monks in the ranks of the Monophysites was, on the other hand, extremely harmful. Without question, it was under their agitation that the oppo- sition to the Council of Chalcedon spread and resulted in the estab- lishment of a separate hierarchy. We must not, however, make an uncalled-for generalization, for there were great monastic figures among the defenders of Chalcedonian orthodoxy; we need only cite St. Euthymius and St. Sabbas. During the Byzantine period, the monks often considered themselves as the expression of the Christian conscience in the face of a hierarchy much too prone toward com- promises with the imperial power; from this position, they often inter- vened in disciplinary questions to defend the rigorist position. A typi- cal illustration of this kind of situation appeared during the ninth century in the conflict between Patriarch Nicephorus and the Studite monks over the restoration of the priest Joseph, previously deposed because he blessed the scandalous marriage of Emperor Constantine VI.[244]

On the subject of secular activities carried out by monks, Zonaras is very strict; he also applies the expression of the canon, "so that the name of God will not be blasphemed," to this trangression of the norm.[245] Balsamon, who does not comment on this expression, insists on the contrary on the legitimacy of such activities when permission is given by the bishop or the emperor; he supports his point of view, which he considers very important, by giving examples.[246] With regard to episcopal jurisdiction over monks and monasteries, the will of the fathers is clearly stated in the final injunction of the canon: "As for the bishop of the city, he must exercise oversight in the monasteries, as is proper." This sentence, in fact, does not appear in the text presented in the name of the emperor Marcian.

Finally, we note that the wording of this canon presents only insignificant differences in its various recensions.

5

Concerning bishops or clerics who wander from one city to another, it has seemed right and proper that the canons issued by the holy fathers with them in mind should remain in force.

In its several recensions, the text of this short canon does not present any variants that affect its meaning. The omission of the adjective ἰδίαν in relation to ἰσχὺν has no particular meaning.[247] In this case, we can make the following translation: "...the canons issued by the holy fathers with them in mind should remain in force." All the ancient Latin versions are unanimous in their witness and, moreover, show that this adjective surely appeared in the primitive Greek text.[248] The previously issued canons which the fathers of Chalcedon were thinking about were those found in the collection mentioned above, whose composition we have already noted: that is, Nicea canon 15, Ancyra canon 18, Antioch canons 16 and 21. We might also mention the canons composed before Chalcedon but which were not found in the collection used at the time of this council: Holy Apostles canon 14, Sardica canons 1 and 2, Carthage canon 48. This simple enumeration shows that the rule was being poorly observed. Its re-enforcement by the fathers of Chalcedon had little more effect than the previous canons. In analyzing canon 15 of Nicea, we explained the causes of this disregard of the norm; they are linked to the sociological changes in Christian society during the fourth century. These changes brought along with them a weakening of the idea of the local church as a tightly structured entity. Custom prevailed over written law for the mass of the clergy, with the exception of the bishops. The translation of bishops from one see to another has always been considered in the Orthodox Church to be a rare exception and not the norm; this remains so despite abuses here and there.[249] The ecclesial tradition has always seen a mystical link between the bishop and his church, one similar to that of marriage, which, moreover, is reflected in the canonical terminology. As proof that the profound reasons for the immovability of other clerics had been forgotten, we can cite canon 17 of the Synod in Trullo: a cleric's moving from one diocese to another is conceived of only as a matter of legality. There is a wrongdoing only if a cleric has not been regularly transferred: in other words, only if he has not received the authorization of his bishop.[250]

Several scholars who have commented on this canon in modern times, notably Beveridge, Heféle and Milash, have thought that the fathers of the council had the case of Bassian in mind when they issued the present ruling; his case was discussed during the twelfth session.[251] This theory supposes that the canon was not adopted at the seventh session but later on. Although this thesis is not completely impossible, it seems to us highly unlikely because it goes against the unanimous testimony which says that the 27 canons were adopted during the seventh session.[252] Let us add that the general character of canon 5 does not at all require us to link it with a specific case.

6

In addition, no one is to be ordained at large, either priest, or deacon, or any member of the clergy in general, unless the ordinand is attached to a city or village church, to a martyr's shrine or to a monastery. As for whoever is ordained at large, the holy council has decided that such an ordination is without value and that, to the shame of the ordainer, he will not be able to exercise his function anywhere.

The decision set out here is closely related with the preceding one. This link, moreover, is very clearly indicated in Greek, by the particle δέ.[253] In effect, according to the conception of the ancient Church, a person is ordained to fulfill a precise function; from then on, there is a link between the man and the function, in principle unchangeable. According to the nature of these stipulations, canon 6 ought to be found before the previous one; that would have been the logical order. In this connection, we must recall that no minutes have been preserved of the session during which the 27 canons were adopted. The adoption of the canons was done, no doubt, with a certain amount of haste. This would also explain the awkward style that is apparent in this canon. The construction of the first sentence is confused because the conditional subordinate clause does not really show the opposition intended in this case. However, despite this editorial awkwardness, the meaning is perfectly clear. To indicate an ordination which is not conferred with a specific charge in mind, the fathers of Chalcedon used two successive adverbial synonyms: ἀπολελυμένως and ἀπολύτως, formed from the same verb ἀπολύω. They have been identically translated in all the ancient Latin versions by the word "absolute."[254]

The prohibition formulated in this canon results from the very finality of ordination, whose *raison d'être* is to look after the needs of the Church's ministry. To confer a ministerial degree and ignore this purpose is an aberration. In addition, no one can be a cleric in general; a priest, a deacon or a subordinate minister necessarily belongs to a local church, and is therefore under the authority of the bishop who assumes its direction. The only fact that can explain why a canon of this kind was necessary is that certain bishops had lost the awareness of the intrinsic relation between the conferring of an order and a clearly defined service in a church. The idea of ministry in the first three centuries of Christian history would not have allowed ordinations at large, but subsequent evolution could not help but have an influence on practice. It sometimes came to the point of considering the priesthood more as an honor than a service. We actually know of cases where the ordination had been conferred at large: St. Paulinus of Nola accepted ordination by the bishop of Barcelona in 394 on the condition that he receive no particular ministry, and this he clearly states himself.[255] Somewhat before this, it seems that St. Jerome agreed to become a priest on the same condition.[256] Most often, it was monks of great repute who were elevated to the priesthood as a purely honorific gesture. P. Canivet thinks, not without some likelihood, that this canon was issued especially to regulate monastic ordinations.[257] Excluding the above-mentioned case of St. Jerome, certain ordinations of monks do in fact appear to be completely aberrant. This is how the anchorite Akepsimas accepted ordination to the priesthood, which was proposed for him to reward his virtue, simply because he had only a few more days to live.[258] The ordination of another ascetic by the name of Marcertonius was carried out without his knowledge and against his will and was done for no pastoral reason whatsoever.[259]

The council declared that an ordination at large is "without value." The Greek word used here is *ἄκυρος*. The adjective has been translated in the ancient Latin versions either as *inefficacis, irrita* or *uacua*.[260] The Old Slavonic version of the *Kormchaya Kniga* uses the word *nevlastno*.[261] The Greek term as well as its translations express an axiomatic principle of traditional church law: according to strictness, all irregular ordinations are null. By making clear that whoever is ordained in this way cannot officiate anywhere, the fathers of Chalcedon wanted to stop these pseudo-clerics from troubling the life of the churches.

If bishops are not mentioned in this canon in connection with ordinations at large, it is simply because such an abuse had not really become widespread even if such cases were not completely unknown.[262] In this text, there is an allusion to clergy serving in a martyr's shrine, *martyrium;* here we are dealing with a non-parochial church built in honor of a martyr. We know that the council itself held its sessions in the shrine of St. Euphemia, which toward the end of the fourth century, Etheria called *famosissimum*.[263] Many such shrines were constructed after Christian worship began to enjoy complete liberty in the Roman Empire.

We note finally that in the text of this canon the word *χειροθεσία* is used to indicate an ordination to any degree of the clergy and is used in connection with the verb *χειροτονεῖν*. This usage shows very clearly, as we have already said, that at this time, no semantic difference at all was made between *χειροτονία* and *χειροθεσία*.

7

We have decided that those who have been admitted into the ranks of the clergy or who have become monks, from now on, must no longer take service in the army or accept any secular dignity; if they dare to do this and do not repent and return to the state which they previously chose for God, they will be excommunicated.

The very minor variants of this canon's text do not at all alter its meaning;[264] the ancient Latin versions are all very faithfully translated as well. In this regard, we note that the technical Greek expression *ἐν κλήρῳ τεταγμένους* has been translated by *"in clero taxati fuerunt"* in the *Hispana*, no doubt under direct Greek influence and to the detriment of easy comprehension.[265] Dionysius correctly translated the term by *"in clero deputati sunt,"*[266] but the most correct interpretation is found in the *Prisca: "in clero ordinati...sunt."*[267]

This canon presupposes that entry into the clergy as well as into monastic life has a lasting character which excludes the exercise of functions not in keeping with a consecrated life. In the same line of thought, canon 3 forbids clerics and monks from managing people's worldly goods; it forbids them from exercising public functions as well. Similar prohibitions on this point can be found in the earlier canons of the Holy Apostles: canon 81 states that:

> we have said that a bishop or a priest must not allow himself to take on public employment but must apply himself to churchly affairs; if he does otherwise, let him be deposed; for no one can serve two masters according to the injunction of the Lord.

Canon 83 states a similar position:

> A bishop, priest, or deacon who takes on military service and wants to remain in possession of both services, the Roman power and the priestly ministry, must be deposed. In effect, the affairs of Caesar are Caesar's and those of God are God's.[267a]

Canon 7 of Chalcedon also prohibits clerics and monks from being in this type of activity; it threatens an across-the-board excommunication to guilty persons who refuse to repent. Generally, as sanctions for these serious wrongdoings, the canons set out deposition for clerics and excommunication for laymen and monks. Why, then, are guilty clerics here threatened with anathema, that is, excommunication in its most rigorous form? The explanation given by Zonaras on this point and taken up by Balsamon seems to us correct: clerics who voluntarily abandon their habit in a decisive and final way have already removed themselves from the priestly dignity (...ἑαυτοὺς τῆς ἀξίας τῆς ἱερατικῆς γυμνώσαντες). From then on, they were punished as laymen.[268] We can, therefore, see here that the will of the legislator is to inflict a punishment and not only to sanction by deposition an already existing situation.

The religious legislation of the emperor Justinian foresaw the case of a monk leaving his monastery to lead a worldly life or to take on a public function. He must be constrained to take up the monastic life again, but if he commits the same offense again, the governor of the province was to re-integrate him into his service, no doubt as a military or paramilitary functionary: τῇ ὑποκειμένῃ αὐτῷ τάξει.[269] This ruling was taken up again in the Basilica;[270] it was abolished, however, by a novella of Leo VI the Wise, who considered it unjust. The twice-guilty monk was to be kept in the monastery.[271] The emperor believed that this was in conformity with the Church's constitution (ἐκκλησια-στικὴ...κατάστασις); he understood this term to refer to canon 7 of Chalcedon. In fact, the ruling of the council set out excommunication but said nothing about the subsequent fate of the guilty person.

Concerning the wording of this canon, we note that our translation of the Greek term στρατεία and its corresponding Latin term *militia* found in all the ancient Latin versions, is "service in the army." It is true that at this period of the late empire, the word could also mean a position at court.[272] This is a lexical vestige showing the military origins of imperial institutions, but we cannot completely dismiss the hypothesis that στρατεία (*militia*) could mean "position at court." However, this interpretation does not seem very likely because the wording of the canon seems to us more logical if the prohibition concerns both service in the army and a public function. If στρατεία here means a position at court, we might expect a statement of this kind: μήτε ἐπὶ ἄλλην ἀξίαν κοσμικήν. Although this argument is not decisive, we must draw attention to the fact that this meaning, our interpretation (excluding both army and public service), has always been given to this canon of the Council of Chalcedon. Thus, we have the same meaning in novella 8 of Leo the Wise and in the Old Slavonic translation of the canon.[273]

Concerning the principle set out in this canon, Bishop Nicodemus Milash most properly makes a reference to the words of the Lord:

> And indeed, which of you here, intending to build a tower, would not first sit down and work out the cost to see if he had enough to complete it? Otherwise, if he laid the foundation and then found himself unable to finish the work, the onlookers would all start making fun of him and saying, "Here is a man who started to build and was unable to finish" (Luke 14: 28-30), and "Once the hand is laid on the plough, no one who looks back is fit for the kingdom of God" (Luke 9:62).[274]

To these words of the Lord is added the following reference from the monastic tonsuring service: "...to you, therefore, who started to go forward on the road leading to the kingdom of God, it is henceforth forbidden to turn back, for, in this case, you will not be worthy of the kingdom of heaven."[275]

8

Let those clerics who serve in centers for the poor, monasteries and martyrs' shrines remain under the authority of the bishops of each city in conformity with the tradition of the holy fathers, and let them not rebel arrogantly against their own bishops.

Those who dare to go against this ruling in whatever way and who do not submit themselves to their proper bishop, if they are clerics, let them be under canonical sentence and if they are monks or laymen, let them be deprived of communion.

Though the meaning of this canon is very clear, we can nonetheless see a certain incoherence in its redaction. In fact, its first part only deals with clerics while the second part envisions sanctions against those who go against the ruling, monks as well as laymen. In our opinion, we have here another indication of how the canons of Chalcedon were hastily edited during the seventh session. Zonaras did not miss this anomaly, and he supposed that the clerics aimed at by this ordinance would not have dared, in and of themselves, to oppose the bishop's authority if they did not feel supported by influential laymen, the δυνατοί; this is why the fathers of Chalcedon set out excommunication for these laymen (ἀκοινωνησία).[276] This sanction must not be confused with the ἀφορισμὸς, that is, exclusion from the Church. In ancient Christianity, and even in our own time in the East, the majority of monks are not part of the clergy; this is why the sanction set out for them is the same as for laymen. As for the penalty given to guilty clerics, it is not clearly determined. However, we can infer from the whole of ecclesiastical legislation that suspension was provided for a first offense and deposition for a second and continued offense. In fact, according to the canons, every priest exercising a sacerdotal activity unknown to the bishop or against his wishes is liable to deposition.[277]

The present canon expresses without ambiguity the basic principle of church law: each bishop exercises his authority over all clergy in the territory of his jurisdiction and not only over those in the parishes. This clarification was necessary because in certain monastic milieus, there was a tendency to withdraw from the hierarchical authority. In addition, for more than a century, the role of the clergy in charitable organizations had grown extensively and this new condition required a clarification of the problem of obedience of clerics attached to these institutions.[278] Zonaras properly understood this ruling as applying to all charitable organizations and not just to homes for the aged.[279] Although the present canon was quite formal, as time went on, especially during the Middle Ages, there were numerous violations of this standard.[280] Balsamon, who deplored the violations, considered those rulings that go against this canon to be null.[281]

9

If a cleric has a dispute with another cleric, let him not bypass his bishop and go to the secular courts, but let him submit the affair first to his own bishop or, of course, on the advice of his bishop, to some agreed-on third party who can judge the case.

If anyone goes against this ruling, let him be subject to canonical penalties.

If, on the other hand, a cleric has a dispute with his own bishop or with another bishop, let him appeal to the synod of the province. Finally if a bishop or a cleric has something against the metropolitan of the province in question, let him appeal either to the exarch of the diocese or to the see of the imperial city of Constantinople, and let him be given justice there.

This is one of those canons which has received very divergent interpretations. This is not due to the transmission of the text itself; there are only minor variants anyway, and none of them affects the meaning in any way.[282] As for the ancient Latin translations, they remain very close to the original Greek and do not interpret the text at all.[283] It is obvious that the westerners did not have any special interest in this canon, either during its composition or later on; this shows very clearly that they did not see in it any important law that could modify the Church's judicial system. The titles that sum up the content of the canons in the *Hispana* and in Dionysius' work are very revealing on this point. In the *Hispana*, we read the following: *"Quod non oporteat clericos praetermisso episcopo ad saecularia iudicia commeare;"*[284] in Dionysius, we read the following: *"Quod non oporteat clericos habentes adversus inuicem negotia proprium episcopum relinquere et ad saecularia iudicia conuolare."*[285] Rusticus uses this heading without any change.[286]

If this canon has been variously interpreted, it is certainly due to the lack of clarity in its redaction. This comes first of all from the fact that this, as well as the 26 other canons of the council, were hastily written.

Just as in the case of canon 6 of Nicea, the authors of this text were implicitly referring to a situation known to them and their contemporaries. They thus had no awareness of the ambiguity of the text. It is proper to note that later on, in a very different church-state context, this canon, like canon 17 of Chalcedon, was to be interpreted in a contestable, indeed completely fantastic, way. It is true that the basic intention of the legislator is not in doubt: clerics who have disputes with other clerics, whatever their places in the hierarchy, ought not appeal to secular courts. The disputes ought to be decided individually by a church court. We are dealing here with what jurists call the *privilegium fori*.[287] Based on the facts we now possess, we cannot categorically state that this was allowed in all matters by imperial legislation.[288] Sometimes, moreover, clerics themselves preferred to go to civil courts.[289]

The first uncertain factor in this canon is precisely about the point of the ruling. The solution depends on the meaning given here to the word πρᾶγμα, which we have translated by "dispute"; more exactly, we have to determine what type of dispute was aimed at. S. Troitsky believed that this term was exclusively related to civil disputes and to transgressions of the common law.[290] This point of view was vigorously contested by Metropolitan Maximus Christopoulos, whose reputation is based on his knowledge of philology; he tried very hard to show that the term πρᾶγμα did not have the limited meaning which the eminent Russian canonist assigned to it.[291] The sharpness of the debate between the professor and the metropolitan is explained by the fact that canons 9 and 17 of Chalcedon were invoked at a relatively recent date to justify the interventions of the see of Constantinople in the jurisdictional conflicts between Orthodox churches. Later on, we will see how these canons were used to support the idea of the universal competence of the see of Constantinople. If we want to remain on scientific grounds, we must recognize that it is not possible to establish, with any absolute certainty, the range of meaning that the authors of this canon wanted to give to the word πρᾶγμα. On the one hand, Metropolitan Maximus certainly was right when, supported by evidence, he affirmed that the Greek word is not restricted to the meaning that Professor Troitsky attributed to it; on the other hand, however, that does not necessarily mean that the fathers of Chalcedon gave to this ruling the universal range of meaning that some have subsequently attributed to it. Two weighty reasons seem to work against the universal scope of this canon; it cannot be applied to all cases: 1) The possibility of the plaintiff's appealing to a court of arbitration is completely inconceivable for wrongdoings which involved ecclesiastical sanctions which only a bishop or a synod could impose; 2) The fact that no appeal procedure is set out equally indicates that we are not dealing with offenses of this sort. Therefore, in all probability, the fathers of Chalcedon had in mind the settlings of contested matters between clergy of all ranks.

Another related problem deals with whether this canon completely excludes appealing to secular courts. The answer depends on the role played by the adverb πρότερον in the wording and consequently its relation with the other adverb γοῦν further along in the text. If we establish a close relation between these two adverbs, the meaning is the following: let them appeal "first off," or else with his permission, to an arbitration court agreed to by the parties. For Metropolitan Maximus Christopoulos, this is the only possible interpretation and those who maintain another opinion, notably Heféle and Troitsky, in his opinion, do so through "an insufficient knowledge of the Greek language."[292] Let us say that the simple reading of the canon gives the impression that this interpretation is more satisfactory; however, it is far from being absolutely certain and uncontestable, contrary to what Metropolitan Maximus might think. In fact, this is not at all how the redactors of the Justinianian legislation understood it: the Code permits a recourse to secular courts *"si vero civilis contentio est"* provided that the ecclesiastical authority is agreeable.[293] As for novella 113, it did not exclude recourse to secular courts either, provided that the disputants had previously (πρότερον) appealed to the bishop.[294] Of course, that does not mean that this was the opinion of the fathers of Chalcedon, but we cannot present this hypothesis as inconsistent.

It is certainly the last part of the canon, related as it is to disputes between bishops or clerics and their metropolitans, that has given rise to the greatest number of divergent interpretations. As we have already noted, this is due to the intrinsic obscurity of the redaction, because in the wording we do not know what the two alternatives are based on: the jurisdiction of the exarchs and that of the see of Constantinople. There is also uncertainty about the "exarchs" mentioned in this passage. It is not surprising, therefore, to note that the very different interpretations of this ruling have arisen; this is especially true from the early Middle Ages on, and perhaps even before, when the historical context differed significantly from that in which the canon was issued. J. Darrouzès thinks that the ambiguity existed from the

beginning and that it was intentional on the part of Archbishop Anatolius, who gave a wide interpretation to this ruling; he wanted to
make an appeal to his see a judicial alternative for the whole East.
Darrouzès also thinks that this interpretation was obviously not that
of the bishops of Syria, Palestine and Egypt, whose independent spirit
was quite evident during the council; he writes that:

> ...even from the very beginning, without even talking about
> the disapproval of the pope, there is a certain ambiguity in
> the use of the term [exarch]; all the legislators did not under-
> stand it in the same way. Once the division into civil dioceses
> disappeared, the ambiguity of the title of exarch could not
> help but increase.[295]

This last point is uncontestable; we have the proof in the discussions
that took place in Byzantium on this subject during the Middle Ages.
By establishing an artificial parallelism between canon 6 of Sardica in
its Greek recension and the present canon,[296] certain scholars have
also maintained that the title of exarch applied to all the metropolitans
in the canons of Chalcedon.[297] This interpretation is not free from a
hidden agenda; the interpretation was placed in the framework of the
continual conflicts, from the ninth century on, over the respective
jurisdictional competences of the patriarch and the metropolitans
under his authority.[298] The term "exarch" in the fourth and fifth centuries did not have a specific meaning in church language; it had not
yet become a title in and of itself; it kept its etymological meaning of
"chief" or "head." In the sixth century, the translator of the *Registri
Ecclesiae Carthaginensis Excerpta* rendered the expression *princeps
sacerdotum* by ἔξαρχον τῶν ἱερέων.[299] Consequently at this period, the
concrete meaning of the term is only indicated by the context. Thus,
for example, when some people complained that Theodoret of Cyrus
had treated Cyril as a heretic, he stated in his defense "...ἐξηκολούθησα
τῷ ἐξάρχῳ μοῦ,"[300] referring to John of Antioch. The bishop of this
great city was ordinarily called exarch, that is head τῆς ἀνατολοκῆς
διοικήσεως.[301] To refer to the heads of extensive church jurisdictions,
another term was soon to become generally used, "patriarch," but at
the time of the Council of Chalcedon, it had not yet taken on this
technical meaning. It was, however, soon to receive official sanction in
the legislation of Justinian.[302]

Does the wording of canons 9 and 17 of Chalcedon suppose that
each civil diocese had an ecclesiastical primate? If we could categorically answer yes or no to this question, we would have the key to the

interpretation of the text. Concretely, the doubt concerns Pontus, Asia and Thrace. In fact, if it were proven that these three civil dioceses had religious leaders at the head of the church's organization, then the following interpretation would have to be adopted: canons 9 and 17 of Chalcedon require that in the case of a dispute between a bishop or a cleric and the metropolitan of the province, the plaintiffs could appeal, according to their preference, either to the exarch of the diocese or to the see of Constantinople. But according to this hypothesis, was the choice given to bishops or clerics of any and all dioceses? Again if we accept this interpretation with the double choice, the logic would require that such be the case. However, even those who maintain this opinion think that the fathers of Chalcedon only had in mind the dioceses of the eastern part of the empire.[303] The position of Pope Nicholas I (858-67) was that "the exarch of the diocese" was none other than the Roman bishop; this is a purely fantastic interpretation and can only be considered here as a matter of curiosity.[304]

A completely different reading of the canon was proposed by K. Müller;[305] for him, the alternate terms "exarch of the diocese" and "see of Constantinople" were not related to the choice of the plaintiffs but were a function of the geography of jurisdictional organization; in the civil dioceses where there was really a religious exarch, the disputants should necessarily appeal to him. On the other hand, where no such church organization existed—in Pontus, Asia and Thrace according to Müller—the judicial authority should be that of the see of Constantinople. This reading of the canon is perfectly possible from the philological point of view. The fact that the medieval commentators on the text did not envision this interpretation cannot be put forward as a decisive negative argument. In many other cases, the real meaning of a canonical prohibition escaped them due to a deficient methodology.[306] On the other hand, the suggestion of Müller has been favorably received by many scholars in our time. A.H.M. Jones wrote that "the most natural interpretation of their rather obscure wording is that the cases in question are to be referred to the head of the diocese (if any), or to the see of Constantinople (if the diocese had no head...). These canons,[307] then, do not imply that every diocese has its 'exarch'; on the contrary, they imply that in some dioceses, Constantinople exercised the jurisdiction which elsewhere fell to the 'exarch.'[308] E. Herman feels that this interpretation is the most satisfying, on the condition that we be able to prove that there were no religious exarchs in these dioceses.[309]

Let us therefore look at things a little bit closer. We note first off that the absence of the term "exarch" would not be sufficient evidence for denying the existence of primates; as we have already noted, "exarch" was not a title in itself used to designate a precise rank in the church hierarchy, but it meant only "head" or "chief." Did the three dioceses really have a primate at their head? The fathers of the Council of Constantinople, 381, made reference to the respective situations in the dioceses of the eastern Roman Empire and considered the bishop of Alexandria to be the adminstrator of the whole church in the diocese of Egypt. They mentioned the prerogatives of the bishop of Antioch in the diocese of the East, probably including canon 6 of Nicea in their understanding of this bishop's rights over the metropolitans of the diocese.[310] On the other hand, for Asia, Pontus and Thrace, there is not the slightest allusion to diocesan primates. Taking into account the minute and nuanced redaction of this text, such a lack of reference cannot be due to a haphazard omission. What we know, moreover, in no way appears to indicate the existence of any exarchal functions in these dioceses. From the founding of Constantinople, it was obvious that the bishop of Heraclea would never be able to exercise a centralizing role in Thrace, even if the civil and ecclesiastical status of the Second Rome placed it outside the administrative limits of the diocese. Thus when Atticus of Constantinople (406-25) consecrated Silvanus for the see of Philippoupolis and then transferred him to Troas, there was no reaction from the bishop of Heraclea.[311] It was certainly in the diocese of Thrace where there were fewer bishops, about 30, that the control of Constantinople was most easily imposed. About Pontus, L. Duchesne observed correctly that, from the Bosphorus to the Euphrates and to Taurus, it was not easy to centralize, and then he adds:

> Caesarea of Cappadocia, residence of the civil vicariate, was very far from the extremities; Ancyra was better placed to challenge Constantinople's control. The province of Bithynia, caught up in this jurisdictional tug of war, was a neighbor to the capital; the city of Chalcedon was like a suburb; Nicomedia and Nicea were also not far away.[312]

Nothing seems to indicate that St. Basil exercised any suprametropolitan rights over the whole of Pontus: moreover, we see that his canonical position even close to home was weakened when a second province was formed in Cappadocia with Tyana as its capital.[313] The hierarchical links that existed until 373 between Armenian Christianity and the church of Caesarea are explained by the origin of the evangelization and not by the exarchal position of the see of Caesarea. When certain relations were established with the Greek East in the 430's, it was in Constantinople and not in Caesarea that the affairs were dealt with.[314]

At first sight, the problem in the diocese of Asia appears more complex. Ephesus was one of the large cities of the empire, and the creation of its church goes back to apostolic times. The influence of the see of Ephesus certainly went beyond the borders of a single province. According to Palladius, the irregularities committed by Antoninus of Ephesus which brought on the intervention of St. John Chrysostom affected the whole diocese of Asia (...ὅλης τῆς ἀσιανῆς διοικήσεως).[315] Maybe this affirmation is a bit of an exaggeration, since to elect a successor to Antoninus St. John Chrysostom assembled a synod of bishops from Lydia, Asia and Caria; they were joined by several bishops from Phrygia.[316] As A.H.M. Jones has remarked, that supposed that the effective influence of Ephesus did not extend beyond these provinces.[317] It is proper to recall that the diocese of Asia still encompassed the following provinces: the Hellespont, Lycia, Pamphylia, Pisidia and Lyaconia. At the council "of the Oak," St. John Chrysostom was criticized because "he meddled in the provinces of others (ἀλλοτρίαις ἐπαρχίαις) and consecrated bishops there."[318] We also note that there was never any mention of his undermining the prerogatives of exarchs in the diocese. The sometimes violent clashes provoked by the meddling of the archbishops of Constantinople in Pontus and Asia between 381 and 451 were not on the diocesan level but on local and provincial ones.[319]

At the sixth ecumenical council, 681, metropolitans of Ephesus and Caesarea respectively signed as Ἔξαρχος τῆς Ἀσιανῶν Διοικήσεως and Ἔξαρχος τῆς Ποντικῆς Διοικήσεως.[320] The fact that the signature of the metropolitan of Ephesus was found at the fifteenth position shows very well that the title was purely honorific, and of course it proves nothing about the situation in the fifth century. Finally, we note that the motion which has been subsequently called "canon 28" of Chalcedon contains no allusion to exarchs and therefore to the suppression of prerogatives that they might have had or previously claimed. In this ruling, we are only dealing with bishops, provincial metropolitans, and the archbishop of Constantinople.

We therefore think that the absence of an exarchal authority in the dioceses of Pontus, Asia and Thrace is highly probable. In this case, the appeal to the see of Constantinople for the settling of disputes was a logical solution. The reading proposed by K. Müller gives to the whole of the canon a very satisfying coherence. The other readings lead to the acceptance of interpretations that are either arbitrary or imply quite unbelievable anachronisms.

10

It is not permitted for a cleric to be enrolled in the churches of two cities at the same time: the one in which he was first ordained and the other where he later went because the second was more important, and he was motivated by vain feelings. Therefore, let those who act in this way be sent back to the church in which they were first ordained, and let them exercise their functions there only.

Whoever has already been transferred from one church to another, he must no longer busy himself with the affairs of the first church, or the martyrs' shrines or the centers for the poor, or the lodging facilities which are attached to them. After the publication of this present ruling of the great and holy council, for those who dare to do anything that is prohibited by it, the holy council has decided that they should be removed from their rank.

This conciliar ruling is to be placed within the general context of ancient canon law which considered each local church as a stable and structured entity. Consequently, ordination implies the appointment to a specific post, normally for life. Based on these same suppositions, the fathers of Chalcedon in canon 5 prohibited clerics from going from one town to another on their own initiative; in canon 6, they declared ordinations at large to be null. Translations were only to be made with the express approval of the competent church authority. What is completely excluded is belonging simultaneously to two churches.[321] Consequently, if a cleric went against this rule and were transferred illegally, he was to be reinstalled (ἀποκαθίστασθαι) in the church to which he had been attached at his ordination. If, on the other hand, he was legally transferred from one church to another, he had necessarily to be removed from the clergy list of the first and not carry on any activities whatsoever in that church.

The wording of the canon is not very clear; there is a seeming inconsistency in the sentence imposed on someone who breaks it. At the beginning, it was only a question of the guilty cleric being sent back to his first church, while at the end of the canon, deposition is set

out. We see here again the proof of a hasty redaction of these disciplinary rulings. It is probably a good idea to accept the explanation
suggested by Balsamon: deposition was only for the cleric who
installed himself permanently in another city.[322] It also makes more
sense to think that the deposition was only for those who refused to
go back to their first church. Balsamon reminds us, moreover, that
this sanction ought not to be applied until after a preliminary warning
and, as evidence, he invokes canons 15 of the Holy Apostles and 17 of
the Synod in Trullo, which dealt with the same subject.[323] Aristenus
emphasizes the anomalous motivation denounced by this canon: the
passion for riches on the part of some clerics.[324]

Montreuil notes that Zonaras "only appeals to civil laws in very
rare occasions."[325] In his commentary on this rule, reproduced in the
Basilica, Zonaras mentions *novella XVI* of Justinian:[326] when a cleric
dies, before ordaining another, the church authorities may eventually
take someone to replace him from a church where the number of
clerics exceeds the number established in earlier times.[327] The different
recensions of this canon contain only small variants, which never
affect its meaning.

11

**We have decided that all the poor as well as those who need
to be helped, after proper investigation, will be issued short
letters called "ecclesiastical [letters] of peace" and not "of
recommendation" because the "letters of recommendation"
are only issued to persons of distinction.**

The difficulty in understanding this canon does not come at all
from the state of the text; the variants are insignificant. There is no
problem in the grammatical construction either; it is perfectly correct.
The problem is found in the expression ἐν ὑπολήψει...προσώποις, which
can be interpreted in two absolutely different ways. In fact, the word
ὑπόληψις can have several meanings which cannot be determined
except in context or by the use of a determinative. It means "reputation," good or bad; from the first meaning, we get "distinction" or
"respectability"; from the second, we get "suspicion" and "doubt."
The first definition seems to have been more widespread in ancient
times;[328] it is the only one that has passed into modern Greek. During
the seventeenth session, Eusebius of Ancyra spoke eloquently for the
archbishop of Constantinople saying that "λάμπει ἡ ὑπόληψις...τοῦ
ἀρχιεπισκόπου Ἀνατολίου."[329] We find this term again in canon 21 of

Chalcedon, but there it is clear that the reputation can be good or bad. This is precisely the intended meaning.[330]

This being the case, we are surprised to note that with no hesitation, the Greek commentators of the Middle Ages have all taken the expression to mean "persons under suspicion."[331] This unanimity is explained, in our opinion, by linking this canon with canon 12 of the Holy Apostles which stipulates that "if a cleric or an excommunicated person or excluded layman goes to another city and is received there without letters of recommendation (ἄνευ γραμμάτων συστατικῶν), let him be excommunicated: him who received and him who was received."[332] We know that in the East during the Middle Ages, these canons were seen as the basis of church legislation having very great prestige. This interpretation was therefore carried over into the wording of the *Pedalion*[333] and also in the translation of the *Kniga Pravil* done by the Russian Holy Synod.[334] On the other hand, the authors of the ancient Latin translation of Greek canonical collections understood the expression "τοῖς οὖσιν ἐν ὑπολήψει...προσώποις" in another sense, that is, "to persons of distinction." The *Hispana* reads *"qui in opinione sunt clariore"*;[335] the *Prisca* says *"qui bona opinione identur,"*[336] and Dionysus says *"honoratioribus...personis."*[337] Of course this unanimity is not in itself an absolutely decisive argument, but it is to be taken into consideration in that the authors of the various Latin recensions did not simply copy each other.[338] Their interpretations are then of equal value with the Greek commentators of the Middle Ages. W. Bright is perfectly right when he says that this understanding, a person of distinction, is the most natural.[339] This is our opinion also, though we still acknowledge, with N. Milash, that we cannot be absolutely certain.[340]

In this canon, we are clearly dealing with two kinds of documents. Those who require them are to receive "brief ecclesiastical letters of peace." The fathers of Antioch had previously stated that "no stranger should be received without letters of peace," and in addition, they made clear that in country areas, these documents could be issued by the country bishops but not by the priests.[341] Canon 33 of the Holy Apostles deals with travelling clerics; it stipulates that:

> no unknown bishop, priest or deacon must be received without letters of recommendation (ἄνευ συστατικῶν), and even if they have them, they must be examined. If they are preachers of piety, let them be received; or else, after having met their needs let them not be received to communion; for often they are

imposters.[342]

Canon 12 of the Holy Apostles is more general since it deals with clerics of all ranks as well as laymen, but it only envisions, as we have already seen, those who have been excommunicated or excluded from the community. Moreover, they should not be received unless they have been issued "letters of recommendation." It is obvious that we are dealing here with an attestation saying that the sanction against them has been lifted. As for canon 41 of Laodicea, it stipulates that it is forbidden for all clerics to travel without being issued "canonical letters."[343]

The precise object of canon 11 of Chalcedon is restricted: the attestation given to Christians in need must not be issued without good reason. This document must not take the solemn form of a long letter of recommendation; this no doubt was to avoid the appearance of being juridically binding on those who might have to examine these letters and make a decision about the person carrying them.[344]

12

It has come to our attention that certain persons, acting against church rules, appeal to public authorities in order to effect the division of a province in two by imperial decree; this they do so that henceforth there may be two metropolitans in the same province. The holy council has, therefore, decreed that in the future, no bishop shall dare to act in this way; if he tries to do so, he must be removed from his rank. As for cities that have already been honored by the title of metropolis by imperial letters, let these cities and the bishops who govern them enjoy only the honor of the title; that is, let the proper rights of the real metropolis be safeguarded.

The intention of the legislators and, therefore, the scope of this canon are only understandable taking the context into consideration. The Church had adopted the general principle of territorial accommodation for its own geographical organization, at least on the provincial level (eparchies). From this came the preeminence of the bishop of the provincial capital, the "metropolitan."

The prerogatives that came with this position had been well defined in the East by conciliar legislation during the fourth century.[345] These texts all appeared in the *Book of the Canons* which was used several times by the fathers of Chalcedon.[346] The very nature of these prerogatives necessarily supposed that they belonged to one single bishop, the primate.[347] By issuing this ruling, the fathers of Chalcedon had no intention of questioning the principle of accommodation or of opposing every modification of the *status quo* inside the provinces, since they themselves foresaw this eventuality in canon 17. In addition, at the previous meeting, they had enthusiastically accepted the proposition of the emperor Marcian for honoring the city of Chalcedon with the title of metropolis, without in any way, however, undermining the metropolitan prerogatives of Nicomedia.[348]

The canon really has two points: the first thing condemned is the collusion of bishops with civil authorities to get a decree from the emperor giving their city the title of metropolis. After the issuance of this ruling, a bishop who acted in this way was liable to deposition. In his commentary, Aristenus properly noted that the canon was aimed at this improper action and not at the emperor's action of giving the city the honorary status of metropolis.[349] Secondly, however, by holding to the letter of the canon, we can deduce that the fathers of Chalcedon were opposed to every future promotion of this kind; this is, in fact, how Zonaras understood it, but he noted that the ruling was not observed very well.[350] Grammatically, such an interpretation is uncontestable since ἐτιμήθησαν is in the aorist, and it is re-enforced by the adverb ἤδη. We should not press the text too far, though. The fathers of the council wanted to regulate the situation such as it was: let the bishops of honorary metropolitan cities not try to arrogate to themselves the real rights of metropolitans. We know very well what had directly motivated the adoption of this canon: the affair of Eustathius of Beirut, dealt with some days before.[351] In this canon, the decision made in the case of Eustathius was made into a general church law. Zonaras noted that it was poorly observed, as we have already seen. Balsamon makes the same observation, but he was on the whole favorable to imperial power. He tried to justify the affair on the juridical level and invoked canons 38 of Trullo and 17 of Chalcedon, but we must recognize that certain scholars do not share this opinion. The legality of such promotions had just been put in doubt, so that it had been necessary to publish an explanatory document (σημείωμα) which according to Balsamon definitively resolved this question.[352] As a matter of fact, the problem then no longer had the same importance as it did at the time of the Council of Chalcedon because the metropolitan system had ceased to be the pivot of church organization.

13

Unknown clerics and readers must in no way exercise their

functions in a city other than their own, without being issued letters of recommendation from their own bishop.

The text of this canon poses a problem. Without any possible doubt, the words "ξένους κληρικοὺς καὶ ἀναγνώστας" appeared in the original text. This is brought out by the perfect agreement of the best Greek tradition[353] as well as the unanimity of the ancient Latin versions.[354] Later on, either by accident or because this phrase seemed strange to them, some Greek copyists replaced ἀναγνώστας by ἀγνώστους, which gives a satisfying meaning: "foreign and unknown cler-ics." This is a classic example of what is called "hypercorrection." We find this modified text in the Trebizond manuscript of 1311, which served as the basis of Rhalles and Potles' edition.[355] The correction was also taken into consideration in the *Kniga Pravil*.[356] On this point, the Russian translations have not followed the *Pedalion*.[357]

We may ask why the fathers of Chalcedon used a formula which could be interpreted to mean that readers were not counted among the clerics. But this conclusion is not at all admissible. A semantic hypothesis presented by Heféle ought to be accepted: ...καὶ ἀναγνώστας could mean "and even readers."[358] In other words, the expression could have an inclusive meaning. On the grammatical level, nothing can be said against this understanding. The fathers of Chalcedon probably thought it useful to introduce the clarification because in the Church, readers were at the limit between the members of the lower clergy and laymen; due to this position, some of them took little note of canonical regulations about the clergy. We note that the Council of Hippo in 393 thought it necessary to stipulate that henceforth readers were considered clerics.[359]

The present canon has a very general scope since it is applied to all clerics without exception, while canon 33 of the Holy Apostles only mentions bishops, priests and deacons. The *commendatiae litterae* of this canon are those required by clerics who travel when they present themselves in a church. It is not a question of incardination in another diocese; for that the cleric would need a dismissory letter.[360]

14

Since, in some provinces, readers and chanters have been allowed to marry, the holy council has decided that none of them should marry a heterodox woman. As for those who have already had children by such a marriage, if they have these children baptized by heretics, they must present them

to the communion of the catholic Church; in case they have not been baptized, they must no longer have them baptized by heretics, or, what is more, give them in marriage to a heretic, to a Jew, or to a pagan, unless the person they are united to promises to embrace the orthodox faith.

If anyone goes against the decree of the holy council let him be submitted to a canonical sentence.

Although the text of this canon has many variants in the manuscript tradition, none affects the very clear meaning in any way.[361] The old Latin translations do not have any special interest here because the Latin and Greek are very close in meaning.[362]

According to the wording of this canon, the possibility of readers and chanters contracting marriage is presented as a simple tolerance allowed in only some provinces (...ἔν τισιν ἐπαρχίαις συγκεχώρηται). This assertion is rather surprising since we find no trace in ancient Christian literature of any prohibition against readers and chanters contracting a *matrimonium iustum*. Such a prohibition only existed for the sacred orders; it has been everywhere and always absolute starting with presbyters.[363] It seems to have been the general rule for the diaconate, while the Council of Ancyra admitted that the rule could be relaxed if, before his ordination, a deacon formally declared that he intended to marry.[364] There was a certain range of practice about the sub-diaconate: in Book 6 of the *Apostolic Constitutions,* marriage is admitted for subdeacons;[365] but canon 26 of the Holy Apostles forbade it for them. In contrast, the same canon expressly authorizes it for readers and chanters.[366] In the West, the discipline on this point was not different from that of the East.[367] The formula used by the fathers of Chalcedon is, therefore, unexpected. Whatever was the case, the fathers did not make any modification to the discipline in force. What was prohibited for readers and chanters was that they be allowed to contract marriage with heterodox women. Such a ruling, in and of itself, is not at all extraordinary. Canon 21 of Carthage had already stipulated that "the children of clerics must not marry pagans or heretics."[368] It is not, however, necessary to appeal to the somewhat shaky hypothesis that the fathers of Chalcedon were motivated by this African decree.[369] The same idea of Christian marriage consecrated in its normal form by a common participation of the couple in the eucharist requires unity in faith.[370] Canons 10 and 31 of Laodicea, appearing in the collection used by fathers of Chalcedon, forbade all

Christians from marrying heretics.[371] Canon 14 of Chalcedon only urges the application of this norm to readers and chanters. No doubt, this ruling was poorly observed by many laymen. Since readers and chanters were at the limit between the clergy and the laity, they neglected it also. Canon 72 of Trullo was to go even further by nullifying absolutely the marriages between orthodox and heretics.[372] It is interesting to note that Balsamon, in his commentary on this canon, applied it to mixed marriages with "Latins."[373] This was also the opinion of Matthew Blastares.[374]

The Church has constantly required members of the clergy to have outstanding characters and exemplary marital and family lives. This is why the tolerances accepted for laymen have always been refused to them, notably when mixed marriage is concerned. In 1835, canon 14 of Chalcedon was invoked by a Russian bishop to forbid such a union for the daughter of a priest.[375] In our own times, however, it would be difficult to extend the strict application of the Church's law to that degree.

15

A woman must not be ordained deacon before the age of 40 and that after a careful inquiry. If after having received ordination and after having exercised her ministry for some time, she wants to marry, thereby scorning the grace of God, let her be excommunicated as well as him who has united himself to her.

In our translation of this canon, we have tightened up the original text by rendering διάκονον...γυναῖκα as "A woman...deacon..." and not by "deaconess," even though the meaning is exactly the same in the two cases. The word "deaconess" is found in all the ancient Latin versions while διακόνισσαν is only found in some manuscripts.[376] In the Old Slavonic, we have *diakonissy...zhenu*, in the *Kniga Pravil*.[377] The whole of the text of this canon is perfectly stable in the Greek manuscript tradition, with one single exception: in the *Synagoge*, we have χειροτονίαν instead of χεροθεσίαν.[378] This difference has no theological significance since the two terms were absolute synonyms at the time. This we have already seen in canon 6 of Chalcedon. On this point C. Vogel most correctly writes that after a detailed examination of the vocabulary, it is not possible "up to the council of Nicea II (787), to find a stable use for the terms expressing the imposition of hands."[379]

The use of the noun διάκονος to designate a woman exercising church functions goes back to the New Testament. St. Paul mentions a certain Phoebe οὖσαν διάκονον τῆς ἐκκλησίας τῆς ἐν Κενχρεαῖς.[380] The terms ἡ διάκονος or γυνή διάκονος are those we find used in the ante-Nicene documents.[381] The feminized form διακόνισσα is attested to for the first time in canon 19 of Nicea. From then on, we find these three forms used concurrently. In the legislation of the emperor Justinian, when it was only a question of deaconesses, the term διακόνισσα[382] was used; concerning the diaconate in general, the noun "deacon" is followed by two adjectives indicating the two sexes respectively.[383] Throughout history, from the origins of Christianity up to and including the Middle Ages, there have been many witnesses to the existence of a feminine diaconate. On the other hand, the functions that deaconesses exercised were not always and everywhere the same, and there were also very important differences in the mode of entering into this ministry.[384]

In contrast to most other terms designating church ministries, there has been no semantic evolution towards a stable usage for the word διάκονος. Like the corresponding verb διακονεῖν, it had a very wide meaning in early Christianity,[385] such that the noun and the verb were synonyms of λειτουργὸς and λειτουργεῖν.[386]

In the *Didascalia of the Apostles*, a work written in Syria in the third century, we find for the first time a description of the tasks assigned to women deacons: they were to visit women of the community, especially those who were sick; they were to take over the teaching of women and above all to assist the bishop in the baptism and chrismation of women.[387] This is also what St. Epiphanius explained, while making clear that there was no question of a priestly function.[388] We have no witness prior to the *Apostolic Constitutions* that makes a reference to the ordination of deaconesses. This document takes us back to the second half of the fourth century, but this information, as valuable as it is, does not allow us to determine for how long such a rite had been in use.[389] The wording of canon 19 of Nicea is rather obscure; we cannot draw any conclusions from it about the practice of the period.[390] According to the *Apostolic Constitutions,* the making of a deaconess takes place in the presence of presbyters, deacons and deaconesses and by the imposition of the bishop's hands, but the presence of the other clerics is not required for the ordination of a subdeacon or a reader. The prayer said by the bishop during the imposition of hands (ἐπιθήσεις....τὰς χεῖρας) is not very explicit about the ministry conferred on the deaconess. There are some references to the Old

Testament: to Mary, Debora, Ann and Hilda. God is asked to give the Holy Spirit to the deaconess "so that she can worthily carry out the task assigned to her." Perhaps we should attribute a precise meaning to the allusions to women who were guardians of the holy doors of the temple.[391] Later on, at the end of antiquity (sixth-eighth centuries), the ordination of deaconesses acquired all the characteristics of accession to higher orders, as professor E. Theodorou has noted, since the formula "the grace divine..." is used. The ordination is carried out during the liturgy at the same place as that of a deacon, that is, immediately after the anaphora.[392]

The text of canon 15 of Chalcedon leaves no doubt about the sacramental nature of the feminine diaconate: note the use of χειροτο-νεῖσθαι, of χειροθεσία (χειροτονία in the *Synagoge*), of λειτουργία to designate their ministry, of the χάρις conferred by the ordination. It is, therefore, clear that at least at this period in the East, we are not dealing with an inferior order. It is no less certain that we cannot speak of a priestly order, for we know that the absolutely constant tradition of the Church, as opposed to that of several sects,[393] has never allowed women to take on priestly functions. On this point, we must note that the feminine diaconate constituted a specific order; this is shown by the fact that the content of the ordination prayers were not identical with those used for the ordination of deacons. Certainly, deaconesses carried out certain tasks similar to those of deacons, but they did not assume all the diaconal functions, notably liturgical, that is, reading the gospel and public prayers. How do we explain that since the feminine diaconate has existed from the beginnings of Christianity, an ordination rite for this ministry seems to have appeared so late? Furthermore, why did it later on fall into disuse?

We have no testimony about the functions conferred on deaconesses in the primitive Church. No doubt, as in the case of Phoebe at Cenchrae, they carried out charitable and welfare duties rather than a liturgical ministry. Later on, the essential role of deaconesses consisted of helping the bishop and the priests at the baptisms and chrismations of women.[394] This participation in the bestowing of sacraments made it seem fitting to impose hands on them, but we do not know when this practice began, as we have already said. J. Daniélou defended the hypothesis that it went back to the third century.[395] With the decline of adult Christian baptisms in the East, there was also a rapid decline in the institution of deaconesses. Apparently, no one thought of reviving this ministry during the great missionary expansion of the ninth and tenth centuries.

We learn through Balsamon that in his time, the twelfth century, no more deaconesses were being ordained. In convents, nuns were called deaconesses, but this title was an improper usage (καταχρηστικῶς...).[396] In the western Church, the feminine diaconate was unknown for a long time, and it has never been successfully and solidly implanted. The prescriptions of the councils manifest on this point an entirely negative attitude.[397] On the other hand, among non-Byzantine oriental Christians, that is, Jacobites and Nestorians, there were even more tasks assigned to deaconesses than in the Greek Church.[398]

According to the present canon of Chalcedon, women deacons are not to be ordained before 40 years of age. As J. Gaudemet remarks, this was "the result of a compromise."[399] According to the law of the emperor Theodosius, no woman could become a deaconess before 60 years of age, and she had to be a widow with children.[400] The reference in this text to *praeceptum apostoli* as well as the fixed age shows that here deaconesses were assimilated to widows mentioned in I Timothy.[401] Such an identification was arbitrary, for at the time—we know nothing on this subject for the first centuries of the Christian era—deaconesses were also recruited from among the virgins and the widows.[402] Certain deaconesses had been ordained very young, for example, St. Olympia.[403] However, the functions that were given to them did not go very well with women of advanced age. Justinian's legislation in its final form agrees with the decision of the Council of Chalcedon in forbidding the ordination of deaconesses below the age of 40.[404] This minimal age as well as the custom of ordaining only virgins and widows shows very well that the feminine diaconate was not a simple variant of the masculine diaconate. The final prohibition of canon 5 carries on in the same line.

Canon 48 of the Synod in Trullo stipulates that the former wife of a newly elected bishop must reside in a monastery, and if she is worthy, she should be raised to the diaconal level (τῆς διακονίας...ἀξίωμα).[405] There is no indication here of a minimum age; this seems to be a relaxing of the norm provided for by novella 6 of the emperor Justinian.[406] The deacon who marries after his ordination is to be dismissed from his functions; his marriage is an irregularity which makes him ineligible for the diaconal ministry.[407] Now the deaconess who marries is to be excommunicated, which meant she is given a double sentence: removal from the ministry and exclusion from the community of the faithful, but this goes against the canonical adage taken from Holy

Scripture: "You will not punish anyone twice for the same fault."[408] This principle is expressly mentioned in canon 48 of the Holy Apostles and canon 32 of St. Basil.[409] In addition, while the fathers of Chalcedon provided for a bishop's relaxing of the sentence for virgins or monks who marry, thus violating their vow of continence, they do not envision any relaxation for deaconesses. We see by this action how serious this act was considered. In the century preceding Chalcedon, St. Basil had already written that "as far as we are concerned, we do not allow the body of a consecrated deaconess (καθιερωμένον) to be used again for carnal purposes."[410] The severity of the ruling issued by the fathers of Chalcedon is perhaps explained by the fact that the admission into the order of deaconesses was only done at a mature age which made a fall all the more inexcusable. We note that the anathema also falls on the husband in such an illegitimate union, for he also is involved in this dirty affair.

16

A virgin who has dedicated herself to the Lord God, as well as a monk, is not permitted to marry. Therefore, if they have gotten married, let them be excommunicated. In addition, we have decided that the bishop of the area has the power to exercise compassion in reference to such persons.

The text of this canon has no significant variants in the various Greek recensions, and there is nothing special to note in the Latin translations of the *Prisca* and the *Hispana*. This is not the case with Dionysius, however. The fact that he translated the Greek noun φιλανθρωπίας by the periphrase "*misericordiam humanitatemque*" is not remarkable since Latin does not have an exact equivalent. However, Dionysius introduced a personal interpretation into this canon by adding "*confitentibus*."[411] The meaning, therefore, is that the bishop can lessen or lift the sanction if the persons involved confess their sin and show repentence. Such an interpretation does not go against the thinking of the fathers, although the idea is not stated expressly in the text itself. The mention of virgins here is related to a specific institution in the ancient Church. These were women who remained in the world but vowed (*propositum*) to remain virgins. In certain places in the fourth century, a liturgical office for the consecration of such women began to evolve.[412] It was the bishop himself who gave the benediction.[413] The development of feminine monasticism contributed to the slow disappearance of this institution.[414] In canon 19 of St.

Basil, we find some interesting information on the status of consecrated virgins at this historical period:

> ...we must now make very clear that we call "virgin" any woman who has voluntarily offered herself to the Lord, has renounced marriage, and has preferred life in sanctification; but we only approve those promises (τὰς...ὁμολογίας) from those who have reached complete maturity, for in these matters, it is not proper to consider childish vows as having any value. But a young girl who is 16 or 17, if she is fully in command of her reasoning and if after having submitted to a rather long trial period and has presevered, if she insistently asks and pleads to be admitted, then she should be enrolled (ἐγκαταλέγεσθαι) among the virgins, the promise should be ratified by suitable guarantees, and she should be severely punished for any violation of her vow. In fact, many young girls are led by their parents or by their brothers or by other relatives without themselves feeling any call to the celibate life; the relatives of these girls do this because they want to make it easier for themselves to live. These girls should not be accepted easily; we should wait until there are clear signs of their own desires.[415]

St. Basil was therefore an advocate of great severity toward those who violated their vows, and he wanted to impose on them the same penance as for unfaithful wives.[416] But he must have recognized that such was not the previous standard when he said that "our fathers condescended with goodness and tenderness to the weakness of those women who had fallen in this way; the fathers ruled that they were to be received after one year, thus assimilating them to those who had been married twice."[417] In effect this was the sentence issued by the Council of Ancyra.[418] St. Basil disapproved of this very light sentence. The adverb ἁπαλῶς that we have translated as "with goodness" most certainly has an unfavorable nuance about it in his thinking; it evokes the idea of softness. The fact that the fathers of Ancyra likened these women to people twice married is explained by the very widely held idea at that time, and shared by St. Basil, that consecrated virgins were bound by a mystical marriage to Christ.[419] In a more judicial approach, the West was to see in the marriage of a consecrated virgin a defective commitment (*pollicitatio*).[420] The fathers of Chalcedon therefore forbade virgins and monks from marrying under sentence of excommunication (ἔστωσαν ἀκοινώνητοι). But what were the concrete implications of the recognized right of the bishop to be merciful toward those who could not keep their vows (φιλανθρωπίας)? Does it mean, as Heféle claimed, that according to this canon, such a marriage was held to be valid?[421] This assertion is ambiguous because it sets the question within a problematic foreign to the fifth century. The ancient Church, even after the normalization of its relations with the state, did not attempt to acquire authority over the juridical validity of marriages, and St. Jerome could declare as an obvious truth that *"aliae sunt leges Caesarum, aliae Christi."*[422] Moreover, until the promulgation of a law by Emperor Leo VI, the Wise (886-912), the marriage blessing did not constitute the only possible legal form for contracting marriage.[423] Of course, that did not mean that the ancient Church was uninterested in marriages contracted by Christians. All of the Church's discipline proves the contrary. Certain categories of marriage were discouraged; others were absolutely forbidden, so that those persons who went beyond the prohibitions of the Church were excluded from the Christian community as long as they remained in that state of sin. If they renounced such relationships, they were reconciled after a more or less long period of penitence. Consequently, those who made a vow of continence and then broke it by marrying were considered in the same irregular situation. The hesitations concerning canonical practice came from the fact that in the early period there were still no official forms for the declaration of such a promise.[424] As soon as the situation changed, the attitude of the Church appeared very clear. According to canon 19 of St. Basil, it is obvious that a sentence could only be handed down as the result of breaking a clearly formulated commitment. St. Basil answered a question of Amphilochius of Iconium by saying that:

> we have not known of (religious) professions of men, except those who have been enrolled in the order of monks; by this action, they have implicitly accepted a celibate life. However, for them also, I think that it is proper to begin by questioning them and by receiving a clear profession from them (ὁ-μολογίαν ἐναργῆ); let them be bound to the sentence imposed on fornicators when they allow themselves to go after the carnal and voluptous life.[425]

From the strictly religious point of view, it is very clear that in church legislation, marriages contracted by persons who have taken a vow of celibacy, that is, monks and nuns, are without any value. In canon 6 of St. Basil, we read that "the fornications of nuns must not be counted as marriages; and in any case, the unions must be broken..."[426] The same father declared elsewhere that:

> she who has made a profession of virginity and then has gone back on her promise, must be under the same sentence as prescribed for adultery. The same thing is to be applied to those who have promised to follow the monastic life and have gone back on their promises.[427]

Dionysius' addition of the term *confitentibus* to the text of the canon clearly shows that he did not understand this conciliar ruling in the sense of a possible recognition by condescension of such a marriage. The eastern tradition is no less clear on this matter. Canon 44 of the Synod in Trullo states that "the monk who is caught in the very act of fornication or who has taken a woman to be his wife or concubine should be judged in conformity with the canons and given the prescribed sentence for those guilty of fornication."[428] Thus we see that the marriage of a monk is assimilated purely and simply to an act of fornication. The Greek canonists of the Middle Ages in no way deduced from canon 16 the possibility of recognizing "by economy" the marriages of persons having already pronounced a vow of continence.[429] On this subject, Balsamon mentioned that the guilty persons were to receive the sentences prescribed by the civil law for *nuptiae damnatae*.[430] According to the canonical collection attributed to Nicephorus of Constantinople, a monk who gave up his monastic vocation and married must be excommunicated and enclosed in a monastery.[431] The unanimity of the tradition before and after Chalcedon allows us to affirm without much chance of error that "the power to exercise mercy" did not relate to an eventual recognition of such a marriage, at least not in the mind of the legislator. The exercise of mercy in this matter relates, rather, to the mitigation of the sentence inflicted for the sin of fornication. Moreover, it is with this meaning that the Greek term $\varphi\iota\lambda\alpha\nu\theta\rho\omega\pi\iota\alpha$ should be interpreted; frequently, we find this word or others of the same root in the ancient canonical literature carrying this connotation.[432] We must not forget that the penances essentially have the character of a spiritual therapy; their rigor must be modeled to the actual state of the repenting person. St. Gregory of Nyssa wrote that:

> in all places, depending on the fault, it is quite proper to take into consideration the disposition of him who is being cared for and not to think that in itself the length of the sentence is enough for successful treatment; what healing is produced

simply by the length of treatment? But the will of him who is being healed must be taken into account, through his own conversion, if he is to be healed.[433]

In the nomocanons, monastic vows were considered to have a definitive and lasting character and to constitute a direct impediment to marriage. This situation prevailed at least until the beginning of the nineteenth century. It was then that some in Russia began to allow monks and nuns to return to the non-monastic state with the possibility of a future marriage; this was seen, however, as exceptional.[434] This was a serious innovation and therefore highly questionable.[435] Up to the present time, Greek legislation does not recognize the right of monks and nuns to leave the monastic life and to marry.[436] It is possible that the legislation of the Greek state, under the growing influence of secularist tendencies, may soon be modified by the introduction of civil marriage.

17

The rural and village communities of each church must without change remain attached to the bishops who possess them, especially if for thirty years one bishop has administered them and had them under his authority without any problems. But if, during these thirty years, anyone has contested or contests this matter, it is possible for those who feel themselves wrongfully treated to bring the affair before the synod of the province. If, on the other hand, someone has been wrongfully treated by his metropolitan, let him make an appeal either to the exarch of the diocese or to the see of Constantinople, as has been said earlier.

Finally, if by imperial authority a city has been founded or is founded in the future, let the rank of the ecclesiastical communities be in conformity with that of the civil and public arrangements.

The present canon deals with the territorial boundaries of episcopal districts in provinces, and it establishes a norm concerning the founding of a new city; according to the "principle of territorial accommodation,"[437] modifications of the political status of cities necessarily entail modifications of the canonical situation inside a province. This was what Heféle explained very clearly in his commentary:

If a village, etc. is raised by the emperor to the dignity of a city, the ancient church of the village must become an epis-

copal church and have its own bishop; the same thing is true
for a newly founded city which is not dependent on the
neighboring city but is under the immediate jurisdiction of
the civil capital of the province. In the same way, the bishop
of the new city must come under the immediate authority of
the ecclesiastical metropolitan of the province and not under
the bishop who before had authority over the village now
become a city.[438]

This stipulation concerning the procedure to be followed in the
Church when a new city is founded was repeated word for word by
the fathers of the Synod in Trullo.[439]

In its original wording, the canon began with the following words:
"τὰς καθ᾽ ἑκάστην ἐκκλησίαν ἀγροικικὰς παροικίας ἤ ἐγχωρίους..."[440]
We find here the term παροικία, which also appears in the last sentence; however, it did not have exactly the same meaning in the two
cases. In the beginning of the canon, it referred to communities situated outside the city in the rural districts dependent on it from a civil
and religious point of view. As for the distinction between ἀγροικικαὶ
and ἐγχώριοι. it was so subtle that the various Latin translations did
not even take it into account and rendered these two adjectives by one
single word taken from the noun rus.[441] According to Aristenus and
Zonaras, the ἀγροικικαὶ παροικίαι were communities far away from the
city having few inhabitants, while the second group was closer to the
city and more populous.[442] This explanation no doubt influenced the
translations of the Kniga Pravil which used the expression v selakh ili
predgradiiakh sushchie prikhody.[443] The noun παροικία was used in
the Septuagint, and it meant "a stay or taking up residence in a foreign country";[444] for a pious Jew, this was a synonym for exile. In
the view of the New Testament, the Christian was always to consider
himself in exile on this earth; the use of the word παροικία came from
this meaning.[445] In canonical language, it came to mean a Christian
community in a definite place, normally presided over by a bishop.[446]
But here the term meant the rural communities around and attached
to an episcopal city; consequently, it would not be incorrect to translate the word by "parish," a word which in the Romance languages
came from the Greek παροικία through the Latin parochia or paro-
ecia.[447] The historian Socrates, who died after 439, used the Greek
term with this meaning.[448] We have not translated it by "parish"
because at the end of the canon, the same Greek word had a different
meaning; the most normal one, as we have said, was "territory of a

bishop" which today is called "diocese" in the West and "eparchy" in the East. This use of the same term παροικία with two different meanings in the same text has led certain copyists to introduce a correction that altered the meaning and the scope of the canon. At the beginning of the canon, they replaced the word ἐκκλησίαν by ἐπαρχίαν.[449] This modification was found in the *Pedalion* and in the Rhalles and Potles edition.[450] This incorrect reading was also taken into the *Kniga Pravil* where we read "*po kazhdoi eparkhii...*"[451] The canon thus dealt with rural episcopal territories in each province.

The jurisdictional disputes that the fathers of Chalcedon foresaw in the present canon were often inevitable because at the time, episcopal districts did not have well-defined geographical boundaries.[452] Beyond the city where he had his seat, the bishop's authority extended to the suburbs, towns and hamlets supposedly dependent on the city. The council set out the principle that the acquired rights should be maintained provided that they were not obtained by force. The adverb ἀβιάστως was related to the adjective of the same origin used twice in the ruling of the fathers of the Council of Ephesus concerning the canonical situation of the churches of Cyprus.[453]

Thus, if a bishop had a rural district under his canonical authority for thirty years without any questioning from neighboring bishops, no claim from any of these bishops was to be received. The bishop in uncontested possession of a rural district was to benefit from the *usucapion* or the acquisitive prescription. The fixing of a thirty-year lapse of time was, like the very notion of prescription or exception, a borrowing from Roman civil law.[454] If no ruling on a matter had been made and a complaint was received, the question should be referred to the provincal synod in conformity with the general norms relating to the competence of this body.[455] But obviously, the metropolitan bishop of the province could be implicated in the appeal, finding himself a defendant. In this case, the person making the complaint was to appeal either "to the exarch of the diocese or to the see of Constantinople."[456] The word for word repetition of this phrase in canon 9 and the supplementary clarification "as it was said before" showed that in the mind of the legislator, we are dealing with a type of procedure that applied to disputes between churchmen. In fact, the litigations which might arise concerning the boundaries of episcopal districts were set in the general framework of canon 9. These litigations were therefore to be appealed to church courts and not to civil tribunals. In his commentary on canon 17, Zonaras made an important remark on the geographical limitations of the judicial competence of the see of Constantinople:

> The bishop of Constantinople is in no way (οὐ...πάντως) the judge of all the metropolitans; he is the judge only of those who are under his authority (ἀλλὰ τῶν ὑποκειμένων αὐτῷ). For it is of course not his place to judge, against their will, the metropolitans of Syria, nor those of Palestine and Phoenecia, nor those of Egypt. The metropolitans of Syria depend on the bishop of Antioch; those of Palestine on the bishop of Jerusalem; and those of Egypt are judged by the bishop of Alexandria; it is by them that they are ordained, and it is on them that they depend (παρ' ὧν καὶ χειροτονοῦται καὶ οἷς περ ὑπόκεινται).[457]

It was not by accident that Zonaras introduced this clarification into his commentary. He was aiming at the tendentious interpretation of an ancient scholion taken up by Aristenus which, based on canons 9 and 17 of Chalcedon, attributed to the see of Constantinople the privilege of judging a metropolitan under the authority of another patriarch.[458] Moreover, it was not the only time that Zonaras refuted Aristenus, without naming him, concerning the see of Constantinople.[459] For Zonaras, it was in fact an axiomatic truth that the judicial competence of the major sees of the universal Church were geographically co-extensive with their respective territorial jurisdictions. We can very clearly see this in his interpretation of canon 5 of Sardica.[460] This restrictive interpretation of the competence of the see of Constantinople was taken up in a long argument in the *Pedalion*.[461] It was equally the opinion of N. Milash.[462] We need not go over this subject, which we have already treated in our commentary on canon 9.

At the beginning of our commentary on canon 17, we explained the meaning of the final stipulation related to the ecclesiastical status of new cities: by virtue of the principle of territorial accommodation, every city created or renewed was to have its own bishop. Such a norm was taken up in a law of the emperor Zeno (474-91) and put into Justinian's code.[463] Of course, there could be properly grounded exceptions,[464] but the legitimacy of a relaxation of the norm, based on "ancient custom" (ἔθος... ἀρχαῖον) had been accepted by the fathers of the Council of Ephesus.[465]

18

Since the crime of plotting and conspiring is repressed

through all possible means by civil laws, even more so is it proper that it should be forbidden by the Church of God. If, therefore, any clerics or monks are found plotting and conspiring, or even thinking about such improper action against bishops or colleagues in the clergy, let them be completely deposed from their rank.

The redaction of this canon has certainly been inspired by the memory of the seditious carryings-on of some clerics and monks during the long period of agitation preceding Chalcedon. During the tenth and eleventh sessions, the attitude of certain clerics of Edessa against Ibas was brought up.[466] According to the minutes of the fifteenth session, we also know of some clerics from Perrha who joined together to carry on a veritable revolt against their bishop, Athanasius. Cyril of Alexandria expressly mentioned this deplorable affair in a letter addressed to Domnus of Antioch.[467] Based on this fact, we could even make an argument in support of the opinion that the 27 canons were adopted only during one of these last sessions of the council; this is not really necessary, however, because the incident was already widely known by most of the fathers at Chalcedon.

In the original text of the canon, we find the word φρατρία, which the Latin translators correctly rendered as *conspiratio*.[468] In the earlier times and in conformity with its Indo-European etymology, this term did not at all have a pejorative meaning.[469] In Homeric Greek, it meant a tribe or a clan. Later on in Greece, it was applied to the politico-religious brotherhoods. In Athens from Solon's time on, it was a tribal subdivision grouping thirty families together. Subsequently, by analogy with the organization of Rome, the term was considered as an equivalent of the Latin word *curia*. The introduction of a pejorative connotation during late antiquity is easily explained. We are aware of exactly the same semantic phenomenon in modern languages, for example in the word "clan." Beside its primitive form, an altered form φρατρία developed during the first centuries of our era; this is attested to in certain readings of the canon.[470] The word was very current in designating a faction involved in intrigues,[471] and it has kept this meaning in modern Greek.

Despite the present canon, the evil that it is aimed at was not at all eradicated; this is why the Synod in Trullo thought it necessary to draw everyone's attention to it.[472] However, neither the fathers of Chalcedon nor those at Constantinople in 691 were able to get to the root of the problem. The unjustified revolt of clerics against their bishop was assuredly a blameworthy thing, and therefore punishable, but often the rebels accused their bishop of unworthy acts as, for example, in the case of Ibas of Edessa. Thus, the First-Second Council (Πρωτοδευτέρα Σύνοδος) of Constantinople, 861, issued its canon 13 as a very important clarification of this matter. We quote the entire text:

> Having sown the tares of the heretics in the Church of Christ and having seen them cut down at the roots by the sword of the Holy Spirit, the evil one among us has come by another twisted route to try to divide the body of Christ through the madness of schismatics. But the holy council having completely put an end to these carryings on, has also decreed that from now on if a priest or a deacon dares to separate himself from the communion of his bishop, under pretext that he himself has something to reproach the bishop for, but acts before the council of bishops has investigated the affair and has made a definitive judgment against the bishop and no longer commemorates his name in the sacred prayers of the liturgies as the Tradition of the Church prescribes, then that priest or deacon shall be deposed and deprived of all priestly honor. In fact, any priest who arrogantly decides to judge his own father and bishop by himself thus taking the place of the metropolitans and condemning him before any judgment has been given, this priest is not even worthy of the honor and name of priest. As for those who follow him, if they are in sacred orders (ίερωμένων) let them be stripped of their honor; if they are monks or laymen, let them be completely excluded from the Church until they have broken all contact with the schismatics and have returned to their bishop.[473]

In issuing this ruling, which made the previous legislation clearer, the fathers of the First-Second Council wanted to put an end to the undisciplined behavior of a part of the clergy and of some monks which had manifested itself in the Byzantine Church since the re-establishment of orthodoxy in 843.[474]

19

It has come to our attention that in the provinces the bishops' councils required by the canons are not being held, and for this reason much Church business which requires attention is being neglected. Thus the holy council has decided that, in conformity with the canons of the holy fathers, the bishops of each province are to gather together

two times a year in the place where the metropolitan judges best, and they will attend to all such business that requires attention. The bishops who will not come to the meetings even though they are in good health in their home cities and free from other urgent and necessary duties are to be fraternally reprimanded.

The various Greek recensions of this canon do not cause any significant problems for its meaning. We only note that according to the best reading of the *Synagoge*, we have κατὰ τοὺς τῶν πατέρων κανόνας.[475] The omission of the adjective ἁγίων before πατέρων no doubt corresponds to the original text since all the ancient Latin versions confirm this short formulation.[476] A gloss has been introduced into the *Prisca*, it makes clear the fact that the fathers are those "*apud Nicaeam Bithyniae constituti.*"[477] This clarification is interesting because it shows the very exceptional authority that the rulings of Nicea had in the West.[478] Of course, this addition was arbitrary because the members of the Council of Chalcedon had in view all the synodal rulings that appeared in the eastern canonical codex and not just those of Nicea. Canon 20 of Antioch is situated in the line of canon 5 of Nicea but with a broadening of its perspective: it was no longer just a question of a judicial proceeding but of an organ which was to examine all the affairs of the life of the Church.[479] As for the obligation on the bishops to participate in these synodal meetings, it was also the point of canon 40 of Laodicea.[480] Although there was no organic relation, we must also note the decision on the same topic adopted by the fathers assembled in Carthage in September 401. They had stipulated that "every time a council must be gathered together, the bishops who are not impeded by age, sickness or some other serious obligation are to come to the meeting as is most proper."[481] The final section of the canon of Chalcedon is quoted by the fathers of the Synod in Trullo.[482]

20

As we have already decreed, clerics serving in one church must not be integrated into the church of another city but must reattach themselves to the church for whose service they were found worthy in the beginning; an exception is to be made for those clerics who have lost their country of origin and therefore are required to go into another church. If after this decree, a bishop receives a cleric under the authority of another bishop, it seems right and proper that

he who received and him who was received should be excommunicated until the cleric who moved into another church returns to his own church.

Purely and simply, this canon adopted the wording of the emperor Marcian's third proposed disciplinary decree which, during the sixth session, he had asked the fathers of the council to adopt.[483] The differences in wording between the proposal and the actual canon are absolutely insignificant; equally unimportant are the differences between the various recensions;[484] obviously the phrase "as we have already decreed" belongs strictly to the text of the canon. This is an allusion to canon 5, which formulated the same prohibition under a shorter and more general form. On the background of this problem, it is enough to refer to the analysis of canons 5 of Chalcedon and 15 of Nicea. However, we note that the present ruling allows for a relaxing of the norm for a very serious reason, that is, when the circumstances that caused the cleric to leave his home country were beyond his control. On this point, the fathers of the Synod in Trullo attempted to suppress the abuses that could derive from such an exception. With this goal in mind, they issued the following ruling:

> Those clerics who under the pretext of barbarian incursions or for any other reason have migrated must return to their own churches and not abandon them for too long a time or for no reason; we require this as soon as the reason for the migration has ceased or as soon as the barbarians have left. If anyone does not conform to the present canon, let him be excluded until he returns to his own church. Let the same sentence be inflicted on a bishop who goes against it.[485]

21

Clerics and laymen who make complaints against bishops or other clergy should not be allowed to make such complaints without first having their reputations examined.

A similar ruling, but more detailed, was issued by the Council of Constantinople in 382, which was later joined to the decisions adopted in the ecumenical council the previous year. We therefore refer the reader to the analysis of canon 6 of the second ecumenical council.

We note, however, the insistence of the canonical legislation on the prudence that should be observed before accepting complaints against bishops and clergy. The complaint must not be accepted "ἁπλῶς καὶ ἀδοκιμάστως," which Dionysius translated by the expression "*passim et sine probatione.*"[486] This expression is related to that used by Numidius, bishop of Maxulitania during the Council of Carthage in 390; it concerned "those people, known for improper conduct, who think they can accuse their fathers, the bishops, for any old reason (*passim uageque*)."[487]

22

Clerics are not permitted to seize the material goods of their bishop after his death; this has already been forbidden by the ancient canons. Those who do such a thing run the risk of losing their rank.

The present translation is based on the best Greek manuscript tradition[488] which is itself supported by all the ancient Latin versions.[489] The proper reading thus goes like this: "...καθὼς καὶ τοῖς πάλαι κανόσιν ἀπηγόρευται." In a whole series of manuscripts, however, we find another reading, unquestionably false: "...καθὼς καὶ τοῖς παραλαμβάνουσιν ἀπηγόρευται."[490] One of the meanings of the verb παραλαμβάνειν is "to receive by transmission." This reading ought not necessarily to hold our attention except that it was the one that Zonaras and Balsamon knew, and they thought that the canon was aimed at the metropolitans who improperly seized the material goods of their dead suffragans.[491] This question was touched on by the fathers of Chalcedon in canon 5. Balsamon opposed an abusive interpretation of canon 81 of Carthage and remarked that the personal goods of a bishop who died without a will ought to revert to his relatives in conformity with the law.[492]

The fathers of Chalcedon made an allusion to the "ancient canons." Now, in the collection that they were using, only one ruling concerns this subject, that is, canon 24 of Antioch, which reads as follows:

> Thus, at the death of a bishop, what belongs to the church, being clearly known, should not be taken away or lost, and the inheritance of the bishop should not be touched on the pretext that it was part of the church's goods. In fact, it is just and agreeable to God and to men that the bishop do with his personal goods what he wants and that the interests of the church also be safeguarded. The church must not suffer in any way, nor should what belongs to the bishop be confiscated in favor of the church...[493]

No other canon in the collection contains a prohibition on this matter; why then the plural: "the ancient canons"? We can think that

many members of the council knew of the existence of canon 40 of
the Holy Apostles, although it did not appear at that time in the
official collection of the Byzantine Church. Its wording is rather close
to the canon of Antioch.[494] In fact, by the middle of the fifth century,
the word κανών had already become a technical term to designate a
written church canon; it appears very improbable, therefore, that the
expression τοῖς πάλαι κανόσιν referred to a rule of customary law.
Canon 35 of the Synod in Trullo was to make clear that the metropolitan is not to seize or appropriate the material goods of a dead
bishop.[495]

23

**It has come to the attention of the holy council that certain
clerics and monks, without any commission from their
bishops, sometimes even excommunicated by them, are
going to the imperial city of Constantinople and staying
there for a long time; they cause trouble, sow disorder in
church affairs, and even shake up some people's houses. The
council has therefore decided that such persons should first
receive a warning from the Advocate of the very holy church
of Constantinople to leave the imperial city; if they persist in
their activities, they should be expelled by the same Advocate
even if they do not want to go, and they should return to
their own countries.**

In the manuscript tradition, the text of this canon contains some
very minor variants which do not change the meaning.[496]

The present ruling is to be put alongside the others adopted by the
Council of Chalcedon to put an end to the lack of discipline among
certain clerics and monks; this was especially necessary where obedience to a bishop or monastic stability was concerned. We can therefore relate this present ruling to canons 4, 5, 8, 10, 13 and 20. The
preconciliar commotion had largely been caused by monks, and the
fathers were able to see for themselves the disdain of these monks for
hierarchical authority during the troubles on Wednesday, October
17.[497]

In the analysis of canon 2, we spoke about the function of the
"Advocate," ἔκδικος. Let us note here the singular, which supposes
that the Church of Constantinople had only one "Advocate." Later
on, he was to be helped by an assistant and was then to carry the title
of προτέκδικος.

The wording of this canon is very clear and as such does not need any special explanation. This is why the commentaries of Zonaras and of Balsamon have nothing to say on this canon; this fact in itself is enough to attract our attention.[498] As for the commentary of Aristenus, it is simply a paraphrase of the text of the epitome.[499]

24

Once monasteries have been consecrated with the consent of the bishop, they must remain forever monasteries, and their material goods must remain in the possession of the monasteries. They must never again become secular habitations. Those who allow them to become secular habitations are to be subjected to the sentences prescribed by the canons.

For this canon, the variants in the manuscript tradition are only minor and do not affect its meaning. We find in the recension of the *Acta Graeca* "*τὰ προσήκοντα αὐτοῖς πράγματα*" whereas the predominant reading elsewhere is "*τὰ ἀνήκοντα αὐτοῖς πράγματα.*"[500] In the *Prisca* and in Dionysius, there is the plural *episcoporum,* which is not supported by any reading of the Greek text; on the other hand, the *Hispana* has the singular *episcopi.*[501]

The present ruling appears to be the logical complement of what was set out in canon 4 of the same council, that is, prohibiting the establishment of a monastery without the consent of the local bishop. The profound spiritual reason for this prohibition contained in canon 24 is given by Zonaras: once dedicated to God by the prayer of the bishop, a monastery cannot be given over to profane usage (*μὴ κοινοῦσθαι*).[502] This ruling of Chalcedon was taken up by the fathers of the Synod in Trullo, who quoted it word for word, but with some additions.[503] In 787, Nicea II threatened serious sanctions for those who would not restore monasteries which had been despoiled by the iconoclasts: deposition for clergy and excommunication for monks and laymen.[504] Such transformations had been frequent under the reign of Constantine V Copronymus (741-775).[505] Moreover, canon 1 of the First-Second Council, 861, held in the church of the Holy Apostles, Constantinople, reminded everyone that it is not permitted for anyone to found a monastery without the authorization of the bishop; furthermore, it made clear that whoever made a gift to help found a monastery could not later on use his gift for his own purpose.[506] The obligation of the bishop to give the first blessing was expressly required by Byzantine civil legislation.[507] The prohibition against the secularization of monasteries was the point of the first chapter of title XI of the *Nomocanon in XIV Titles*.[508]

By issuing this canon, the fathers of Chalcedon wanted to make sure that monasteries were not used for purposes other than as monasteries; in addition, monasteries should be exempted from taxes and seizures that would destroy their ability to support themselves. At this time, it was not possible to foresee the fantastic extension of monastic properties during the Middle Ages. Concerning the inalienability of monastic property, it is interesting to note that Balsamon studies the scope of the verb φυλάττεσθαι in this canon and maintained the opinion that its untouchable character is not absolute, and he makes reference to the legislation of the Basilica.[509] We equally note that Aristenus only mentions the inalienability of monastic real estate (ἀκίνη-τους...κτήσεις).[510]

In the sixteenth century, when the great controversy about monastic properties broke out in Muscovite Russia, this canon of Chalcedon was one of those which shocked the partisans of absolute monastic poverty;[511] they thus made a new arrangement of the *Kormchaya Kniga* and eliminated the offending texts. For this, they were severely censured in 1531 by Metropolitan Daniel of Moscow.[512]

The fathers of Chalcedon ruled that those monks who broke this canon were to become subject to the sentence set out in the canons (...ὑποκεῖσθαι τοῖς ἐκ τῶν κανόνων ἐπιτιμίοις). Now nothing in the canons prior to those of Chalcedon specifically relates to this question. Perhaps the fathers were thinking that the sanctions applied to those who seized or used sacred objects for profane purposes should also apply to those who confiscate monastic property. This offense was the aim of canons 72 and 73 of the Holy Apostles which, as we have already said, were known by most fathers of the council.[513]

25

Since certain metropolitans, as we have learned, neglect the flock which has been given to them and put off the ordinations of bishops, it has seemed right and proper to the holy council that the ordinations of bishops take place within three months unless an absolute necessity requires a longer delay. If he does not act in this way, let the metropolitan be subjected to an ecclesiastical sentence. As for the revenue of the widowed church, let it be maintained intact by the treasurer of this church.

In the text of this canon, the single variant which merits attention, even though the general meaning is not affected, is the plural ἐκκλησιαστικοῖς ἐπιτιμίοις found in numerous manuscripts;[514] this reading appears also in the *Pedalion* and Rhalles and Potles. It is translated in the singular, however, in the *Kniga Pravil, tserkovnoi epitimii*, thus supposing a singular in the Greek text.[515] The ancient Latin versions also support a singular reading.[516] We note also the expression τῆς χηρευούσης ἐκκλησίας (*uiduatae ecclesiae*): a church which has lost its bishop is considered to be "widowed," for the link between the bishop and his church is compared to the union of marriage.[517] This terminology is still used by the Orthodox Church even if its canonical and spiritual meaning is lost on many people.

The most ancient and most important prerogative of the metropolitan consists in controlling the elections and consecrations of bishops on the territory in which he is primate.[518] This right obviously implies that the metropolitan ought to watch over the vacant episcopal sees and see to it that they are filled as soon as possible; however, the legislation before Chalcedon had not really touched on the question of the delay before naming a new bishop. A council in Carthage in 401 had decreed that a bishop who was the temporary administrator of a widowed church (*intercessor*) was not to exercise this charge for more than a year.[519] If the canon of Chalcedon sets a time limit not to be exceeded, it does not indicate a requisite minimum interval. The tradition on this matter varied from place to place. According to the witness of Liberatus, in Alexandria the custom (*consuetudo*) required that the newly elected bishop conduct the funeral of his predecessor.[520] This happened in Constantinople, as a most rare occasion, when Proclus presided at the funeral of Maximian.[521] It seems completely justified that a certain lapse of time occur between the death of one bishop and the installation of his successor. It is necessary to find a candidate and make an inquiry about him. The nomocanical legislation allowed a delay of three months before the consecration, if there were a dispute.[522] Balsamon, in his commentary on this canon, correctly made reference to this ruling.[523] As for the conditions which might delay the consecration of a new bishop beyond the delay prescribed, Zonaras sees only the impossibility of communications due to a barbarian invasion as a proper cause for delay.[524] Balsamon also takes up this explanation.[525]

The metropolitan who neglects his duty to make sure that widowed churches are provided with bishops within three months, except in exceptional cases, is to be subject to an ecclesiastical sentence ("ὑποκεῖσθαι αὐτὸν ἐκκλησιαστικῷ ἐπιτιμίῳ"). It is not clear, however, just what this sanction might be and who would have the right to pronounce it. Balsamon admitted his perplexity on this question, suggesting that it was in the competence of the provincial synod.[526]

During the vacancy of the see, the revenue is to be kept by the treasurer, that is, as Balsamon made clear, it is not to go to the metropolitan.[527] The following canon requires, moreover, that each church have a cleric who fulfills this function.

26

As we have learned, in some churches, the bishops administer the material goods of the church without a treasurer; it has seemed right and proper that every church with a bishop should also have a treasurer taken from the clergy who will administer the church's goods with the advice of his own bishop. In this way, the administration of the church will not be without checks and balances, the goods of the church will not be dissipated, and the priesthood will be free from all suspicion. Let anyone who will not follow these instruction be subjected to the divine canons.

In the whole of the canonical legislation, several rulings deal with the administration of the material goods of each church. As these rulings develop, we can see some basic underlying principles emerge. First of all, it is clear that the local bishop as head of the local church has the upper hand in the administration not only of the spiritual but also the material affairs of his church. This is what is clearly set out by canons 38 and 41 of the Holy Apostles.[528] St. Cyril of Alexandria wrote the following: "Such a thing would deject the very pious bishops all over the world if they were obligated to justify the expenditures that they have made either concerning the church's goods or private goods."[529] However, the bishop must not be suspected of abuses in using the material goods of his church, and it is exactly this that the fathers of Chalcedon wanted to eliminate by the present canon. On the other hand, in order to avoid all dispute after the death of a bishop, canons 40 of the Holy Apostles and 24 of Antioch make it clear that the personal goods of the bishop must be carefully distinguished from those of the church.[530] The best solution was therefore for the bishop to name a treasurer from among his clergy. This institution was no doubt widely established from the fourth century on.[531] In the following century, it was to become the nearly general practice, all the more so because the material riches of the churches were steadily increasing. Churches which did not have an administrative treasurer were rare. According to the *Gesta Tyri* read at the tenth session of the Council of Chalcedon, Ibas of Edessa had decided to have the revenue of his church administered by treasurers taken from the clergy according to the model of the church in Antioch ("*κατὰ τὸν τύπον τὸν ἐν τῇ μεγίς τῃ Ἀντιοχέων ἐκκλησίᾳ διοικεῖται τὰ πράγματα διὰ οἰκονόμων ἐκ τοῦ κλήρου προβαλλομένων*").[532] A letter of St. Cyril to Domnus of Antioch tells us that the treasurers of the church of Perrha had been driven out by a group of rebellious clerics.[533] The historian Socrates wrote that Theophilus of Alexandria had taken two clerics as treasurers, but that when they saw the way in which he operated, they abandoned their function.[534] This last allegation may only be a slander, because the hostile feelings of Socrates towards Theophilus are well known.[535] In a letter of instruction (Ὑπομνηστικὸν) addressed to Ammon, Theophilus stated that the treasurer must be named after consultation with the clergy.[536] According to Balsamon and Zonaras, the requirement that the treasurer be from the clergy is a very important one.[537] The fathers of the seventh ecumenical council reminded everyone that all churches without exception must have an administrative treasurer.[538] Despite the imperative character of the canons, Zonaras observed that in his time many bishops did not have such treasurers.[539] During the Byzantine period, the "Great Treasurer," that is, of the patriarchate of Constantinople, was a very important person. As chief administrator, his role was especially important during the vacancy of the patriarchal see.[540]

27

Those who carry off women by force under the pretext of marriage, as well those who aid and approve those who carry out such actions, the holy council has decided that if they are clerics, they are to be deposed from their position, and if they are laymen, they are to be excommunicated.

Although the meaning of this conciliar ruling has remained the same throughout its many recensions, we note that the manuscript tradition is rather fluid. The recension of the *Synagoge* is considerably different from the *Acta Graeca*.[541] An internal critical examination of the text leads us to the conclusion that John the Scholastic, or else the author of the recension that he used, knowingly reworked the initial text found in the *Acta*. He substituted the word *κόρας* "young girl," for the word γυναῖκας "women," thinking it more appropriate in the context. He also replaced συναινοῦντας "those who approve," by συν-αιρομένους "those who give aid," perhaps because he thought that the notion of consent or approbation was too imprecise from a juridical point of view. Finally, he thought it useful to add the monks (μονά-ζοντες) among the guilty parties liable to be excommunicated. The text in the *Syntagma in XIV Titles*, according to the *Recensio Trullana*, is the same as in the *Acta* except that the form συναιρομένους has been added as in the *Synagoge*.[542] In some recensions, we also find the reading συναιρουμένους.[543] This alteration is easily explained both phonetically and orthographically; there is also a semantic similarity. The verb συναιρεῖν means "to aid someone to seize." The ancient Latin versions are of little interest in determining the primitive Greek text of the canon; they only show that the recension of the *Synagoge* clearly departed from the initial wording of this canon.[544]

The illegal nature of abduction was obviously not in doubt in the canon, but in the pre-Chalcedonian legislation there was no universally accepted penance for this crime. St. Basil recognized as much when he wrote that "on this subject of abductions, we do not have an ancient canon...."[545] The question had only been touched on partially by canons 67 of the Holy Apostles and 11 of Ancyra.[546] St. Basil gave his personal opinion and ruling in the absence of any existing rule (ἰδίαν γνώμην); his position was itself not without ambiguity: "During three years, let them [the abductors] and their accomplices be excluded from the prayers. But if there was no violence, there is no guilt unless there was seduction or theft in the affair."[547] In canon 22, on the other hand, St. Basil dealt with the question that the Council of Ancyra had touched on:

> Those who have wives who have been abducted while they were engaged to others must not be admitted before the women have been given back to their fiancés who can then choose, if they want to, to take the women back or to dissolve the engagement. If anyone abducts a woman who is not engaged, she must be taken from her abductor and returned to her own family....[548]

Later on in this same text, St. Basil stated that it was proper to apply the sentence prescribed for the sin of fornication to the seducer of a woman, either in secret or by force.[549] By decreeing excommunication for a layman guilty of this crime, the fathers of Chalcedon showed themselves more severe than St. Basil. This canon is taken up word for word by the Synod in Trullo.[550]

In his commentary on this canon, Zonaras underlined the fact that abduction constituted an impediment to marriage in the sense that the abductor is not permitted to marry the woman he has taken by force. Concerning the accomplices, he explained the difference between συμ-πράττοντας and συναιρομένους: the first are those who directly partici-pate in the abduction, while the others are those who indirectly give them aid. An interesting psychological note is found in this commen-tary: the accomplices are to be justly punished (εἰκότως) all the more because they do not have the excuse, like the abductors themselves, that they were carried away by the passion of love.[551] In large part, Balsamon accepted the explanation of his predecessor and referred to novella 35 of Leo the Wise.[552] We also note the appreciation of Mat-thew Blastares in his *Alphabetical Syntagma:* abduction must be consi-dered as a most serious crime, more serious than adultery.[553]

This decree on abduction is the last of the 27 disciplinary canons which were issued by the Council of Chalcedon and which appear in the ancient canonical collections. The three others that we find in later Byzantine collections are called canons only by stretching the term, as we have shown in our introduction. However, we do not think that this fact is really essential or significant. This is not an isolated case. It is enough to recall the so-called "canons" of the Council of Ephesus, which in fact are only a selection of various decisions of this assembly.

A vote of the same holy council, taken in favor of the preroga-tives of the see of the very holy Church of Constantinople.

28

Following in every detail all the decrees of the holy fathers and knowing about the canon, just read, of the 150 bishops dearly beloved of God, gathered together under Theodosius the Great, emperor of pious memory in the imperial city of Constantino-ple, New Rome, we ourselves have also decreed and voted the same things about the prerogatives of the very holy Church of this same Constantinople, New Rome. The fathers in fact have correctly attributed the prerogatives [which belong] to the see of the most ancient Rome because it was the imperial city. And thus moved by the same reasoning, the 150 bishops beloved of God have accorded equal prerogatives to the very holy see of New Rome, justly considering that the city that is honored by

the imperial power and the senate and enjoying [within the civil order] the prerogatives equal to those of Rome, the most ancient imperial city, ought to be as elevated as Old Rome in the affairs of the Church, being in the second place after it. Consequently, the metropolitans and they alone of the dioceses of Pontus, Asia and Thrace, as well as the bishops among the barbarians of the aforementioned dioceses, are to be ordained by the previously mentioned very holy see of the very holy Church of Constantinople; that is, each metropolitan of the above-mentioned dioceses is to ordain the bishops of the province along with his fellow bishops of that province, as has been provided for in the divine canons. As for the metropolitans of the previously mentioned dioceses, they are to be ordained, as has already been said, by the archbishop of Constantinople, after harmonious elections have taken place according to custom and after the archbishop has been notified.

This motion was submitted for the approval of the council members at the last session, which took place, according to the most probable calculations, on Thursday, November 1st; it most certainly constitutes the text as amended after objections raised during the unofficial session of the night before. Although we do not have the minutes of this preceding evening's meeting, many clues lead us to believe that some modifications were introduced into the initial text. The somewhat strange character of the redaction has not escaped the attention of researchers who have studied this text; however, they have not investigated the cause of this oddity. Martin Jugie has written that "this text comes from a laborious redaction and calls for numerous comments for it is far from being clarity itself."[554] G. Dagron has also noted that "the jurisdictional consequences are set out in a very clumsy way, in a restrictive form (μητροπολίτας μόνους), as if the purpose of the canon was rather to prohibit the bishop of the see of Constantinople from directly consecrating the bishops of non-metropolitan sees."[555] It is obviously here that the unexpected character of the redaction appears. In fact, after a solemn introduction emphasizing the reasons for granting an eminent place to the see of New Rome, the jurisdictional content of the prerogatives which flow from this position is immediately expressed by a restrictive formulation. In addition, the procedure for electing bishops described in the last part excludes the intervention of the archbishop of Constantinople with the exception, of course, of the metropolitans. This exclusion of a role for Constantinople was expressly mentioned in the official interpretation of the motion that was given by the imperial commissioners:

> As for the very venerable local bishops, let them be consecrated by all the very pious bishops of the province or by the majority of them, the confirmation being within the competence of the metropolitan, which is in conformity with what the fathers have ruled; this is to be done *without any reference being made to the very venerable archbishop of the imperial city of Constantinople concerning these consecrations.*[556]

This restrictive aspect of the ruling was also underlined by Archbishop Anatolius in his letter to Pope Leo. Anatolius reminded the pope that the consecration of numerous bishops was taken away from the see of Constantinople, despite the prevailing custom for more than sixty years.[557] We can infer that in its primitive form, the motion did not contain a clause safeguarding the rights of the metropolitans; this seems likely from the statement of the imperial commissioners at the conclusion of the fourteenth session concerning the dispute over Vasilinoupolis. The prerogatives of the metropolitan of Nicomedia concerning episcopal consecrations were effectively recognized, but the commissioners took great care to reserve those rights which could have been given to the see of Constantinople when the questions was to be examined.[558] Now this took place on Tuesday, October 30; the day after, the evening of October 31, the unofficial session previously mentioned took place. We can therefore be certain that the safety clause concerning the rights of the metropolitans was inserted into the primitive text during the meeting of October 31 because of objections raised by some participants. This addition explains the awkward wording of the text in its final form, the only text that has come down to us.

Let us examine the text itself. First of all, we note that it has been recopied with minute care, no doubt because of its importance; we therefore cannot point out any variant worthy of mention in the manuscript tradition.[559] The ancient Latin translations are of little interest: the one given by the two manuscripts of the *Prisca*, combined with canon 3 of Constantinople, is mediocre and incomplete.[560] Rusticus faithfully follows the text of the *Acta Graeca.*[561] There is no translation of the motion in Dionysius because at the time, this text did not appear in the Greek canonical collections. For the same reason, we do not find it in the Syriac version made in Hierapolis, 500-1.[562]

Despite the last minute reworking of the text, the source of its awkwardness, we realize that it had been well prepared by the chancery of the church of Constantinople. In contrast to the redaction of the 27 canons, the language is polished and the terminology precise. The decree contains two very distinct parts: the second is presented as a consequence of the first; the coordinate conjunction καί followed by the subordinate conjunction ὥστε adequately shows this. First of all there is a preamble expressing the canonical situation of Constantinople. It constitutes a whole in itself, in that it seems to be an interpretation of canon 3 the council of 381. It serves, however, as a justifying reason for the following part. The intrinsic importance of the preamble comes from the fact that it is clearly longer than the following part, which itself can be subdivided into three sections: 1) the affirmation of the suprametropolitan rights of the see of Constantinople in the dioceses of Pontus, Asia and Thrace; 2) an appendix concerning the right of the archbishop of New Rome to ordain bishops "among the barbarian nations," which on the jurisdictional level were an extension of the above-mentioned dioceses; and 3) clarifications concerning the promotion of the bishops and metropolitans of the three dioceses.

Let us now look at things in more detail. First of all we note the solemn style of the inital formulation: "πανταχοῦ τοῖς τῶν ἁγίων πατέρων ὅροις ἑπόμενοι...." The relation to the dogmatic definition of the council seems obvious: ἑπόμενοι τοίνυν τοῖς ἁγίοις πατράσιν..."[563] This is certainly not a coincidence. As with the dogmatic definition, there is here a clear intention to show the continuity of tradition while at the same time explaining it. Consequently, the authors of the motion tried very hard to set out *a posteriori* the reasons for the decision adopted by the council of 381 concerning the see of Constantinople. They based themselves entirely on the principle of territorial accommodation, that is, the canonical arrangement of the church must correspond to the political and administrative order. Constantinople enjoyed the status of imperial capital; it was honored by the presence of the emperor and the senate; in the civil sector, it enjoyed privileges equal to those of ancient Rome. These assertions faithfully reflected the situation at the time of the Council of Chalcedon, but they did not reflect the exact political and administrative circumstances of Constantinople in 381. Concerning the privileges of the new capital, we note that the projection of a later stage of development into the past was a current practice of historical works at this time.[564]

In fact, the process evolved rather slowly and not without some bumps along the road.[565] G. Dagron rightly spoke of "a slow promotion to the rank of capital."[566] At first, there was no question of denying the superiority of Rome. Even in the most laudatory formulations, we only hear of Constantinople being called "Second Queen" (ἡ τὰ δεύτερα...βασιλεύουσα); only Rome surpassed Constantinople in dignity (μόνη σεμνοτέρα).[567] An important step toward the juridical equality of the two cities was taken in the reign of Constantius (337-61). An abrupt halt in this ascension took place with the extinction of Constantine's dynasty in 363. The climb started again after the reign of Valens (364-78).[568] From the solemn entry of Theodosius into the city, November 24, 380, the political situation of Constantinople was to be stabilized in a positive sense. The emperor established his definitive residence there and really made it the capital of the eastern part of the Roman state. The reestablishment of orthodoxy by the council of 381 gave to the city a religious consciousness that it did not have before. In this context, the paragraph concerning the prerogatives of the bishop of New Rome, found in the text adopted by this council of 381, stand out even more.[569] The political rise of Constantinople, while it accentuated the decline of Rome and announced the decomposition of the empire in the West, was necessarily to raise hostile reactions in the Latin world. The strongest opposition came from the regent Stilico, "the perfect image of a Romanized German barbarian,"[570] who directed the affairs of the empire in the West in the name of the young Honorius (394-423). It was then that the poet Claudian, a follower of Stilico, launched his invectives against Constantinople as "*quae dicitur aemula Romae.*"[571] This injured Latin sensibility of course was felt in the Church as well; we note the sharp reaction of the Roman legates at Chalcedon and then later on of Pope Leo himself when he saw the motion on the see of Constantinople. On the level of civil law, the movement toward full equality between the two capitals evolved slowly. No doubt rather early, but we do not know at what exact date, Constantinople became the beneficiary of the privileges of the *Jus italicum,* and this was confirmed in the early 370's by a law of the emperors Valens and Gratian.[572] It was, however, only in 421 that the complete juridical equality of the two Romes was officially proclaimed in civil legislation.[573] From then on, it was understood that all the privileges of Old Rome were extended to New Rome. Thus, a wish expressed by Themistius in a speech to the emperor Constantius II in 357 was finally realized: Constantinople participated in the destiny and in the name of Rome (καὶ τῆς τύχης καὶ τοῦ ὀνόματος).[574] This idea of a veritable assimilation was to be translated into juridical terms by a law of Justinian in which we read that *"Romam autem intelligendum est non solum veteram, sed etiam regiam nostram."*[575] It is not at all surprising that such a conception had repercussions in the Church. We find a faithful echo, for example, in what the archbishops of Constantinople, Anatolius (449-58) and John II (518-20), wrote;[576] for them, the assimilation took on a spiritual dimension.[577]

The presence of the senate is mentioned as one of the reasons motivating the fathers of the council of 381 in issuing their decision ("...καὶ συγκλήτῳ"). In his *Church History,* written between 439 and 450, Sozomen had already noted that the reason for the elevation of New Rome was the presence of the senate.[578] This is not an anachronism, for from the reign of Constantius II (337-61) this assembly had acquired a certain importance, and this situation was consolidated under the reign of Theodosius I (379-95). It is significant, however, to note that its role had grown again near the middle of the fifth century.[579] It is therefore altogether understandable that in the motion edited in collaboration with the imperial commissioners, the presence of the senate was mentioned as a source of honor for Constantinople.

Thus, the first part of the motion was presented as a paraphrastic exegesis of the ruling on the see of Constantinople adopted by the council of 381; in fact, however, the authors of the motion were looking at things from the perspective of the political and administrative realities of the mid-fifth century. Nonetheless, the consequences for the Church of this juridical evolution were not taken to their logical conclusions. While the text of 381 spoke of "prerogatives of honor" (τὰ πρεσβεῖα τῆς τιμῆς), Chalcedon made clear that the prerogatives were "equal" (ἴσων) to those of Old Rome. It added that Constantinople "was also to be just as elevated as Old Rome in church affairs" (καὶ ἐν τοῖς ἐκκλησιαστικοῖς ἐκείνην μεγαλύνεσθαι πράγμασι). Yet, at once this daring interpretation of the text of 381 was watered down a bit by a serious corrective: Constantinople only occupied the second place (δευτέραν μετ' ἐκείνην ὑπάρχουσαν). It was quite obvious that without this restriction it would have been difficult to make reference to the text of 381. Moreover, neither the authors of the motion nor the fathers of Chalcedon who approved it had any intention of putting in doubt the primacy of Old Rome. The authorized commentary of the decree given by the imperial commissioners and the letter of the council to Pope Leo were absolutely clear on this point.[580] We note in addition that in the text of the motion different verbal forms are used to indicate the origin of the prerogatives of Rome and Constantinople. In the first case, we find ἀποδεδώκασι, and in the second ἀπένειμαν. The verb ἀποδιδόναι evokes the idea of "giving to someone what is his due" while ἀπονέμειν means "to assign" or "to award." In this document, prepared with such care, the use of two different verbs is certainly not an accident. In this way, the authors very discreetly avoided too radical an assimilation: they did not claim, in fact, that the first place of the Roman Church came from a precise canonical act; the fathers, those of the past as well as those at the time of the Council of Constantinople, only recognized a reality which at least in its principle was not questioned.[581] The prerogatives of Constantinople, however, were the result of a definite canonical decision. The Latin translation of the acts edited by Rusticus is aware of this distinction in the Greek verbs.[582] This difference is stressed even more in Greek by the respective use of the perfect and the aorist.[583]

Later on, in a totally different historical context, these subtle nuances were to be lost on certain writers who maintained that the preposition μετά in canons 3 of Constantinople and 28 of Chalcedon indicated not the hierarchical order but the chronological succession; and, to support this assertion, they affirmed that the term "equality" (τὴν ἰσότητα) used by Chalcedon excluded the idea of hierarchical order.[584] This fantastic interpretation was vigorously refuted by Zonaras.[585]

The second part of the decree defines the rights of Constantinople over certain episcopal ordinations. The link with the preceding part, introduced by the conjunctive expression "and consequently" (καὶ ὥστε), clearly shows that from the legislator's point of view, these rights derived from what is contained in the preamble, and this, according to them, was nothing else but an amplification of the canon adopted in 381. Does this mean that they regarded the dispositions of the decree as simply making explicit the "prerogatives of honor" (τὰ πρεσβεῖα τῆς τιμῆς) of the bishop of Constantinople recognized by the council in 381? In reality, things are more complicated. Without doubt there have been advocates of such a simplistic interpretation. Thus during the twelfth session of Chalcedon, when the question was raised of who should have the canonical right to ordain the future bishop of Ephesus, the clerics of Constantinople cried out "Let the decisions of the 150 holy fathers be observed! Let the privileges of Constantinople not be lost! Let the ordination be done here by the archbishop according to custom!"[586] But the explanations of the decree such as we find them in the letters of the council and of Anatolius to Pope Leo, were much more nuanced. The fathers of the council declared that they had sanctioned by a synodal vote ("κατὰ συνοδικὴν ἐκυρώσαμεν ψῆφον...") the custom that had existed for a long time about the role of the see of Constantinople in the promotion of the metropolitans. They added that they had, on the other hand, confirmed ("ἐβεβαιώσαμεν δὲ...") the canon of the 150 fathers on the prerogatives of the see of Constantinople.[587] From his side, Anatolius wrote that the council had confirmed the canon of the 150 fathers and gave the wording of the canon with a notable modification: in the text of this stipulation where "prerogatives of honor" are mentioned, Anatolius spoke of "honor and prerogatives."[588] This is significant. The purpose of this change was to put aside a purely honorific interpretation of the canon of 381. This was obviously the reason why the determinative τῆς τιμῆς was omitted from the text of the motion. That such a reductionist interpretation of the canon of 381 could have been given is proven by what we find in an edict of the emperor Theodosius II: "According to the prescriptions of the canons, and our wish also, the bishop of Constantinople should find it sufficient to have the honor of the prerogatives after that of Rome because this city is a New Rome."[589]

This decree was no doubt issued in 449, and it showed how great the influence of Dioscorus was in religious affairs; this influence was exercised, however, through the intermediary of the eunuch Chrysaphius.[589a] Along with the letters of the council and Anatolius, both most likely written by the same person,[590] we must also mention the letter of the emperor Marcian to Pope Leo; in this document, however, there was not the slightest allusion to the suprametropolitan jurisdiction acknowledged as belonging to the archbishop of Constantinople. The decision adopted at Chalcedon was conceived as recalling that of the council of 381 concerning New Rome's second place in the church hierarchy.[591] The problem of the relation between the jurisdictional right of Constantinople and the stipulations of the council of 381 was thus dodged. We can imagine that in the imperial chancery they must have thought that there was no reason for the emperor to enter into details; they had been sufficiently expressed in the letters of the council and Anatolius. In any case, the two first documents allow us to get an idea of the manner in which the redactors of the motion looked at the relation between this canon and the one issued in 381. They especially did not want the expression "the prerogatives of honor" to be understood in the sense of a simple honorific precedence. They meant to imply the responsibilities that fall to the major sees and especially to those of Old Rome and to New Rome in the universal Church. For this second see, such concern was especially applicable to the eastern part of the *oikoumene*. From this position flowed the right analogous to the one that all the major sees enjoyed, that is, the control of episcopal consecrations in neighboring areas.[592] Such was at least the manner of seeing things in the official circles of the church in Constantinople. Thus, from this point of view, the jurisdictional power mentioned in the motion was based directly on the custom which was a consequence of the status attributed to the church of New Rome by the second general council.

Just how exact was the assertion contained in the letters of the council and of Anatolius, that is, to what extent was the decision about the suprametropolitan jurisdiction of Constantinople a simple ratification of a long custom? A preliminary remark is necessary: we cannot establish any parallel between the extension of Constantinople's ecclesiastical jurisdiction over the three dioceses and the prerogatives of Rome, Alexandria and Antioch relating to episcopal consecrations. In fact, for these three great sees, their preponderant influence had been prior in time to the establishment of the metropolitan system. For Constantinople, the jurisdictional expansion developed in the territories where this system was already in place and working; thus this expansion worked to the detriment of the metropolitan system. This is the source of the uncertain jurisdictional character of the custom which only slowly imposed itself and not without running into opposition based on the canons. References were made to the canons during the twelfth and fourteenth sessions of the Council of Chalcedon. The greater part of the interventions made by the archbishops of Constantinople as well as the reactions to these interventions are well known; history has kept them alive. They are fully listed and noted from 381 on in the first fascicle of the *Regéstes*.[593] It is still proper to remark that these interventions had already begun previously, especially in the time of Macedonius (314-60).[594] The episcopate of St. John Chrysostom is properly considered to be a decisive step in the establishment of Constantinople's authority over Asia and Pontus.[595] In the affair of the simoniac bishops of Asia, he not only presided over the synod that deposed the guilty persons, but he proceded with their replacement. Coming back to Constantinople from Ephesus by land, he deposed Gerontius of Nicomedia; this action provoked the anger of the city's population. At the Synod of the Oak, we saw some of the complaints put forward against St. John Chrysostom; one of them was the following: "...he encroached on the provinces of others and consecrated bishops in them."[596] It is true, however, that he acted in Asia only on the pressing request of a number of bishops in this diocese, so that formally there was no transgression of the rule set out by the fathers of the council of 381: "If they are not invited, let the bishops not go outside their own dioceses for an ordination or any other ecclesiastical act."[597] But closer to the truth is another explanation of St. John Chrysostom's conduct: up to a certain point, it was an accepted point that the major sees of the Church by reason of their moral authority had the right to intervene in exceptional circumstances in the affairs of local churches to re-establish order. If St. John Chrysostom was accused of getting mixed up in other people's affairs, it was because he had made many enemies, and especially Theophilus of Alexandria was greatly upset to see the growing influence of the see of Constantinople. Thus, rather than just dwell on exceptional cases and spectacular interventions, it would be interesting to have information on the whole process by which Constantinople assured itself the control over the consecrations of the metropolitans and bishops in the three dioceses. Now the historical sources give us only very fragmentary information on this subject. Some interesting data has been given to us, however, in the explanations of the votes taken during the seventeenth session of the Council of Chalcedon.[598]

The jurisidictional expansion of the see of Constantinople was not accomplished in exactly the same way in each of the three dioceses. We must take for granted that from the episcopate of Nectarius (381-97) such a control was imposed on the six provinces of Thrace where, moreover, the local churches were not very numerous. Even if Socrates incorrectly affirmed that Thrace was attached to the see of the capital, this statement being based on the decision of the council of 381, his statement nonetheless expressed a factual reality.[599] Moreover, it is significant that the jurisdictional control over the diocese of Thrace did not seem to run into any resistance. It was not at all the same situation for Pontus and Asia. Thus around 426-7, when Sisinnius of Constantinople chose Proclus for the see of Cyzicus, metropolitan of the Hellespont, he ran into the insurmountable opposition of the inhabitants, who had their own candidate ordained. According to Socrates, there may have been a law prescribing that no episcopal ordination be carried out without the consent of Constantinople; but it seems that this was a special decree issued only for Atticus ("...ὡς

Ἀττικῷ μόνῳ εἰς πρόσωπον παρασχεθέντος").[600] Nonetheless, at the Council of Chalcedon, Diogenes of Cyzicus was one of the convinced supporters of the right of Constantinople over the consecration of metropolitans.[601] His point of view was not shared by the bishops of the province of Asia, who asked that the canons be respected, making an obvious allusion to the rules established by the councils of Nicea, Antioch and Laodicea.[602] Concerning the diocese of Pontus, we have proof that the prerogatives of Constantinople over consecrations were not taken for granted because we have the refusals of Eusebius of Ancrya and Thalassius of Caesarea to approve the motion.[603] There was a conflict between two conceptions of church organization: according to the more ancient law, each province was normally to enjoy autocephaly; strictly limited exceptions were allowed in the cases of Rome, Alexandria and Antioch. According to the new law which had not yet received official approval, there was a tendency for a generalized control by the major sees to develop over vast areas. This was to result in the constitution of the patriarchates. Since this phenomenon involved all the major sees, it is hard to understand why certain Roman Catholic scholars have exclusively concentrated their criticisms on the growth of Constantinople.[604]

The decree, therefore, recognized a suprametropolitan jurisdiction for the archbishop of New Rome in the dioceses of Pontus, Asia and Thrace, leaving to the metropolitans of these territories their prerogatives in the promotions of bishops. In the Middle Ages, certain writers gave another meaning to the phrase "...τοὺς τῆς Ποντικῆς καὶ τῆς Ἀσιανῆς καὶ τῆς Θρακικῆς διοικήσεως μητροπολίτας μόνους." They thought that μόνος designated a geographical restriction; that is, this adjective indicated the fact that the archbishop of Constantinople had not received jurisdiction over other dioceses from the Council of Chalcedon.[605] This interpretation was fully accepted by Aristenus, although the text of the *Epitome* did not contain the adjective μόνους.[606] Zonaras gave preference to the first interpretation; however, at the end of his commentary on canon 28, he mentioned the existence of this other opinion.[607] Since he did not criticize it openly, he no doubt considered it less probable but not impossible. As we have already shown at the beginning of our analysis of the text, only the first interpretation effectively corresponds to the intention of the legislator. Because the motion expressly indicated the dioceses over which the archbishop of Constantinople was to exercise his suprametropolitan jurisdiction, this meant that he was not to have an analogous right

over the provinces of Illyricum. Since the final attachment of the civil
dioceses of Macedonia and Dacia to the eastern empire in 395, the
churches of Illyricum had felt the attraction of the see of Constantinople, but we do not see that the archbishops of New Rome tried to
impose their suprametropolitan jurisdiction in this area.[608] On the
other hand, before the Council of Chalcedon, as well as after it, they
never renounced their right to intervene in exceptional cases, thus
showing by their conduct that they did not regard these territories as
Old Rome's exclusive sphere of influence.[609] They were upheld in their
view and actions by the civil power. There was also a law of July 14,
421, which stipulated that if any doubt was ever raised (*quid dubietatis*)
in the province of the Illyricum, it was necessary to make an appeal to
the archbishop of New Rome.[610] At the instigation of Pope Boniface,
the emperor of the West, Honorius, appealed to his colleague of the
East, Theodosius II, asking him to postpone this measure. In a reas-
suring answer, Theodosius seems to have acceded to this request.[611]
But there was no abrogation by a juridical act of the contested law;
otherwise it would not have been put into the Code of Theodosius
and reproduced in the Code of Justinian.[612]

In the second part of the motion, that is, between the affirmation of
Constantinople's supremetropolitan jurisdiction and the remarks about
the promotion of metropolitans and their suffragans, we find a stipulation about episcopal consecrations among the barbarians of the
three dioceses: "ἔτι δὲ καὶ τοὺς ἐν τοῖς βαρβαρικοῖς ἐπισκόπους τῶν
προειρημενῶν διοικήσεων." This phrase constitutes an addition that
modified the declared norm on this point. In fact, according to the
general principle set forth, Constantinople had authority only over the
consecrations of metropolitans. Before examining the scope of this
ruling, it is no doubt useful to note that in the thought of the legislator
it had a very secondary importance in relation to the rest of the text;
this is important because of the speculations concerning this clause
that have been put forth in our own time. During the seventeenth
session, the imperial commissioners withdrew the motion to make
some clarifications; they did not think it was necessary to mention this
stipulation. Nor do we find the slightest allusion to this point in the
later correspondence between Rome and Constantinople. It is, therefore, very obvious that this section was only a detail within the
framework of the jurisdiction over the three dioceses accorded to
Constantinople. As we will see, this was how the Byzantine canonists
also considered it.

The present ruling should be placed in the context of the general canonical organization such as it had been sanctioned by the fathers of Nicea and other councils of the fourth century: according to the principle of territorial accommodation, metropolitan districts with only a few exceptions were to have the same boundaries as the provinces of the Roman Empire; the bishop of the capital city of each province, that is, the metropolitan, *ipso facto* enjoyed primatial prerogatives, most importantly concerning the control of episcopal elections in the province. Such a system, therefore, was only fully applicable where the Roman political system was in force. The borders of the empire were not conceived of as a fixed and immovable line. Such an idea would run against the potential universality of the empire. As G. Dagron has correctly written, "the Roman world was a totality whose divisions could only be inside; there were no foreign countries; there were only outlying districts."[613]

Most certainly "*τῶν προειρημένων διοικήσεων*" is the grammatical determinant of "*τοὺς ἐπισκόπους*" and not of "*ἐν τοῖς βαρβαρικοῖς.*"[614] However, the whole phrase in question forms a grammatical unit which should be understood globally, for if the "barbarian" bishops were dependent on the named dioceses, *it was very obviously for geographical reasons.* This is exactly how the phrase was understood in the Byzantine canonical tradition. Aristenus wrote that "only the metropolitans of Pontus, Asia and Thrace are subject" to the bishop of Constantinople and "are to be ordained by him; equally, in the diocese in question, the bishops of the barbarians are included."[615] This way of understanding the ruling is all the more significant because the formulation of the *Epitome* on which Aristenus commented lends itself to a different interpretation.[616] We see, however, that Aristenus based himself not on the wording in the *Epitome* but on the complete text of the motion. Zonaras spoke of "*τῶν ἐπισκόπων τῶν ἐν τοῖς βαρβαρι-κοῖς ἔθνεσι, τοῖς οὖσιν ἐν ταῖς ῥηθείσαις διοικήσεσιν*";[617] therefore, the meaning is "of barbarian nations finding themselves in the named dioceses" and not just of bishops jurisdictionally attached to these dioceses. Matthew Blastares wrote that the archbishop of Constantinople was to ordain "also the bishops among the neighboring barbarian nations (*ὁμόροις*) of the dioceses under his authority."[618]

In order to understand correctly the meaning of this ruling, it is necessary to refer to what the Council of Constantinople decided in 381: after having set out the principle of non-interference of one diocese's episcopate in the affairs of other dioceses and after having restated the competence of provincial synods, the fathers of this council immediately added that "in what concerns the Church of God among the barbarian nations (ἐν τοῖς βαρβαρικοῖς ἔθνεσι), it is important that they be administered according to the established custom of the times of the fathers."[619] The Christian communities within the boundaries of the Roman Empire were under the jurisdictional authority of the great cities where their bishops were canonically elected and consecrated. In the text of the Chalcedonian motion, the ruling on the bishops among the barbarian nations was only a logical extension of the decision on the status of the metropolitans of these three dioceses. At the same time that they officially lost their autocephaly,[620] the major cities involved saw their rights over episcopal ordinations "among the barbarians" given over to the see of Constantinople. Of course, this transfer of authority, which nonetheless affected only a very small number of metropolitan sees, was by no means without political implications.

The fathers of the council of 381 had used the expression "ἐν τοῖς βαρβαρικοῖς ἔθνεσι"; in the Chalcedonian motion, we simply find "ἐν τοῖς βαρβαρικοῖς."[621] Does this slight difference in wording indicate any particular intention, as Metropolitan Maximus of Sardis claimed,[622] or are the two expressions strictly equivalent, as Zonaras and Blastares thought?[623] In either case, there would only be a slight nuance of difference. At the time, the term τὸ βαραρικὸν (in Latin, barbaricum) designated all the territories which de facto were not directly integrated into the cultural and administrative sphere of "Romania."[624] The very imprecise character of this name stood for very diverse political and cultural situations. For example by using a metonymic formulation, the fathers of the Synod in Trullo used the expression "ἐν ταῖς βαρβαρικαῖς ἐκκλησίαις" with this meaning.[625] In this case, it was a question of churches in the West which were not under the Byzantine influence and where, consequently, it was practically impossible to expect that the general law would be applied.[626] Concerning the term "ἐν τοῖς βαρβαρικοῖς" in the motion of Chalcedon, it is probable that it meant the regions situated within the borders of the civil dioceses of Thrace and Pontus; the question was not relevant to Asia, which was encircled by other dioceses. The interpretation of the Pedalion seems correct to us; it says "......οἱ ἐπίσκοποι οἱ εἰς τοὺς βαρβαρικοὺς τόπους εὑρισκόμενοι τοὺς γειτονεύοντας εἰς τὰς ῥηθείσας αὐτὰς διοικήσεις."[627] Referring to the situation of his own time, Zonaras mentioned the Alans, near the diocese of Pontus, and the Russians, neighbors of Thrace.[628] This precise statement was repeated verbatim by Balsamon and then Blastares;[629] it was also integrated into the explanation of the *Pedalion*.[630] H. Leclercq maintained that this stipulation gave to the see of Constantinople the right to ordain bishops "in the dioceses established among the barbarians."[631] This interpretation is completely fantastic because it is in contradiction with the wording of the motion. However, the ruling on the bishops "ἐν τοῖς βαρβαρικοῖς" is frequently invoked in our own time by supporters of the jurisdiction of the ecumenical patriarch over what is called the diaspora; they understand it to mean all the Orthodox churches situated outside the geographical limits of autocephalous churches.[632] We do not need to set out the history of the origin and development of this theory because the relation between such a claim and the clause about the bishops *"inter barbaros...praefatarum dioceseum"* is purely artificial. Even among the Greek-speaking Orthodox, this interpretation has run into resistance. Metropolitan Christophoros of Leontopolis, subsequently patriarch of Alexandria, has made a sharp refutation of it.[633] Among the Russians, we note also the criticism of S. Troitsky.[634] Let us be sure not to confuse two separate issues: 1) the unduly extended interpretation of the clause in question, a recent phenomenon, and 2) the global use of the motion to justify the primacy of the see of Constantinople in the East. This second use claims support because the proposed decree was submitted to the council for approval in order to give a solid canonical base, on the level of *jus scriptum,* to an already established situation.

After the clause on the ordination of bishops *in barbaricis,* the decree ends by outlining the procedure flowing from the decision about the suprametropolitan rights of Constantinople in the three dioceses. This passage starts with the adverb δηλαδή, which here has the post-classical meaning "that is to say." The case of suffragan bishops is clearly distinguished from that of the metropolitans. For the bishops, the election and consecration must be carried out in conformity with the rules of written law, that is, those in the *Book of Canons*.[635] In other words, the exclusive authority of the synod of the eparchy and of the metropolitans was confirmed.[636] The archbishop of Constantinople was not to interfere in this process, as the imperial commissioners were to state expressly at the end of the meeting. With regard to the promotion of the metropolitans, the prescribed procedure did not exclude the participation of the rest of the provincial bishops: the election of the future metropolitan fell to them as well as to the clergy and notables of the locality, this was equally made clear by the imperial commissioners.[637] During the thirteenth session, Archbishop Anatolius made it clear that there was no intention of depriving them of this right.[638] According to the wording of the decree, the archbishop of Constantinople was then either to do the consecration himself or to allow it to be done in the province itself. It is difficult to know when this procedure fell out of use. From the year 1000 on, the promotion of metropolitans was done differently; the patriarchal synod composed of metropolitans and archbishops present in the capital selected three candidates, and the patriarch chose one to be ordained.[639]

After having analysed this decree point by point and before seeing the reactions it provoked, it is proper to try to understand what were the real intentions of its authors. Many questions have been asked about their motivations and objectives, but the hypotheses put forward on this subject have most often been seriously undermined by a methodological error: instead of taking into account the historical context and the concrete problems being faced at the time, scholars have tended to consider the decree in the perspective of later developments.[640] In addition, insufficient attention has been paid to the fact that *this motion did not have the purpose of defining the primatial prerogatives of the see of Old Rome but only those of the see of Constantinople.* In this context, the mention of Rome only came into the picture as a point of reference and consequently only where the analogy seemed proper. This same thing was true for canon 6 of Nicea which concerned the ancient jurisdictional customs in Italy and which were used to justify those of Egypt.[641] We must not be surprised then to find no reference to the apostolicity of the church of Rome; the fathers of Chalcedon had no intention of minimizing the importance of this apostolicity, as their letter to the pope showed.[642] With discretion, it is true, the authors of the motion had marked the nuance in the situation of each of the two sees by the respective use of ἀποδεδώκασι and ἀπέμειναν as well as by the reminder of the second place in rank of the see of Constantinople: "δευτέραν μετ᾽ ἐκείνην ὑπάρχουσαν." If the first part of the decree strongly brings out the legitimacy of the rights of New Rome and if there really were a polemical point in the mind of the redactors, it could only have been aimed at the see of Alexandria, which from the foundation of Constantinople had never stopped trying, by various means, to undermine the position of the bishops of the new capital. But it is not certain that this was the main reason for the solemnity of the statement. Let us not forget that this first part was a preamble used to introduce justifications for the concrete proposals set out in the rest of the text. These dealt with the jurisdiction of Constantinople over the three dioceses and the means of its application. In the mind of the motion's redactors, they wanted to put into written law what had only been a developing practice; it was, however, far from being unanimously accepted as the norm by the bishops concerned. By underlining the eminent dignity of the see of Constantinople, we can see that they were trying to establish a solid basis for its jurisdictional claims. It was precisely over these claims that the debate took place during the sixteenth session. After the council, the opposition of St. Leo was determined essentially by the same issue. Later on, when the suprametropolitan jurisdiction of the patriarch of Constantinople had become an unquestioned fact and when in addition the ecclesiastical relations between East and West had deteriorated, the accent began to be put on the affirmations of the preamble and to use them for apologetical ends against the papacy. The first witness to such an interpretation is found in a scholion that goes back to the seventh century:

> It must be known that they [that is the members of the fourth ecumenical council] had called the church of Constantinople second because then the older Rome was also a capital. If, therefore, as the holy council affirms, the fathers attributed the [primatial] prerogatives (τὰ πρεσβεῖα) to older Rome because it was the capital, now that by the good will of God, this city [Constantinople] is the only capital, it is the one who rightly holds the first place position (τὴν προτέραν).[643]

It was probably at this time that the theme of the transfer of power from the old capital to the new one was born: the Byzantines called this ἡ τῶν σκήπτρων μετάθεσις, using a metonymic expression. This expression appeared in the epitome of the canons probably made in the seventh century by Stephen of Ephesus.[644] This theory of only one legitimate imperial power, that of the emperors in Constantinople, was to be a constant in the political philosophy of the Byzantines in their confrontations with the West after the *renovatio imperii* of the ninth century. Emperor Michael III was to mention it in his correspondence with Pope Nicholas I.[645] A current interpretation of the Chalcedonian decree on Constantinople's privileges was reproduced in the *Alexiad* of Anna Comnena; it represented an opinion in the cultured circles of the eastern empire during the Middle Ages. This document said:

When the seat of the empire was transferred from there to here in our country and in our imperial city, the senate and the whole administration was transferred; by the same act, the first place in the episcopal hierarchy was also transferred. Thus from the beginning the emperors have accorded honors to the see of Constantinople; but especially the Council of Chalcedon raised the bishop of Constantinople to the highest position [in the hierarchy] and subordinated all the dioceses of the universe to him.[646]

The great Byzantine canonists did not fall into such extravagances. Aristenus was very sober: he said that the bishop of Constantinople was equal in dignity (ἰσότιμος) to the bishop of Rome and possessed the same prerogatives by reason of the presence of the emperor and the senate. He went on to say that only the metropolitans of Pontus, Thrace and Asia were under his authority "as well as the bishops of the barbarians in these dioceses." He thus showed that he probably understood the adjective "only" as relating to geography; he made clear that Illyricum was in the past under Rome's jurisdiction.[647]

Zonaras was opposed to those who deformed the meaning of the expression "being the second after it," and on this subject, he referred back to his explanation of canon 3 of Constantinople. As for the equality of prerogatives decreed by the Council of Chalcedon in favor of the church of Constantinople, he considered that it was a decision made under the inspiration of the Holy Spirit because of the future doctrinal deviation of Rome.[648] Balsamon wrote two commentaries on canon 28.[649] Their most outstanding aspect was the interest he attached to *Constitutum Constantini*, currently but improperly called the *Donatio Constantini*.[650] Very diverse opinions have been put forward on the origins of this forged document and on the motives of its author. Let us simply say that it was written in Rome but probably not in the papal curia, either in the second half of the eighth century or at the beginning of the ninth.[651] It is very difficult to determine when the Greek East first became aware of the document. F. Dölger supposed that already by 958 it was known, at the time of the mission of Liutprand of Cremona; on the other hand, P. Alexander suggested that it was known and used only during the time of Manuel Comnenus (1143-80).[652] This diversity of opinions comes from the difficulty of identifying certain allusions to this or that other related document, for example the *Vita Silvestri*.[653]

The motion on the privileges of the see of Constantinople was definitively adopted during the last meeting of the council, November 1. We do not know how many fathers were at this session; it was considered to be the seventeenth session in the *Acta Graeca* and the sixteenth in the *Versio a Rustico edita*. The roll which appears at the beginning has a stereotyped character; it does not claim to be exact since besides the 58 names, it contains the normal formula: "...καὶ τῆς λοιπῆς ἁγίας καὶ Οἰκουμενικῆς Συνόδου."[654] The meeting opened in a tense atmosphere. Paschasinus and Lucensius immediately asked for the floor, and they contested what had taken place the night before, the form as well as the content. The session in question, so they said, had been held in their and the imperial commissioners' absence. As for the decisions made, in their view they went *"praeter canones ecclesiasticos et disciplinam."* Consequently, they asked that the council, this time gathered in official session, take a stand on this issue.[655] The imperial commissioners agreed to the request. Aetius, Anatolius' archdeacon, observed that it was normal practice in the councils to deal with pressing questions after having settled essential matters, and this was what happened in the case of the church of Constantinople. He added that the legates had been invited to participate in the deliberations. They declined to come saying they had not received instructions in this matter. They were then referred to the imperial commissioners who allowed the council to examine the problem in question. Aetius ended his statement saying that this was what they had done, not acting in secret or in a furtive manner. Therefore everything was normal and regular (ἀκόλουθος καὶ κανονική).[656] The commissioners then asked that the minutes of the session in question be read. Aetius gave to Beronician, secretary of the sacred consistory, a document which is called σχεδάριον in the *Acta*. It was not at all an exact word for word version of the session; it was only a brief text; it was later on to be called "canon 28" and also contained the signatures of the bishops in attendance. It is surprising that the Roman legates did not make any objection to this sleight-of-hand trick.

The number of 185 signatures has only an approximate value[657] because several signatures were made by proxy; several metropolitans signed in their own names and then for their suffragans also. In any case, it is impossible to know what idea a good portion of the members had on this question. How many of them, moreover, were still in Chalcedon on October 31 and November 1? It is not out of the question to think that some of them did not attend these meetings just to avoid having to take a stand on the matter. We note the curious absence of Eunomius of Nicomedia who during the fourteenth session, October 30, had stated some reservations on the rights of the see of Constantinople.[658]

Anatolius of Constantinople, the principal winner in the affair, naturally signed the motion first. Then came the signature of Maximus of Antioch followed by Juvenal of Jerusalem. The decree did not seem to embarrass them in the slightest. The relations between Constantinople and Antioch were always good, and the bishops of the great city of the diocese of the East never felt slighted by the ascension of New Rome; besides, Maximus owned his episcopal promotion to Anatolius. As for Juvenal, he had contracted a debt of gratitude toward the archbishop of Constantinople who had supported his territorial claims. We note the names of Eusebius of Doryleum, Ibas of Edessa, and Theodoret of Cyrus among the signatures. Unquestionably, they found nothing in the motion that could undermine the authority or dignity of the see of Rome. Two African bishops, Aurelius and Restitutianus, also signed. The only members of the council present at the session of October 31 (the sixteenth) who refused to sign were the metropolitans of Ancyra and of Caesarea as well as their respective suffragans. Theirs were not insignificant refusals since these metropolitans were holders of two principal sees in the civil diocese of Pontus.[659] We note that the see of Ephesus was vacant because of the rejection of the legitimacy of both Bassian and Stephen; this greatly facilitated the adoption of the decree by paralyzing the reaction of the bishops of Asia, who were hostile to the hegemony of Constantinople. Even more important in this matter was the absence of Egyptian bishops after the deposition of Dioscorus.

After the reading of the motion, Lucensius asked the commissioners to verify that no one had signed under pressure (*coacti*); cries were then raised in the assembly to affirm that there had not been any pressure.[660] They then went on to the essential matters and got down to the core of the question. We need to make a preliminary note here: the debate was strictly in the canonical realm and did not get onto the ecclesiological level. The debate stayed precisely within the limits of the *jus scriptum*, that is, which canons ought to prevail. It was also in this line that Pope Leo showed his opposition after the council.

Lucensius then declared that:

> It is clear that the decrees of the 318 [fathers of Nicea] have been put aside and that mention has only been made of the canons of the 150 [fathers of Constantinople], whose decrees do not appear among the synodical canons; and [the Con-

stantinoplitans] recognize that these were adopted almost 80 years ago. If, therefore, during this period, they have enjoyed this privilege, what are they looking for? If they have not enjoyed this privilege, why are they seeking after it?[661]

Thus, the decision of the council of 381 was brought into question because it was not contained *in synodicis canonibus* and because this decision went against the rulings of Nicea. The canons of Constantinople were not unknown in the West; they had been translated into Latin and appeared in the private collection improperly called *Isidoriana*. This work had been done either at Rome or in Africa between 419 and 450.[662] But the only canonical collection used by the Roman curia at the time of Chalcedon contained only the canons of Nicea and of Sardica, put together in a single whole.[663] Although certain scholars have maintained the opposite, it does not seem that the decision of Constantinople, 381, on the place of the bishop of Constantinople had provoked a hostile reaction on the part of the Roman see.[664] Moreover, when Eusebius of Doryleum read the canon in question to Pope Leo, he did not protest at all.[665] At the beginning of the Council of Chalcedon, the Roman legates associated themselves with the general indignation towards Dioscorus, who had given the fifth place to Flavian at the Council of Ephesus in 449. Paschasinus made an unambiguous statement concerning the rank of Anatolius: "*Ecce nos Deo uolente domnum Anatolium primum habemus; hi quintum posuerunt beatum Flavianum.*"[666] Diogenes, metropolitan of Cyzicus, remarked on this question that the legates knew the canons.[667] During the council, Anatolius always had the first place after the Roman legates, and it was also in this position that he signed the dogmatic definition.[668] The use and the interpretation of canon 3 of Constantinople, 381, in the preamble of the motion moved the legates of the pope, and after them the pope himself, to take a negative attitude towards this canon.

When the statement of Lucensius had been translated into Greek, Aetius asked the legates to make known the instructions they had received. The priest Boniface then produced a papal document and read the following passage:

> You will not allow that the rulings established by the holy fathers be recklessly violated; by all means you will protect the dignity of our person that you represent, and if, by chance, anybody tries to gain any advantage because of the position of their cities, you will oppose the attempt with solid firmness.[669]

Where could the Roman delegation have gotten such a document since on the night before they were still claiming that they had not received any instructions on the question to be discussed? V. Grumel thought that it was the substance of a verbal answer that the pope had given to his legates after having received a statement in November of 450 on the privileges of the see of Constantinople from Anatolius' representatives.[670] This is not absolutely inconceivable, but it is a pure conjecture based on a very slender indication, that is, an allusion to a question which it was not necessary to deal with in a letter and which the legates would answer orally. Could the pope then have attributed so little importance to this affair when later on he was to manifest so much passion about it? In addition, up to the last session of the council, the legates, as we have already said, manifested no attitude of defiance to the action of the see of Constantinople. Fr. Dvornik suggested an ingenious hypothesis: the document in question may have been edited in Rome to be used against any eventual claims of Dioscorus. But since it was of a general scope, it could find a new application.[671] This hypothesis seems to be the most plausible.

The reading of these papal instructions caused no commentary, and the imperial commissioners asked each party to refer to their canonical sources. Paschasinus then read "the sixth canon of the 318 holy fathers"; in fact, he read also canon 7. According to the *Versio a Rustico edita,* which only contained insignificant variants in relation to the *Versio antiqua,* the text had the following wording:

> *Trecentorum decem et octo sanctorum patrum canon sextus//*
> *(quod) ecclesia Romana semper habuit primatum. teneat autem*
> *et Egyptus// ut episcopus Alexandriae omnium habeat potes-*
> *tatem, quoniam et Romano episcopo haec est consuetudo. simi-*
> *liter autem et qui in Antiochia constitutus est, et in ceteris pro-*
> *vinciis primatus habeant ecclesiae ciuitatum// ampliorum//.*
> *per omnia autem manifestum sit, ut si quis praeter uoluntatem*
> *metropolitani episcopi fueri ordinatus, quia hunc statuit haec*
> *sancta synodus non debere esse episcopum. sane si// communi*
> *(omnium)// consensu et// rationabiliter probato et secundum*
> *ecclesiasticam regulam// statuto// duo aliqui aut tres// per*
> *contentionem suam// contradicunt, illa obtineat sententia in*
> *qua plures fuerint numero sacerdotes. quoniam//uero//mos*
> *antiquus optinuit et uetus traditio ut//Heliae id est Hierosoly-*
> *morum episcopo deferatur, habeat consequenter honorem suum*
> *sed et metropolitano sua digitas salua sit.*[672]

This formulation of canon 6 of Nicea was rather strange and naturally has greatly intrigued scholars.[673] As a whole, this text did not correspond to any known ancient Latin recension. It put two versions together: until *"civitatum ampliorum"* inclusively, it was the version found in the *Codex Ingilrami* except for a detail here and there. Following that, the quotation of Pachasinus faithfully reproduced the wording of the *Isidoriana.*[674] But was it really in this combined form that the Roman legate read canons 6 and 7 of Nicea? Nothing is less certain, all the more so because the later Greek version of the *Acta* is not at all clear on this point.[675] The beginning of the text of this later version, however, gives us an interesting element for the reconstitution of what Paschasinus really said. We read that "*ἡ ἐκλλησία Ρώμης πάντοτε ἔσχεν τὰ πρωτεῖα...*" This plural leads us to think that Paschasinus must have said that *"Ecclesia Romana semper habuit primatus."* This corresponds very exactly to what we find in the *Codex Ingilrami.* It is therefore not at all impossible that the papal legate did use this single version; the partial quotation of the *Interpretatio Isidori,* then, would come from later redactors.

Whatever was the initial goal sought after by the authors of this addition to canon 6 of Nicea, this interpolation was later on most certainly understood in a general sense to favor the power of the papacy in the universal Church.[676] According to the *Acta Graeca* and the *Emendatio Rustici,* Aetius asked that the canon be read according to the official collection of the church of Constantinople, and this was done.[677] However, many scholars have thought that this re-reading, for purposes of verification, was never done. The mention of a re-reading was the interpolation of a copyist. In support of this hypothesis, we note that otherwise a controversy would have erupted just at this time over the exact wording of the canon in question.[678] Other scholars, however, have defended the authenticity of this re-reading.[679] It is difficult to make a categorical judgment. The question is in any case a secondary matter since there was no debate about the text. Moreover, the problem of the Roman primacy was not really posed at Chalcedon, at least not directly.[680]

Later on, using the same book ("*ἀπὸ τοῦ αὐτοῦ βιβλίου*"), the *synodikon* of the council of 381 was read from the beginning up to the passage concerning the see of Constantinople, that is, what in later Greek collections constituted canons 1 to 3.[681] After that, the imperial commissioners asked the bishops of the dioceses of Pontus and Asia, who the night before had approved the decree on the see of Constantinople, to say if they had done so freely or under pressure. These bishops then came to the middle of the assembly.[682] Their principal spokesmen then spoke one after the other: Diogenes, metropolitan of Cyzicus in the Hellespont, Florentius, metropolitan of Sardis in Lydia, Romanus of Myra in Lycia, Kalogeros, metropolitan of Claudioupolis in Honoriad, Seleucus of Amasea in the Helenopont, Eleutherius, metropolitan of Chalcedon in Bithynia, Peter, metropolitan of Gangra in Paphlagonia, Nounechius, metropolitan of Laodicea in Pacatian Phrygia, Mariamnus, bishop of Synnados in Salutarian Phrygia, Pergamius, metropolitan of Antioch in Pisidia, Krikonianos, metropolitan of Aphrodisias in Caria: all affirmed that they had signed freely; certain ones mentioned the fact that they and several of their predecessors had been consecrated by the archbishop of Constantinople.[683] After these metropolitans, Eusebius of Doryleum stated that "I signed of my own free will since I myself read this canon to the very holy pope in Rome in the presence of clerics from Constantinople, and he accepted it ($\dot{\alpha}\pi\epsilon\delta\dot{\epsilon}\xi\alpha\tau o$)."[684] On this point, Heféle observed that:

> Eusebius of Doryleum is here in error, for Pope Leo had always affirmed that he had neither approved nor received the canon as being part of the laws approved by the Church. When Eusebius read this canon to the pope, it could be true that he made no observation and that Eusebius could have interpreted this silence in a completely wrong way.[685]

The reality, as we have already seen, was no doubt more complex. The canon in question certainly did not appear in the *synodicum* used by the Church of Rome, but before anyone had made a reference to this canon in the motion on which the authority of Constantinople over the three dioceses was based, there had not been the slightest criticism of it. We can even speak of a tacit approval; Eusebius probably quoted this canon to the pope to show that the attitude of Dioscorus, who was acting as the head of the episcopate of the whole East, was going against the canonical norm.[686]

After Eusebius of Doryleum, Antiochus, bishop of the city of Sinope in the Helenopont, stated that "of my own free will, I signed following my metropolitan and the canon of the 150 [fathers]."[687] Finally the other bishops having approved the motion yelled out that "of our own free will we signed!"[688] The imperial commissioners concluded that no one had signed under constraint, and they asked those who had not signed the motion to explain their refusal.[689] Eusebius of Ancyra took the floor. Instead of speaking about principle, he went into a personal apology for having consecrated a bishop in Gangra. He was interrupted by a priest of Constantinople, Philip, who said to him that Proclus had intervened in the matter; he did not deny this. Then he expressed his opinion on the question at hand: he affirmed that the authority of a provincial synod over the election of bishops should not be lessened. Anatolius asked him to say who had consecrated him, and he had to admit that it was Proclus.[690] Héfele wrote that "...his speech shows well enough that, without openly contesting the right of Constantinople to carry out ordinations in so extended an area, he did not however look on it in a positive way."[691] The other metropolitan who had refused to sign the motion then said that "we will go to my lord archbishop Anatolius and regulate this affair."[692] This meant that he wanted to avoid a conflict. As L. Duchesne noted with an ironic twist, "he was an accommodating man."[693]

The imperial commissioners then made a statement which summed up the content of the motion, also adding a few clarifications. Here is the wording of their statement:

> After what has happened and after having heard what was said from various speakers, we declare that in conformity with the canons the primatial rights and exceptional honor (τὰ πρωτεῖα καὶ τήν ἐξαίρετον τιμὴν) of the dearly beloved-of-God archbishop of Old Rome have been preserved, but that it is necessary that the very venerable archbishop of the imperial city of Constantinople, New Rome, enjoy the same prerogatives of honor and, therefore, he should have the authority to ordain the metropolitans in the dioceses of Asia, Pontus and Thrace. So, let them be elected by the clerics, the notables and persons of high rank (λαμπροτάτων ἀνδρῶν) of each capital city as well as by all the very pious bishops of the province or by the majority of them so that the most worthy candidate may be chosen as the bishop of the metropolitan city. Then the electors will refer the matter to the very venerable archbishop of the imperial city of Constantinople who will decide if the ordination will be done there [that is, in Constantinople] or else, with his permission, in the province where the election to the vacant episcopal chair took place. As for the very venerable bishops of each city, let them be ordained by all the very pious bishops of the province or by the majority of them, the confirmation (τὸ κύρος) of the candidate falling to the metropolitan, in conformity with the prescribed rule of the fathers, without having to refer these

ordinations to the very venerable archbishop of the imperial
city of Constantinople. This is what we have envisioned; it is
just that this proposal be adopted by the holy ecumenical
council.[694]

The assembly approved the motion by acclamation. The bishops
asked at the same time that the council be ended.[695] They no doubt
had not thought that it would last as long as it did. Already at the
sixth session, Thursday, October 25, they had asked for the right to go
home.[696]

The papal delegation made one last attempt to oppose the adoption
of the decree on the see of Constantinople. Lucensius solemnly
declared that:

The apostolic see must not be humiliated in our presence;[697] this
is why we ask your Sublimeness to abrogate everything that was
done yesterday in our absence, to the detriment of the canons
and the rules; if it is not abrogated, let our protest *(contradictio)*
be inserted into the Acts so that we may know what we must
carry to the knowledge of the apostolic man, the pope of the
universal Church, so he can make a judgment on the undermining of his see and on the violations of the canons.[698]

The minutes of the session do not mention any spontaneous reaction
of the assembly after this peremptory statement. Probably many
bishops thought that the pope would not approve the position taken
by the legates at this time. In the Latin minutes of the session, the
brief intervention of Bishop John of Sebaste, metropolitan of Armenia
Prima, was recorded; he spoke to the imperial commissioners saying
that "all of us remain in agreement with your Magnificence."[699] The
commissioners then decided to close the session officially by recognizing that the motion had been adopted.[700] Concerning the clarification
of the imperial commissioners when they tried to explain the motion,
we note that they tried to avoid aggravating the controversy: the primacy of the see of Old Rome was given its proper recognition and
value; they even used the term that we find in the interpolated version
of canon 6 of Nicea, τὰ πρωτεῖα, stronger than the normal Greek
expression τὰ πρεσβεῖα. For the metropolitans, they underlined the
preservation of their exclusive prerogatives over the consecration of
bishops. Finally we note that there was not really any common front
of opposition groups: Eusebius of Ancyra and Thalassius of Caesarea
did not join together with the legates. As for the bishops of the diocese
of Asia who had defended the rights of the see of Ephesus during the

twelfth and thirteenth sessions, they did not join with the opponents of the motion at this time. This in no way means that they accepted the motion with open arms. The independentist feelings remained strong in the diocese of Asia. We see it very clearly in 476 at the synod that was held in Ephesus. The primatial rights of the bishop of this city were recognized over the whole of the diocese of Asia, but this was a decision that had no real consequences.[701]

Contrary to what the authors and the supporters of the motion were hoping for, Pope Leo completely accepted as his own the point of view expressed by his legates at the last session of the council. However, he took some time to reflect on the matter before answering the requests coming from Constantinople. On May 22, 452, he sent out several letters; one went to the emperor Marcian, one to the empress Pulcheria, and one to archbishop Anatolius.[702] To the emperor, he expressed his joy at the happy result of the council on the question of faith, but he was surprised, and he regretted, that after having reached its goal, the peace of the Church had been put in danger by Anatolius' thirst for honors: *"miror et doleo quod pacem universalis ecclesiae divinitus reformatam ambitionis rursus spiritus inquietat."*[703] The decisions concerning the see of Constantinople are *"contra reverentiam tamen canonum paternorum, contra statuta spiritus sancti, contra antiquitatis exempla."*[704] The pope contested the application in this case of the principle of territorial accommodation: *"alia tamen ratio est rerum saecularium, aliam divinarum."*[705] In his letter to Pulcheria, St. Leo condemned what he called *"alienum ius."*[706] As we might have expected, it was in his letter to Anatolius that he stated most of his objections: he defended the metropolitan system and the rights of the sees of Alexandria and Antioch, considered to be Petrine. He reproached Anatolius for having ordained Maximus of Antioch, thus clearly showing his apprehensions; he feared that the archbishop of Constantinople wanted to extend his authority beyond the three dioceses mentioned in the motion to the whole of the eastern section of the empire. In the same set of letters, he sent an answer to Julian of Cos, his representative in Constantinople:[707] he showed his bewilderment at Julian's suggestion that he come to terms with the motion. The theme throughout all these letters is the lasting and unchangeable character of the rulings of Nicea. They have been in force *"ad totius ecclesiae regimen"* and *"usque in finem mundi."*[708] This absolutizing of the legislation of Nicea and more precisely of canon 6 implied the downgrading of any other later canons, and at first glance it appears somewhat strange. It is true that Nicea canon 6 was known in Rome in the interpolated form that we mentioned before. In addition, the Nicene corpus of the papal curia also contained the canons of Sardica, favorable to the Roman primacy, even though their real origin had been known at the time for a good twenty years. We note that on this point the pope made an allusion to *canonibus* of Nicea.[709] This plural form is important. In addition, since the end of the fourth century, canon 6 was understood as indicating a hierarchical order among the "petrine" sees: Rome, Alexandria and Antioch, the second having been established by Peter through Mark. This hierarchy carried with it a certain inconsistency on the part of St. Leo which F. Dvornik rightly brought out:

> The pope did not realize that his argumentation contained a weak point. In fact, according to the theory of apostolic origin, Antioch ought to have the second place since Peter had founded an episcopal chair there. Moreover, Nicea canon 6 most certainly had the principle of accommodation to the political situation of the empire as its basic point.[710]

In any case, for the pope, the Nicene order was unchangeable since it had been adopted under the inspiration of the Holy Spirit (*"Spiritu Dei instruente"*).[711]

Months passed without the pope's giving his formal approval to the decrees of the council; this inaction created a certain malaise among the orthodox of the East, all the more so because the Monophysite opposition was growing. Finally, he gave his approval to what had been decided at Chalcedon but *"in sola...fidei causa."*[712] The emperor urged Anatolius to renew his contacts with the pope, and so the archbishop wrote to St. Leo. In the letter, Anatolius affirmed that he had not personally been in favor of any particular position regarding the rights of Constantinople; in any case, the confirmation of this act belonged to the pope.[713] The pope interpreted this last statement as an implicit recognition of the nullity of the contested decree and exhorted the archbishop to remain faithful to the rulings of Nicea.[714] In a letter addressed to the emperor, the pope made known his satisfaction at the normalization of relations which had come to pass in Church relations.[715] In fact, everyone was caught in complete ambiguity because there had been no withdrawal of the contested decree and in practice, it was applied. In any case, we do not see how anyone could have reversed a process already widely in practice before the council. When the decree was inserted into the canonical collection of the

Byzantine Church toward the end of the sixth century, there had already been a long history of Constantinople's suprametropolitan jurisdiction and there was no longer any problem about the matter in the East. Later on in the controversies between the Greeks and the Latins, interest was displaced toward the affirmations contained in the preamble of the decree, but this constitutes a subject going beyond the framework of this present study. As we have already said, the text of the motion did not appear in the *Synagoge* of John the Scholastic, but this fact ought not to be interpreted as a rejection of the decree or even a suspicion of it, because all the religious legislation of Justinian supposed the recognition of this conciliar ruling. We see this particularly in the way novella 131:2 was edited.[716] The refusal of Pope Leo and his successors to accept this disciplinary decree manifested a total lack of awareness of the ecclesiastical situation in the East. As for the argumentation based on the canons of Nicea, it was very artificial since it in no way took into account the later historical developments. Certainly the fears of the pope, not clearly admitted in his correspondence, of the establishment in the East of an ecclesiastical power independent of Rome and dominating the other primatial sees in that part of the empire were not without foundation. This was in fact what happened. But canon 28 of Chalcedon did not bring about any real change in this matter. The weakening of the sees of Alexandria and Antioch was first of all the result of quarrels concerning the dogmatic definition worked out at Chalcedon; then of course, there was the Arab conquest which considerably worsened things.

The official recognition by the Roman Church of Constantinople's second place in the Church's hierarchy took place in the thirteenth century. This was the work of the Fourth Lateran Council, 1215.[717] But this recognition was placed in a completely different context: Constantinople was in the hands of the crusaders, who had created a Latin patriarchate. In addition, on the ecclesiological level, the doctrine of papal power, such as it was conceived by the westerners, greatly reduced the importance of this recognition. This decision was nothing really new in Roman Catholicism because since the end of the eleventh century, the anti-Photian assembly of 869-70 had been considered by the western canonists as the "eighth ecumenical council."[718] Now canon 21 of this council declared, among other things, that

...we ordain that absolutely no one among the powers of this world is to injure or force to abdicate from their sees those who occupy the position of patriarch; they should be accorded, on the contrary, honor and respect, first of all to the very holy pope of Old Rome and then to the patriarch of Constantinople, and then those of Alexandria, Antioch and Jerusalem.[719]

[An extract] of the same holy council, from the session concerning Photius, bishop of Tyre, and of Eustathius, bishop of Beirut.

29

The very magnificient and glorious rulers said the following: "On the subject of the bishops who have been consecrated by the very pious bishop Photius and then dismissed by the very pious bishop Eustathius and reduced to the rank of priest after exercising their episcopate, what does the holy council think?" Paschasinus and Lucensius, the very pious bishops, and the priest Boniface, legates of the church of Rome, said the following: "To reduce a bishop to the rank of a priest is a sacrilege; if a valid reason can be given for his dismissal from the exercise of the episcopate, he must not, however, take the position of a priest; if, on the other hand, he has been dismissed from his charge without being found guilty, he must be reinstated in his episcopal dignity." Anatolius, the very pious archbishop of Constantinople, said the following: "Those bishops who have been reduced to the rank of priests, if they have been condemned for just reasons, must not be considered worthy of the rank of priests. But if without valid reason, they have been reduced to a lower degree, provided that their innocence has been shown, it is just that they should again take up the dignity of the episcopate and the priesthood."

All the pious bishops cried out that the judgment of the fathers is just! We all say the same thing! The fathers have justly spoken! Let the sentence of the archbishops be in force!"

The very magnificient and glorious imperial commissioners said the following: "Let what the holy council has decided keep its force for ever!"

We cannot determine with any precision when these extracts from the minutes of the nineteenth session of Chalcedon were added to the *Syntagma in XIV Titles* after the motion on the see of Constantinople.

We cannot doubt that this insertion was relatively ancient, since it was already attested to in the *Recensio Trullana* of the *Syntagma.* However, in the index, only 28 canons were attributed to the Council of Chalcedon. Following this there was the mention "From the same holy council..."[720] What is certain is that the insertion of this text was not made at the same time as canon 28, which was introduced into the *Syntagma* right at the time of its composition.[721] If we compare this text of the *Syntagma* with that of the acts of the council, we see that only the statement on the downgrading of bishops to the rank of priest was taken from the minutes of the session; even more pruning of the text was carried out: among the interventions of the bishops, we do not find those of Paschasinus and Lucensius or that of Anatolius.[722] Later on, another shortening took place: the intervention of the legates was left but without mentioning that it came from them; then followed Anatolius' statement, but this time naming him as its source.[723] A final shortening was done to give the text the form of a canon: only the opinion of the legates was quoted, without naming the source. This then is what we find in the *Pedalion* and the *Kniga Pravil.*[724] We have already spoken of the session of October 20. Photius complained of having been excommunicated because he continued, as before, to consecrate suffragans in the metropolitan territory of Beirut. In doing this, he had not taken account of the imperial decree that raised the see of Beirut to the level of metropolitan city. The bishops that he had consecrated were reduced to the rank of simple priests, probably because the ordinations done in these conditions were held to be against the canons. In fact, if we allow that as metropolitan Photius no longer had the right to exercise his control over ordinations, then the bishops consecrated for these sees were not really bishops at all in terms of Nicea canon 6.[725] But the Council of Chalcedon refused to recognize the value of the imperial pragmatic sanction; it followed that the bishops consecrated by Photius were perfectly regular. Consequently, their downgrading to the rank of priest constituted an arbitrary action. There had been sacrilege, in fact, to the degree that the sacred acts carried out by these bishops had been held to be null and void.[726] On this occasion, the fathers of Chalcedon set out the principle that a bishop judged guilty of some serious wrongdoing must be deposed from the priesthood and not simply reduced to the rank of priest. If that was obvious for a serious wrongdoing, which according to canonical law represented an obstacle to the exercise of any sacred function,[727] we note that a bishop could be authorized to function only

as a priest. Two canons, one before, one after Chalcedon, admitted that
possibility. Canon 18 of the Council of Ancyra said the following:

> If any bishops are nominated for (κατασταθέντες) a commun-
> ity but not accepted by it and if they get involved in other
> communities, cause trouble, and promote commotion for the
> bishops already established there, let them be excommuni-
> cated. As for those who would like to sit among the presby-
> ters where they themselves previously sat as priests, let them
> not be rejected from this position of honor; but if they pro-
> voke quarrels against the local bishops, let them be removed
> also from the honor of the priesthood and let them be
> banished.[728]

We note here that the right to sit among the college of presbyters,
far from being a punishment, was considered to be a way of giving a
place of honor in the priesthood to a bishop, thus avoiding the possibility of having two bishops in one place.[729]

We come now to canon 20 of the Synod in Trullo: "Let no bishop
preach publicly in a city that is not under his authority. If he is caught
doing this, let him be removed from the episcopate (τῆς ἐπισκοπῆς
παυέσθω); let him only exercise presbyteral functions."[730] This canon
seems to go against the decision adopted by the Council of Chalcedon. Were the authors of this ruling aware of the contradiction? It
was certainly possible in Constantinople to inspect the acts of the
Council of Chalcedon; on the other hand, we cannot affirm categorically that the extract from the acts was part of the *codex canonum* that
they used. But up to what point is there a contradiction? The difficulty
resides in the manner of understanding the verb παυέσθω. It is possible
that this word was a synomym for καθαιρείσθω and therefore indicated deposition properly speaking, but it is also possible that it designated the cessation of the activity that went with a function.[731] This
second interpretation was that of Balsamon, who wanted to avoid the
contradiction between this canon and the one of Chalcedon.[732] An
interpolation in the text of the *Nomocanon in XIV Titles* already
marked a similar concern:[733] closer to our own times, John Sokolov
and Nicodemus Milash took up Balsamon's interpretation.[734] Aristenus thought that there was really a contradiction, and he declared
that this stipulation represented a exception to the general norm
expressed in canon 29 of Chalcedon.[735]

If we make a link between the present canon and canon 3 of the
same Synod in Trullo where we find the same verb used, it clearly

appears to be a sort of deposition since the sanction had a definitive character without, however, implying an exclusion from the body of priests.[736] This seems to have been the intention of the fathers of the Synod in Trullo. To justify the exceptional character of this sentence, Zonaras emphasized the canonical and pedagogical considerations: the wrongdoing mentioned in the canon was not one which constituted an impediment to the exercise of the priesthood; it was a sin of ambition and vanity. The appropriate punishment seemed to consist in the humiliation, for a bishop, of being reduced to the rank of a priest.[737] This interpretation was taken up word for word by Balsamon.[738] St. Nicodemus the Hagiorite also accepted and justified it in his commentary of canon 35 of the Holy Apostles: the bishop guilty of this wrongdoing

> sinned directly against the episcopal dignity by acting as if
> there were two bishops in the same see; this is why he was
> deposed ($\kappa\alpha\theta\alpha\iota\rho\epsilon\tilde{\iota}\tau\alpha\iota$) from this dignity. However, he did not
> sin against the dignity of a priest since nothing says that there
> cannot be two priests and more in the same see. This is why
> he is not deposed from this dignity.[739]

This explanation is very subtle. Whatever may be the case, in fact, regarding canon 29 of Chalcedon, it seems that the sentence prescribed by canon 20 of the Synod in Trullo has never been concretely applied in its rigor, at least as far as we are aware.

[An extract] of the fourth session of the same holy and great council in which the question of the bishops of Egypt was examined.

30

The very magnificient and glorious imperial commissioners and the very great senate have said the following:

"As the bishops of Egypt have not agreed up to the present time to sign the letter of the very venerable Archbishop Leo, not by opposition to the catholic faith but because they say that in the diocese of Egypt, a custom prevails which does not allow such a thing without the consent and the decision of the archbishop, they therefore ask for a delay until the consecration of him who will become bishop of the great city of the Alexandrians; it has seemed reasonable and humane to us that they be given the right to remain in the imperial city, with their present status, until the consecration of the

archbishop of the great city of the Alexandrians."

Paschasinus, the very pious bishop, legate of the apostolic see, said the following: "If your Authority prescribes it and since you ask that proof of humanity be made on this point, let them give guarantees that they will not leave this city until the day when the city of the Alexandrians will receive a bishop."

The very magnificient and glorious imperial commissioners and the very great senate said the following: "Let the motion of the very venerable bishop Paschasinus be confirmed! Consequently, the very pious bishops of the Egyptians with their present status will either give guarantees, if that is possible for them, or they will promise under oath to wait here for the consecration of him who will become bishop of the great city of the Alexandrians."

The study of the manuscript tradition of the *Syntagma in XIV Titles* shows that this text, taken from the minutes of the fourth session, was not inserted into the canonical collection until some time after the so-called "canon 29."[740] If the conciliar decision on the affair of Beirut could be seriously considered, if not in form at least in content, as a canon, that is, a ruling capable of being applied in the future, this was certainly not the same situation for this *ad hoc* decision concerning the Egyptian bishops. The adding of extracts from the minutes of the nineteenth session spoke to a very precise purpose: to set up a framework so that the decree on the see of Constantinople would appear to be "canon 28" of Chalcedon. This objective was reached, and there was no further need to add more texts. In any case, the same procedure was used on this canon as for the previous one: pruning took place. First of all the preamble disappeared: "The very magnificient..."[741] At this stage, the text contained the statement of the commissioners and the senators, followed by the proposed amendment of Paschasinus. There was then the indication of the fact that the commissioners and the senators were going to speak; finally there was a new statement taking into account the observation of Paschasinus.[742] Later on, more pruning and an amalgamation were made; the result was the following: "As for the bishops of Egypt..., with their present status, until the consecration of the archbishop of the great city of Alexandrians. Consequently with their present status either they will give guarantees, if they can, or else they will promise under oath." Such is the form of the resolution in Rhalles and Potles.[743] It is also what is found in the *Kniga Pravil*.[744] A somewhat similar formulation appears in the *Pedalion*, but the end was slightly modified; it appeared as follows: "They will therefore give guarantees such that they will not leave this city until the city of the Alexandrians has received a bishop."[745] This modification was introduced by St. Nicodemus the Hagiorite himself, and he explained it this way: the oath required from the Egyptian bishops is a proposition of the imperial commissioners and not a decision of the fathers of the council. The holy canons never ask that anyone take an oath.[746] Let us remark that the order to give the guarantees somewhat embarrassed Byzantine commentators because of canon 20 of the Holy Apostles, which said that "a cleric who becomes a guarantor for someone must be deposed."[747] However, Zonaras and Balsamon thought that this Apostolic canon did not apply to all cases without distincton; to support their argumentation, they referred precisely to the decision of the Council of Chalcedon on the subject of the bishops of Egypt.[748] This is what Aristenus had already maintained.[749]

We have translated the two expressions ἐπὶ τοῦ ὁμοίου σχήματος and ἐπὶ τοῦ οἰκείου σχήματος by "in their present status."[750] In other words, taking into account the reason that they gave, they were to keep their episcopal dignity, not being deposed therefore for their refusal to sign the tome of Pope Leo. H. Alivizatos quoted this resolution of the Council of Chalcedon with regard to the bishops of Egypt as an example of an application of "economy" in the sense of condescension. He observed, however, that in this case, the local tradition of Egypt concerning the primatial authority was taken into consideration.[751] In fact, the bishops in question did not rally at all to the dogma of Chalcedon, and they did not participate in the election of a successor to Dioscorus. The consecration of Proterius was done by four Egyptian bishops who from the first session of the council disassociated themselves from their archbishop: Athanasius of Busiris, Nestorius of Phragonis, Ausonius of Sebennytus and Macarius of Cabasa.[752]

CHAPTER IV FOOTNOTES

[1]*ACO* II, I, 2, pp. 20-3 (216-18); *ibid.*, II, V, p. 113.

[2]See in this chapter the section on the 10th and 11th sessions.

[3]A. Van Roey, "Eutyches," *DHGE* XVI, col. 87-91.

[4]*ACO* II, II, 1, p. 24 (*Epistola papa Leonis ad Flavianum de Eutychem*).

[5]Martin, (Abbé), *Le pseudo-synode connu dans l'histoire sous le nom de brigandage d'Ephèse* (Paris, 1875), pp. 89-90. E. Stein, *Histoire du Bas-Empire*, t. I, French edition (Paris, 1959), p. 308.

[6]*Regestes*, nos. 98, 99, 100. On the origins and working of this form of this synod, see J. Hajjar, "Le synode permanent dans l'Eglise byzantine des origines au XIᵉ siècle," *OCA* 164 (Rome, 1962); Bl. Phidas, Ἐνδημοῦσα σύνοδος (Athens, 1971).

[7]We are dealing with the gnostic heretic of the second century and not with the Apollinarian of the same name of the fourth or beginning of the fifth century.

[8]Schwartz, *Der Prozess des Eutyches, Sitzungsberichte der Bayerischen Akademie der Wissenschaften*, philos.-philol.-Hist. Klasse, 5, pp. 1-93.

[9]*ACO* II, I, 1, p. 175.

[10]Answer of Peter Chrysologos, *PL* 54, col. 739-43. The archbishop of Ravenna refused to take part without knowing the arguments of Eutyches' adversaries. He declared, moreover, that the judgment of the affair belonged to the pope of Rome "quoniam beatus Petrus, qui in propria sede et vivit et praesidet, praestat quaerentibus fidei veritatem" (col. 743A).

[11]This is what Facundius of Hermiania affirmed; *Pro trium defensione capitulorum*, VIII, 5, *PL* 68, col. 723C-24A.

[12]*Regestes*, nos. 101, 102, 103.

[13]*ACO* II, II, 1, pp. 24-33. On this famous text, see also A. Grillmeier, *Le Christ dans la Tradition chrétienne*, French edition (Paris, 1973), pp. 528-546. See also V. V. Bolotov, *Lektsii po istorii drevnei tserkvi, IV, Istoriia tserkvi v period vselenskikh soborov, III, Istoriia bogoslovskoi mysli* (Petrograd, 1918), pp. 266-279.

[14]*ACO* II, I, 2, p. 28 (224).

[15]*Regestes*, no. 105.

[16]*Liberati Breviarium, ACO*, II, V, p. 117.

[17]F. Haase, "Dioskur von Alexandria und das Konzil von Chalkedon im Lichte der monophysitischen Quellen," *Kirchengeschichtliche Abhandlungen* (Breslau, 1908), VI, pp. 183-233, especially p. 194.

[18]Letter 112, *SC* no. 111, pp. 48-9.

[19]*ACO* II, I, 1, pp. 68-9; p. 71.

[19a]*Ibid.*, II, IV, pp. 9-10: S. Leonis epist. 29.

[20]*Ibid.*, II, I, 1, pp. 77-82: list of participants. The minutes of the first meeting of the assembly of Ephesus have been transmitted to us by the acts of the council of Chalcedon: *Gesta actionis primae, ibid.*, pp. 55-196. For a more complete account of what happened at Ephesus, we must turn to the Syriac version: J. Flemming, *Akten der ephesinischen Synode vom Jahre* 449 (Berlin, 1917). We there learn what happened at the session of August 22.

[21]*ACO* II, I, 1, pp. 83-5.

[22]"Κοντραδικίτουρ, ὅ ἐστιν ἀντιλέγεται," *ibid.*, p. 191.

[23]H. Chadwick, "The Exile and Death of Flavian of Constantinople," *JTS*, n.s., 6 (1955), pp. 16-34.

[24]*ACO* II, III, 1, p. 187.

[25]Ep. 95, *ibid.*, II, IV, p. 51: "...non iudicio sed latrocinio."

[26]*Ibid.*, II, II, 1, pp. 77-9.

[27]*Ibid.*, pp. 79-81.

[28]Letter 113, *SC* 111, pp. 56-67; see also Letter 116 to the priest Renatus, *ibid.*, pp. 68-73. On the idea of the role of the papacy which comes out of these three appeals, see our article, "Problèmes primatiaux au temps du concile de Chalcédoine," *Messager*, no. 77 (1972), pp. 35-62, especially pp. 37-8.

[29]Ep. 44, *ACO* II, IV, p. 21.

[30]Hamilton Hess, *The Canons of the Councils of Sardica* (Oxford, 1958), pp. 49-55.

[31]Ep. 46, *ACO* II, IV, pp. 27-8; "...cum omni Occidentali concilio," p. 28.

[32]Ep. 44, *ibid.*, pp. 19-21 and Ep. 43, *ibid.*, pp. 26-27.

[33]Inter epist. s. Leonis, 55 and 56, *PL* 54, col. 857-859 and 859-861.

[34]*Ibid.*, 62, col. 875-8. No doubt intentionally, Theodosius qualified Leo as "patriarch" (col. 876A), letting it be known that as such he ought not to get mixed up in the affairs of the East.

[35]On the exact date of the election of Anatolius, see R. V. Sellers, *The Council of Chalcedon* (London, 1953), p. 94, note 4.

[36]Ep. 69, *ACO* II, IV, pp. 30-31.

[37]This is what stands out in a letter of pope Leo to him, epist. 60. See P. Goubert, "Le rôle de sainte Pulchérie et de l'eunuque Chrysaphios," *Das Konzil von Chalkedon*, t. I (Würtzburg, 1951), pp. 303-321; *ACO* II, IV, p. 29.

[38]*Regestes*, nos. 116 and 117.

[39]*Ibid.*, no. 120.

[40]Ep. 78-86, *ACO* II, IV, pp. 38-45.

[41]*Ibid.*, II, I, 1, pp. 27-28.

[42]Ep. 89 and 90, *ibid.*, II, IV, pp. 47-48. The following expression is very characteristic of this reticence: "...vestris dispositionibus non renitor," epist. 90, *op. cit.*, p. 48, line 15.

[43]Epist. 92, Juliano episcopo, *ibid.*, p. 49. Paschasinus was the head of the delegation. The pope wrote to the emperor Marcian: "...vicem praesentiae meae possit implere," epist. 89, *ibid.*, p. 47, lines 22-23. As for Julian, he was not, properly speaking, a legate; he was there in his capacity as representative of the pope in Constantinople and thus became part of the Roman delegation. These were permanent representatives whose only role, apart from special mandates, was to be intermediaries. On this subject, see L. Brehier, *Les institutions de l'Empire byzantin* (Paris, 1949), pp. 455-456. On this bishop Julian, see A. Wille, *Bischof Julian von Kios* (Würtzburg, 1909). According to the author, he could not have been bishop of the island of Kos in the Aegean Sea but of the city of Kios in Bithynia. However, this hypothesis has not been universally accepted.

[44]Epist. 93 "sanctae synodo apud Nicaeam constitutae," *ACO ibid.*, II, IV, pp. 51-53.

[45]W. de Vries, *Orient et Occident* (Paris, 1974), pp. 107-110.

[46]Security measures were nonetheless put in place. See the letter of Pulcheria to the governor of Bithynia, *ACO* II, I, 1, p. 29.

[47]On this church, see the description of Evagrius, *Historia ecclesiastica* II, 3, edition of J. Bidez and L. Parmentier (London, 1958), pp. 39-42.

[48]As for the number of participants, the figures we use are based on the unedited work of E. Gerland and reviewed by V. Laurent, *Le quatrième concile ou de Chalcédoine*, pp. 47-48 of this typed work. See also V. Laurent, "Le nombre des Pères du concile de Chalcédoine (451)," Academie roumaine, *Bulletin de la section historique*, t. XXVI, 1 (1945), pp. 33-46. About the officially quoted number of later times, M. Goemans has written: "Diese Zahl 600 oder 630, die sonst noch genannt wird, ist frielich mehr symbolisch zu nehmen," *Chalkedon als Algemeines Konzil, Das Konzil von Chalkedon, loc. cit.*, p. 261. The number "630" has been taken from the numerical value of the first two consonants of the name in Greek of the city Chalcedon: χλ′.

[49]Four African bishops, at least, can be identified: Aurelian of Hadramyttium, Restitutianus of an unknown see, Valerian of Puppius and Valerian of Bassiana. See V. Laurent, "Les évèques d'Afrique au concile de Chalcédoine (451)," Academie roumaine, *Bulletin de la section historique*, t. XXV, 2 (1944), pp. 1-22. On the canonical status of the bishops of Illyricum at this time and their attitude towards the Roman See, see B. Phidas, Προϋποθέσεις διαμορφώσεως τοῦ θεσμοῦ τῆς πενταρχίας τῶν Πατριαρχῶν (Athens, 1969), pp. 279-280.

[49a]*ACO* II, I, 1, pp. 55-56. On the conciliar procedure, see H. Gelzer, "Die Konzilien als Reichsparlamente," *Ausgewählte Kleine Schriften* (Leipzig, 1907), pp. 142-156. See also Ch. Walter, "L'iconographie des conciles dans la tradition byzantine," *Archives de l'Orient chrétien* 13 (Paris, 1970), pp. 145-149.

[50]*Op. cit.*, II, 18, pp. 67-93.

[51]E. Chrysos, "Ἡ διάταξις τῶν συνεδριῶν τῆς ἐν Χαλκηδόνι οἰκουμενικῆς συνόδου," *Kleronomia*, t. 3, vol. 2 (1971), pp. 259-284. We have taken into account the wise corrections proposed by the author as to the order and the date of the sessions except in one case, that of the seventh session during which the 27 canons were issued. The convergence of the ancient witnesses seems to us to require that we place this redaction during the session which followed the one during which the decree on the faith was proclaimed. This is what Evagrius affirms: *Historia ecclesiastica* II, 18, *op. cit.*, p. 92. This is also what Pope Pelagius II wrote: *Epist. III ad episcopos Histriae, ACO* IV, II, p. 127. The canons are also placed at this point in the *Acta graeca* of the council: *ibid.*, II, I, 2, pp. 158-163 (354-359).

[52]A. Schonmetzer, *Schrifttums-Verzeichnis zur Geschichte des Konzils von Chalkedon, Das Konzil von*

Chalkedon, III, pp. 825-865, especially for the sources, pp. 826-828. About later reworkings, see our analysis of canon 28.

[53]*ACO* II, I, 1, p. 65.

[54]*Ibid.*.

[55]*Gesta actionis primae, passim, ibid.*, pp. 55-196.

[56]*Ibid.*, II, I, 2, p. 29 (225).

[57]*Ibid.*.

[58]*Ibid.*, pp. 72-83 (331-342).

[59]*Ibid.*, p. 124 (320). It was probably at Nicea, therefore before the opening of the council at Chalcedon, that Dioscorus excommunicated Pope Leo. The Roman legates seemed not to know about this act at the first session since they made no mention of it.

[60]*Ibid.*, pp. 41-2 (237-238).

[61]N. Charlier, "Dioscore," *DHGE* XIV, col. 508-14.

[62]*Art. cit.*, pp. 262-266.

[63]*ACO* II, I, 2, p. 80 (276).

[64]*Ibid.*, pp. 81-83 (277-279).

[65]For the affair "de Juvenali et consortibus," see *ibid.*, pp. 109-110 (305-306); "de episcopis aegyptiis," pp. 110-14 (306-10).

[66]"De Caroso et Dorotheo," *ibid.*, pp. 114-121 (310-317).

[67]*Ibid.*, II, I, 3, pp. 100-1 (459-460). Previously, canon 5 of Antioch had already been quoted in the case of the disputants: *ibid.*, II, I, 2, p. 118 (314) (Actio IV). Concerning this canonical collection and its continuous numbering system, see our commentary on canon 1.

[68]*Ibid.*, II, I, 3, pp. 99-101 (458-460).

[69]*Ibid.*, pp. 101-110 (460-469).

[70]"...Εἰ σύνοδον χρὴ καλεῖν τῶν ἐπιδημούντων τῇ Βασιλίδι πόλει τὴν συνέλευσιν," *ibid.*, p. 106 (465), lines 40-41.

[71]*Ibid.*, lines 37-40.

[72]*Ibid.*, p. 107 (466), lines 5-11.

[73]Metropolitan Maximus of Sardis has written the following about the intervention of Anatolius: "Seeing that none of the fathers of the council made any remark about this declaration of Anatolius, as clear and categorical as it was, it is obvious that the legality of the permanent synod was thereby ratified with the simple reservation that the synod not take decisions that condemned absent persons," *Le Patriarcat oecuménique*, French edition (Paris, 1975), p. 166. This affirmation of the metropolitan of Sardis seems to us rather peremptory. Is it really possible to base the legitimacy of an institution on an argument from silence? We note that during this debate the fathers of Chalcedon emphasized the value of the canons of Nicea. In fact, they did not even speak on the legitimacy of this type of episcopal meeting; some even doubted that it could be called a "synod."

[74]*ACO, ibid.*, p. 105 (464), line 36-37; cf. *ibid.*, p. 110 (469), lines 1 and 2.

[75]*CJ*, I, 2, 12, CJC, II, p. 13: "Omnes sane pragmaticas sanctiones, quae contra canones ecclesiasticos interventu gratiae et ambitionis elicitae sunt, robore suo et firmitate vacuatas cessare praecipimus." The imperial constitutions were called "pragmatics"; they did not have a general purpose, nor did they have anything to do with a personal case as with the "adnotationes" and the decrees. On this subject, see J. Gaudemet, *La formation du droit séculier et du droit de l'Eglise aux IVe et Ve siècles*, second edition (Paris, 1979), pp. 39-42.

[75a]*ACO, ibid.*, pp. 108-109 (467-468).

[76]*Ibid.*, II, I, 2, pp. 121-130 (317-26).

[79]R. V. Sellers, *The Council of Chalcedon* (London, 1953), pp. 116-117.

[78]A. Fliche and V. Martin, *Histoire de l'Eglise*, t. 4 (Paris, 1937), p. 235, note 1; de Vries, p. 145.

[79]*ACO, ibid.*, p. 129 (325), line 23, p. 130 (326) line 3.

[80]Sellers, pp. 121-123.

[81]*ACO* II, II, 2, pp. 20-1 (112-113).

[82]*Ibid.*, p. 20 (112).

[83]*Ibid.*, II, I, 2, pp. 130-158 (326-54).

[84]*Ibid.*, II, I, 2, pp. 139-140 (335-6) and II, II, 2, pp. 5-6 (97-8). On the fact that the empress Pulcheria was present at this session, we have the categorical witness of the "Rerum Chalcedoniensium collectio Vaticana," *ibid.*, II, II, 2, pp. 5 (97) and 21 (113).

[85]*Ibid.*, II, I, 2, pp. 126-130 (322-6). For the theological analysis of the conciliar decree, see

Grillmeier, *op. cit.* pp. 551-559. On the scope of the prohibition against composing a different formula, see our commentary on canon 7 ("διαλαλία") of the council of Ephesus.

[86]*ACO* II, I, 2, pp. 141-55 (337-51).

[87]*Ibid.*, p. 156 (354).

[88]A.H.M. Jones, *The Later Roman Empire* (Oxford, 1964), vol. I, pp. 333-341. The consistory was the supreme council of state.

[89]*ACO, ibid.*, p. 157 (353).

[90]*Ibid.*

[90a]*Ibid.*, pp. 157-158 (353-354).

[91]*Ibid.*, pp. 158-163 (354-359). In the *Acta Graeca*, these "ὅροι ἐκκλησιαστικοί," as they are called (p. 158, line 6), do not contain any subscription. It is completely inconceivable that there never were any signatures. Moreover, in the Latin version "a Rustico edita," we read the following after the text of the the 27 canons: "Bonifacius presbyter sanctae ecclesiae Romanae statui et subscripsi et ceteri episcopi diversarum provinciarum vel civitatum subscripserunt," *loc. cit.*, *ACO* II, III, 3, p. 98 (537). In the *Prisca*, there are 165 signatures including that of the three main Roman legates at the head; then follows that of Anatolius of Constantinople and that of Julian of Kos; *ibid.*, II, II, 2, pp. 40-45 (132-137). The *Hispana, ibid.*, p. 93 (185), gives a certain number of signatures; among them are those of the Roman legates. Then at the end of the list of names is added the following sentence: "Item omnes episcopi quingenti uingenti definientes subscripserunt." Seeing that the protocols of the conciliar sessions have not come down to us in their original forms, this obviously teaches nothing about the number and quality of the fathers who gave their expressed approval to the 27 conciliar canons. In contrast, it shows that in the sixth century, the Latin authors of the compilations saw nothing improper in the fact that the Roman delegates at Chalcedon would have approved this series of canons. If pope Leo seemed to have accepted only what had been decreed "in...fidei causa" (*ibid.*, II, IV, pp. 70-71), this restriction was aimed in fact only at the motion on the privileges of Constantinople. Nothing in his writings or in those of his successor allows us to accept any other interpretation. Otherwise, how could the 27 canons have appeared in the very official Dionysian versions?

[92]See note 51. We see, however, a very strong probability. An absolute certainty is impossible due to the absence of the protocols in their original form.

[93]E. Honigmann, "Juvenal of Jerusalem," *DOP* 5 (1950), p. 146.

[94]Actio VIII, *ACO* II, I, 3, pp. 4-7 (362-366).

[95]*Ibid.*, II, II, 2, p. 18 (110). That this is an addition to the version made by Maximus has been clearly shown by Honigmann, p. 255.

[96]Nicephorus of Constantinople, Χρονογραφικὸν σύντομον. "Μάξιμος ὁ ἐν τῇ τετάρτῃ συνόδῳ ἐν Χαλκηδόνι, ὃ καὶ ἐξεβλήθη διὰ πταῖσμα, ἔτη δ'," *Opuscula historica*, edition of C. de Boor (Leipzig, 1880), p. 131.

[97]*ACO* II, I, 3, pp. 7-11 (366-370), *loc. cit.*, p. 9 (368).

[98]*Ibid.*, p. 11 (370).

[99]*Ibid.*, pp. 11-16 (370-375). On the affair of Ibas, see R. Devreesse, *Le Patriarcat d'Antioche depuis la paix de l'Eglise jusqu' à la conquête arabe* (Paris, 1945), pp. 56-60. See also Chrysostomos Papadopoulos, Ἱστορία τῆς Ἐκκλησίας Ἀντιοχείας (Alexandria, 1951), pp. 376-384 and 404-408. On the workings of Church justice at this time, we can also profitably consult the work of N. Zaozersky, *Tserkovnyi sud v pervye veka khristianstva* (Kostroma, 1878).

[100]We do not know who was the addressee of the letter, all the more so since Maris could have been the simple hellenization of the Syriac "Mar," the normal title for a bishop.

[101]*ACO* II, I, 3, pp. 32-34.

[102]"...οὐ φθονῶ τῷ Χριστῷ γενομένῳ Θεῷ ἐφ' ὅσον γὰρ αὐτὸς ἐγένετο, κἀγὼ ἐγενόμην," *ibid.*, p. 27 (386) lines 3-4.

[103]*Ibid.*, pp. 21-22 (380-381).

[104]*Ibid.*, pp. 17-37 (376-396).

[105]*Ibid.*, p. 30 (389), lines 32-33: "...ἐξηκολούθησα τῷ ἐξάρχῳ μου."

[106]*Ibid.*, pp. 14-16 (373-375).

[107]See note 104.

[108]*ACO, ibid.*, pp. 38-42 (397-401), especially p. 42 (401), lines 11-15; the anathema against Nestorius.

[109]*Anathematismi adversus "tria capitula,"* XIV-XV, *COD*, pp. 97-98.

[110]*Actio de Domno, ACO* II, II, 2, pp. 19-20 (111-112) and II, III, 3, pp. 5-6 (444-445).

[111]*Ibid.*, II, I, 3, pp. 42-53 (401-412). On this subject, see P. Batiffol, "L'affaire de Bassianos d'Ephèse (444-448)," *EO* XXIII (1924), pp. 385-394.

[112]*ACO, ibid.*, p. 48 (407).

[112a]*Ibid.*, pp. 51-53 (410-412).

[113]*Ibid.*, pp. 53-56 (412-415).

[114]*Ibid.*, p. 54, lines 8-14.

[115]*Op. cit.*, pp. 167-168.

[116]*ACO, ibid.*, pp. 56-62 (415-421).

[117]See note 51.

[118]*ACO, ibid.*, p. 62 (421), intervention of Aetius, lines 17-25; exclamations of the bishops, line 26.

[119]*Ibid.*, lines 26-33. The intervention of Aetius and the remark of the imperial commissioners clearly show that a project for resolving the question of the prerogatives of the see of Constantinople was already being prepared as V. Monachino observed in "Il canone 28 di Chalcedonia e San Leone Magno," *Gregorianum* 33 (1953), p. 536; metropolitan Maximus of Sardis also notes the same thing, *op. cit.* p. 169. It is probable that at least a certain number of the fathers had learned of such a project. This was the case of Eunomios of Nicomedia who, after having thanked the commissioners, made this wise statement: "...ἀγαπῶ τὸν ἀρχιεπίσκοπον τῆς μεγαλωνύμου Κωνσταντινουπόλεως κρατούντων τῶν κανόνων," *ACO, ibid.*, lines 35-6.

[120]*Ibid.*, pp. 63-83 (422-442D); *Gesta Antiochiae*, pp. 69-81 (428-440).

[121]*Ibid.*, p. 83 (442D), line 12.

[122]*Ibid.*, pp. 83-5 (442-444). The original text of the letter, *ibid.*, II, IV, pp. 51-52 (letter 93); Greek translation, *ibid.*, II, I, 1, pp. 31-2.

[123]*Ibid.*, II, III, 3, pp. 91-8 (530-537).

[124]Chrysos, *art. cit.*, p. 276.

[125]*Ibid.*, pp. 276-277.

[126]*ACO*, II, III, 3, pp. XVII-XVIII.

[127]Greek text: *ibid.*, II, I, 3, pp. 86-99 (445-458); Latin text (Versio a Rustico edita), *ibid.*, II, III, 3, pp. 98-114 (537-553). For the date see Chrysos, *art. cit.*, p. 280.

[128]*ACO* II, I, 3, pp. 110-14 (469-473). For its attribution to Theodoret, see the conclusive argumentation of Schwartz, *ibid.*, II, I, 3, pp. XII-XVI.

[129]*Ibid.*, pp. 114-6 (473-475).

[130]*The Church Universal and the See of Rome* (London, 1939), p. 114.

[131]*ACO, ibid.*, pp. 116-118 (475-477).

[132]See note 89.

[133]*Synagoge*, p. 7, pp. 215-217 and 234-235. Text of the canons in the Greek acts of the council: *ACO*, II, I, 2, pp. 158-163 (354-359) ("ὅροι ἐκκλησιαστικοί"); Latin translation in the Versio a Rustico edita: *ibid.*, II, III, 3, pp. 91-98 (530-537); translations in the ancient Latin collections: *ibid.*, II, II, 2, pp. 31-109 (123-201). As P. P. Joannou has noted concerning the absence of the motion on the rights of the see of Constantinople in the Dionysian versions: "Le 28ᵉ canon de Chalcédoine ne fut probablement pas omis a cause de l'indignation suscitée dans l'église romaine, mais parce qu'il manquait aussi et pour cause à la collection d'Antioche qui ne compte que 27 canons," *CCO*, p. 10.

[134]On the wide consensus among scholars on this period's being the one in which the *Syntagma*, (first recension) was composed, see Ernest Honigmann, "Le concile de Constantinople de 394 et les auteurs du Syntagma des XIV titres," *Subsidia Hagiographica* 35 (1961), pp. 3-83, especially p. 56.

[135]*Syntagma*, pp. 124-125: the primitive form of the text presented as a "ψῆφος." Index, *ibid.*, p. 58: "Συνόδου τῆς Καλχηδόνι (*sic*) τῶν ΧΛ΄ ᾿Αγίων Πατέρων κανόνες ΚΗ΄." Cf. V. N. Beneševič, *Kanonicheskii sbornik XIV titulov* (St. Petersburg), p. 76.

[136]We are dealing here with the manuscript of Chieti and with that of Justell; they are dated from the sixth century and come from Italy. Canon 3 of Constantinople is combined with the motion adopted at Chalcedon. See the text in *ACO*, II, II, 2, pp. 46-47 (138-139). For the explanation of the affair, see Fr. Maassen, *Geschichte der Quellen und der Literatur des canonischen Rechts im Abendlande* (Graz, 1870), pp. 94-99 and 526-536. See also Fr. Dvornik, "The See of Constantinople in the First Latin Collections of Canon Law," *Mélanges G. Ostrogorsky* (Belgrade, 1963), pp. 97-101. This article is reproduced with the same pagination in the collection entitled *Photian and Byzantine Ecclesiastical Studies*, Variorum reprints XVII (London, 1974).

[137]*ACO* II, I, 3, pp. 108-9 (467-8). *Syntagma*, pp. 126-128. In the *Pedalion*, p. 210, and in the *Kniga Pravil* (*Pravila* I, p. 426), canon 30 is reduced to the declaration of the Roman legates, without

preamble. In the *Syntagma* of Rhalles and Potles II, pp. 286-287, there is first this statement but without mention of its authors, then the intervention of Anatolius is quoted with mention of the canon.

[138]*ACO*, II, I, 2, p. 114 (310). *Syntagma*, pp. 128-129. In the *Pedalion*, p. 210, we find the resolution of the council as it was formulated by the imperial commissioners with an addition, more or less reproducing the corrective proposed by Paschasinus. In the edition of Rhalles and Potles II, pp. 288-289, this amendment is given according to the definitive formulation approved by the imperial commissioners. In the *Kniga Pravil* (*Pravila*, I, p. 428), an abridged formulation of the corrective is given.

[139]*Syntagma*, p. 112.

[140]A. Van Hove has written the following: "Controvertitur utrum concilium Chalcedonense approbaverit syntagma Antiochenum, an simpliciter agnoverit quaedam principia canonica quae in syntagmate occurent," *Commentarium Lovaniense in codicem iuris canonici*, vol. I, t. I, Prolegomena, *editio altera* (Malines, 1945), *loc. cit.* p. 144, note 3. W. M. Plöchl seems to us to be much too categorical when he declares that "das Konzil hat diese Kollection nicht *de lege* approbiert, beruft sich jedoch auf die Approbation der darin enthaltenen Normen durch frühere Kirchenversammlungen," *Geschichte des Kirchenrechts*, I (second edition, Vienna, 1960), *loc. cit.* p. 274.

[141]"Le concile de Constantinople de 394 et les auteurs du 'Syntagma des XIV titres'," *Subsidia Hagiographica* 35 (Brussels, 1961), pp. 1-83; for this question, see p. 48.

[142]See the introduction to the council of Chalcedon.

[143]*ACO* II, I, 3, pp. 100-1 (459-60).

[144]*Ibid.*, p. 48 (407).

[145]*Ibid.*, p. 96 (455).

[146]*Ibid.*, p. 95 (454). In fact, the original Greek does not correspond at all to the text adopted at Nicea. See our analysis of canon 6 of Nicea.

[147]*Ibid.*, p. 107 (466).

[148]*Ibid.*, p. 60 (119).

[149]*Ibid.*, II, V, p. 51.

[150]*Synagoge*, p. 5.

[151]On the double appearance of the code, see J. Gaudemet, *Institutions de l'antiquité* (Paris, 1967), pp. 756-7.

[153]E. Herman, "Jean III le Scholastique," *DDC* VI, col. 118-120. Certain scholars think that it was when he was still at Antioch that he composed this work: H. G. Beck, *Kirche und theologische Literatur im Byzantinischen Reich* (Munich, 1959), p. 144. This was also the opinion of C. Leclercq who observed that "...videtur Joannes potius illae sedi (i.e. of Antioch) quam Constantinopolitanae favisse, ergo collectio sua redegit ante adventum suum Constantinopolim," *Fontes iuridici Ecclesiarum Orientalium* (Rome, 1967), *loc. cit.* p. 41. In our opinion, that proves only that he edited his *Synagoge* before his promotion to the see of Constantinople in 565.

[143]Honigmann, pp. 55-57.

[154]J. A. B. Mortreuil, *Histoire du droit byzantin* (Paris, 1843), pp. 200-201. A. Christophilopoulos, Δίκαιον καὶ Ἱστορία (Athens, 1973), pp. 138-140.

[155]Photius wrote that "in this letter, he still gives canon 2 of the second holy synod of Constantinople as canon 166 which brought together 150 fathers; I do not know where he takes this figure from, and it agrees with the other authors; it is not only in this letter, but also in his other writings; he gives it the same rank" (*Bibliothèque*, codex 228, edition of "Les Belles Lettres," t. IV [Paris, 1965], *loc. cit.*, p. 116). On the particularities of the numbering system of Ephrem, see note 180 below. It was the competition among the collections to invent a systematic classification which brought about the eclipse and then the complete oblivion of this collection, as E. Schwartz has noted, "Die Kanonessamlungen der alten Reichskirche," *Gesammelte Schrifte*, IV (Berlin, 1960), pp. 159-275, especially 159-160.

[156]*Rhalles-Potles* II, p. 217.

[157]Fr. Schulthess, *Die syrischen Kanones der Synoden von Nicaea bis Chalcedon* (Göttingen, 1908). Folios 1-151 of the manuscript in the British Museum, *Add. 14, 528*. A description of the content of the article of Schwartz is found on pp. 161-169.

[158]*PL* 67, col. 139A-230B. He wrote in his preface addressed to bishop Stephen of Salonis that "...sub ordine numerorum, id est a primo capite usque ad centesimum sexagesimum quintum, sicut habetur in Graeca auctoritate, digessimus," *loc. cit.* col. 142A. The opinion of Wilhelm Peitz,

according to which Dionysius could have been himself the compiler of this 'Graeca auctoritas' ("Dionysius Exiguus als Kanonist" *Schweitzer Rundschau*, XLX, [1945-6]) is unacceptable, as is the whole of his theory on the foundation of the ancient canonical collections. Charles Munier has shown in a definitive way what were the methodological errors of W. Peitz, "L'oeuvre canonique de Denys le Petit d'après les travaux du R.P. Wilhelm Peitz, SJ," *Sacris Erudiri* XIV (1963), pp. 236-250. On the person and work of Dionysius, see J. M. Versanne, *Denys le Petit et le droit canonique* (Paris, 1913). See especially J. Rambaud-Buhot, "Denys le Petit," *DDC*, IV, 1131-1152.

[159]In writing this, we are thinking especially of E. Revillout, *Le concile de Nicée d'après les textes coptes et les diverses collections canoniques* (Paris, 1881).

[160]On this council, see *Héfele-Leclercq* I[1], pp. 298-326. On the number of the canons, see below.

[161]J. Lebon, "Sur un concile de Césarée", *Le Museon*, t. LI, cahiers 1-2 (Louvain, 1938), pp. 89-132.

[162]This division only appeared very late in the manuscript tradition of the *Syntagma in XIV Titles* as we can realize from the examination of the various recensions of this work: V.N. Beneševič, *Kanonicheskii sbornik XIV Titulov* (St. Petersburg, 1905). Of course, the *Synagoge* only indicates 14 canons, pp. 6, 203 and 237.

[163]*Héfele-Leclercq* I[1], pp. 326-334.

[164]Schwartz, *Kanonessamlungen...*, pp. 174-175.

[165]*Héfele-Leclercq* I[2], pp. 1029-1045. For the date of this council, see W. A. Jurgens, "The Date of the Council of Gangra," *The Jurist* 20 (1960), pp. 1-12.

[166]F. Maassen, *Geschichte der Quellen un der Literatur des canonischen Rechts im Abendlande* (Graz, 1870), p. 13 and pp. 924-938. Also see H. Leclercq, "Conciles grecs dans les collections d'Orient," *Héfele-Leclercq* III[2], Appendix I, pp. 1149-1200.

[167]We thus read in the *Prisca* (end of the fifth century): "Incipit constituta canonum Antiochensium in Dedicatione," EOMIA, t. II, *pars altera, loc. cit.* p. 228. On the council which issued these canons, see Ed. Schwartz, *Gesammelte Schriften, III (Zur Geschichte des Athanasius)* (Berlin, 1959), pp. 216-230. By the same author see *ibid.*, IV, *Kanonessamlungen...*, pp. 192-3.

[168]Balleriniorum disquisitiones "De antiquis collectionibus et collectoribus canonum," Pars I-a, *PL* 56, col. 35-41.

[169]P.-P. Joannou (*CSP*, pp. 100-1) holds to the position that the council *in encaeniis* is the source without indicating the reasons for his choice. However, it is clear that this author, like those before him holding the same opinion, has been influenced by the wording of canons 4, 12, and 15; he considers them to have been "fabricated against Athanasius to exclude his appeal to Rome," *op. cit.* p. 101.

[170]A. Boudinhon, "Note sur le concile de Laodicée," *Comptes-rendus du Congrès scientifique international des catholiques* (Paris, 1888), t. II, pp. 420-27. G. Bardy, "Laodicée," *DDC* IV, col. 337-43. See the testimony of Theodoret: *Interpretatio Epist. ad Coloss.*, II, 18, *PG* 82, col. 613B, and *ibid.*, III, 17, col. 620D.

[171]Joannou, p. 128.

[172]Dionysius Exiguus, *Stromata*, p. 52.

[173]Schwartz, *Kanonessamlungen...*, p. 194, Epist. CCXVIII, edition of "Les Belles-Lettres," t. II (Paris, 1961), pp. 217-218.

[174]Palladius, *Vita Joannis Chrys.*, chapter IX, *PG* 47, col. 31. Cf. Socrates, *Héfele-Leclercq* VI, 18, *PG* 67, col. 720A. Pope Innocent I rejected them, Epist. VII, *ad clerum et populum Constantinopolitanum*, §3, *PL* 20, col. 503C-505B. Later on, the attitude of Rome towards these canons changes. In 534, Pope John II quoted canons 4 and 15 of Antioch to Caesarius of Arles so he could use them in the affair of bishop Contumeliosus. Mansi, 8, col. 810.

[175]F. Cavallera, *Le schisme d'Antioche* (Paris, 1905), pp. 211-2.

[176]See note 145.

[177]"...ἀπὸ τοῦ αὐτοῦ βιβλίου," *ACO* II, I, 3, p. 96 (455).

[178]Van Hove, p. 143.

[179]J. Rambaud-Buhot affirms categorically that "la collection dont on a fait usage à Chalcédoine renfermait sous une seule numération les canons des conciles orientaux jusqu'au concile d'Antioche inclusivement," col. 1143. This is an example of an hypothesis which does not sufficiently take into account all the data.

[180]Such a fusion is also found in the manuscript tradition of the *Syntagma in XIV Titles*: Codex Vallicell. F. 10, see *Syntagma*, p. 231, note 3.

[181]EOMIA II, pars III, pp. 405-21.

[182]*Ibid.*, pp. 411-21.

[183]Schulthess, *Syrischen Kanones...*, pp. 109-10. This arrangement of the text was later on preserved in the ancient Arab-Melkite collection; on this subject, see E. Jarawan, *La collection canonique arabe des Melkites et sa physionomie propre* (Rome, 1969), p. 73.

[184]*PL* 67, col. 142A. On the Antiochian origin of this "Graeca auctoritas," see P.-P. Joannou, *CCO*, pp. 8-9.

[185]"Incipiunt regule ecclesiastice sanctorum apostolorum prolate per clementem ecclesie Romane pontificem (quae ex grecis exemplaribus in ordine primo ponuntur; quibus quamplurimi quidem consensum non prebuere facile, et tamen postea quaedam constituta pontificum ex ipsis canonibus adsumpta esse uidentur)," EOMIA, fasc. I, pars prior, *loc. cit.* p. 8. Unfortunately for our information, Dionysius did not make clear who were these "quamplurimi." Moreover, he took for granted that the Roman pontiffs had used these canons. It is difficult to verify this assertion. What is certain, however, is that a pre-Dionysian Latin version of these canons had existed; it has been edited by C. H. Turner, EOMIA I, fasc. I, pars prima, p. 8. 32n. 32hh. John the Scholastic appears to have accepted without hesitation the apostolic origin of the collection (*Synagoge*, p. 5). On the other hand in the preface of the *Syntagma in XIV Titles* ("Τὰ μὲν σώματα..."), an allusion is made to the doubts of certain scholars about the authenticity of these canons (*Syntagma*, p. 2). The fathers of the Synod in Trullo spoke prudently of the 85 canons "which have been transmitted to us under the name of the holy and glorious apostles" (canon 2, *ibid.*, p. 142).

[186]H. Hess, *The Canons of the Council of Sardica* (Oxford, 1958), pp. 51-2 and 151-2.

[187]Letter to Pope Hormisdas (around 520?), Maassen, *Geschichte der Quellen...*, p. 965.

[188]See the introduction to the council of Ephesus.

[189]In the first recension, the canons of Chalcedon are separated from the canons of the previous Greek councils by the canons of Sardica and by those of Carthage in causa Apiarii (*Stromata*, pp. 19-22 and 61-98). In the second recension, they come immediately after canon CLXV (on the illicit ordination of Maximus), however, without their own numbering, independent of the rest of the collection (*PL* 67, col. 171B-176D). The canons of Sardica come next.

[190]See note 157.

[191]The expression is from Cardinal Gasparri in his preface to the code of 1917 (ed. Westminster, Md., 1949), i.

[192]*Héfele-Leclercq* II[2], p. 1221.

[193]W. Plöchl, *Geschichte des Kirchenrechts*, I (Vienna, 1960), pp. 330-4.

[194]*ACO* II, II, 2, p. 33 (125) and p. 54 (146).

[195]*Ibid.*, p. 54 and p. 87.

[196]*Ibid.*, II, III, 3, p. 93 (532).

[197]*Ibid.*, II, II, 2, p. 33.

[198]A. Faivre, *Naissance d'une hiérarchie* (Paris, 1977), *passim*.

[199]In the ancient Latin versions, the Greek word is either transliterated (Hispana, Prisca) or translated (Rusticus, Dionysius).

[200]*ACO* II, II, 2, p. 87: Hispana; *ibid.*, p. 33: Prisca; *ibid.*, p. 54: Dionysius: II, III, 3, p. 93: Rusticus.

[201]"qui rebus ecclesiae temporaliter praeficitur," *Lexil.*, I, p. 307. *Héfele-Leclercq*, "Mansionarius," *DACL* X[2], col. 1582-1585. On the etymology of the Russian word "ponomar'," see B. Volin and S. Uchakov, *Tolkovyi slovar russkogo iazyka* (Moscow, 1939), t. 3, col. 579.

[202]*Pedalion*, p. 186.

[203]Carthage, canon 97. These defenders must not be confused with those spoken of in canon 75 of the same African collection; they were supposed to protect the poor against the rich. These two canons appear in the edition of Ch. Munier on the councils of Africa: *CC*, series Latina CLIX, respectively p. 215 and p. 202. We are following the chronological indications given by this author. B. Fischer, "Defensor ecclesiae," *Reallexikon f. Antike u. Christentum*, fasc. 21, col. 656-8.

[204]*Le livre des cérémonies*, edition "Les Belles-Lettres," I (Paris, 1935), first book, chapter I, text p. 23, commentaries on p. 74.

[205]J. Goar, *Euchologion sive Rituale Graecorum* (Venice, 1730), p. 229.

[206]C. Vogel, "L'imposition des mains dans les rites d'ordination en Orient et en Occident," *La Maison-Dieu* 102 (Paris, 1970), pp. 57-72.

[207]*Ibid.*, pp. 65-7. A Michel, "Ordre, Ordination." *DTC*, XI[2], col. 1193-1405.

[208]*Rhalles-Potles* II, p. 218.

[209]*Ibid.*, p. 219. This meaning of "φραγίζειν" is clearly explained in a text of Symeon of Thessalonica, "De sacramentis," chapters 158-9, *PG* 155, col. 364C-365D.

[210]*Ibid.*, chapter 156, col. 361D-364A.

[211]Goar, *op. cit.*, pp. 194-204. The Russian pontifical (*Chinovnik*) uses the word "khirotonia" not only for the hierarchical orders but also for the subdiaconate: synodal edition, p. 118. For the orders of reader and chanter, the title "Chin na postavlenie," is used, *ibid.*, p. 115.

[212]Nicea, canons 16, 17 and 19; for this last canon, we find the variant "'Εν τῷ κλήρῳ ἐξεταζομένων" (*Syntagma*, p. 93, note 2); in this case, there is to all intents and purposes perfect agreement.

[213]Nicea, canon 2, *Syntagma*, p. 84. In the work of P. Panagiotakos, Τὸ ποινικὸν δίκαιον τῆς Ἐκκλησίας (Athens, 1962), pp. 266-267, we find an inventory of periphrases used in ancient Church literature to designate the deposition of clergy.

[214]The term "Σιμωνιανός" appears with this meaning in St. Theodore the Studite, epist. 53, *PG* 99, col. 1105B. On simony in general, the following definition is given by Thomas Aquinas: "Studiosa sue deliberata voluntas emendi vel vendendi aliquid spirituale vel spirituali adnexum" (IIa-IIae, q.c., a 1).

[215]II Maccabees 4:7-24.

[216]*Hist. Arian.*, 73, *PG* 25, col. 781B.

[217]In the canonical collections, this letter 53 appears as canon 90 of St. Basil. It is addressed "πρὸς τοὺς ὑφ' ἑαυτῶν ἐπισκόπους [ὥστε] μὴ χειροτονεῖν χρήμασιν" (edition "Les Belles-Lettres," vol. I, pp. 137-9; *Syntagma*, pp. 509-511; *CPG*, pp. 175-178).

[218]*Regestes*, 20; Palladios, *De vita Chrys.*, XV, PG 47, col. 51-52.

[219]*ACO* II, I, 3, p. 24 (383).

[220]*Syntagma*, pp. 598-603.

[221]Justinian, novella 123, I, *CJC*, III, p. 594. Cf. *CJ*, I, 3, 30, *CJC*, p. 22.

[222]*Epist. XLVI, ad Isacium, loc. cit. PL* 77, col. 1166A.

[223]*Syntagma*, pp. 159-160, 209-212, 224-245; for the encyclical of St. Tarasius: *CPG*, pp. 315-322.

[224]*Regestes*, 2005, 2006, and 2008.

[225]On simony at the time of the Ottoman domination, see J. Panagopoulos, Ἡ σιμωνία κατὰ τὸ Δίκαιον τῆς Ὀρθοδόξου Ἀνατολικῆς καὶ τῆς Δυτικῆς Ἐκκλησίας (Athens, 1946), pp. 69-73. On the scandals that took place in Greece between 1874-8 about simoniac ordinations, see Sp. Makris, "Σιμονιακά," *Th. ith. E* t. ii, col. 160-162.

[226]*ACO* II, I, 2, p. 157 (353).

[227]P. Noailles and A. Dain, *Les novelles de Léon VI le Sage* (Paris, 1944), pp. 288-291.

[228]*Syntagma*, p. 63; *CC*, p. 122.

[229]*De Lapsis*, 6, Ed. Hartel, pp. 240-241.

[230]Epist. LII, 16, "Les Belles-Lettres," t. II, pp. 190-191.

[231]Nicea II, canon 10, *Syntagma*, pp. 216-217; the First-Second council, canon 11, *CSP*, pp. 467-468; commentary of Zonaras for canon 3 of Chalcedon: *Rhalles-Potles* II, pp. 221-222.

[232]The text of the proposed decree: *ACO* II, I, 2, p. 157 (353).

[233]Jones, vol. III, pp. 799-803.

[234]*CJ*, I, 3, 36, *CJC*, p. 24. Novellae of Justinian, CXXIII, C. 35, *ibid.*, pp. 618-619.

[235]L. Ueding, *Die Kanones von Chalcedon in ihrer Bedeutung für Mönchtum und Klerus. Das Konzil von Chalcedon* (Würtzburg, 1953), pp. 569-676.

[236]At the time of the ceremony of vesting according to the Orthodox tradition, the following question is asked of the candidate: "Will you stay in the monastery and in the ascetic way until your last breath?," Goar, *Euchologion* (Vienna, 1730), p. 383. See the saying of St. Syncletica, 6, Γέροντηκόν (Athens, 1961), p. 120.

[237]*Syntagma*, p. 226; *CSP*, pp. 453-55.

[238]*Rhalles-Potles* IV, p. 428: first series, can. 17.

[239]Fr. Sophrony (Sakharov) has written that "in many lives of the saints, we meet with the voluntary or involuntary abandonment of the monastery where they have received the habit; however, this is not considered as a fall nor even as a relaxation of their monastic calling. Many of them were taken from their monasteries for hierarchical service in the Church; many were transferred to another place for some reason; certain monks, for some praiseworthy reason, left with the blessing of the superior; finally, there were even cases where they escaped from their monasteries looking for the 'discomfort of salvation.' " "Des fondements de l'ascèse orthodoxe," *Messager* 18 (1954), p. 73.

[240]*CJ*, I, 3, 46, *CJC*, pp. 33-34.

[241]The adjective "σταυροπιγιακός" comes from the verb "πήγνυμι," meaning "to attach with

nails" as well as the noun "σταυρός" meaning "cross." These monasteries are thus designated because at their foundation, the patriarchal cross was attached to them, marking the direct jurisdiction of the patriarch. On this status, see the decree of patriarch Germanus II and his synod, issued at Nicea, June, 1232: *Rhalles-Potles* V, pp. 110-12, *Regestes*, 1259. On the strictly limited territorial character of the stavropigial status see *Rhalles-Potles, ibid.*, pp. 112-113; cf. *Regestes* 1260.

[242]See the many examples of monasteries having enjoyed this status of total independence and as such qualified as "ἐλεύθερα καὶ αὐτοδέσποτα ἥ αὐτοεξουσία" in the work of Fr. Placide de Meester, "De monachico statu iuxta disciplinam byzantinam," *Fonti*, series II, fasc. X (Rome, 1942), pp. 105-106. On the removal of this status of independence from the Athonite federation in 1312, see the "sigillion" of Patriarch Niphon, *Archives de l'Athos, VII, Actes du Protaton*, edition of D. Papachryssanthou (Paris, 1975), pp. 245-8. It is recognized in this document that the status of independence had constituted a relaxation of the wise canonical rules and that it had been an error, p. 247. From that time on, the Protos was to receive confirmation from the ecumenical patriarch.

[243]For example, see Theodoret of Cyrus, *Correspondence*, Letter 113: " Ἀλυπίου τοῦ ἐξάρχου τῶν παρ' ἡμῖν μοναζόντων," *SC*, 111, p. 66. On the exarchs, inspectors of monks, see de Meester, pp. 185-187.

[244]Constantine VI repudiated his wife Maria in January, 795, and married his mistress, Theodotia. On this subject, see G. Ostrogorsky, *History of the Byzantine State* (New Brunswick, N.J., Rutgers University Press, 1969), pp. 180-181; *Regestes* 368, 377-379, 387-388.

[245]*Rhalles-Potles* II, p. 227.

[246]*Ibid.*, pp. 228-9.

[247]*ACO* II, I, 2, p. 159 (355); *Synagoge*, p. 55; for the variants in this collection, see note 5.

[248]Hispana: *ACO* II, II, 2, p. 88 (180); Prisca: *ibid.*, p. 36 (126); Dionysius, *ibid.*, p. 55 (147); Rusticus, *ibid.*, II, III, 3, p. 94 (533). The received text omits the adjective: *Pedalion*, p. 189; *Rhalles-Potles* II, p. 229. The *Kniga Pravil*, however, introduced the equivalent of the Greek word into the translation: "...svoei sile," *Pravila* I, p. 342.

[249]See our article, "Les translations épiscopales," *Messager* 57 (1967), pp. 24-38.

[250]*Syntagma*, p. 157.

[251]*SP* I, p. 118; *Héfele-Leclercq* (11,2), p. 787; *Pravila*, I, p. 342.

[252]See note 51. It is true that Rusticus attributed the redaction of the canons to the Actio XV, but in the Introduction, we have already explained the reason for this.

[253]In the *Synagoge*, p. 85, the particle is obviously omitted since the two canons are not placed together.

[254]Hispana: *ACO* II, II, 2, p. 88 (180); Prisca: *ibid.*, pp. 34-35 (126-127); Dionysius: *ibid.*, p. 55 (147); Rusticus: *ibid.*, II, III, 3, p. 94 (533).

[255]"...nam ea conditione in Barcinonensi Ecclesia consecrari adductus sum, ut ipsi ecclesiae non alligarer, in sacerdotium tantum Domini, non etiam in locum ecclesiae dedicatus," Epist. I, 10, *PL* 61, col. 159B.

[256]Vallarsi, *S. Hieronymi Vita*, ch. XII, 3, *PL* 22, col. 41.

[257]*Le monachisme syrien selon Théodoret de Cyr* (Paris, 1977), p. 233. Nicodemus Milasch established a connection between the redaction of this canon and the intervention of some Eutychian monks of unknown origin in the council at the time of the previous session (*De Caroso et Dorotheo*), *Pravila, I², pp.* 343-4. This is plausible.

[258]Theodoret, *Religiosa Historia*, XV, *PG* 82, col. 1416CD.

[259]*Ibid.*, XIII, col. 1401-4.

[260]Prisca: "inefficacem," *ACO* II, II, 2, p. 35 (127); Dionysius: "irritam," *ibid.*, p. 55 (147); Hispana: "uacuam," *ibid.*, p. 88 (180); Rusticus: "irritam," *ibid.*, II, III, 3, p. 94 (533).

[261]*Syntagma*, p. 115. In the *Kniga Pravil*, the term "nedeistvitel'nym" is used, *Pravila*, I, p. 343.

[262]Sozomen told of the case of two monks, Barses and Eulogius, who thus became bishops "οὐ πολεώς τινος, ἀλλὰ τιμῆς ἕνεκεν," *Historia ecclesiastica* VI, 34, PG 67, col. 1393C. There were some abuses in the Celtic Church. In Ireland, some bishops without sees and, therefore, without jurisdiction, were used by the abbots of monasteries to confer orders. L. Gougaud, *Les Chrétientés celtiques* (Paris, 1911), pp. 215-219.

[263]*The Travels of Egeria*, 23, SC 21, p. 186. On the churces built in honor of martyrs, see André Grabar, *Martyrium, recherches sur le culte des reliques et l'art chrétien antique*, 2 volumes (Paris, 1946). Canon 9 of Laodicea forbids Orthodox from going to the so-called martyrs' shrines of heretics, *Syntagma*, p. 269.

[264]In certain manuscripts, instead of "τεταγμένους," we find "κατειλεγμένους." *ACO* II, I, 2, p. 159 (355); the meanings are very close.

[265]*ACO* II, II, 2, p. 88 (180).

[266]*Ibid.*, p. 55 (147). The translation of Dionysius is reproduced unchanged by Rusticus, *ibid.*, II, III, 3, p. 94 (533).

[267]*Ibid.*, II, II, 2, p. 35 (127).

[267a]*Syntagma*, pp. 79-80.

[268]*Rhalles-Potles* II, pp. 232-233.

[269]Novella CXXIII, c. 42, *CJC*, III, p. 623.

[270]IV, I, 14, edition of J. J. Scheltema and N. Van der Wal, vol. A.I. (Groningen, 1955), p. 117.

[271]Novella VIII, edition of P. Noailles and A. Dain (Paris, 1944), pp. 38-41.

[272]Du Cange, *Glossarium*, t. V (Niort, 1885): "militia," p. 377.

[273]"V voinstvo": *Syntagma*, p. 115. This is also the interpretation adopted in the *Kniga Pravil*. "v voinskuiu sluzhbu," *Pravila* I, p. 345.

[274]*Pravila* I, pp. 346-7.

[275]Goar, "'Ακολουθία τοῦ μικροῦ σχήματος," p. 384.

[276]*Rhalles-Potles* II, p. 235.

[277]Apostolic Canon 31; Trullo canon 31; First-Second council canon 13; *Syntagma*, pp. 67, 164; *SPC*, pp. 470-2.

[278]St. Gregory the Theologian wrote that "our very honorable son, well beloved of God, Sacerdos, our colleague in the priesthood, is the head of a well known center for the poor which serves many people because of his piety and zeal for this type of work"; Ep. CCXI, *loc. cit.*, I, edition of "Les Belles-Lettres," t. II (Paris, 1967), p. 103. At Ephesus, Bassian had founded a similar center which, according to him, had aroused the jealousy of his adversaries; *ACO* II, I, 3, p. 46 (405).

[279]*Rhalles-Potles* II, pp. 234-5.

[280]See note 242.

[281]Balsamon puts special stress on the wishes expressed in the foundation documents ("κτητορικῶν τυπικῶν διατάγματα"), *Rhalles-Potles* II, p. 236.

[282]The conjunctive particle in front of "τὸν ἔξαρχον τῆς διοικήσεως" is attested to in the most ancient manuscript, and we find the equivalent in the pre-Dionysian Latin translations, the Hispana (*ACO* II, II, 2, p. 89 [181] and the *Prisca* (*ibid.*, p. 35 [127]).

[283]In the Prisca, in the place of a precise translation of "exarch of the diocese," we find "ad dioceseos primam sedem." In the Hispana, we find "ad ipsius metropolitanum episcopum"; in neither case is the meaning profoundly altered. Dionysius correctly translates the expression as "primatem dioceseos" (*ibid.*, p. 56 [148]). We do not see why in the Hispana there is the adverb "certe" in front of "ad Constantinopolitanae regiae civitatis sedem," since that does not correspond to any variant known in the Greek text.

[284]P. 89 (181).

[285]*Ibid.*, p. 56 (148).

[286]*Ibid.*, II, III, 3, p. 94 (533).

[287]The clerical privilege of being judged only by Church courts even in secular matters was still maintained by the *Codex juris canonici* of 1917, but with certain restrictions; canon 120.

[288]J. Gaudemet, *L'Eglise dans l'Empire romain* (Paris, 1958), pp. 242-243.

[289]Sp. N. Troianos, Ἡ ἐκκλησιαστικὴ οἰκονομία μέχρι τοῦ θανάτου τοῦ 'Ιουστινιανοῦ (Athens, 1964), p. 14.

[290]"O smysle 9 i 17 Kanonov Khalkidonskogo sobora," *JMP* (1961), 2, pp. 57-65.

[291]*Le Patriarcat oecuménique dans l'Eglise orthodoxe*, French translation (Paris, 1975), p. 233.

[292]*Ibid.*, p. 233. In the apology for the permanent jurisdictional primacy of the see of Constantinople, metropolitan Maximus Christopoulos gives a considerable weight to canons 9 and 17 of Chalcedon: in this work, 84 pages are dedicated to these two canons alone.

[293]*CJ*, I, 4, 29, *CJC* II, pp. 45-6, p. 45.

[294]Novella CXXIII, c. 22, *ibid.*, II, p. 611-2.

[295]*Documents inédits d'ecclésiologie byzantine* (Paris, 1966), p. 79.

[296]*Syntagma*, p. 284: "...διὰ γραμμάτων τοῦ ἐξάρχου τῆς ἐπαρχίας, λέγω δὴ τοῦ ἐπισκόπου τῆς μητροπόλεως." The original Latin of this intervention by Ossius was probably as follows: "per litteras primatis episcopi provinciae, hoc est metropolitani." On this subject, see H. Hess, *The canons of the Council of Sardica* (Oxford, 1958), p. 99. Another translation of the exact term is especially

heavy: "...eius qui provinciae illius sortitus est" (*Codex Vaticanus lat.* 1319), EOMIA, I, fasc. alta., pars IIIA, p. 501.

[297]For example, Zonaras, *Rhalles-Potles* II, pp. 237-8. This opinion was not shared with Balsamon, for whom the exarch mentioned here was "the metropolitan of all the diocese." He noted that the prerogative we are dealing with here no longer existed in his time although the title of exarch was used by certain metropolitans, *ibid.*, pp. 238-40. J. Darrouzès has properly noted that "le commentaire des deux principaux canonistes nous apprend surtout qu'ils ne concevaient pas une juridiction du patriarche en dehors des limites de son territoire," p. 81. On the different meanings of the team "exarch" in the canonical tradition of the Orthodox Church, see A. Pokrovsky, "Ekzarkh i Ekzarkhat," *Bogoslovsk. Encyclop.* t. 5, col. 368-373. See also K.M. Kuev, *Kat v'prosa za titulata "ekzarkh" v starob'vlgarskata literatura, Izvestiia na instituta za istoriia,* t. 14-15 (Sofia, 1964), pp. 334-336. See also T. Sabev, *Ugrediavane i diotsez na b'lgarskata exzarkhia do 1878 g.* (Sophia, 1973). This author has especially studied the discussions that preceded the promulgation of the firman of February 27, 1870, and underlined the fact that the title of "exarch" then given to the head of the Bulgarian Church corresponded to the usage of the fifth century, pp. 42-7. In Church language during the High Middle Ages, the title "exarch" had completely lost its primitive meaning of "head." It had become a purely honorific title for the metropolitans of certain sees; then a galloping inflation of titles took over so that at the present time in the eastern patriarchates, nearly all the residential metropolitans are called "ὑπέρτιμος καὶ ἔξαρχος." In addition, since the Middle Ages, the title of "patriarchal exarch" has been given to certain ecclesiastical charges, either for an exceptional mission or for some kind of ambassadorial task.

[298]Bl. Phidas, Προϋποθέσεις διαμορφώσεως τοῦ θεσμοῦ τῆς πενταρχίας τῶν πατριαρχῶν (Athens, 1969), p. 291.

[299]Canon 39, *Syntagma*, p. 339; Latin text *Concilia Africae*, edition of C. Munier, *CC*, Latin series, CCLIX, p. 185. We find many examples in Church literature of the fifth century on the use of this word with the meaning of "important person." Thus for the Cyrillians, John of Antioch was among the opponents "ἔξαρχον τῆς ἑαυτῶν ἀποστασίας," *ACO* I, I, 3, p. 26. Theodoret spoke in his letters of the "exarch of the monks who live with us," letter 113 (to Leo, bishop of Rome), *SC* 111, p. 6. In this edition, Y. Azema presents the following explanation of this matter: "The name currently given to the elder of a monastery or to a group of religious," *op. cit.*, p. 66, note 3. E.A. Sophocles, *Greek Lexicon of the Roman and Byzantine Periods* (Cambridge, Mass., 1887), p. 480: "Overseer of monasteries."

[300]*ACO* II, I, 3, p. 30 (389).

[301]*Ibid.*, p. 79 (438).

[302]Novella CIX, *praefatio*: "Οἱ ἁγιώτατοι πάσης τῆς οἰκουμένης πατριάχαι," *CJC* III, p. 518. Novella CXXIII, 3: "Τοὺς μὲν μακαριωτάτους ἀρχιεπισκόπους καὶ πατριάρχας," *CJC, ibid.*, p. 597. According to Bl. Phidas, the title of "patriarch" was imposed for bishops of major sees in place of "exarch" because this latter term was too tied up with the diocesan borders, and this did not correspond to the jurisdictional areas of the sees which became patriarchal, Ἰστορικὰ προβλήματα περὶ τὴν λειτουργίαν τοῦ θεσμοῦ τῆς πενταρχίας τῶν πατριαρχῶν (Athens, 1970), p. 29. This explanation seems quite excellent to us.

[303]St. Nicodemus the Hagiorite has very clearly shown the lack of logic in this position, *Pedalion*, p. 192, note 1.

[304]Epist. VIII (*ad Michaelem imperatorem*), Mansi XV, col. 201-202. "Quem autem primatem dioeceseos sancta synodus dixerit, praeter apostoli primi vicarium," col. 201E. This strange exegesis was no doubt not invented by pope Nicholas himself. The real author of the letter where it is found was Anastasius the Librarian, and there is every reason to believe that he was the author of this fantastic interpretation. Nicodemus Milasch dedicates several pages to the presentation and the refutation of this particular theory, *Pravila* I, pp. 353-358.

[305]*Kirchengeschichte*, 1, second edition (Tübingen, 1929), pp. 656-658.

[306]A striking example of the misinterpretation of a canon is found in the commentary of Balsamon concerning canons 6 and 7 of Nicea; anachronistically, he saw in them the constitutions of the patriarchates of Rome, Alexandria, Antioch and Jerusalem, *Rhalles-Potles* II, pp. 129-131.

[307]Canons 9 and 17 of Chalcedon.

[308]*The Later Roman Empire* (Oxford, 1964), vol. III, p. 300.

[309]"Die von K. Müller vorgeschlagene Lösung wäre die beste, wenn man nicht grund hätte zu vermuten, das den Metropoliten der drei kleineren Diozesen ebenfalls der titel 'Exarch' gegeben

worden wäre. So ist vorlaufig eine sichere Lösung der Frage noch möglich," *Chalcedon und die Ausgestaltung des Konstantinopolitanishen Primats, Das Konzil von Chalkedon*, vol. II (Würtzburg, 1953), pp. 459-90, p. 477.

[310]See our commentaries on canon 2 of Constantinople and especially canon 6 of Nicea.

[311]*Regestes*, 48a.

[312]*Histoire ancienne de l'Eglise*, III, 4th edition (Paris, 1911), p. 461.

[313]See letters XLVII, XLVIII, XLIX, and L of St. Basil, "Les Belles-Lettres," t. I (Paris, 1964), pp. 60-66. Also see the introduction of P. Gallay, *ibid.*, pp. XI-XIII.

[314]See the very well documented study of G. Amadouni, "L'autocéphalie du katholicat arménien," *OCA* 181 (Rome, 1968), pp. 137-78, especially pp. 141-65. This author writes that "l'église, ou mieux la hiérarchie armenienne naissante n'était considerée que comme le prolongement de l'evangelisation de Césarée en Armenie, St. Grégoire n'étant que l'un de ses plus illustres missionnaires," p. 143. However, G. Amadouni, without bringing forth any proof, speaks about the exarchate of Caesarea.

[315]*De vita s. Joannis Chrys.*, XIV, *PG* 47, col. 50.

[316]*Ibid.*.

[317]*Op. cit.*, pp. 299-300.

[318]Photios, "Bibliothéque," codex 59, t. I, p. 56, in the edition of R. Henry, "Les Belles-Lettres" (Paris, 1959).

[319]For example, see the case of Proklos: Sisinnius, archbishop of Constantinople (426-427), wanted to impose him on Cyzicus, but he ran up against the opposition of the inhabitants of the city. The emperor Theodosius II seems to have forbidden any episcopal ordination carried out against the wish of the bishop of Constantinople, but according to the Cyzicians, this provision was only a privilege given to Attikos personally; Socrates, *Historia ecclesiastica* VII, 28 and 41, *PG* 67, col. 801B and 829C. Effectively, this law was not put into the code of Theodosius. On the subject of the interventionist policy of the see of Constantinople from a more general point of view, see our commentary on canon 28 of Chalcedon.

[320]Mansi, XI, pp. 689-690.

[321]Balsamon (*Rhalles-Potles* II, p. 241) explains very well why the thing is impossible: a cleric could not be attached to two bishops at the same time.

[322]*Ibid.*, p. 242.

[323]*Ibid.*.

[324]*Ibid.*.

[325]*Histoire du droit byzantin*, 3 (Paris, 1846), p. 424.

[326]*CJC*, III, pp. 115-117B=III, 3, 1, edition of H.J. Scheltema and N. van der Wal (Groningen, 1955), pp. 108-109.

[327]*Rhalles-Potles* II, p. 241.

[328]St. John Chrysostom spoke of "ὑπόληψις ἀγαθή," *Ad pop. Antiochenum homil. VII*, 5, *PG* 49, col. 98. Zonaras in his commentary on canon 44 of Carthage speaks of "οὐκ ἀγαθὰς ὑπολήψεις," *Rhalles-Potles* III, p. 410.

[329]*ACO* II, I, 3, p. 98 (457). See canon 6 of Constantinople, *Syntagma*, p. 98: "...χραίνειν τὰς τὸν ἱερέων ὑπολήψεις."

[330]See the commentary on this canon.

[331]*Rhalles-Potles* II, pp. 243-6.

[332]*Syntagma*, p. 64. See canon 33 of the same collection, *ibid.*, p. 68.

[333]P. 14.

[334]*Pravila*, I, p. 360: "...litsam, nakhodiashchikhsia pod somneniem."

[335]*ACO* II, II, 2, p. 89 (181).

[336]*Ibid.*, p. 37 (128).

[337]*Ibid.*, p. 57 (149).

[338]On these ancient Latin versions, see W. M. Plöchl, *Geschichte de Kirchenrechts* I, second edition (Vienna, 1960), pp. 277-279.

[339]*The Canons of the First Four General Councils*, second edition (Oxford, 1892), p. 185.

[340]*Pravila* I, pp. 362-363.

[341]Canons 7 and 8, *Syntagma*, pp. 255-6.

[342]*Syntagma*, p. 68.

[343]*Ibid.*, p. 275. It seems proper to adopt the best attested reading in the manuscript tradition: "κανονικῶν γραμμάτων" (=canonicis litteris). The reading "κοινωνικῶν γραμμάτων" which we find

in the so-called "Tarasian" recension of the *Syntagma in XIV Titles* is an easily explained error due to phonetic similarity. Although certainly false, this reading is not absurd in meaning; it could mean "letters of communion."

[344]We find a model for such a letter in the *Pedalion* pp. 758-759.

[345]Nicea, canons 4 and 6; Antioch, canons 9, 11, 14, 19, 20; Laodicea, canon 12, *Syntagma*, pp. 84-5, 86, 256, 257-8, 259, 261, 262, 269.

[346]See our commentary on canon 1 of Chalcedon.

[347]Canon 34 of the Holy Apostles: "It is important that the bishops of each nation know who among them is the first and let them consider him as their head...," *Syntagma*, p. 68. The term "nation" here means "population of a province." On this subject, see Sozomen, *Historia ecclesiastica*, VII, 9, *PG* 67, col. 1436BC.

[348]"...σωζομένου δηλαδὴ τῇ Νικοδημέων πόλει τοῦ οἰκείου ἀξιώματος," *ACO* II, I, 2, p. 157 (353).

[349]*Rhalles-Potles* II, pp. 249-250.

[350]*Ibid.*, p. 427.

[351]See our treatment of this meeting (19th in the Greek acts of the council).

[352]*Rhalles-Potles* II, pp. 247-9. On the question of the identity of the imperial "σημειώματα," see F. Dölger and J. Karayannopoulos, *Byzantinische Urkundenlehre* (Munich, 1968), p. 86.

[353]*ACO* II, I, 2, p. 160 (356). *Synagoge*, p. 75; *Syntagma*, p. 118.

[354]Hispana: "Extraneum clericum et lectores...," *ACO* II, II, 2, p. 90 (182). Prisca: "Peregrinos clericos et lectores...," *ibid.*, p. 37 (129). Dionysius: "Peregrinos clericos et lectores...," *ibid.*, p. 57 (149).

[355]*Rhalles-Potles* II, p. 250.

[356]"K lirakat chuzhit' i neznaetyt'...," *Pravila* I, p. 364.

[357]P. 196.

[358]*Héfele-Leclercq* II², p. 801.

[359]Canon 19 B: "Clericorum autem nomen etiam lectores retinebunt," *Breviarium Hipponense, CC*, Concilia Africae, p. 39.

[360]Trullo, canon 17: "...absolutely no cleric, whatever is his rank, is authorized, without a letter of dismissal (ἐγγράφου ἀπολυτικῆς) from his own bishop, to take up service in another Church," *Syntagma*, p. 157. Apostolic Canons 33, *ibid.*, p. 68.

[361]*ACO* II, I, 2, p. 161 (357); *Synagoge*, p. 87, *Syntagma*, pp. 118-119.

[362]Hispana, *ACO* II, II, 2, p. 90 (182); Prisca, *ibid.*, p. 37 (129); Dionysius, *ibid.*, pp. 57-58 (149-150). It is to be noted that the Greek adjective "ἑτερόδοξον" was not transliterated in Latin. In the Hispana and Dionysius, we find the expression "sectae alterius" and in the Prisca "alterius hereseos."

[363]Neocaesarea, canon 1, *Syntagma*, p. 328.

[364]Ancyra, canon 10, *Syntagma*, p. 233.

[365]VI, 17, 3, edition of F.X. Funk (Paderborn, 1905), I, p. 341.

[366]*Syntagma*, p. 66.

[367]*Breviarium Hipponense*, canon 18, p. 38. St. Leo, epist. CLXVII, 3, *PL* 54, col. 1204A.

[368]*Canones in Causa Apiarii*, 21, *CC*, p. 141 cf. *Breviarium Hipponense*, canon 12, *ibid.*, p. 37.

[369]This hypothesis was advanced by A. Faivre, *Naissance d'une hiérarchie* (Paris, 1977), p. 232. He proposed it, moreover, prudently. The ancient discipline of the universal Church was more marked by similarities than by dissimilarities. Thus, in order to retain the non-accidental character of the agreement between certain stipulations, we must be sure that a specific canonical collection was known by those who issued a rule analogous to the one appearing in the collection. Now, it is highly doubtful in the case of the canons of Carthage before the fourth century.

[370]K. Ritzer, *Le mariage dans les Eglises chré*tiennes, French edition (Paris, 1970), pp. 140-141. On the significance of the link between marriage and the eucharist, see J. Meyendorff, *Marriage, an Orthodox perspective*, second edition (Crestwood, 1975), pp. 22-26.

[371]*Syntagma*, pp. 269-273. On the presence of the canons of Laodicea in the official collection used at Chalcedon, see our commentary on canon 1 of Chalcedon.

[372]*Ibid.*, pp. 188-189.

[373]*Rhalles-Potles* II, pp. 253-254.

[374]*Ibid.*, VI, p. 173 (Alphabetical Syntagma, letter Γ, chapter, 12).

[375]*Polnoe sobranie postanovlenii i rasporia tenii po vedotstvu pravoslavnago ispovedaniia*, vol. I (St. Petersburg, 1870), p. 623.

[376]Hispana, *ACO* II, II, 2, p. 90 (182): Prisca, *ibid.*, p. 37 (129); Dionysius, *ibid.*, p. 58 (150). The

Greek text of the acts, *ibid.*, II, I, 2, p. 161 (357).

[377]*Syntagma*, p. 119: Greek text and Old-Slavonic version, *Pravila* I, p. 367.

[378]Pp. 81-82.

[379]"L'imposition des mains...," *La Maison-Dieu*, 102 (1970), pp. 57-72, especially 63.

[380]Romans 16:1. This is the translation in Latin: "...quae est in ministerio Ecclesiae, quae est in Cenchris." According to the opinion of many exegetes, both ancient and modern, women deacons are also referred to in I Timothy 3:11.

[381]Faivre, p. 138.

[382]Novella CXXIII, cc. 13 and 37, *CJC* III, pp. 604 and 620; CXXXI, c. 13, 3, *ibid.*, p. 662.

[383]Novella III, prol. *CJC, ibid.*, p. 19: "διακόνους ἄρρενάς τε καὶ θηλείας"; III, c. 1, *ibid.*, p. 21; III, c. 2, *ibid.*, p. 22.

[384]C.H. Turner, editor, *Catholic and Apostolic*; collected papers (London and Oxford, 1931), chapter XI: "Ministries of Women in the Primitive Church," pp. 316-351, especially pp. 328-343. P. H. Lafontaine, *Les conditions positives de l'accession aux ordres dans la première législation ecclésiastique* (Ottawa, Ontario, Canada, 1963), pp. 27-55. R. Gryson, *Le ministère des femmes dans l'Eglise ancienne* (Gembloux, 1971), *passim*. E. Theodorou, "Διακόνισσα," Θρησκευτικὴ καὶ Ἠθικὴ Ἐγκυκλοπαιδεία, Th. 1 E, t. IV, (1964), col. 1144-1151. A. G. Martimort, *Les diaconesses, Essai historique* (Rome, 1982). These works give a rich bibliography on the question.

[385]For example, see I Cor. 3:5; II Cor. 3:6; 6:4, etc. The same remark for the word "διακονία."

[386]For example, see Acts 13:2; Phil. 2:17. See II Cor. 9:12 for the combination of the two words "...ἡ διακονία τῆς λειτουργίας ταύτης."

[387]Fr. Funk, *Didascalia et Constitutiones Apostolorum* (Paderborn, 1905), III, 12, 1-3, pp. 208-10.

[388]*Haereses*, LXXIX, 3, *PG* 42, col. 744D-745A.

[389]Funk, p. 524; VIII, 19-20.

[390]See our analysis of this text. See also A. Kalsback, *Die altkirchliche Einrichtung der Diakonissen bis zu ihrem Erloschen* (Freiburg-in-Breisgau, 1926), pp. 46-9.

[391]This is Faivre's opinion, p. 87. Lafontaine, p. 31, who gives references in support of this position, attributes to deaconesses "the keeping of the entrance door for women and the space reserved for them in the church."

[392]*Art. cit.*, col. 1146. See the text of the office in the Byzantine tradition of this time: Goar, pp. 218-9. Matthew Blastares referred to the ancient books where the ritual was precisely described; he noted that the deaconesses bent their heads and not their knees at the moment of their ordination, in contrast to deacons, Alphabetical Syntagma, letter "Γ," chapter 11, *Rhalles-Potles* VI, p. 172. The problem raised by some Roman Catholic theologians as to whether the ordination of women deacons imprints a sacramental character or not is a question that only has meaning within the bounds of western scholastic doctrines. As such, it does not concretely interest Orthodox theologians or historians of ancient Church institutions.

[393]See the detailed explanation of Lafontaine, pp. 8-24.

[394]See notes 387 and 388.

[395]*Nouvelle Histoire de l'Eglise*, I (Paris, 1963), p. 196.

[396]*Rhalles-Potles* II, p. 255; Answer 38 to Mark of Alexandria, *ibid.*, IV, p. 477.

[397]Thus, for example, canon 2 of the council of Nimes, 396, says that "equally it has been noted by certain persons that, contrary to the apostolic discipline—an unheard of thing up to now—we saw, I do not know where, women elevated to the ministry of deacons (*in ministerium faeminae...leviticum ...adsumptae*); Church discipline does not admit such a thing. It is improper. Let such an irregular ordination be annulled; and let us be very careful that no one in the future has the audacity to act in this way," "Conciles gaulois du IVᵉ siècle," *SC* 241 (Paris, 1977), pp. 126-9.

[398]Lafontaine, pp. 32-33

[399]*L'Eglise dans l'Empire romain (IVᵉ-Vᵉ siècles)* (Paris, 1958), p. 123.

[400] The law of June, 390, *CTh* XVI, 2, 27, edition of Mommsen (Berlin, 1905), pp. 843-844. It was also stipulated that the deaconess was then to leave her wealth to her children, only keeping control over her personal properties. Clerics who get themselves put on wills or receive inheritances through fraud or unworthy means are not to receive any benefit from their doubtful double dealings. This law set a limit of 60 years of age for becoming a deaconess, and it is mentioned by Sozomen, *Historia ecclesiastica* VII, 16, *PG* 67, col. 1461C.

[401]V, 9-13.

[402]*Constitutiones Apostolorum* III, 16, 1, edition of Funk, p. 209.

[403]*Vie d'Olympias la diaconesse*, *SC* 13bis (Paris, 1968).

[404]Novella CXXIII, c. 13, *CJC* III, p. 604. Previously, novella VI, c. 6, ibid., p. 43, indicated the age at about 50 years while allowing for a lower age in cases of necessity on the condition that the deaconess live in a convent.

[405]*Syntagma*, p. 177.

[406]See note 404.

[407]Ancyra, canon 10, *Syntagma*, p. 233.

[408]Nahum 1:9. This is the interpretation according to the Septuagint. The meaning of the Hebrew text is not clear.

[409]*Syntagma*, pp. 66 and 489.

[410]Canon 44, *Syntagma*, p. 492.

[411]"Virginem quae se deo domino consecrauit, similitier et monachum non licere nuptialia iura contrahere, quodsi hoc inuenti fuerint perpetrantes excommunicentur; confitentibus autem decreuimus ut habeat auctoritatem eiusdem loci episcopus misericordiam humanitatemque largiri"; *ACO* II, II, 2, p. 58 (150).

[412]J. Gaudemet, *L'Eglise dans l'Empire romain (IVe-V·^e siècles)* (Paris, 1958), pp. 206-11.

[413]Carthage, canon 6, *CC*, Concilia Africae, p. 102.

[414]Balsamon, *Rhalles-Potles* II, p. 257.

[415]*Syntagma*, p. 482.

[416]According to St. Basil, the sin of adultery brought with it a sentence of 15 years: canon 58, *ibid.*, p. 499. For the same sin, canon 20 of Ancyra imposed a sentence of 7 years, *ibid.*, p. 236.

[417]*Syntagma*, p. 480. There was also a certain indulgence that St. Cyprian showed on this point. Did he not write "...si autem perseuerare nolunt uel non possunt, melius nubant quam in ignem delictis suis cadant," Epist. 6, 2, Hartel's edition (*CSEL* III, IIa), p. 474.

[418]Canon 19, *Syntagma*, p. 236.

[419]"...what must we think of the the virgin who is the bride of Christ and a sacred vessel consecrated to the Master?," *Syntagma*, p. 481. Cf. council in Trullo, canon 4, p. 147.

[420]Gaudemet, p. 209.

[421]*Héfele-Leclercq* II², p. 804. This opinion is vigorously refuted by Nicodemus Milasch, *Pravila* I, p. 372.

[422]Epist. 7, 3, *PL* 22, col. 691.

[423]Novella 89, P. Noailles and A. Dain, *Les Novelles de Léon VI le Sage* (Paris, 1944), pp. 294-7. P. Mitsopoulos, Ἡ νομικὴ καὶ ἐκκλησιαστικὴ μορφὴ τοῦ γάμου (Athens, 1939), especially pp. 56-67. For the period before the Early Middle Ages, this remark of K. Ritzer seems to us very correct: "...the ecclesiastical tradition of the Greeks was inclined even more to limit the categories of persons apt to receive the blessings of the Church than to make of this blessing an obligatory precept," *Le mariage dans les Eglises Chré*tiennes, French edition (Paris, 1970), p. 163. C. Vogel, "Les rites de la célébration du mariage: leur signification dans la formation du lien durant le haut moyen âge," *Il matrimonio nella società altomedi-evale* (Spoleto, 1977), pp. 397-465.

[424]Concerning the ways of entering monasticism at its beginnings, J. Gaudemet observes that "the period of the early development is not that of well defined juridical structures. The status of the monk is still uncertain," p. 199.

[425]*Syntagma*, p. 483.

[426]*Ibid.*, p. 469. The genitive plural "τῶν κανονικῶν" does not allow us to determine the gender. The title of the canon in the *Codex Vallicellianus F-47* (10th century) indicated in the note by Beneševič supposed that the noun was understood in the feminine: "περὶ κανονικῶν πορνευοῦσαν..." This has influenced contemporary translators: *CPG* p. 103; St Basil, *Lettres*, vol. 2, collection *Les Belles-Lettres*, text established and translated by Y. Courtonne (Paris, 1961), p. 126. The annotated epitome of Aristenus contains ἡ κανονική, which is unambiguous; *Rhalles-Potles* IV, p. 409. On the other hand, Zonaras and Balsamon supposed that the noun was masculine and gave it a very broad meaning including clerics, monks, nuns, and virgins, *ibid.*, pp. 408-9.

[427]Canon 60, *Syntagma*, p. 499.

[428]*Ibid.*, p. 175.

[429]Zonaras: *Rhalles-Potles* II, pp. 256-7; Balsamon, *ibid.*, pp. 257-8; Aristenus, *ibid.*, p. 258.

[430]*Ibid.*, p. 258. It is a reference to the Basilica 27, 6, 1, edition of H.J. Scheltema and N. Van der Wal, 4 (Groningen, 1962), pp. 1354-6 ("περὶ ἀθεμιτογαμιῶν"). This passage is taken from Novella of Justinian, c1-3, *CJC* 3, pp. 75-78. Quotation from Balsamon: Novella 12, c. 1, p. 75 = Basilica, p.

1354.

431*Rhalles-Potles* IV, p. 430: Canon 35 of the first series.

432For example, see canons 5 and 12 of Nicea; in Trullo, canon 3, *Syntagma*, pp. 86, 89, and 145.

433Letter to Letoios, *Syntagma*, p. 630. Cf. in Trullo, canon 102, *Syntagma*, pp. 203-204.

434J. Rezac, "De monachismo secundum recentiorem legislationem russicam," *OCA* 138 (Rome, 1952), pp. 283-287.

435Nicodemus Milasch, *Pravoslavno tsrkveko pravo* (Belgrade, 1926), pp. 710-11.

435A.P. Christophilopoulos, Ἑλληνικὸν ἐκκλησιαστικὸν δίκαιον, second edition (Athens, 1965), p. 226. P. Panagiotakos emphatically states that the Holy Synod of the Church of Greece grants no dispensation in this matter, Ἐγχειρίδιον περὶ τῶν κολυμάτων τοῦ γάμου (Athens, 1959), p. 52.

437See our analysis of Nicea canon 4. The expression "principle of territorial accommodation" with this precise meaning is widely used by F. Dvornik, *Byzantium and the Roman Primacy,* (New York: Fordham University Press, 1966), *passim*.

438*Héfele-Leclercq* II², p. 806.

439Canon 38, *Syntagma*, pp. 169-70. However, the term "παροικιῶν" with the ambiguous meaning was replaced by "πραγμάτων."

440*ACO* II, I, 2, p. 161 (357); *Synagoge*, p. 36; *Syntagma*, p. 120.

441Prisca: "Rusticas," *ACO* II, II, 2, p. 37 (129); Dionysiana; "rusticas," *ibid.*, p. 58 (150); Hispana: "rusticanas," *ibid.*, p. 90 (182).

442*Rhalles-Potles* II, pp. 259 and 263.

443*Pravila*, I, p. 372.

444Wisdom of Solomon 19:10.

445I Peter 1:17; Acts 13:17.

446Canon 34 of the Holy Apostles: "τῇ αὐτοῦ παροικίᾳ...καὶ τοὺς ὑπ' αὐτὴν χώραις," *Syntagma*, p. 68; Antioch, canon 9: "τῇ ἐκάστου...παροικίᾳ,...καὶ τοὺς ὑπ' αὐτὴν χώραις"; "τῆς ἑαυτοῦ παροικίας...," *ibid.*, p. 256.

447Plöchl, pp. 170-173.

448*Historia ecclesiastica* I, 27 and VII, 25, *PG* 67, col. 156A and 793A.

449*ACO* II, I, 2, p. 161 (357); a variant for line 17 of several manuscripts.

450*Pedalion*, p. 199; *Rhalles-Potles* II, p. 258.

451*Pravila* I, p. 372. In fact it is difficult to know how the authors of the *Kniga Pravil* understood the text because in this work, they did not always translate the word "ἐπαρχία" in the same way. Sometimes the Greek word kept its Greek but Russified form "eparkhiia"; sometimes it was translated by the term "obchast." In addition, in this canon 17 of Chalcedon, "παροικία" was translated by "prikhod" at the beginning and at the end.

452J. Gaudemet notes correctly that "in fact we have to get rid of our modern idea of a border, imaginary line, that we can go across in one step," p. 326.

453" Ἀνεπηρέαστον καὶ ἀβίαστον"; "καθαρὰ καὶ ἀβίαστα," *Syntagma*, pp. 107-8; cf. also the participle "βιασάμενος" in the same text, p. 108.

454R. Naz, "Prescription," *DDC* VII, col. 178-194. The period of 20 years goes back to a law of the emperor Theodosius II, *CJ* VII, 39, 3, *CJC* II, p. 311.

455Canon 37 of the Holy Apostles, *Syntagma*, p. 69; Constantinople, canon 2, pp. 96-7; Antioch, canon 20, p. 262.

456The reading in a manuscript of the 9th century (Nan. 22) of the *Synagoge* which gives "ἐπάρχῳ" that is, "prefect" instead of "ἐξάρχῳ" is completely aberrant. *Synagoge*, p. 36, note 23.

457*Rhalles-Potles* II, p. 260.

458See the text of this scholion in the work of V.N. Beneševič, *Kanonicheskii sbornik XIV titulov* (St. Petersburg, 1905), *Prilozheniia*, pp. 25-26. See the commentary of Aristenus on canon 9, *Rhalles-Potles* II, p. 240.

459See our commentary on canon 3 of the council of Constantinople.

460*Rhalles-Potles* II, pp. 240-241.

461Pp. 192-193, in the note.

462*Pravila* I, p. 374.

463*CJ* I, 3, 35, *CJC* II, pp. 23-24.

464*Ibid.*, cf. *Nomocanon in XIV Titles*, I, 20, *Rhalles-Potles* I, p. 57.

465*ACO* I, I, 7, pp. 122-123: We are dealing with a request presented by two bishops of the province of "Europe" in the diocese of Thrace. We note also that one of the exceptions sanctioned by the law of Zeno mentioned above also concerned a province of the civil diocese, "Scythia minor": there was no other bishop than the one from Tomi.

466*ACO* II, I, 3, pp. 11-42 (370-401).

467*Ibid.* pp. 63-83 (422-442); Letter of St. Cyril, pp. 66-67 (425-426).

468Prisca: *ibid.*, II, II, 2, p. 38 [130]; Hispana, *ibid.* p. 91. Dionysiana, *ibid.*, p. 58 [150]. Hispana, *ibid.*, p. 91 [183]. This last translation makes a clarification: "...conspirationum crimen, quod apud graecos dicitur fratrias."

469K. Latte, "Phratrie," Pavly-Wissowa-Kroll, *Realencyclopädie der Klassischen Altertumswissenschaft* (Stuttgart), XX, 1, col. 746-756.

470*Synagoge*, p, 79; *Syntagma*, p. 121; *Rhalles-Potles* II, p. 263. This altered form is found in the verb which is derived from it: φατρίαζειν, φατριάζειν.

471St. Gregory of Nazianzus, epist. 41, 10: "...κατὰ φατρίας καὶ συγγενίας," which P. Gallay translated by "by cliques and relatives," t. I, *Les Belles-Lettres* (Paris, 1964), p. 53. Socrates, *Historia ecclesiastica* VI, 4, concerning the intrigues against St. John Chrysostom: "φατρίας συνίστασαν κατ' αὐτοῦ," *MGH*, 67, col. 672A.

472Canon 34, *Syntagma*, pp. 167-168.

473Canon 13, *Les conons des Synodes Particuliers* (Fonti), pp. 470-1; we have modified the translation of P. Ioannou on several points.

474On this agitation see D. Stiernon, *Constantinople IV* (Paris, 1967), pp. 11-68.

475*Synagoge*, p. 150.

476Prisca, *ACO* II, II, 2, p. 38 (130); "secundum canones patrum"; Dionysiana, *ibid.*, p. 59 (151); idem; Hispana, *ibid.*, p. 91 (183); "secundum patrum regulas."

477*Op. cit.*, p. 38 (130).

478Pope Innocent I made a remark to Theophilus of Alexandria that the Roman Church does not recognize any others, Ep. V, *PL* 20, col. 496A.

479*Syntagma*, p. 262. This ordinance of the council of Antioch is to be linked in its wording with canon 37 of the Holy Apostles, *ibid.*, p. 69. This one is possibly prior in time to the canon of Antioch but not much. For canon 5 of Nicea (*ibid.*, pp. 85-6). See our commentary on this text.

480*Syntagma*, p. 275.

481This decision was inserted into the canonical corpus of the Church of Africa: canon 76, *op. cit.*, pp. 202-3, *loc. cit.*, p. 202.

482Canon 8, *Syntagma*, pp. 150-151, quotation p. 151.

483A proposed decree, read by Beronician, secretary of the imperial consistory: *ACO* II, I, 2, p. 157 (353), lines 19-24.

484Acts: *ACO* II, I, 2, p. 162 (358); *Synagoge*, pp. 72-3; *Syntagma*, pp. 121-122.

485Canon 17, *Syntagma*, pp. 157-158.

486*ACO* II, II, 2, p. 59 (151).

487*CC*, pp. 14-5. This text is taken up in the African codex as canon 8 of this collection, *ibid.*, p. 103.

488*ACO* II, I, 2, p. 162 (358); (Acta): *Synagoge*, p. 40; *Syntagma*, p. 122.

489Prisca: "...sicut et anterioribus canonibus cautum est," *ACO* II, II, 2, p. 39 (131). Dionysiana: "...sicut antiquis quoque est canonibus constitutum," *ibid.*, p. 59 (151). Hispana: "...sicut iam et praecedentibus regulis statutum habetur," *ibid.*, p. 91 (183).

490*Synagoge*, p. 40, note 47. This is also the text that we find in *Rhalles-Potles* II, p. 268. On the other hand, the *Pedalion* gives the correct reading, p. 202. The *Kniga Pravil* gives an exact translation: "Kak sie vospreshcheno i drevnimi pravilami," *Pravila* I, p. 380.

491*Rhalles-Potles* II, pp. 268-9.

492*Ibid.*, p. 269. Canon 80 of Carthage, *CC* p. 204.

493*Syntagma*, p. 264.

494*Ibid.*, p. 70.

495*Syntagma*, p. 168.

496See the notes of the *Synagoge*, p. 76.

497Meeting of "de Caroso et Dorotheo," *ACO* II, I, 2, pp. 114-121 (310-317).

498*Rhalles-Potles* II, pp. 270-271.

499*Ibid.*, p. 271.

500*ACO.* II, I, 2, p. 162 (358); *Synagoge*, p. 100; *Syntagma*, p. 123; *Rhalles-Potles* II, p. 271; *Pedalion*, p. 203.

501Prisca: *ACO* II, II, 2, p. 39 (131): Dionysius: *ibid.*, p. 60 (152); Hispana, *ibid.*, p. 92 (184).

[502]*Rhalles-Potles* II, p. 272.

[503]Canon 49, *Syntagma*, p. 177.

[504]Canon 13, *Syntagma*, p. 219.

[505]A. Vasiliev, *Histoire de l'Empire byzantin*, vol. I (Paris, 1932), pp. 336 and 347-348.

[506]*Les canons des Synodes Particuliers* (Fonti), pp. 447-449.

[507]Justinian, Novella 5, c. 1, *CJC* III, p. 29: this is the section of the novella inserted into the *Basilica* 4, 1, 1, edition of H. J. Scheltema and N. Van der Wal, vol. AI, p. 112.

[508]"Περὶ ποιήσεως μοναστηρίων, καὶ τοῦ γίνεσθαι αὐτὰ ἰδιωτικά...," *Rhalles-Potles* I, pp. 247-250.

[509]*Rhalles-Potles* II, p. 272; *Basilica* 5, 2, pp. 130-140.

[510]*Rhalles-Potles* II, p. 273.

[511]J. Meyendorff, *Une controverse sur le rôle social de l'Eglise* (Chevetogne, 1956).

[512]This intervention of the metropolitan is quoted by A. S. Pavlov in his work, *Istoricheskii ocherk o sekularizatsii tserkovnykh zemel' v Rossii* (Odessa, 1871), p. 91.

[513]*Syntagma*, p. 77.

[514]*ACO* II, I, 2, p. 162 (358), note for line 27; *Synagoge*, p. 48, note 10; *Syntagma*, p. 124, note 1.

[515]*Pedalion*, p. 204; *Rhalles-Potles* II, p. 273; *Pravila* I, p. 386.

[516]Prisca, *ACO* II, II, 2, p. 40 (132); Dionysius, p. 60 (152); Hispana, p. 92 (184).

[517]J. Trummer, "Mystisches im alten Kirchenrecht. Die geistliche Ehe zwischen Bishof und Diozese," *Oesterreichisches Archiv für Kirchenrecht* II (1951), pp. 62-75.

[518]Nicea, canons 4 and 6; Antioch, canon 19; and Laodicea, canon 12.

[519]*Codex can. eccl. africanae*, canon 74, *CC*, p. 202.

[520]*Breviarium*, 20, *PL* 68, col. 1036D.

[521]Socrates, *Historia ecclesiastica* 7, 40, *PG* 67, col. 829B.

[522]Justinian, Novella 137, c. 3, *CJC* 3, p. 697; this text is taken up in the Basilica 3, 1, 8, vol. AI, p. 84.

[523]*Rhalles-Potles* II, p. 276.

[524]*Ibid.*, p. 274.

[525]*Ibid.*, p. 275.

[526]"Οἷον δὲ τοῦτό ἐστιν, οὐκ οἶδα· νομίζω δὲ παρὰ τῆς συνόδου ὁρισθησόμενον," *ibid.*, p. 275.

[527]*Ibid.*, p. 275.

[528]*Syntagma*, pp. 70-1.

[529]Letter to Domnos, pp. 566-7.

[530]*Ibid.*, p. 70 and pp. 263-4.

[531]The council of Antioch did not yet know this institution; we do not find any allusions to this matter in its canons. Canon 7 of the council of Gangra mentioned this concerning the bishop: "He who is the one in charge (τοῦ ἐγκεχειρισμένου) of receiving and making the offerings," *Syntagma*, p. 246. Canon 8 of the same council spoke of "him who is charged with the administration of charity" (τοῦ ἐπιτεταγμένου εἰς οἰκονομίαν εὐποιΐα), *ibid.*, p. 246. St. Basil had several "treasurers" in his Church, Letter 232, 1, edition of *Les Belles-Lettres*, t. 3 (Paris, 1966), p. 55. St. Gregory of Nyssa also had "administrators of the sacred monies" (οἱ ταμίαι τῶν ἱερῶν χρημάτων), Letter 225, p. 22.

[532]*ACO* II, I, 3, pp. 15-6 (374-5).

[533]Actio 15, *ibid.*, pp. 66-7 (425-6).

[534]*Historia ecclesiastica* 6, 7, *PG* 67, col. 685AB.

[535]On the causes of this hostility, see Glenn F. Chesnut, *The First Christian Histories* (Paris, 1979), pp. 170-1.

[536]*Syntagma*, p. 537: canon 9 (canon 10 in all later collections).

[537]*Rhalles-Potles* II, pp. 277-8.

[538]*Syntagma*, pp. 217-8.

[539]*Rhalles-Potles* II, p. 278.

[540]J. Goar, *Euchologion*, p. 228. On the dignity of "treasurer" in the Orthodox Church, see Nicodemus Milasch, *Dostoianstva u pravoslavnoi tsrkvi* (Zadar, 1879), pp. 130-1.

[541]*ACO* II, I, 2, p. 163 (359); *Synagoge*, pp. 130-131.

[542]*Syntagma*, p. 124; for the ancient form, that is, of the Trullan recension, see footnote 5.

[543]Recensio Tarasiana, *ibid.*, p. 124. This is also what is found in the *Pedalion*, p. 205.

[544]Prisca, *ACO* II, II, 2, p. 40 (132). The expression "...aut consensum rapientibus praebere" assumes the original Greek of the Acta: "Ἡ συναινοῦντας τοῖς ἁρπάζουσιν." Dionysius, p. 60 (152).

Hispana, p. 92 (184).

[545]Canon 30, *Syntagma*, p. 489.

[546]Apostolic Canon 67: "If anyone keeps an unengaged virgin in his home by force, let him be excommucated. He will not be permitted to take another woman (as his wife), but he will keep her that he has chosen, even if she is poor," *Syntagma*, p. 76. Ancyra, canon 11: "Concerning young, engaged girls who are kidnapped by someone else, it seems right and proper that these girls be returned to their fiances, even if the kidnappers have abused them by force," p. 233.

[547]*Syntagma*, p. 489.

[548]*Ibid.*, pp. 484-485.

[549]*Ibid.*, p. 485.

[550]Canon 92, *ibid.*, p. 197.

[551]*Rhalles-Potles* II, p. 279.

[552]*Ibid.*, pp. 279-280. Novella of Leo: edition of P. Naiolles et A. Dain, pp. 140-143. This law set out the death penalty for the perpetrator of a ravishing if it was done violently as well as corporal punishments for accomplices.

[553]A, 13, *Rhalles-Potles* VI, p. 104.

[554]*Le schisme byzantin* (Paris, 1941), p. 13.

[555]*Naissance d'une capitale: Constantinople et ses institutions de 330 à 451* (Paris, 1974), p. 478.

[556]*ACO* II, I, 3, p. 99 (458).

[557]*Ibid.*, II, I, 2, p. 54 (250).

[558]Here is what the commissioners said exactly: "Concerning the competence of the see of the very holy Church of illustrious Constantinople concerning the consecrations in the provinces, this matter will be examined at the proper time by the holy council," *ACO* II, I, 3, p. 62 (421). We note the sibylline remark made after that by Eunomios of Nicomedia: "...I love the archbishop of illustrious Constantinople provided the canons are observed."

[559]The Recensio Tarasiana does not have "βασιλίδι" in this clause: *Syntagma*, p. 125. The presence of this adjective is moreover universally attested to, including in the Recensio Trullana of the *Syntagma* in *XIV Titles*. See *ibid.*, note 10; cf. *ACO* II, I, 3, p. 89 (448) and *Rhalles-Potles* II, p. 281. For the text as a whole, see *ACO* II, I, 3, pp. 88-89 (447-448); *Syntagma*, pp. 124-6; *Rhalles-Potles* II, pp. 280-281; *Pedalion*, p. 206; *CCO*, pp. 91-93. We note this variant in the main recension chosen by P.-P. Joannou, p. 92; "Τοὺς ἐν τοῖς βαρβαρικοῖς ἐπισκόπους." No note, however, tells us from what manuscript(s) it is taken. G. Dagron, p. 484, note 1, thinks that the proper understanding is "the (territories) in barbarian (territory)." If this is not a printing error, pure and simple, forgotten from the list of the errata, we think that it is only the error of a copyist; this is easily explained by the similar pronunciation of βαρβαρικῆς and βαρβαρικοῖς due to the linguistic phenomenon of iotacism.

[560]*ACO* II, II, 2, pp. 46-47 (138-139). On the presence of this canon in two Italian manuscripts of the sixth century, see F. Maassen, *Geschichte der Quellen und der Literatur des canonischen Rechts im Abendlande* (Graz, 1870), pp. 94-99 and 526-36.

[561]*ACO* II, III, 3, p. 102 (541). Rusticus, in the middle of the sixth century in Constantinople, had corrected the "versio antiqua" by using a manuscript of the monastery of the Acemetes. This is why we often speak of the "Emendatio Rustici."

[562]On this matter, see the remark of Ed. Schwartz, "Die Kanonessamlungen der alten Reichskirche," *Gesammelte Schriften*, 4 (Berlin, 1960), p. 164, note 1. The ancient canonical Arabic collection used by the Melkites, that is, the partisans of the council of Chalcedon, only contained the 27 canons. On this subject, see Elias Jarawan, *La collection canonique arabe des Melkites et sa physionomie propre* (Rome, 1969), p. 95.

[563]*ACO* II, I, 2, p. 129 (325).

[564]For example, see Socrates, *Historia ecclesiastica* I, 17, *PG* 67, col. 116C. The work was composed in Constantinople between 438 and 443.

[565]On this subject, see the excellent work of Maciej Salamon, *Rozwoj idei Rzymu. Konstantynopola od IV do pierwszei potowy VI wieku* (Katowice, 1975).

[566]*Op. cit.*, p. 47.

[567]*Themistii orationes*, vol. I, Disc. III, edition of G. Downey (Leipzig, 1965), pg. 59.

[568]Such is the opinion of G. Dagron, p. 84. On the other hand, M. Salamon thinks that after 370, Valens gave his favor to Constantinople and emphasized the equality of status with Old Rome, p. 89.

[569]See our analysis of this passage above; it was later on numbered as canon 3 of the second ecumenical council.

[570]Vasiliev, p. 115. On this person, see E. Demoygeot, "La politique orientale de Stilicon, de 405 à 407," *Byzantion*, XIV-XX (1950), pp. 27-37.

[571]In Rufinum, II, 54, *MGH*, a.a., x.

[572]*CT* XIV, 13, 1, p. 789: "De iure Italico urbis Constantinopolitanae." The fact that a city was called "iuris Italici," from the third century on, no longer represented a very exceptional privilege. See the list of cities which enjoyed this status in the *Digest* L, XV, 1, and 8, *CJC* I, pp. 908-9. On the "Jus Italicum," see G. Luzzatto, "Appunti sul ius Italicum," *Melanges de Visscher*, 4 (1950), pp. 79-110.

[573]*CJ* XI, 21: "Constantinopolitana non solum iuris Italici, sed etiam ipsius Romae veteris praerogativa laetetur," *CJC* II, p. 434.

[574]Disc. II, vol. I, p. 60.

[575]*CJ* I, 17, 10, *CJC* II, p. 70.

[576]On this subject, we find these significant passages in the letter written by archbishop Anatolius to pope Leo; the council did not know about his letter. On the proposed decree on the see of Constantinople, he states that "we have taken the initiative in this action, rightly having confidence in your Beatitude who will consider as his own the honor of the see of Constantinople, seeing that certainly for a long time, your apostolic see has assumed the guardianship and the concord (of the see of Constantinople) (κηδεμονίαν καὶ ὁμόνοιαν), and in all things, as was necessary, it (Rome) abundantly made it (see of Constantinople) participate in its influence," *ACO* II, I, 2, p. 53 (249). A little further along in the same letter, we read that "in fact the see of Constantinople has for father your apostolic see to which it (see of Constantinople) is joined in a very special way," p. 54 (250). Archbishop John II of Constantinople, in the preamble that he inserted into the formulary of Hormisdas, said that "I assuredly accept that the two very holy Churches of God, that is, of your Old Rome and of this New Rome, are one; I admit that the see of the apostle Peter and the see of this imperial city are one," Collectio Avellana, Epist. 159, *CSEL* 35 (edition of O. Günther), p. 608.

[577]P. Stephanou, "Sedes Apostolica, Regia Civitas," *OCP* 33, 2 (1967), pp. 563-82.

[578]*Historia ecclesiastica* 7, 9, *PG* 67, col. 1436C.

[579]Dagron, pp. 206-208.

[580]*ACO* II, I, 3, p. 99 (458) and pp. 116-8 (475-7), especially p. 118 (477).

[581]Of course, that did not imply that Rome and the East had the same conception of this primacy, as the historical dossier shows quite clearly. On this matter, see the excellent study of W. De Vries, *Orient et Occident, les structures ecclésiales vues dans l'histoire des sept premiers conciles oecuméniques* (Paris, 1974).

[582]In the version of the conciliar acts published by Rusticus, "ἀποδεδόκασι" is translated by "reddiderunt," and "ἀπένειμαν" by "tribuerunt," *ACO* II, III, 3, p. 102 (541). The translation of the whole of the motion is rather mediocre in the Prisca. Here the first Greek verb has been translated by "statuerunt," which is rather a contradiction or at least a false meaning; on the other hand the second Greek verb has been rather correctly translated by "obtineat," *ibid.*, II, II, 2, p. 47 (139).

[583]V. Monachino doubts that it is necessary to give importance to this difference in verb tense in the ordinary Greek of the fifth century, "Il Canone 28 di Calcedonia e S. Leone Magno," *Gregorianum* 33 (1952), p. 542, note 21. That does not seem to us to be correct because, as we have already shown, in contrast with the 27 canons, the motion is written in a polished style.

[584]V.N. Beneševič, *Kanonicheskii sbornik XIV Titulov*, Prilozheniia (St. Petersburg, 1905), p. 26, n. 203, cf. *ibid.*, p. 21, n. 147.

[585]*Rhalles-Potles* II, p. 282. He refers us for more details to his commentary on canon 3 of Constantinople, *ibid.*, pp. 173-4. Aristenus adopted the chronological explanation of the preposition "after" in his interpretation of the resolution of the second ecumenical council: *ibid.*, p. 176. He is the one therefore that Zonaras has especially in mind even though in his normal manner, he does not name him.

[586]*ACO* II, I, 3, p. 53 (412).

[587]*Ibid.*, p. 118 (477).

[588]"...τὴν τιμὴν καὶ τὰ πρεσβεῖα," *ibid.*, II, I, 2, p. 54.

[589]This edict is known by its presence in the Syriac collection published by F. Schulthess, *Die syrischen Kanones der Synoden von Nizäa bis Chalcedon* (Göttingen, 1908), Document 13, p. 146. The later Greek version was done by E. Schwartz, "Die Kanonessamlungen der alten Reichskirche," *Gesammelte Schriften* 4 (Berlin, 1960), p. 167.

[589a]According to E. Schwartz, this pragmatic sanction may have been tied to the conflict between Bassian and Stephen concerning the see of Ephesus. But this opinion is contested by E. Honigmann

for whom the pragmatic sanction had Flavian of Constantinople in mind. This in fact seems to be more in relation with the paragraph that we have quoted. Honigmann put it chronologically in the first half of 449 and more precisely in April, when the legality of Flavian's action against Eutyches was questioned. He thinks that one of the consequences of the victory of Stephen was perhaps the choice by the emperor Theodosius II of Ephesus as the site of the projected council. He observes that all that would explain the mysterious and ironic remark of Kekropios of Sebastopolis, addressed to Stephen during the 12th session of the council of Chalcedon: "My lord Stephen ("Κύρι Στέφανε") learn how still powerful is bishop Flavian, even after his death!" (*ACO* II, I, 3, p. 51 [410]. On this subject, see E. Honigmann, "Stephen of Ephesus (April 15, 448-October 29, 451) and the Legend of the Seven Sleepers," *Studi e Testi* 173 (Rome, 1953), 17, pp. 125-168, on this question, pp. 161-162.

590For V. Grumel, there was no doubt that it was the one of Anatolius himself, *Regestes*, n. 129.

591*ACO* II, I, 2, p. 55.

592J. Meyendorff, *Orthodoxie et Catholicité* (Paris, 1965), p. 70.

593Nos. 20, 21, 23, 29, 48, 49a, 71, 83, 86b, 93, 95, 108, 109.

594Dagron, pp. 436-442.

595See the version of Palladius in his life of St. John Chrysostom, *PG* 47, col. 5-82 and more especially col. 51-52. See also Sozomen, *Historia ecclesiastica* 8, 6, *PG* 67, col. 1529B and 1532B. See also *ACO* II, I, 3, p. 52 (411): the intervention of the priest Philip during the 12th session.

596This is the 10th of the accusations of bishop Isaakios: "... Ἐπιβαίνει ἀλλοτρίαις ἐπαρχίαις καὶ χειροτονεῖ ἐπισκόπους," apud Photium, *Bibliotheka cod. 59*, edition of *Les Belles-Lettres*, t. I (Paris, 1959), p. 56.

597Canon 2, *Syntagma*, pp. 96-97. This point is underlined by C. Baur, *Der heilige Johannes Chrysostomus und seine Zeit*, t. II (Munich, 1930), p. 139.

598*ACO* II, I, 3, pp. 96-98 (455-457).

599*Historia ecclesiastica* V, 8, *PG* 67, col. 580A: "...καὶ κληροῦται Νεκτάριος μὲν τὴν μεγαλόπολιν καὶ τὴν Θρᾳκήν."

600*Historia ecclesiastica* VII, 28, *PG* 67, col. 801B. See *Regestes* n. 49a: In fact, it was most probably an imperial decree in favor of Attikos, clarifying the applications of canons 2-3 of Constantinople.

601*ACO* II, I, 3, p. 52 (411).

602*Ibid.*, pp. 52-53 (44-12). G. Dagron has written that "La resistance de l' Eglise d' Ephèse...n'avait pas non plus situé le débat au plan du droit," pp. 479-480.

603*ACO* II, I, 3, pp. 97-8 (456-7).

604Thus for S. Vailhé, it was a question of "usurpations of power," "Constantinople (Eglise de)," *DTC* III-2, col. 1323. M. Jugie spoke of "l'ambition des évêques de Byzance décorée par Constantin du titre de *Nouvelle Rome*," *Le schisme byzantin* (Paris, 1941), p. 10.

605V.N. Beneševič, *Kanonicheskii sbornik XIV Titulov* (St. Petersburg, 1905), Prilozheniia, n. 201, p. 26.

606*Rhalles-Potles* II, p. 286.

607*Ibid.*, pp. 283-284.

608E. Demougeot, *De l'unité à la division de l'Empire romain* (Paris, 1951); Ch. Pietri, *Roma Christiana* (Rome, 1976), vol. II, pp. 1069-1147. An excellent analysis of the jurisdictional situation of Illyricum in the fourth and fifth centuries is provided by Bl. Phidas, Προϋποθέσεις διαμορφώσεως τοῦ θεσμοῦ τῆς πενταρχίας τῶν Πατριαρχῶν (Athens, 1969), pp. 258-89; also F. Dvornik, *The Idea of Apostolicity in Byzantium* (Cambridge, Mass., 1958), pp. 25-29, where we find a complete bibliography on this delicate historical question.

609On this matter, see Bl. Phidas, Ἱστορικοκανονικὰ προβλήματα περὶ τὴν λειτουργίαν τοῦ θεσμοῦ τῆς πενταρχιαστῶν πατριαρχῶν (Athens, 1970), pp. 75-104.

610*CT* 16, 2, 45, p. 852.

611C. Silva-Tarouca, *Epistularum Romanorum pontificum ad vicarios per Illyricum aliosque episcopos collectio Thessalonicensis* (Rome, 1937), 15, pp. 43-44 and 16, pp. 44-45. The authenticity of these two letters has been put in doubt by Friedrich and Mommsen, but they have not been followed by very many scholars.

612*CJ* I, 2, 6, *CJC* II, p. 12.

613*Ibid.*, p. 486.

614Metropolitan Maximus of Sardis, *Le Patriarcat oecuménique dan l'Eglise orthodoxe*, French edition (Paris, 1975), pp. 281-282.

615*Rhalles-Potles* II, P. 286.

[616]*Ibid.*, "ὅθεν οἱ Ποντοῦ καὶ Θρᾴκης καὶ ᾿Ασίας, καὶ οἱ Βάρβαροι, τῷ τῆς Κονσταντινουπόλεως κερειοτόνηται."

[617]*Ibid.*, p. 283.

[618]Alphabetical Syntagma, letter E, chapter II, *Rhalles-Potles* VI, p. 257.

[619]*Syntagma*, p. 97.

[620]The adjective "αὐτοκέφαλος" is attested to for the first time in the sixth century in Theodore the Reader; he used it to describe the situation of the capital of Cyprus: II, 2, *PG* 86, col. 184BC.

[621]In the Prisca, we read "in barbaricis," *ACO* II, II, 2, p. 47 (139). The *Versio a Rustico edita* reads "inter barbaros," *ACO* II, III, 3, p. 102 (541).

[622]*Ibid.*, p. 275.

[623]*Rhalles-Potles* II, p. 283 and VI, p. 257.

[624]See the note on canon 28 of Chalcedon in Migne: "in Barbaris: Omnia nimirum loca imperio Romano non subjecta barbara olim et barbarica a Romanis ipsis appellata sunt; ut totus orbis Romanus, una voce Romania dicta sunt," *PG* 137, col. 484CD, note 39. J. Gaudemet has written that "En face de peuples nouveaux qui s'établissent dans l'Empire, apparait un concept de' 'romanité'... Ce ne peut être une notion territoriale, car au Vᵉ siècle le sol de l'empire n'appartient plus aux seuls Romains. Il s'agit d'une forme de civilisation, continuant les traditions classiques, mais ralliée au Christianisme, qui unit ses adeptes, vieilles familles romaines ou lointains provinciaux, en face des '*barbari*' qui peu à peu s'imposent." *Institutions de l'Antiquité* (Paris, 1967), p. 727. Despite appearances, there is a contradiction between these two definitions of "barbarica"; we have here two different approaches; there are zones where, practically, the imperial authority could not be applied or where the Greco-Roman civilization was in decline, but there could be no legal recognition of such a situation, which was considered only temporary in principle. The term "τό βαρβαρικόν" in the singular as well as the plural "τά βαρβαρικά" designated the regions where the barbarians had installed themselves. See, for example, John Malalas (491-578), *Chronography* 12, *PG* 97, col. 445B: The emperor Severus died "εἰς τό βαρβαρικόν." In canon 52 of Carthage, we read the following: "...Tunc de provincia Mauritania, propterea quod in finibus Africae posita sit, nihil statuimus, siquidem vicinae sunt barbarico," *CC*, p. 189. This passage was translated into Greek this way: "...τότε περὶ τῆς τῶν Μαυριτανῶν χώρας οὐδέν ὡρίσαμεν, διὰ τό εἰς τὰ τέλη τῆς ᾿Αφρικῆς κεῖσθαι αὐτήν, καί ὅτι τῷ βαρβαρικῷ παράκειται," *Syntagma*, p. 348. Zonaras commented on this passage and used the plural: "Καί τοῖς βαρβαρικοῖς παράκεται," *Rhalles-Potles* III, p. 431. Balsamon wrote, "Πλησίον τῶν βαρβάρων παρακεῖσθαι," *ibid.*

[625]Canon 30, *Syntagma*, pp. 163-165, p. 163.

[626]R. Gryson noted about this canon that the "'barbarian' or 'foreign' countries, in the eyes of the Greeks who edited this canon, were obviously the Latin countries"; *Les origines du célibat ecclésistique* (Gembloux, 1970), p. 120. This is not completely exact. The fathers of the council in Trullo wanted to make it apparent that they stood for the norm, at Rome and in Africa where the imperial authority was still exercised. They envisioned an exception only for countries which were not under this authority; cf. canon 12 and 13, *Syntagma*, pp. 151-154.

[627]*Pedalion*, p. 209.

[628]*Rhalles-Potles* II, p. 283.

[629]*Ibid.*, respectively, II, p. 285 and VI, p. 257.

[630]P. 209.

[631]*Héfele-Leclercq*, II², p. 818, note 1.

[632]For example, see Gennadios, Metropolitan of Heliopolis and Thira, ᾿Ιστορία τοῦ Οἰκουμενικοῦ Πατριαρχείου (Athens, 1953), pp. 175-176.

[633]"La position du patricat oecuménique dans l'Englise orthodoxe," French translation in *EO* 24 (1925), pp. 41-55; the original Greek text was published in the periodical *Pantainos*, 39-41 (1924).

[634]"O granitsakh rasprostraneniia prava vlasti konstantinopolskoi patriarkhii na 'diasporu'," *JMP* 11 (1977) pp. 34-45. The argumentation of this canonical scholar is perfectly valid even if his interpretation of the expression "ἐν τοῖς βαρβαρικοῖς" is not totally clear.

[635]For the composition and the content of this collection, see our commentary on canon 1 of Chalcedon.

[636]The words "μετὰ τῆς ἐπαρχίας ἐπισκόπων" do not constitute a later addition, contrary to what is affirmed in a note of Migne (*PG* 137, col. 484D, note 40). They are solidly attested to in the most ancient manuscript tradition, both Greek and Latin.

[637]See further along the complete text of their intervention.

[638]*ACO* II, I, 3, p. 54 (413).

[639]See the commentaries of Zonaras and Balsamon, *Rhalles-Potles* II, pp. 283-4. Also J. Darrouzès, *Documents inédit d'ecclésiologie byzantine* (Paris, 1966), pp. 11-19.

[640]For example see A. Wuyts, "Le 28ieme canon de Chalcédoine et le fondement du Primat romain," *OCP* 17 (1951), pp. 265-282. In this article useful references on this subject are given.

[641]See our comentary on this canon of Nicea.

[642]*ACO* II, I, 3, pp. 116-118 (475-477).

[643]This scholion was inserted into a treatise on the privileges of the most holy see of Constantinople ("Περὶ προνομιῶν τοῦ 'Αγιωτάτου Θρόνου Κωνσταντινουπόλεως") edited by A.S. Pavlov: "Anonimnaia grecheskaia stat'ia o primushchestvakh konstantinopol'skoga patriarshego prestola i drevneslavianskii perevod ee s dvumia vazhnymi dopolneniiami," *VV* 4 (1987) 143-154, *loc. cit.,* pp. 149-150. On the origins and the date of this scholion, see the article of S. V. Troitsky, "Kto vkliuchil papisticheskuiu scholiiu v pravoslavnuiu Kormchuiu," *BTr* 2, pp. 5-62. The question is envisioned in relation to the refutation of this scholion that we find in three manuscripts of the *Kormchaya* according to a recension called "Efremovskaia."

[644]"The bishop of New Rome is equal in dignity (ὁμότιμος) by reason of the transfer of scepters...," *Rhalles-Potles* II, p. 286. We note that, in an anachronistic manner, they considered the affair already accomplished at the time of the council of Chalcedon when the empire still existed in the West.

[645]This is what the pope wrote to Hincmar of Rheims recalling the content of the imperial letter he had received, *PL* 119, col. 1152D-1161A, especially cols. 1155-7.

[646]*Alexiade* I, 4, edition of *Les Belles-Lettres,* t. I (Paris, 1937), p. 48.

[647]*Rhalles-Potles* II, p. 286.

[648]*Ibid.,* p. 282.

[649]*Ibid.,* pp. 284-286.

[650]The best edition of this text was made by H. Fuhrmann, *Das Constitutum Constantini (Konstantinische Schenkung) Text: Fontes iuris Germanici Antiqui in usum scholarum ex MGH separatim editi,* X (Hanover, 1968).

[651]Y. Congar, *L'ecclésiologie du haut Mayen-Age* (Paris, 1968), p. 199, note 15. For a more recent bibliography see N. Huyghebaert, "La Donation de Constantin ramenée à ses véritables dimensions," *Revue d'Histoire Ecclésiastique* 71, 1-2 (Louvain, 1976), pp. 45-69.

[652]F. Dölger, *Rom in der Gedankenwelt der Byzantiner, Byzanz und die europäische Staatenwelt* (Ettal, 1953), pp. 70-115. P. Alexander, "The Donation of Constantine at Byzantium and its Earliest Use against the Western Empire," *Melanges G. Ostrogorsky,* 1 (Belgrade, 1924), pp. 11-26.

[653]W. Levison, *Konstantinische Schenkung und Silvesterlegende, Miscellanea F. Ehrle* (Rome, 1924), pp. 159-247.

[654]*ACO* II, I, 3, pp. 86-7 (445-6) (Gr.) and *ibid.,* II, III, 3, pp. 99-101 (538-540).

[655]*Ibid.,* II, 111, 3 p. 101 [540].

[656]*Ibid.,* II, III, 3, p. 88 (447). On Aetios, see the article on him, M. Jugie, *Dictionnaire d'histoire et de geographie ecclésiastique,* I, col. 668-669.

[657]*ACO* II, I, 3, pp. 89-94 (448-453); cf. *ibid.,* II, III, 3, pp. 102-8 (541-547).

[658]*Ibid.,* II, I, 3, p. 62 (421).

[659]On the administrative situation of Ancyra, see Jones, vol. II, p. 892, also Dagron, pp. 476-7.

[660]*ACO* II, I, 3, p. 94 (453), cf. *ibid.,* II, III, 3, p. 108 (547).

[661]*Ibid.,* II, III, 3, p. 109 (548). Approximate Greek translation: *ibid.,* II, I, 3, p. 95 (454).

[662]Plöchl, pp. 277-8; J. Gaudemet, *La formation du droit séculier et du droit de l'Eglise aux IVe et Ve siècles,* second edition (Paris, 1979), pp. 167-8.

[663]This collection, if we can really give it this name, is generally called "'Vetus Romana," Plöchl, p. 277.

[664]See our commentary on canon 3 of Constantinople.

[665]See above.

[666]*ACO* II, III, 1, p. 53.

[667]"'Επειδὴ ὑμεῖς τοὺς κανόνας οἴδατε," *ibid.,* II, I, 1, p. 78.

[668]*Ibid.,* II, I, 2, p. 141 (337).

[669]*Ibid.,* II, III, 3, p. 109 (548).

[670]*Regestes,* n. 119.

[671]*The Idea of Apostolicity in Byzantium and the Legend of the Apostle Andrew* (Cambridge, Mass., 1958), pp. 90-91. We read this in a letter of Leo to Anatolius: "De commonitorio uera a clericis dilectionis tuae nobis oblato, necessarium non fuit epistulis quid uideretur inserere, cum sufficeret

legatis cuncta committi, quorum sermone ex omnibus diligentius instrueris," Letter 85 of June 9, 351, *ACO* II, IV, pp. 44-5, *loc. cit.*, p. 45.

[672]*ACO* II, III, 3, p. 109 (548).

[673]The classic study of this text was done by E. Schwartz, *Der sechste nicaenische Kanon auf der Synode von Chalcedon* (Berlin, 1930) (Sonderausgabe aus den Sitzungsberichten der Preussischen Akademie der Wissenschaften, Phil.-Hist. Klasse, 27).

[674]*EOMIA* I, pars altera, p. 121 (codex Ingilr.) and pp. 197-201 (Isid.).

[675]*ACO* II, I, 3, p. 95 (454). After the words "κατὰ τὴν Ἀντιόχειαν," there is a confused passage.

[676]See our analysis of canon 6 of Nicea.

[677]*ACO* II, I, 3, p. 95 (454) and II, III, 3, pp. 109-110 (548-9).

[678]For example see, E. Caspar, *Geschichte des Papsttums*, I (Tübingen, 1930) p. 523, note 3; also *Héfele-Leclercq* II², p. 831.

[679]H. R. Percival, *The Seven Ecumenicaal Councils of the Undividied Church: Select Library of Nicene and Post-Nicene Fathers*, vol. 14 (Grand Rapids, 1899, 1977), pp. 293-294.

[680]A. Wuyts, "Le28ᵉ canon de Chalcédoine et le fondement du Primat romain," *OCP 17* 1951, pp. 265-282.

[681]*ACO* II, I, 3, pp. 96 (454) *ibid.* II, III, 3, p. 110 (549) (Latin translation). In the Acta Graeca, we find the following appellation, "Συνοδικὸν τῆς Β΄ συνόδου," which supposes that this assembly was considered to be the second ecumenical council. In the Latin translation, we find "...primi concilii sub Nectario episcopo Constantinopolis episcoporum centum quinquaginta."

[682]*Ibid.*, II, I, 3, p. 96=II, III, 3, p. 111.

[683]*Ibid.*, II, I, 3, pp. 96-7 (455-6).

[684]*Ibid.*, p. 97.

[685]*Héfele-Leclercq* II², p. 832.

[686]We are speaking of the synodicum used by the Roman Church rather than the official collection. In fact, the first collection which really merits this title was the work of Dionysius Exiguus at the end of the fifth century.

[687]*ACO* II, I, 3, p. 97 (456).

[688]*Ibid.*

[689]*Ibid.*

[690]*Ibid.*, p. 98 (457).

[691]*Héfele-Leclercq* II², pp. 832-3.

[692]*ACO* II, I, 3, p. 98 (457).

[693]*Histoire ancienne de l'Eglise*, t. III, 4th edition (Paris, 1911), p. 463.

[694]*ACO* II, I, 3, pp. 98-9 (457-8).

[695]*Ibid.*, p. 99 (458).

[696]*Ibid.*, II, I, 2, p. 157 (353).

[697]"Sedes apostolica, nobis praesentibus, humiliari non debet... ." This is what we read in the version of Rusticus. This text is little different from that of the Versio Antiqua: "...nobis praecepit praesentibus ut humiliari non debeat." The Greek version presents a sweetened form: "Ὁ ἀποστολικὸς θρόνος ἡμῶν παρόντων προσέταξε πάντα πράττεσθαι."

[698]*ACO* II, III, 3, pp. 113-14 (552-553) (Latin text); cf. *ibid.*, II, I, 3, p. 99 (458) (Greek interpretation).

[699]*Ibid.*, II, III, 3, p. 114.

[700]*Ibid.*, II, I, 3, p. 99.

[701]This happened in the short reign of Basiliscus. The emperor gave the force of law to this act, but for reasons of political expediency, he had to withdraw his approval a little while later. On this subject, see Evagrius, *Historia ecclesiastica* III, 6 and 7, edition of Bidez and Parmentier (London, 1898), pp. 106-107.

[702]*ACO* II, IV, pp. 55-57; Ep. 104, *ad Marcianum*; *ibid.*, pp. 57-9, Ep. 105, *ad Pulcheriam Aug.*; *ibid.*, pp. 59-62, Ep. 106, *ad Anatholium episcopum.*

[703]*Ibid.*, pp. 55-56.

[704]*Ibid.*, p. 56.

[705]*Ibid.*

[706]*Ibid.*, p. 58.

[707]*Ad Julianum episcopum*, ep. 107, *ibid.*, p. 62.

[708]*Ibid.*, pp. 56 and 61.

709For example, see *ibid.*, p. 56; on the same page "statuta," *ibid.*, p. 58: "regulis." We could multiply the quotations.

710*Byzance et la primauté romaine* (Paris, 1964), p. 48.

711*ACO* II, IV, p. 56.

712*Epist. ad Synodum Chalcedonensem*, 114, March 21, 453, *ibid.*, p. 71.

713*Ibid.*, pp. 168-169.

714*Ibid.*, Ep. 135, pp. 88-9.

715*Ibid.*, Ep. 136, pp. 90-1.

716"Καὶ διὰ τοῦτο θεσπίζομεν, κατὰ τοῦς αὐτῶν ὅρους ἁγιώτατον τῆς πρεσβυτέρας Ῥώμης πάπαν πρῶτον εἶναι πάντων τῶν ἱερέων, τὸν δὲ μακαριώτατον ἀρχιεπίσκοπον Κωνσταντινουπόλεως τῆς νέας Ῥώμης δευτέραν τάξιν ἐπέχειν μετὰ τὸν ἁγιώτατον ἀποστολικὸν θρόνον τῆς πρεσβυτέρας Ῥώμης, τῶν δὲ ἄλλων πάντων προτιμᾶσθαι," *CJC* III, p. 655.

717Constitutio V: De dignitate patriarcharum. "Antiqua patriarchalium sedium privilegia renovantes, sacra universali synode approbante sancimus, ut post Romanam ecclesiam, quae disponente Domino super omnes alias ordinariae potestatis obtinet principatum, utpote mater universorum Christi fidelium et magistra, Constantinopolitana primum, Alexandrina secundum, Antiochene tertium, Hierosolymitana quartum locum obtineant...." *Conciliorum Oecumenicorum Decreta* (Freiburg-in-Breisgau, 1962), p. 212.

718Dvornik, *The Photian Schism* (Cambridge, 1948), pp. 309-330.

719Latin text: *CCO*, p. 331. We have reproduced the French translation of D. Stiernon, *Constantinople IV* (Paris, 1967), p. 294.

720Beneševič, *Kanonicheskii sbornik XIV titulov* (St. Petersburg, 1905), p. 232. However, the term "Recensio Trullana" must not be misinterpreted. Probably the extract in question did not appear in the codex used by the fathers of the council in Trullo.

721*Ibid.*, p. 76, lines 8-9.

722*ACO* II, I, 3, p. 108 (467), lines 32-36 and p. 109 (468), lines 1-6.

723*Rhalles-Potles* II, pp. 286-287. This is the family of manuscripts to which the one from Trebizond (1311) belongs. This recension was used by Zonaras and Balsamon.

724*Pedalion*, p. 210; *Pravila* I, p. 426.

725"Let this be perfectly clear: if anyone has become a bishop without the consent of the metropolitan, the great council decrees that such a one is not even a bishop," *Syntagma*, p. 86.

726Zonaras, commentary on canon 29 of Chalcedon, *Rhalles-Potles* II, p. 287.

727For example, see St. Basil, canon 32, *Syntagma*, p. 489; Apostolic canon 25, *ibid.*, p. 66.

728*Syntagma*, pp. 235-6. The French translation shown in *CSP*, p. 69, can lead into error. It is not a question of "elected bishops" but non-consecrated ones. In fact κατασταθέντες is, as Zonaras justly notes, a synonym for χειροτονηθέντες, *Rhalles-Potles* III, p. 58.

729Later on, the council of Antioch was to rule that a bishop in this situation keep his episcopal dignity, canon 18, *Syntagma*, pp. 260-1. Cf. canon 36 of the Holy Apostles, *ibid.*, p. 69: without getting into specifics, this rule stipulates the same thing.

730*Ibid.*, p. 159.

731P. Panagiotakos, *Τὸ ποινικὸν δίκαιον τῆς Ἐκκλησίας* (Athens, 1962), pp. 266-267 and pp. 313-314 (Παῦσις=ἔκπτωσις ἀπὸ τοῦ θρόνου).

732*Rhalles-Potles* II, p. 351.

733After the mention of the extract from the conciliar acts concerning Photios and Eustathius, we read "Συνόδου στ΄. κανὼν κ΄. καὶ τὰ ἐν αὐτῷ λύοντα τὴν ἐναντιοφάνειαν τῶν κανόνων," *ibid.*, I, p. 185. Cf. the non-interpolated text: *Syntagma*, p. 29 (title 9, chapter 11).

734Archimandrite John (Sokolov), *Opyt kursa tserkovnogo zakonovedeniia* II (St. Petersburg, 1851), p. 380. Nicodemus (Milasch), *Pravila* I, p. 494.

735*Rhalles-Potles* II, pp. 351-352.

736"...πεπαῦσθαι μὲν πάσης ἱερατικῆς λειτουργίας ἤτοι ἐνεργείας...τῆς δὲ τιμῆς τῆς κατὰ τὴν καθέδραν καὶ στάσιν μετέχειν, ἀρκουμένους τῇ προεδρίᾳ," *Syntagma*, p. 146. Cf. Ancyra, canon 2, *ibid.*, p. 229.

737*Rhalles-Potles* II, p. 350.

738*Ibid.*, p. 351.

739*Pedalion*, p. 39.

740It is not mentioned in the index of the Trullan redaction of the *Syntagma*; Beneševič, p. 232.

741It does not appear in many later manuscripts of the Recensio Tarasiana; *Syntagma*, p. 128.

[742]*ACO* II, I, 2, p. 114 (310), lines 1-18.

[743]*Op. cit.*, II, pp. 288-9, with the complete form given on page 289.

[744]*Pravila* I, p. 428.

[745]*Op. cit.*, p. 210.

[746]*Ibid.*, p. 211 note 2.

[747]*Syntagma*, p. 65.

[748]*Rhalles-Potles* II, pp. 27-28.

[749]*Ibid.*, p. 29.

[750]This Greek expression is rendered in the *Kniga Pravil* by "v svoem sane," *Pravila* I, p. 428, while in the Old Slavonic *Kormchaya*, there was a literal translation: "vo svoiem obraz," *Syntagma*, p. 129. We can relate this formulation of the council of Chalcedon to what we read in canon 8 of Nicea about the Novatianist clergy: "...οἱ εὑρισκόμενοι ἐν τῷ κλήρῳ ἔσονται ἐν τῷ αὐτῷ σχήματι," *Syntagma*, p. 87.

[751] Ἡ οἰκονομία κατὰ τὸ κανονικὸν δίκαιον τῆς Ὀρθοδόξου Ἐκκλησίας (Athens, 1949), p. 36.

[752]*Liberati Breviarium*, 14, *ACO* II, V, p. 123. We note that these four bishops belonged to the same province, Second-Egypt; see E. Honigmann, *La valeur historique du "Thronos Alexandrinos,"* *Subsidia Hagiographica*, n. 35 (Brussels, 1961), p. 157.

INDEX